DATE DUE

NY 20 '04			
JE 9 '04			
AP 3 06			
JE 2 7 '06			
MY 2 8 '10			
OC 19 '10			

DEMCO 38-296

· THE ·
KILLING
STATE

THE
KILLING
STATE

Capital Punishment in
Law, Politics, and Culture

EDITED BY AUSTIN SARAT

New York   Oxford
Oxford University Press
1999

Oxford University Press

Oxford   New York
Athens   Auckland   Bangkok   Bogotá   Bombay   Buenos Aires   Calcutta
Cape Town   Chennai   Dar es Salaam   Delhi   Florence   Hong Kong   Istanbul
Karachi   Kuala Lumpur   Madrid   Melbourne   Mexico City   Mumbai
Nairobi   Paris   São Paulo   Singapore   Taipei   Tokyo   Toronto   Warsaw
and associated companies in
Berlin   Ibadan

Copyright © 1999 by Oxford University Press, Inc.

Published by Oxford University Press, Inc.
198 Madison Avenue, New York, New York 10016

Oxford is a registered trademark of Oxford University Press

Library of Congress Cataloging-in-Publication Data
The killing state : capital punishment in law, politics,
and culture / edited by Austin Sarat.
p.   cm.
"This book emerged out of a conference entitled
"Capital punishment in law and culture" held at
Amherst College in April, 1997"—p. viii.
Includes bibliographical references and index.
ISBN 0-19-512086-8
1. Capital punishment—United States—Congresses.
I. Sarat, Austin.
KF9227.C2K56   1998
364.66'0973—dc21   97-53268

3 5 7 9 8 6 4 2
Printed in the United States of America
on acid-free paper

To my children,
Lauren, Emily, and Benjamin,
with the hope that someday
they will not live
in a killing state.

ACKNOWLEDGMENTS

This book emerged out of a conference entitled "Capital Punishment in Law and Culture," held at Amherst College in April 1997. That conference took the occasion of the twenty-fifth anniversary of the Supreme Court's decision in *Furman v. Georgia* (declaring the death penalty as then administered unconstitutional) to launch a broad inquiry into the question of how state killing affects our law, politics, and culture. I am grateful to all the participants and to those who attended for their lively engagement with those issues. The conference was sponsored by Amherst College's Charles Hamilton Houston Forum on Law and Social Justice and its Department of Law, Jurisprudence, and Social Thought. I am grateful for that sponsorship as well as for the encouragement and support of colleagues, especially William Bowers, Kristin Bumiller, David Delaney, Tom Dumm, Lawrence Douglas, Joseph Hoffmann, Nasser Hussain, Thomas R. Kearns, and Martha Umphrey.

CONTENTS

III. THE DEATH PENALTY AND THE CULTURE OF RESPONSIBILITY

CONTRIBUTORS

ANTHONY AMSTERDAM is Judge Edward Weinfeld Professor of Law at New York University.

HUGO ADAM BEDAU is Austin Fletcher Professor of Philosphy at Tufts University.

WILLIAM E. CONNOLLY is Professor of Political Science at Johns Hopkins University.

JENNIFER L. CULBERT is Visiting Assistant Professor of Justice Studies at Arizona State University.

PETER FITZPATRICK is Professor of Law at Queen Mary and Westfield College, University of London.

ANNE NORTON is Professor of Political Science at the University of Pennsylvania.

AUSTIN SARAT is William Nelson Cromwell Professor of Jurisprudence and Political Science, Amherst College. He is currently president of the Law and Society Association.

JONATHON SIMON is Professor of Law, University of Miami.

CHRISTINA SPAULDING is Assistant Public Defender, Dade County, Florida.

JULIE M. TAYLOR is Associate Professor of Anthropology at Rice University.

FRANKLIN E. ZIMRING is William G. Simon Professor of Law at the University of California, Berkeley.

· THE ·
KILLING
STATE

CAPITAL PUNISHMENT AS A LEGAL, POLITICAL, AND CULTURAL FACT: AN INTRODUCTION

AUSTIN SARAT

Political power . . . I take to be the right of making laws with the penalty of death.

John Locke, *Second Treatise of Government*

From birth control to death control, whether we execute people or compel their survival . . . , the essential thing is that the decision is withdrawn from them, that their life and their death are never freely theirs.

Jean Baudrillard, *Symbolic Exchange and Death*

Today Americans live in a killing state in which violence is met with violence, and the measure of our sovereignty as a people is found in our ability both to make laws carrying the penalty of death and to translate those laws into a calm, bureaucratic bloodletting.[1] We live in a state in which killing increasingly is used as an important part of criminal justice policy and of the symbolization of political power. At a time when life and the sensibility necessary to a meaningful life are extremely fragile,[2] we are told that life must be taken to preserve our lives and sensibilities. The killing state is thus a state of being as well as the state we are in.

As we contemplate the end of the twentieth century, the most prominent manifestation of our killing state, capital punishment, defying the predictions of Foucault,[3] Elias,[4] and others, is alive and well in the United States. Not only does this country cling tenaciously to capital punishment long after almost all other democratic nations have abandoned it,[5] but today the number of people on death row as well as the number executed grows steadily.[6] For a brief period after *Gregg v. Georgia* reinstated capital punishment[7] there was tight legal supervision of the death penalty and great restraint in its use, yet that period is now long gone.[8] The pressure is on to move from merely sentencing people to death and then warehousing them to carrying out executions by reducing procedural protections and expediting the legal process.[9] While the full result is yet to be seen, it now appears that the killing state will be a regular part of the landscape of American politics for a long time to come.

What will the persistence of capital punishment mean for our law, politics, and culture? Will it contribute to or undermine democracy and the rule of law? Will it nurture a culture of respect and responsibility or of resentment and recrimination? It is to these questions that the essays collected in this volume are addressed.

Readers looking for a balanced assessment and response to these questions, or a representative sampling of opinion on the death penalty, should be warned; they will not find it in this book. Though quite different in their politics and theoretical approaches, the authors whose work is brought together here are united in the belief that, as the epigrams from Locke and Baudrillard suggest, capital punishment has played, and continues to play, a major, and dangerous, role in the modern economy of power. While several of them are well-known experts on the death penalty, others are new to this subject. Nevertheless, they are united in their belief that scholarship on the death penalty has to go beyond treating it as simply a terrain of moral argument and policy contest.[10] Their work brings to that scholarship broader interests in the connections of capital punishment to basic issues facing our legal, political, and cultural systems. The contributors to this volume address the powerful symbolic politics of the death penalty, the way capital punishment pushes to, and beyond, the limits of law's capacity to do justice justly, and the place of the politics of state killing in contemporary "culture wars." In each of these areas they highlight the insidious and destructive presence of capital punishment.

What is the political meaning of state killing in a democracy? Does it express or frustrate popular sovereignty, strengthen or weaken the values on which democratic deliberation depends? Or, we might ask more directly, is capital punishment compatible with democratic values? Surely there must be serious doubts that it is.[11] Capital punishment is the ultimate assertion of righteous indignation, of power pretending to its own infallibility. By definition it leaves no room for reversibility. It expresses either a "we don't care" anger or an unjustified confidence in our capacity to recognize and respond to evil with wisdom and propriety. Democracy cannot well coexist with either such anger or such confidence. For it to thrive it demands a different context,[12] one marked by a spirit of openness, of reversibility, of revision quite at odds with the confidence and commitment necessary to dispose of human life in a cold and deliberate way.[13]

"The death penalty," as Terry Aladjem writes, "strains an unspoken premise of the democratic state" that may variously be named respect for the equal moral worth or equal dignity of all persons.[14] Democratically administered capital punishment, punishment in which citizens act in an official capacity to approve the deliberate killing of other citizens, contradicts and diminishes the respect for the worth or dignity of all persons that is the enlivening value of democratic politics.[15] And a death penalty democratically administered, a death penalty that enlists citizens to do the work of dealing death to other citizens, implicates us all as agents of state killing.[16]

Along with the right to make war,[17] the death penalty is the ultimate measure of sovereignty and the ultimate test of political power. It is the contention of the essays contained in this volume that we can learn a lot about the kind of society we live in by examining the way that society punishes,[18] including whether it uses death as a punishment. One lesson of such an examination is, as George Kateb notes, that "the state's power deliberately to destroy innocuous (though guilty) life is a manifestation of the hidden wish that the state be allowed to do anything it pleases with life."[19] In this wish we again confront a deep threat to democracy, to the tentativeness and scrupulousness of democratic politics and to democratic respect for persons.

The right to dispose of human life through sovereign acts was traditionally thought to be a direct extension of the personal power of kings.[20] With the transition from monarchical to democratic regimes, one might have thought that such a vestige of monarchical power would have no place and, as a result, would wither away. Yet, at least in the United States, the most democratic of democratic nations, it persists with a vengeance. How are we to explain this?

It may be that our attachment to state killing is paradoxically a result of our deep attachment to popular sovereignty. Where sovereignty is most fragile, as it always is where its locus is in "the People," dramatic symbols of its presence, like capital punishment, may be most important. The maintenance of capital punishment is, one might argue, essential to the demonstration that sovereignty could reside in the people. If the sovereignty of the people is to be genuine, it has to mimic the sovereign power and prerogatives of the monarchical forms it displaced and about whose sovereignty there could be few doubts. Rather than seeing the true task of democracy as the transformation of sovereignty and its prerogatives in the hope of reconciling them with a commitment to respecting the dignity of all persons, the death penalty is miraculously transformed from an instrument of political terror used by "them" against "us," to our instrument used by some of us against others.[21] Thus understanding state killing may be a key to understanding modern mechanisms of consent.[22]

As any attentive American who lived through the 1970s, 80s, and 90s knows, the politics of law and order have been at center stage for a long time. From Richard Nixon's "law and order" rhetoric to Bill Clinton's pledge to represent people who "work hard and play by the rules," crime has been such an important issue that some now argue that we are being "governed through crime."[23] In the scurry to show that one is tough on crime, the symbolism of capital punishment has been crucial. It has also been crucial in the processes of demonizing young, black males and using them in the pantheon of public enemies to replace the "evil empire."[24] No American politician today wants to be caught on the wrong side of the death penalty debate. Thus in the 1992 campaign Bill Clinton showed he was a different kind of Democrat through his visible support for the death penalty and his use of it while governor of Arkansas.[25]

The politics of capital punishment is crucial in an era of neoliberal withdrawal from other kinds of state intervention. It helps to shift the symbolic capital of the state to an area where, whatever one's doubts about the capacity of government to govern effectively, there can be demonstrable results. As Aladjem puts it, "It is significant that just when there is doubt as to whether rational democratic institutions can generate a public sense of justice, there has been a resurgence of pre-democratic retributivism and a renewed insistence that it is a 'rational' response to an increase in violent crime."[26] This helps explain the energy behind recently successful efforts to limit habeas corpus and speed up the time from death sentences to state killings. A state unable to execute those it condemns to die would seem almost too impotent to carry out almost any policy whatsoever.

Yet it is precisely this hydraulic political pressure that threatens to undermine important legal values, for example, due process and equal protection. To take but one particularly striking example, the much publicized execution of Robert Alton Harris is a telling reminder of the pressure on law to compromise its highest values and aspirations in order to turn death sentences into state killings.[27] During the twelve-hour period immediately preceding Harris's execution, no fewer than four separate stays were issued by the Ninth Circuit Court of Appeals.[28] Ultimately, the Supreme Court ordered that "no further stays shall be entered . . . except upon order of this court."[29] With this unusual and perhaps unconstitutional order, the Court stopped the talk and took upon itself the responsibility for Harris's execution.

In so doing it paid an enormous price. What kind of law is it that would do something arguably illegal solely to ensure the death of one man? The Court's action in the Harris case was symptomatic of just such a state of affairs, one in which the act of responding to the crime was, in Foucault's words, rightly "suspected of being in some undesirable way linked with it. It was as if the punishment was thought to equal, if not exceed, in savagery the crime itself . . . to make the executioner resemble a criminal, judges murderers."[30] The impatience of the law to facilitate state killing arouses anxiety and fear; it suggests that law's violence bears substantial traces of the violence it is designed to deter and punish.[31] The bloodletting that the law seems so eager to let loose strains against and ultimately disrupts all efforts to normalize or routinize state killing as just another legally justifiable and legally controlled act. It may be that law is controlled by, rather than in control of, the imperatives of the killing state.[32]

In this situation there is, and must be, a truly uneasy linkage between law and violence. Law it seems cannot "work its lethal will" and ally itself with the killing state while "remaining aloof and unstained by the deeds themselves."[33] As pervasive and threatening as this alliance is, it is, nonetheless, difficult to understand that relationship, or to know precisely what one is talking about when one speaks about it.[34] This difficulty arises because law is violent in many ways—in the ways it uses language and in its representational practices,[35] in the silencing of perspectives and the denial of experience,[36] and in its objectifying epistemology.[37] It arises from the fact that the linguistic, representational violence of the law is inseparable from its literal, physical violence. As Peter Fitzpatrick suggests,

> In its narrow perhaps popular sense, violence is equated with unrestrained physical violence. . . . A standard history of the West would connect a decline in violence with an increase in civility. Others would see civility itself as a transformed violence, as a constraining even if not immediately coercive discipline. . . . The dissipation of simple meaning is heightened in recent sensibilities where violence is discerned in the denial of the uniqueness or even existence of the 'other.' . . . These expansions of the idea of violence import a transcendent ordering—an organizing, shaping force coming to bear on situations from outside of them and essentially unaffected by them.[38]

Violence, as both a linguistic and physical phenomenon, as fact and metaphor,[39] is integral to the constitution of modern law.[40] And a thoroughly nonviolent legality is inconceivable in a society like this one. Yet to say that modern law is a creature of both a literal, life-threatening, body-crushing violence, and of imaginings and threats of force, disorder, and pain, is not to say that it must embrace all kinds of violence under all conditions. If law cannot adequately define the boundary between life and death, guilty killing and innocent execution, then what is left of law? If law cannot adequately effect a reconciliation between violence and reason,[41] then how can law itself survive?

It is only in and through its claims to legitimacy that what law does is privileged and distinguished from "the violence that one always deems unjust."[42] Legitimacy is thus one way of charting the boundaries of law's violence. It is also the minimal answer to skeptical questions about the ways law's violence differs from the turmoil and disorder that law is allegedly brought into being to conquer. But the need to legitimate law's violence is nagging and continuing, never fully resolved in any single gesture.[43] Where law, as in the Harris case, goes too far to facilitate state killing, it undermines its own claims to legitimacy and thus casts a pervasive doubt on all its violent acts.

This helps explain the lively contestation that today marks the legal debate over capital punishment as well as the emergence of what I have elsewhere called "the new abolitionism."[44] Both were vividly on display when, in February 1994, Justice Harry Blackmun of the United States Supreme Court announced, "From this day forward I no longer shall tinker with the machinery of death."[45] This dramatic proclamation capped his evolution from long-time supporter of the death penalty to tinkerer with various procedural schemes and devices designed to rationalize death sentences and ultimately to outright abolitionist. Twenty-two years before his abolitionist announcement, he dissented in *Furman v. Georgia*, refusing to join the majority of his colleagues in what he labeled the "legislative" act of finding execution, as then administered, cruel and unusual punishment.[46] Four years after *Furman* he joined the majority in *Gregg v. Georgia*, deciding to reinstate the death penalty in the United States.[47] However, by the time he underwent his abolitionist conversion, Blackmun had left a trail of judicial opinions moving gradually, but inexorably, away from this early embrace of death as a constitutionally legitimate punishment.[48] As a result, the denunciation of capital punishment that he offered in 1994 was as categorical as it was vivid— "I will no longer tinker with the machinery of death." It was most significant as a moment in the transformation of abolitionist politics and as an example of "abolition as legal conservatism."[49]

Blackmun's abolitionism found its locus in neither liberal humanism nor radicalism, nor even in the defense of the most indefensible among us. It was, instead, firmly rooted in mainstream legal values of due process and equal protection. Blackmun did not reject the death penalty because of its violence, argue against its appropriateness as a response to heinous criminals, or criticize its futility as a tool in the war against crime. Instead, he shifted the rhetorical grounds. Harkening back to *Furman*, as if rewriting his opinion in that case, he focused on the procedures through which death sentences were divided. "[D]espite the efforts of the states and the courts," Blackmun noted, "to devise legal formulas and procedural rules . . . , the death penalty remains fraught with arbitrariness, discrimination, caprice, and mistake. . . . Experience has taught us that the constitutional goal of eliminating arbitrariness and discrimination from the administration of death . . . can never be achieved without compromising an equally essential component of fundamental fairness—individualized sentencing."[50]

Two things stand out in Blackmun's argument. First he acknowledges law's effort to purge death sentences of any taint of procedural irregularity. As he sees it, the main implication of *Furman* is that a death penalty is constitutional only if it *can be* administered in a manner compatible with the guarantees of due process and equal protection. Here Blackmun moves the debate away from the question of whether capital punishment is cruel or whether it can be reconciled with society's evolving standards of decency. Second, Blackmun identified a constitutional conundrum in which consistency and individualization—the twin commands of the Supreme Court's post-*Furman* death penalty jurisprudence—cannot be achieved simultaneously. As a result, Blackmun concluded that "the death penalty cannot be administered in accord with our Constitution."[51] The language that Blackmun uses is unequivocal; after more than twenty years of effort Blackmun says, in essence, "enough is enough."

The new abolitionism that Blackmun championed presents itself as a reluctant abolitionism, one rooted in acceptance of the damage that capital punishment does to central legal values and to the legitimacy of the law itself. It finds its home in an embrace, not a critique, of those values. Those who love the law, in Blackmun's view, must hate the death penalty for the damage that it does to the object of that love. "Rather than continue to coddle the Court's delusion that the desired level of fairness has been achieved . . . ," Blackmun stated, "I feel morally and intellectually obligated simply to concede that the death penalty experiment has failed. It is virtually self-evident to me now that no combination of procedural rules or substantive regulations ever can save the death penalty from its inherent constitutional deficiencies."[52] In this admonition we again see Blackmun's categorical conclusion that nothing can "save" capital punishment, a conclusion spoken both from within history, as a report of the result of an "experiment," but also from an Archimedean point in which the failure of the death penalty is "self-evident" and permanent.

Blackmun's brand of abolitionism reminds us of the ways state killing damages law, the ways the killing state cannot be the "legality" state, the ways state killing kills the state itself. Blackmun opened an important new avenue for engagement in the political struggle against capital punishment, providing abolitionists a position of political respectability while simultaneously allowing them to change the subject from the legitimacy of execution to the imperatives of due process. The rhetoric Blackmun made available to opponents of capital punishment enables them to deflect the overwhelming political consensus in favor of death as a punishment.[53] They can say that the most important issue in the debate about capital punishment is one of fairness not one of sympathy for murderers; they can position themselves as defenders of law itself, as legal conservatives. One can believe, new abolitionists now were able to concede, in the retributive or deterrence-based rationalizations for the death penalty and yet still be an abolitionist; one can be as tough on crime as the next person yet still reject capital punishment. All that was required to generate opposition to execution was a commitment to the view that law's violence should be different from violence outside the law as well as a belief that that difference could/should be rooted in the fairness and rationality of the violence that law does.

Yet, despite the new rhetorical and strategic terrain that Blackmun opened up, abolition has by no means prevailed. Quite to the contrary. Proponents of capital punishment have responded with a mean-spirited constitutional revisionism. Numerous recent decisions of the Supreme Court have eroded, not enhanced, the procedural integrity of the death-sentencing process.[54] Moreover, in 1996 Congress delivered a one-two punch directed against Blackmun's brand of abolitionist politics, first enacting Title I of the Anti-Terrorism and Effective Death Penalty Act, which severely limited the reach of federal habeas corpus protections for those on death row,[55] and then defunding postconviction defender organizations, which provided legal representation for many of those contesting their death sentences.[56] Thus even those procedural guarantees that Blackmun found inadequate to secure fairness and reliability in capital sentencing have been openly and enthusiastically jettisoned.

American society seems even more impatient with the procedural niceties and delays attendant to what many now see as excessive scrupulousness in the handling of capital cases. What good is having the death penalty, so the refrain goes, if there are so few executions?[57] Blood must be let; lives must be turned into corpses; the charade of repeated appeals prolonging the lives of those on death row must be brought to an end.

The impact of state killing is, however, not limited to our political and legal lives. It has a pervasive effect in constituting our culture as well. This volume seeks to trace those cultural effects. It takes up the argument of David Garland, namely that we should attend to the "cultural role" of legal practices, to their ability to "create social meaning and thus shape social worlds," and that among those practices none is more important than how we punish.[58] This book extends that argument to the domain of the death penalty.

Punishment, Garland tells us, "helps shape the overarching culture and contribute to the generation and regeneration of its terms."[59] Punishment is a set of signifying practices that "teaches, clarifies, dramatizes and authoritatively enacts some of the most basic moral-political categories and distinctions which help shape our symbolic universe."[60] Punishment lives in culture through its pedagogical effects. It teaches us how to think about categories like intention, responsibility, and injury, and it models the socially appropriate ways of responding to injuries done to us.[61] Moreover, it exemplifies relations of power and reminds us of the pervasiveness of vulnerability and pain. Most powerfully, "penalty highlights the characteristics of the normal self by policing its failures and pathologies and spelling out more precisely what one is expected minimally to be."[62]

But punishment also lives in culture as a set of images, as a spectacle of condemnation. The semiotics of punishment is all around us, not just in the architecture of the prison, or the speech made by a judge as she sends someone to the penal colony, but in both "high" and "popular" culture iconography, in novels, television, and film. Punishment has traditionally been one of the great subjects of cultural production, suggesting the powerful allure of humankind's fall from grace and of our prospects for redemption. But perhaps the word "our" is inaccurate here since

Durkheim[63] and Mead,[64] among others, remind us that it is through practices of punishment that cultural boundaries are drawn, that solidarity is created by marking difference between self and other, though disidentification as much as imagined connection. "[M]ass-mediated representations of prisoners function as a public display of the transgression of cultural norms; as such, they are a key site at which one may investigate the relationship of the individual to the culture in general, as well as the cultural articulation of 'proper behavior.'"[65]

And what is true of punishment in general is certainly true of those instances in which the punishment is death. Traditionally the public execution was one of the great spectacles of power and instructions in the mysteries of responsibilities and retribution.[66] Yet the privatization of execution, has not ended the pedagogy of the scaffold.[67] It has been redirected into the medium of the capital trial.[68] If, as I argued earlier, the death penalty persists, on this account, as the ultimate test of whether sovereignty can reside in the people, capital trials, not executions, are the moment when that sovereignty is most vividly on display.[69] Indeed, capital trials have displaced execution itself as the venue for the display of sovereignty since, in regard to the death penalty, "[p]unishment," as Foucault notes, "(has) become the most hidden part of the penal process."[70] Yet execution itself, the moment of state killing, is even now an occasion for rich symbolization, for the production of public images of evil or of an unruly freedom whose only containment is in a state-imposed death,[71] and for fictive recreations of the scene of death in popular culture.[72]

Traditionally, the cultural politics of state killing has focused on shoring up status distinctions and distinguishing particular ways of life from others.[73] Thus it is not surprising that the death penalty marks an important fault line in our contemporary culture wars. To be for capital punishment is to be a defender of traditional morality against rampant permissivism, of the rights of the innocent over the rights of the guilty, of state power against its anarchic critics.[74] To oppose it is to carry the burden of explaining why the state should not kill the killers, of producing a new theory of responsibility and of responsible punishment, and of humanizing inhuman deeds.

Yet all of this may miss the deepest cultural significance of state killing. As Baudrillard suggests, in regard to capital punishment, "[T]he thought of the right (hysterical reaction) and the thought of the left (rational humanism) are both equally removed from the symbolic configuration where crime, madness and death are modalities of exchange."[75] And, all of this is carried on against the background of cultural divides that are becoming ever more intense as they become more complex and unpredictable.

The essays in *The Killing State: Capital Punishment in Law, Politics, and Culture* are divided into three parts. The first, "The Politics of State Killing," takes up the relationship between the death penalty and democracy. It locates the conversation about capital punishment in the United States historically and comparatively before drawing it back to the contemporary American situation. The second part, "Capital Punishment and Legal Values," explores what death penalties say about law's possibilities and its limits. The third, "The Death Penalty and the Culture of Responsibility," explores how state killing and its cultural representations constitute us as particular kinds of subjects while at the same time enacting a denial of the un-settling possibilities in contemporary cultural transformations.

The first essay in the book, by Anne Norton, is neither about the United States nor state killing in the literal sense. Yet this rich description of the uses to which "killing the state" (or at least its sovereign representatives) has been put in transi-tions from monarchical to democratic regimes opens an exploration of the vexing relationship of capital punishment and democracy on a contrarian note. Today, Norton notes, capital punishment is a tool of the powerful against dominated groups. As such, it appears as an enactment of the finality of state power, a finality quite at odds with the spirit and substance of democracy. The death penalty always calls us to certainty, and, in so doing, invites us to forget the limits of our reason. However, in moments of political turmoil—exemplified in the English Civil War, the French Revolution, and colonial uprisings, the political valence of capital pun-ishment is reversed.

In those moments, killing, killing of the state, becomes an instrument of the dominated, a way of bringing low the powerful, a signification of a desire for equal-ity. In these moments we are reminded, Norton contends, of the violent origins of liberal constitutionalism. We are reminded that there is no space of freedom or equality that has been, or can be, secured without bloodletting. If we remember this lesson, we can evaluate the political meaning of killing, not in terms of a hu-manist revulsion against violence but in terms of politics itself, of the ends it serves, the purposes to which it is put. The death penalty is less an assault on the dignity of the condemned, Norton argues, than it is a stark reminder of the responsibility that comes with all political engagement. For us, in our time, the lesson is that we need less of an absolute condemnation of state killing than a commitment to use it, and all political power, to create a more just and egalitarian politics.

Norton's critique of absolutist rejections of state killing, and her insistence on a politically grounded assessment of it, is a theme taken up in the next three essays. It would seem, at first glance, to be directed against Hugo Adam Bedau, one of this nation's most important abolitionist voices. Indeed Bedau's contribution to this book directly engages the question "Is absolute abolition a tenable policy?" Here Bedau carefully and skeptically reviews the major arguments for absolute aboli-tion—for example those centered on the sanctity of life, the dignity of the person, the failure of deterrence. In his view, each fails to present a convincing case. Yet Bedau suggests that there is such a case.

The best case for abolition rests on a commitment to respecting substantive due process, to respecting liberty, autonomy, and privacy except when there is no alternative but to limit them in order to accomplish some pressing social objective. What this means is that "[s]ociety must not use laws that impose more restriction on, or interference with, human liberty, privacy and autonomy than are absolutely necessary." In Bedau's view, the most pressing social objective that might satisfy this criterion is crime reduction, or the protection of innocent life. Yet focusing on the experience of Michigan and Wisconsin, two long-time abolitionist states, demon-strates, on his account, that this goal can be satisfied as well without the death penalty as with it.

If Bedau is right, then the only absolutist case against capital punishment is not absolutist at all, but instead rests on the contingent demonstration of necessity. State killing, even as it is shown to be, in its present practice, demonstrably incompatible with substantive due process values, cannot be shown, under all conditions, to be unacceptable. Bedau, like Norton, directs us to think politically about state killing, to ask when and for what purposes it is used and to gear our reactions to the worth of those purposes and the necessity, not just the desirability, of killing as a method of attaining them.

Julie Taylor's essay shows what happens when state killing is unleashed for purposes of advancing domination not equality, of abridging liberty rather than advancing it. The particular form of state killing with which she is concerned is police violence; the cultural context is contemporary Argentina. In Argentina, Taylor notes, the end of dictatorship was marked by a dispersion of, rather than an end to, state killing. It moved from the carefully controlled discipline of the disappearance to the proliferation of the use of lethal force by the police. This change represents a move from an internalization in which the victims of state killing "disappeared" into the state itself to an externalization in which state killing enters the quotidian world and becomes pervasive in its presence.

Because, as Michael Taussig argues, "the 'law' of the police . . . is independent of the rest of the law,"[76] state killing, when it takes the form of the trigger-happy policeman, does not present itself as policy, subject to the stringent demands of necessity. It is fact not possibility, it is imperative not escapable contingency. The killing state thus seems spectral, formless when its instrumentality is police violence. "[I]n Argentina," Taylor notes, "the functioning of a second penal system, parallel to the strict penal code, has been historically institutionalized through the police edict, removing constitutional guarantees that, while never absolute, when in place serves to impede abuses." In this sense the killing state leads parallel lives, at once inside and outside, unknowable and yet known, subject to law and yet lawless. Far from the grand gestures of democratic opening that Norton describes, lethal police violence is, as Taylor portrays it, "formless, like its nowhere tangible, all-pervasive ghostly presence in the life of civilized states." It is a form of delinquency in which a delinquent state proliferates violence while both denying its existence and promising an end to violence.

Unlike the majesty of the capital trial, and the rituals of the gallows or its contemporary equivalent, death at the hands of the trigger-happy police is neither majestic nor ritualized. It does not respond to the demand to know why, precisely because it exists in a quiet denial rather than a proud proclamation. The killing state insinuates itself into civil society where it intimidates and fragments. Its logic is the logic of terror, a logic that defies logic. Police violence controls those who remain alive through fear. As a result, while democratic forms exist, democracy cannot be realized in anything other than its formalities.

Jonathan Simon and Christina Spaulding, like Taylor, are interested in the proliferation of violence or the promise of violence as an instrument of state policy. But they return us to the United States and to the practices of capital punishment. In this insightful analysis of the politics of capital punishment, Simon and Spaulding analyze patterns of change in the statutory aggravating factors that, under American law, define who among the population of murderers is "death eligible."

They do so to show how the death penalty has become implicated in a shift of governance strategies toward "governing through crime" and in the movement toward symbolic recognition rather than substantive benefit as the major output of neoliberal politics.

Simon and Spaulding trace the evolution of death penalty politics over a twenty-year period by focusing on the kinds of persons and crimes covered by statutory aggravating factors. The post-*Gregg* aggravators had three central characteristics: First, they were directly responsive to the dictates of the Supreme Court; they aspired to be, as well as to satisfy, the law. Second, the primary object of protection was the state and its officials. Third, they gave little heed to mollifying the private fears of the citizenry.

Today, because the Supreme Court has largely abandoned the effort to discipline the death penalty, aggravating factors have proliferated in such a way as to provide symbolic recognition to this or that political constituency. New aggravators are concerned more with managing risks than with responding to harms to specific persons. They are passed out to constituencies as "tokens of our esteem." They reflect both a new populism and a new spirit of privatization, and they encourage resentment and reprisal rather than responsible engagement in solving social problems. They divide rather than unite, giving an appearance of democratic responsiveness to our fears while diminishing the likelihood of genuine democratic deliberation.

The next section of this book—"Capital Punishment and Legal Values"—begins with an essay by Peter Fitzpatrick, which returns us to Norton's concerns about the temptations and dangers of finality, of a ferocious use of power in the service of death. Like Norton, Fitzpatrick worries about what state killing does to our most important public institutions; only here the concern is to assess what such a use of power means for law itself. Following Derrida, Fitzpatrick claims that law is the "impossible union of determination with all that is beyond determination." Law's integrity depends upon its never being complete, fully determined, and fully determining because its presence and its reach must extend toward the always deferred possibility of justice. For law to be law, Fitzpatrick contends, it must always be able "to do more." Thus death sets the limits of law and exposes law's radical incompleteness. Death does this by marking law's determinate being and asserting its finality against law's openness. Thus, when law deals in death, it acts against itself in a dramatic and damaging way.

Law always runs out when it engages in capital punishment. In those moments law can present only one side of itself, its "naked determining force." When the state kills, it makes an irremediable exclusion and ensures that the borders securing law will no longer be places pointing toward expansionary promises, what Derrida calls the "fading horizon of justice." In this moment something "rotten" is exposed in the fabric of law; its violence overwhelms and extinguishes its legitimating promises. Law's legitimacy, Fitzpatrick argues, depends on its promise that "one day to come" it could actually be more and be extended to the previously excluded. Capital punishment denies this promise, and the whole edifice of legality is, as a result, rendered more fragile rather than more secure.

Deploying a very different vocabulary and addressing himself specifically to the

United States, Franklin Zimring takes up Fitzpatrick's concern with the impact of state killing on law and legal values. He argues that there is a deep and fundamental clash between the operational needs of the execution system and the most important principles of American legal culture. There is, he notes, an inherent momentum in the death penalty system pushing for expeditious execution. This momentum comes from the promise to satisfy the demands of vengeance that inescapably is part of the politics of state killing. So strong is this momentum that in a series of important decisions, for example, *Penry v. Lynaugh*,[77] *McCleskey v. Kemp*,[78] *Herrera v. Collins*,[79] the Supreme Court has committed itself to expediting the process of turning death sentences into state killings while sacrificing due process, equal protection, and law's refusal ever to risk punishing the innocent.

Zimring details three points of conflict between state killing and legal values. The first is its conflict with substantive principles of human dignity. Second is the conflict between state killing and the integrity of the process through which legal judgments are made. Third is the possibility that the changes and accommodations necessary to facilitate state killing may spill over and threaten "respect for due process throughout the criminal justice system." He worries that the drive to kill expeditiously, which seems now to be the highest priority in death penalty cases, will set the tone for the entire criminal justice system. The death penalty, he notes, "can only be principled if it is not efficient and only efficient if it is morally and procedurally arbitrary." Like Fitzpatrick, Zimring argues that the damage state killing does to law cannot be contained. Death radiates throughout law and damages whatever it touches.

This trade-off between principled and arbitrary decision making is the take-off point for Anthony Amsterdam's careful examination of cases in which the Supreme Court has lifted stays of execution. In these cases, the Court has consistently sacrificed fairness to expedite state killing. In its decisions lifting stays, the Court sends a message to judges throughout the country that they do not have to commit themselves to the excruciatingly difficult work of providing conscientious review of claims of constitutional error in death cases. Moreover, the opinions vacating stays display a tone of rage; they are petulant and present what Amsterdam considers a demonstrably false picture of defendants and their lawyers "abusing" the legal system by taking unfair advantage of opportunities to delay and draw out the process of turning death sentences into state killings.

Amsterdam argues that the Court avoids the moral burden of deciding to let someone be killed at the hands of the state by consistently denying that it has a choice and by elevating the alleged need to protect the orderly process of criminal justice to the status of an absolute value. Because the Court speaks in euphemisms, Amsterdam insists, it never confronts the reality of the killing that it unleashes. He examines two of the rhetorical devices that make it possible for the Court to avoid this confrontation with reality. The first—metaphoric coding—is exemplified in the phrase "abuse of the writ." This phrase suggests that law itself is what is in danger in these cases and allows the Justices to imagine that lives must be taken in order to put an end to this attack on law. The second, closely related device involves the construction of a "conspiracy myth" in which the condemned and their lawyers are portrayed as manipulating the process and taking advantage of conscientious judges. This myth gives the Justices someone to be mad at and explains why, until recently, so few executions had been carried out. Making relief harder to obtain became one way to resist the conspiracy. Finally, in Amsterdam's view, the rhetorical devices used in the Supreme Court's stay opinions become readily available capital in the struggle over capital punishment in the wider culture.

It is to that culture that the essays in the third part of this volume address themselves. William Connolly's "The Will, Capital Punishment, and Cultural Wars" contends that the contemporary politics of state killing must be understood as part of a broad cultural contest over the integrity and stability of ideas of free will and responsibility. In order to understand that cultural contest, Connolly says that we need to understand the history of theorizing about the will. Theorists who place a timeless and undivided will at the center of their understandings of freedom and responsibility "assert great confidence" in their judgments about punishment. Through a careful reading of Augustine, Kant, and Nietzsche, among others, Connolly shows that within the story of the will is a recognition, often repressed, of its uncertain, divided, opaque character. Even Kant, theorist of responsibility par excellence, occasionally acknowledged that the propensity to evil resided within the will itself and is not extirpable by the will itself. Yet, if punishment is to be grounded in ideas of freedom and responsibility, such complexities must be forgotten.

Forgetting, Connolly argues, is at the heart of the contemporary debate about capital punishment. Forgetfulness accommodates a cultural quest for revenge, which, he notes, is always inextricably linked to state killing. Connolly uses the book and film of *Dead Man Walking* to point out how difficult it is to carry on the struggle against capital punishment in an era when the basic categories through which we judge murderers and assess penalties are being called into question. In the face of this development the cultural contest over, and the meaning of, capital punishment becomes ever more important. What looks like a struggle over a penological device is really part of a debate over basic ideas of freedom and responsibility.

Instead of confronting the divided nature of the will and the resulting instabilities in ideas of freedom and responsibility, supporters of the death penalty would rather sacrifice lives. They would do almost anything rather than give up the purity of the concepts through which persons are now judged and sentenced. The intensity of these cultural demands for "categorical integrity" is a response, Connolly contends, to increased globalization with its threats to state sovereignty as well as to radical increases in the tempo of cultural life that call into question fundamental aspects of our identity. The state responds to threats to itself by becoming a theater of punitive power. Moreover, the insistence on freedom and responsibility confirmed in state killing is one device through which the most insecure segments of our society can reaffirm their social worth.

The result of globalization and acceleration of tempo is culture war in which the death penalty plays a central role. State killing mobilizes, and expresses, divisions between those who seek to return to a world of responsible individuals and vengeful punishments and those who seek more generous responses to new experiences of contingency. It creates and sustains powerful cultural tropes that underwrite particular ways of being in the world.

Like Connolly, Jennifer Culbert contends that one of those tropes, the image of the normal, rational, self-determining individual, is central to contemporary thinking about capital punishment. Challenged by both psychiatry and philosophy, law responds by reaffirming its faith in the normal person. It does so by adapting legal doctrine and devising new standards of responsibility. This is precisely the work done by the Supreme Court in *Tison v. Arizona*,[80] a case of two sons charged in a murder committed by their father during his flight after a prison break that they helped to orchestrate. In that case the Court held that a person can be sentenced to death for a crime he did not commit, intend to commit, desire, or anticipate if he can be said to have displayed "reckless indifference to human life."

The *Tison* opinion is dependent, Culbert suggests, on assumptions about how normal persons act and ought to act. In *Tison* the Court had to confront the possibility that a normal person might be perfectly incapable of telling right from wrong. Borrowing from Hannah Arendt's notion of the "banality of evil," Culbert contends that horrific acts can occur as small, thoughtless gestures under mundane circumstances. The Court responded by accommodating, without acknowledging, this fact. Its refusal to consider the psychology of the defendants showed its anxiety about the relationship between normality and indifference. The Court also acted against the challenge of a philosophical argument that holds all action to be ultimately reckless in that it takes place in a preexisting context that is both uncontrollable and that regularly defeats intention.

Tison's doctrinal innovation seeks to reinforce responsibility in the face of the rapidly eroding figure of the "normal person" and, as such, is an important moment in the law's resistance to the cultural contingencies Connolly describes. However, the figure of the normal person is, of course, not a formal legal category, but is instead a norm reflective of a customary understanding. Its importance in death penalty cases, like *Tison*, reminds us that the cultural meaning and legitimacy of decisions about state killing hinge on implicit moral norms instead of formal legal principles. Every legal decision, but especially decisions in which life and death are at stake, sends powerful signals about who we are and how we are expected to act. Each of those decisions becomes part of the cultural fabric as much as of the body of legal precedent or of the capital of particular political struggles. *Tison* shows how far the Court will go in protecting, rather than rethinking, the norms against which state killing is said to be justified.

But the cultural fabric constituted by state killing is not just knit together by and through legal decisions and practices. It is, in addition, constituted in the complex cultural politics through which state killing is represented. The last essay in this book, by Austin Sarat, turns its attention to those cultural politics by examining capital punishment in popular culture. It takes as its focus two recent films about the death penalty, *Dead Man Walking* and *Last Dance*. Because execution is no longer public, Sarat contends, it lives in images conveyed, in repressed memories, and in horrible imaginings. It is a hidden reality, known if it can be known at all, by indirection. Most people get whatever images and representations of state killing they do from popular culture. Consequently, film becomes the crucial site of spectatorship.

Sarat examines *Dead Man Walking* and *Last Dance* for what they tell us about the politics of popular cultural representations of capital punishment. Those representations are, he contends, deeply invested in the constitution of a modern, responsible subject as the proper object of punishment. They serve to stabilize the categories that Connolly argues are increasingly being put into question, and they remind us that there is an important difference between being responsible and taking responsibility. The former does some of the legal work necessary for the assignment of guilt; the latter is important in determining blameworthiness and in deciding on punishment. By focusing their attention on the question of whether particular people deserve to die, death penalty films position their viewers as if they were jurors in the penalty phase of a capital trial.

In addition, they present "you are there," behind-the-scenes representations of execution itself. They show the instrumentalities of state killing and, through their showing, seek to convey knowledge of death at the hands of the state. They depend on a type of representational realism and endeavor to inspire confidence that their viewers can know the truth about the death penalty even as they raise questions about its appropriateness in particular cases. In both of these gestures, Sarat suggests, films like *Dead Man Walking* and *Last Dance* enact and depend on a conservative cultural politics in which conventional notions of will and responsibility are left unchallenged, broad, systemic questions about the death penalty go unmasked, and the equation of seeing and knowing is treated as adequate even where death is concerned.

As the essays in this book suggest, in law, politics, and culture state killing is as significant as it is controversial. While it may weaken both democracy and the rule of law, and while it may distract us from confronting the fragility and contingency of basic cultural categories, the machinery of death does its work at an ever escalating pace. The juxtaposition of this increased momentum for state killing and the dangers of the practice is disquieting, if not destabilizing. As Benjamin suggests, "[I]n the exercise of violence over life and death more than in any other legal act, law reaffirms itself. But," he continues, "in this very violence something rotten in law is revealed, above all to a finer sensibility, because the latter knows itself to be infinitely remote from conditions in which fate might imperiously have shown itself in such a sentence."[81] As a result,

> Anglo-American law has traditionally suffered a serious identity crisis over its awkward relation to violence. . . . Our system assumes that law is to hold a monopoly on violence, but this is a monopoly viewed as both necessary and discomforting. It is necessary because it is viewed as the alternative to something worse—unrestrained private vengeance—and it is discomforting because those who make and enforce the law would like us to believe that, though they may be required to use force, force is somehow categorically distinguishable from violence. . . . [T]he efforts of modern jurisprudence to finesse or deny the role of violence have not ceased.[82]

Nor, it might be said, have they succeeded.

These efforts put enormous pressures on events like the capital trial to demonstrate and affirm the difference between state killing and killing that the state condemns. Death sentences and executions can never speak for themselves. While they convey the authority and the desire that someone should be put to death by the state, they represent the ultimate public embrace of law's special brand of violence. In the end, they leave us in a killing state, living more precariously though perhaps more blindly in the face of the danger that that state will erode our legal, political, and cultural sensibilities and swallow up the innocent as well as the guilty, leaving nothing but killing as the currency of social life.[83]

Notes

1. Austin Sarat and Thomas R. Kearns, "A Journey through Forgetting: Toward a Jurisprudence of Violence," in *The Fate of Law*, ed. Austin Sarat and Thomas R. Kearns (Ann Arbor: University of Michigan Press, 1991).

2. As Baudrillard puts it, "Identity is untenable: it is death, since it fails to inscribe its own death. Every closed or metastable, functional or cybernetic system is shadowed by mockery and instantaneous subversion. . . . Hence their fragility increases in proportion to their coherence . . . that is why the only strategy is catastrophic. . . . Things must be pushed to the limit. . . . Death must be played against death." Jean Baudrillard, *Symbolic Exchange and Death* (London: Sage, 1993), 4.

3. Michel Foucault, *Discipline and Punish: The Birth of the Prison*, trans. Alan Sheridan (New York: Vintage Books, 1979).

4. Norbert Elias, *The Civilizing Process*, trans. Edmund Jephcott (New York: Pantheon Books, 1982).

5. Franklin Zimring and Gordon Hawkins, *Capital Punishment and the American Agenda* (Cambridge: Cambridge University Press, 1986).

6. As of January 1, 1996, 313 people had been executed since the reinstatement of capital punishment in 1976. More than 3,100 were on death row.

7. Gregg v. Georgia, 428 U.S. 153 (1976).

8. Robert Weisberg, "Deregulating Death," 1983 *Supreme Court Review* (1983): 305.

9. Samuel Gross, "The Romance of Revenge: Capital Punishment in America," 13 *Studies in Law, Politics, and Society* (1993): 71.

10. Franklin Zimring recently called on scholars to broaden the focus of death penalty research and claimed that the increasing unresponsiveness of policy makers and courts to social science evidence concerning capital punishment sets researchers "free of the constraints that might apply if such work was relevant to immediate decisions on executions." Franklin Zimring, "On the Liberating Virtues of Irrelevance," 27 *Law & Society Review* (1993): 12.

11. For the opposite case see Walter Berns, *For Capital Punishment: Crime and the Morality of the Death Penalty* (New York: Basic Books, 1979).

12. Carl Cohen, *Democracy* (New York: Free Press, 1971).

13. Terry Aladjem, "Revenge and Consent: The Death Penalty and Lockean Principles of Democracy," unpublished manuscript (1990), 36. Robert Burt has recently suggested that "[t]he retaliatory force justified by the criminal law . . . has the same place in democratic theory as majority rule. Each is a form of coercion and neither is legitimate as such. Criminal law penalties and majority rule are both rough equivalents, tolerably consistent with the democratic equality principle only if all disputants (but most particularly, the dominant party) see their application of defensive coercion as a limited way station working ultimately toward the goal of a consensual relationship among acknowledged equals." See "Democracy, Equality and the Death Penalty," *Nomos* 36, *The Rule of Law*, ed. Ian Shapiro (New York: New York University Press, 1994), 14.

14. See A. J. Meldren, "Dignity, Worth, and Rights," in *The Constitution of Rights*, ed. Michael Meyer and William Parent (Ithaca: Cornell University Press, 1992). Also Jordan

Paust, "Human Dignity as a Constitutional Right: A Jurisprudentially Based Inquiry into Criteria and Content," 27 *Howard Law Journal* (1984): 150.

15. See Justice Brennan, in his concurring opinion in *Furman v. Georgia*, 408 U.S. 238, 270 (1972); and Hugo Adam Bedau, "The Eighth Amendment, Dignity, and the Death Penalty," in *The Constitution of Rights: Human Dignity and American Values*, ed. Michael Myer and William Parent (Ithaca: Cornell University Press, 1992).

16. See Austin Sarat, "Violence, Representation, and Responsibility in Capital Trials: The View from the Jury," 70 *Indiana Law Journal* (1995): 1103.

17. See Elaine Scarry, "The Declaration of War: Constitutional and Unconstitutional Violence," in *Law's Violence*, ed. Austin Sarat and Thomas R. Kearns (Ann Arbor: University of Michigan Press, 1992).

18. David Garland, *Punishment and Modern Society: A Study in Social Theory* (Chicago: University of Chicago Press, 1990).

19. George Kateb, *The Inner Ocean* (Ithaca: Cornell University Press, 1992), 192.

20. Foucault, *Discipline and Punish*, 9.

21. John Locke, *Second Treatise of Government*, 1st ed., ed. C. B. Macpherson (Indianapolis, Ind.: Hacket, 1980).

22. Aladjem, "Revenge and Consent." Also Thomas Dumm, *Democracy and Punishment: Disciplinary Origins of the United States* (Madison: University of Wisconsin Press, 1987).

23. Jonathan Simon, "Governing through Crime," in *The Crime Conundrum: Essays on Criminal Justice*, ed. Lawrence Friedman and George Fisher (Boulder, Colo.: Westview Press, 1997).

24. Michael Tonry, *Malign Neglect: Race, Crime, and Punishment in America* (New York: Oxford University Press, 1995).

25. Marshall Frady, "Death in Arkansas," *New Yorker*, February 22, 1993, 105, 132.

26. Terry Aladjem, "Vengeance and Democratic Justice: American Culture and the Limits of Punishment," unpublished manuscript (1992), 8.

27. See Judge Stephen Reinhardt, "The Supreme Court, the Death Penalty, and the *Harris* Case," 102 *Yale Law Journal* (1992), 205. Also Evan Camiker and Erwin Chemerinsky, "The Lawless Execution of Robert Alton Harris," 102 *Yale Law Journal* (1992): 2225.

28. Beneath the headline "After Night of Court Battles, a California Execution," the April 22, 1992, edition of the *New York Times* reported the tangled maze of last-minute legal maneuvers that immediately preceded the death in California's gas chamber of Robert Alton Harris, the 169th person to be executed since the Supreme Court restored capital punishment in 1976. As in many previous executions, the hope for clemency or the possibility of a stay of execution was in Harris's case pursued until the last minute.

29. The Court scolded Harris's lawyers for "abusive delay which has been compounded by last minute attempts to manipulate the judicial process" (New York Times, April 22, 1992, p. 22). In so doing it displaced Harris as the soon-to-be victim of law, and portrayed law itself as the victim of Harris and his manipulative lawyers. To defend the virtue of law required an assertion of the Court's supremacy against both the vexatious sympathies of other courts and the efforts of Harris and his lawyers to keep alive a dialogue about death.

30. Foucault, *Discipline and Punish*, 9.

31. See Thomas Dumm, "Fear of Law," 10 *Studies in Law, Politics, and Society* (1990): 29, 44–49. As Dumm puts it, "In the face of the law that makes people persons, people need to fear. Yet people also need law to protect them. . . . Hence fear is a political value that is valuable because it is critical of value, a way of establishing difference that enables uncertainty in the face of danger" (p. 54).

32. The capital trial is one particularly important event through which law seeks to dis-

tinguish the killings that it opposes and seeks to avenge from the force that expresses its opposition and through which its avenging work is done. In such trials, illegal violence is juxtaposed to the "legitimate" force that the state seeks to apply to the killer.

33. Sarat and Kearns, "A Journey through Forgetting," 211.

34. As Ronald Dworkin argues,

> Day in and day out we send people to jail, or take money away from them, or make them do things they do not want to do, under coercion of force, and we justify all this by speaking of such persons as having broken the law or having failed to meet their legal obligations. . . . Even in clear cases . . . , when we are confident that someone had a legal obligation and broke it, we are not able to give a satisfactory account of what that means or why it entitles the state to punish or coerce him. We may feel confident that what we are doing is proper, but until we can identify the principles we are following we cannot be sure they are sufficient. . . . In less clear cases, . . . the pitch of these nagging questions rises, and our responsibility to find answers deepens."

See *Taking Rights Seriously* (Cambridge, Mass.: Harvard University Press, 1977), 15.

Another version of this difficulty is described by Samuel Weber. As he says, "To render impure, literally; to 'touch with' (something foreign, alien), is also to violate. And to violate something is to do violence to it. Inversely, it is difficult to conceive of violence without violation, so much so that the latter might well be a criterion of the former: no violence without violation, hence, no violence without a certain contamination." See "Deconstruction before the Name: Some [Very] Preliminary Remarks on Deconstruction and Violence," unpublished manuscript (1990), 2.

35. See Catharine MacKinnon, *Feminism Unmodified* (Cambridge, Mass.: Harvard University Press, 1987). For an interesting treatment of representation as violence in a nonlegal context see Nancy Armstrong and Leonard Tennenhouse, eds. *The Violence of Representation: Literature and the History of Violence* (London: Routledge, 1989).

36. See Martha Minow, *Making All the Difference* (Ithaca: Cornell University Press, 1989). Also see Joan Scott, "The Evidence of Experience," 17 *Critical Inquiry* (1991): 773; and Teresa de Lauretis, "The Violence of Rhetoric: Considerations on Representation and Gender," in *The Violence of Representation*, ed. Nancy Armstrong and Leonard Tennenhouse (London: Routledge, 1989).

37. Robin West, "Disciplines, Subjectivity, and Law," in *The Fate of Law*, ed. Austin Sarat and Thomas R. Kearns (Ann Arbor: University of Michigan Press, 1991).

38. See Robert Paul Wolff, "Violence and the Law," in *The Rule of Law*, ed. Robert Paul Wolff (New York: Simon & Schuster, 1971), 55.

39. Drucilla Cornell suggests that the violent "foundation" of law is allegorical rather than metaphorical; "[T]he Law of Law is only 'present' in its absolute absence. The 'never has been' of an unrecoverable past is understood as the lack of origin 'presentable' only as allegory. The Law of Law, in other words, is the figure of an initial fragmentation, the loss of the Good. But this allegory is inescapable because the lack of origin is the fundamental truth." See "From the Lighthouse: The Promise of Redemption and the Possibility of Legal Interpretation," 11 *Cardozo Law Review* (1990): 1687, 1689.

40. See Thomas Hobbes, *Leviathan*, ed. C. B. MacPherson (New York: Penguin Books, 1986). See also Hans Kelsen, *General Theory of Law and the State*, trans. Anders Wedberg (New York: Russell & Russell, 1945); Noberto Bobbio, "Law and Force," *Monist* 48 (1965): 321; Walter Benjamin, "Critique of Violence," in *Reflections*, trans. Edmund Jephcott (New York: Harcourt, Brace, 1978).

41. On the general problematic of violence and reason see Sarat and Kearns, "A Journey through Forgetting," 265–273.

42. Jacques Derrida, "The Force of Law: The 'Mystical Foundations of Authority,'" 11 *Cardozo Law Review* (1990): 927.

43. Robert Weisberg, "Private Violence as Moral Action: The Law as Inspiration and Example," in *Law's Violence*, ed. Sarat and Kearns.

The imperatives of violence may be so overwhelming as to distort and destroy prevailing normative commitments. Two powerful examples are provided by Justice Powell in McCleskey v. Kemp, 481 U.S. 279 (1987) (holding that statistical evidence of racial discrimination may not be used to establish prime facie case of discrimination in death penalty cases), and by Justice Rehnquist in *Payne v. Tennessee*, 501 U.S. 808, (1991) (devising new understanding of the bindingness of precedent to overturn two decisions forbidding the use of victim impact information in death penalty litigation).

Unfortunately, except in the utopian imagination, there is no symmetry in the relation of law and violence. Law never similarly threatens violence. Even when we realize the way law itself often exaggerates the threat of violence *outside* law, we can never ourselves imagine that law could ever finally conquer and undo force, coercion, and disorder; its best promise is a promise to substitute one kind of force—legitimate force—for another.

44. Austin Sarat, "Abolitionism as Legal Conservatism: The American Bar Association, the Death Penalty, and Our Continuing Anxiety about Law's Violence," 1 *Theory & Event* (1997), <http://muse.jhu.edu/journals/theory_&_event/v001/1.2sarat.html>.

45. See *Callins v. Collins*, 510 U.S. 1141 (1994).

46. *Furman v. Georgia*, 408 U.S. 405 (1972).

47. *Gregg v. Georgia*, 428 U.S. 153 (1976).

48. See Jeffrey King, "Now Turn to the Left: The Changing Ideology of Justice Harry A. Blackmun," 33 *Houston Law Review* (1996): 296, 297. Also Randall Coyne, "Marking the Progress of a Humane Justice: Harry Blackmun's Death Penalty Epiphany," 43 *University of Kansas Law Review* (1995): 367.

49. In the United States, opposition to the death penalty traditionally has been expressed in several guises. Some have opposed the death penalty in the name of the sanctity of life. See Albert Camus and Arthur Koestler, *Reflections on the Guillotine* (Paris: Calman-Levy, 1958). Even the most heinous criminals, so this argument goes, are entitled to be treated with dignity. In this view, there is nothing that anyone can do to forfeit the "right to have rights." Justice William Brennan in *Furman*, 257. Others have emphasized the moral horror, the "evil," of the state willfully taking the lives of any of its citizens. Kateb, *The Inner Ocean*, 191–192. Still others believe that death as a punishment is always cruel and, as such, is incompatible with the Eighth Amendment prohibition of cruel and unusual punishment. See Hugo Adam Bedau, *Death Is Different: Studies in the Morality, Law and Politics of Capital Punishment* (Boston, Mass.: Northeastern University Press, 1987).

Each of these arguments has been associated with, and is an expression of, humanist liberalism or political radicalism. Each represents a frontal assault on the simple and appealing retributivist rationale for capital punishment. Each has put the opponents of the death penalty on the side of society's most despised and notorious criminals; to be against the death penalty one has had to defend the life of Sirhan Sirhan or John Gacey, of cop killers and child murderers. Thus it is not surprising that while traditional abolitionist arguments have been raised repeatedly in philosophical commentary, political debate, and legal cases, none of them has ever carried the day in the debate about capital punishment in the United States. By the time Blackmun wrote his opinion in *Callins v. Collins* it looked like none ever would.

50. *Callins*, 3546.

51. Id., 3549.

52. Id., 3547.

53. Phoebe Ellsworth and Samuel Gross, "Hardening of Attitudes; Americans' Views on the Death Penalty," 50 *Journal of Social Issues* (1994): 48.

54. For example, *Teague v. Lane*, 489 U.S. 288 (1989) and *Penry v. Lynaugh*, 492 U.S. 302 (1989).

55. Pub. L. No. 104–132, 110 Stat. 1214 (1996).

56. See Harvey Berkman, "Costs Mount for Indigent Defense," *National Law Journal*, August 7, 1995, A18.

57. Samuel Gross, "The Romance of Revenge: Capital Punishment in America," 13 *Studies in Law, Politics, and Society* (1993): 71.

58. David Garland, "Punishment and Culture: The Symbolic Dimension of Criminal Justice," 11 *Studies in Law, Politics, and Society* (1991): 191.

59. Id., 193.

60. Id., 195.

61. Weisberg, "Private Violence as Moral Action."

62. Garland, "Punishment and Culture," 210.

63. Emile Durkheim, *The Division of Labor in Society*, trans. G. Simpson (New York: Free Press, 1933).

64. George Herbert Mead, "The Psychology of Punitive Justice," 23 *American Journal of Sociology* (1918): 577.

65. See John Sloop, *The Cultural Prison: Discourse, Prisoners, and Punishment* (Tuscaloosa: University of Alabama Press, 1996), 3.

66. Foucault, *Discipline and Punish*.

67. Michael Madow, "Forbidden Spectacle: Executions, the Public, and the Press in Nineteenth Century New York," 43 *Buffalo Law Review* (1995): 461.

68. As Robert Weisberg argues, such trials provide "a representational medium that . . . serves as a grammar of social symbols. . . . The criminal trial is a 'miracle play' of government in which we carry out our inarticulate beliefs about crime and criminals within the reassuring formal structure of disinterested due process." See "Deregulating Death," 385.

69. Austin Sarat, "Speaking of Death: Narratives of Violence in Capital Trials," 27 *Law & Society Review* (1993): 19.

70. Foucault, *Discipline and Punish*, 9. See also Austin Sarat and Aaron Schuster, "To See or Not to See: Television, Capital Punishment, and Law's Violence," 7 *Yale Journal of Law & the Humanities* (1995): 397.

71. See, for example, Norman Mailer, *The Executioner's Song* (New York: Warner Books, 1979).

72. Wendy Lesser, *Pictures at an Execution: An Inquiry into the Subject of Murder* (Cambridge, Mass.: Harvard University Press, 1993).

73. Writing about the end of public executions in the mid-nineteenth century Masur notes that it "marked the triumph of a certain code of conduct and set of social attitudes among the middle and upper classes; it symbolized a broader trend toward social privatization and class segmentation; it turned the execution of criminals into an elite event centered around class and gender exclusion rather than communal instruction." See Lewis Masur, *Rites of Execution: Capital Punishment and the Transformation of American Culture, 1776–1875* (New York: Oxford University Press, 1989), 6.

74. Berns, *For Capital Punishment*.

75. Baudrillard, *Symbolic Exchange and Death*, 169.

76. Michael Taussig, "The Injustice of Policing: Prehistory and Rectitude," in *Justice and Injustice in Law and Legal Theory*, ed. Austin Sarat and Thomas R. Kearns (Ann Arbor: University of Michigan Press, 1996), 20.

77. 492 U.S. 302 (1989).

78. 107 S. Ct. 1756 (1987).

79. 507 U.S. 1001 (1993).
80. 481 U.S. 137 (1987).
81. Benjamin, "Critique of Violence," 286.
82. See Weisberg, "Private Violence as Moral Action," 175–176.
83. Dumm, "Fear of Law."

· I ·

THE POLITICS OF
STATE KILLING

• 1 •

AFTER THE TERROR: MORTALITY, EQUALITY, FRATERNITY

ANNE NORTON

Capital punishment, in this historical moment, in this political space, is visited by the powerful upon the dominated, by the state upon the subject. Death is the culmination of a long series of procedures, performed by technicians under the surveillance of diverse, carefully trained administrators, recorded in scrupulous detail. In this historical moment, capital punishment appears as an enactment of the finality of the power of the state. In it, the subjection of the dominated is confirmed. The execution of the condemned marks the boundary dividing writing from violence. Death removes the condemned from the reach and power of the law, of writing, of constitutional guarantees. Death marks that point at which the rule of law finds itself exhausted.

Yet we moderns, we liberals, we constitutionalists are subjects of (and subject to) a history in which capital punishment serves not the powerful but the dominated, not the state, but the subject. This history records the founding of the modern, liberal, constitutional order. In this history, capital punishment figures not as the exhaustion of law but as its inauguration.

I look here to instances of capital punishment that reverse the valences of power underwriting contemporary debates over capital punishment. The first set is drawn from the founding violence of Regicide and Reign of Terror that marked the English and French Revolutions. The second set of executions is drawn from those acts of violent terror that sought to end European colonial rule, and, as Fanon and Sartre taught us, reminded the colonized of their equality.

The revolutionaries and the regicides inverted the customary application of capital punishment in two respects. The powerful were executed by the dominated. Sentences were handed down (or rather, up) by the many rather than the few who ruled. Often there were no formal sentences at all. The condemned were denied all the procedural securities that surround the apparatus of justice in the contemporary United States. Not only the powerful, but entire systems of dominion were condemned. These instances provide a critical vantage point on contemporary debates. They place in question the assumed dichotomies of law and violence, justice and death. They remind us ("pain is the most powerful aid to mnemonics") of the foundation of politics in guilt.

Regicide and Terror

In the regicides of Louis Capet and Charles Stuart, the death penalty is not an instance of closure or the exhaustion of law, but an opening to a more democratic, more lawful order. These executions, and those accomplished less formally in the Terror, did not secure existing hierarchies, they assaulted them. These instances of the death penalty remind us that we—we moderns, we liberals, we constitutionalists, we democrats—have our political origins not only in the word that becomes law but in the violent confirmation of our common mortality.

"The beginnings of everything great on earth," Nietzsche affirmed, are "soaked in blood thoroughly, and for a long time."[1] The liberal constitutional orders of France, England, and the United States had their soaking in the regicides of Charles Stuart and Louis Capet, the bloodletting of the Terror, and the violence of revolution. In regicide, capital punishment is capital indeed: directed at the head of state, accomplished in decapitation. Capital punishment answers capital crimes.

Natural equality, Hobbes had argued in *Leviathan*, is evinced by the fact that anyone can kill anyone else. Civil society, however, had found that distinction in death—treating different deaths differently—secured distinctions among the living. The guillotine put the institution of capital punishment in accord with the principle of equality manifest in a common mortality.[2] The French revolutionaries' liberal use of the guillotine extended and institutionalized the principle of equality, giving to each of the convicted a common death. The guillotine, a machine unable to recognize the distinctions of birth and rank that marked off aristocrats and commons, the powerful and the powerless, gave the same death to every citizen. The aristocracy, no longer set apart in death, bore witness in their executions to the principle of equality.

The guillotine accomplished this equality in execution not by diminishing the aristocracy, but by raising the common people. Beheading had been a punishment reserved for errant aristocrats. Indeed, in the debates on capital punishment in the National Assembly, Verninac de Saint-Maur had objected to the guillotine on those grounds. "Rather than elevate the masses to the dignity of the block, we should reduce the nobility to the modesty of the gibbet."[3] The adoption of beheading as the means of execution for all guilty of capital crimes was thus the extension of a privilege formerly reserved to the aristocracy. Moreover, as Robespierre had earlier observed, the means of punishment formerly allotted to commoners "disgrace the family of those who perish by these means, but the blade that severs the head of the criminal debases his family not at all." Because the traditional imaginary did not "associate the idea of family dishonor" with beheading, the guillotine limited its punishment to the guilty.[4] The means of execution punished only the condemned. This singular punishment, which divided the body into two and united so many in death, made each of the condemned an individual. The guillotined were not only mortals, they were individuals and citizens subject to a formal institutional equality.

This equality embraced all citizens—indeed, all mortals. The guillotine proved its leveling capacity in the execution of Louis Capet. Capet was treated as an ordinary prisoner; his death marked with no special pageantry of state. At the Temple, Louis Capet was confronted with a drawing of the guillotine, with the irreverent caption "Louis spitting in the sack."[5] On the day of the execution, his valet was not permitted to cut his hair, for, as the guard declared, "The executioner is good enough for him."[6] Another guard refused to deliver a package for him to his wife, saying, "That is no concern of mine. I am here to conduct you to the scaffold."[7] At the scaffold, officers insisted on binding his hands.

Louis Capet and his confessor read the denial of personal services, particularly the insistence on binding his hands, as profound insults to his person. They were wrong. Insults make distinctions. Louis Capet was merely subject to the ordinary regulations governing the transport and restraint of prisoners. Charles Stuart, confronting a similar situation in his trial, declared, "I am no ordinary prisoner!"[8] He was not, and his captors recognized it. Each sign of distinction they allowed him — in his accomodations, in his trial, in his execution, and in the disposal of his body — secured the monarchy against further assault. In insisting, however, on trying Charles Stuart as if he were "an ordinary prisoner" and they had the right to do so, the English revolutionaries secured the primacy of parliamentary authority in England.[9]

The English Parliament did not, under ordinary circumstances, have the authority to make of itself a court of law. Charles Stuart had not been slow to point this out. His first act during the trial was to ask "by what lawful authority I am seated here." He was told (after some debate) that he was called by the authority of the Commons of England assembled in Parliament. "The Commons of England" he declared "was never a court of judicature. I would know how they came to be so."[10] Throughout the trial, Charles Stuart continued to dispute the legality of the proceedings. In the ordinary understanding of English law, Charles was entirely in the right. Many of the English revolutionaries had refused or avoided participation in the trial. But as Charles had observed, he was no ordinary prisoner and his no ordinary trial. In giving itself the right to try and to condemn the king, the Commons seized a right to which they had no right and made it their own.

In France, the mechanism of the guillotine enacted the revolutionary claims of an emerging democracy. The literal opening of the bodies of deposed monarchs and a condemned aristocracy revealed an all-too-visible humanity. The claim to the possession of power by right of blood was answered by rites that opened these once sacred bodies and let out that power in the blood. The people of the Terror had blood on their hands, but it was blood that carried right within it.

Violence, as Nietzsche observed, does not simply destroy, it establishes. Nietzsche asks, "How can one create a memory for the human animal?" and answers, "Man could never do without blood, torture, and sacrifices when he felt the need to create a memory for himself. . . . [P]ain is the most powerful aid to mnemonics." Violence, he writes, is essential to those promises by which men bind themselves to one another in politics.[11]

Freud's myth of primal rebellion, which so illuminates the role of violence in the establishment of identity, is particularly appropriate to a consideration of the attacks on authority in the French Revolution.[12] For (let us give Filmer his due) what is the killing of a king if not the killing of the father? Robespierre, arguing before the Convention for the death of Louis, saw the possibility of a revisionist history, and a change in regime that might "even, perhaps, treat faithful friends of liberty as *cannibals*, as anarchists, as factious men."[13] Images of cannibalism haunted the Revolution. A dissenting deputy described the National Assembly as "this cavern of Anthropophages."[14] It is reported in some histories, and many myths, that after Louis Capet's head was cut off, bystanders tasted the blood. His jailers had earlier written on the walls of the prison, "We're going to put up the big pig of the regime."

It is not necessary to see Louis as an edible, to see Louis consumed, to recognize in his execution the enactment of a totem meal. In killing and consuming Louis and the aristocrats, the people of France absorbed their sovereignty. They disinterred the kings of France and laid them in a common grave, mingling their ashes not only with one another, but with those of the people. They came to comprehend in their collective character the authority that had once resided, hidden, in the bodies of the kings, and the sacred body of Saint Louis. In opening those bodies they opened the hidden places, they revealed the title held in blood to the gaze of all. In consuming those bodies, in mingling their ashes in a common grave, they incorporated the sovereignty these persons once possessed. They incorporated the divine right of their kings.

These sacramental gestures were supplemented by a sacramental language. Louis's confessor, a man occupationally attentive to such matters, discoursed to Louis and in his memoirs, on the resemblance of the king to Christ. Certainly, Capet's death, like the death of other lords, was linked to the creation of a corpus mysticum. Freud's band of brothers killed the father and consumed him, found that they had become one body. They shared a common flesh. The flesh of the father that each had consumed now bond them together in a single body. Once bound by the father's word, external to themselves, they now find themselves bound by the flesh of the father within them. They are guilty, and their guilt binds them together.

"I knew," Burke writes, "that the sufferings of monarchs make a delicious repast to some sort of palates," but he is horrified to see bodies serve similarly.[15] Accepting the veracity of the *Times* correspondents (or perhaps recognizing that the truth of the matter mattered very little) he wrote of the revolutionaries' "devouring as a nutriment of their ferocity some part of the bodies of those they have murdered; their drinking the blood of their victims." Burke, like the editor of *Revolutions de Paris*, recognized that the people had become "mangeurs de rois."

The British had no taste for the totem meal, they had eaten earlier.

Flesh was not to be the food of the French for long. They, like the British, would not need to kill another king. The regicides of Charles Stuart and Louis Capet put an end not only to those men, but to the system of absolute monarchical authority.

"The Revolution begins when the tyrant ends," Saint Just declared in a speech before the Convention, marking the execution of Louis Capet as the inaugural moment of the Revolution.[16] John Cook had argued of Charles Stuart, "He must die, and monarchy must die with him."[17] Oliver Cromwell affirmed, "I'll cut off his head with the crown on it." Those who undertook to condemn Charles Stuart and Louis Capet were acutely conscious that they sat in judgment not on particular men but on systems of right and sovereignty. "No man can reign innocently," Saint Just argued.[18] With those deaths, more than a person was cast into oblivion. The executions of Charles Stuart and Louis Capet both began eras of more liberal, more lawful politics. Each put an end to absolute monarchy. Those who executed Charles Stuart were, for the most part, men of faith, who believed that they were engaged in divine work. Few of the French regicides shared that faith. Not all of us share it now.

For the faithful, execution lacks finality. The executed is sent to another place, another time, and another judgment. The death penalty may entail a more fearful judgment and a more demanding responsibility for the uncertain and the unbelieving. When we execute, we elect to cast the dead into oblivion. This will not, however, always argue against execution. Where there is no certainty of an afterlife, the character and conditions of life in the world take on an unchallenged importance. The uncertain and the unbelieving may understand themselves to be not only willing but obliged to cast another into oblivion. If, as the history of regicide suggests, executions may cast more than mortals into oblivion, we may be obliged to take those deaths upon ourselves.

Yet we will be haunted, we unknowing ones, by the arrogant imposition of this all-too-partial closure.

Frantz Fanon and the Violence of Liberation

The capacity of violence to put an end not only to particular lives but to a political order was asserted again in Frantz Fanon's *Wretched of the Earth*. The "morality" of decolonization with regard to the settler is simple, Fanon writes; the imperative is "to put him out of the picture." The native "has already decided to eject him and to take his place." As Fanon writes, "[I]t is a whole material and moral universe that is breaking up."[19]

"The naked truth of decolonization evokes for us the searing bullets and blood-stained knives which emanate from it."[20] The truth of decolonization, and its power to dismantle a moral universe, began in a great refusal: "[W]e only become what we are by the radical and deep-seated refusal of that which others have made of us."[21] The violence of decolonization was, like the violence of regicide and the Terror, an assault on privilege. As Albert Memmi observed, the colonizers, even those of good will, share a guilt consequent on the enjoyment of undeserved privilege. The violence of anticolonial terror was not, therefore, as random as it seemed. In his notorious introduction to Fanon's work, Jean-Paul Sartre (mindful, perhaps, of Saint Just's argument that no reign is innocent) endorsed these informal executions. "Make no mistake about it," Sartre insists, "by this bitterness and spleen, by their ever-present desire to kill us, by the permanent tensing of powerful muscles which are afraid to relax, they have become men."[22] Sartre regards anticolonial violence as redemptive not only for the colonized but for the colonizer: "[V]iolence, like Achilles' lance, can heal the wounds it has inflicted."[23]

The colonial order had employed violence to conquer and pacify the colonized, to terrorize them and render them subject. Colonial violence stripped the colonized of their humanity, depriving them of the exercise of will, the right of dominion, and the integrity of their bodies. The killing of the colonizer, Fanon argued, returned to the colonized the humanity that colonization had denied them. "The colonized man finds his freedom in and through violence," Fanon wrote. Through violence "the 'thing' which has been colonized becomes man."[24]

"At the level of individuals," Fanon writes, "violence is a cleansing force. It frees the native from his inferiority complex and from his despair and inaction; it makes him fearless and restores his self-respect." Violence not only makes the colonized human, it makes them a nation. Fanon writes, "The practice of violence binds them together as a whole."[25] Following Freud, Fanon affirms that violence secures the capacity for self-government. "Yesterday they were completely irresponsible; today they mean to understand everything and make all decisions."[26] They had acquired the right to make promises.

Fanon's account turns on the recognition of responsibility. That the killings are done on behalf of the state does not absolve the individuals who commit them of responsibility. On the contrary, it is the assumption of responsibility, of guilt, that binds the nation together.

In the penultimate chapter of *Wretched of the Earth*, "Colonial War and Mental Disorders," Fanon recounts a series of cases that came to his psychiatric practice. These cases seem at first to offer a cautionary coda to the approbation of revolutionary violence that Fanon offers in the text proper. Yet Fanon's moral tales of justice and responsibility resist this undemanding reading.

Case No. 1 concerns an Algerian, a soldier in the National Liberation Front (FLN), who became impotent following the rape of his wife. His impotence, we learn, is more than sexual. He was troubled by sleeplessness and absent-mindedness, and his superiors, thinking him ill, sent him for a medical examination. "He avoided political discussion and showed a marked lack of interest in everything having to do with the national struggle. He avoided listening to any news which had a bearing on the war of liberation."[27]

The revolutionary had learned that his wife had been questioned by the French, refused to reveal her knowledge of his whereabouts or those of his comrades in the FLN, and was, in the course of questioning, raped by the French. "That wasn't a simple rape, for want of something better to do, or for sadistic reasons like those I've had occasion to see in the villages; it was the rape of an obstinate woman, who was ready to put up with anything rather than sell her husband. And the husband in question, *it was me*."[28]

Ethics, Kant taught, is found in the triangulation of the general and the particular. Kant instructs us to look for the general principle in particular acts, to accord personal conduct to a general standard. The recognition of that general standard was not, however, sufficient for Fanon's revolutionary. He had, after all, "seen peasants drying the tears of their wives after having seen them raped under their very eyes." He had, with his comrades, "intervened in such circumstances in order to explain matters to the civilians."[29] He knew, and he had explained to others, where one's duty lay in such general circumstances. He had accepted it. What he had not expected was the recognition of an all-too-private debt: "the husband in question, *it was me*."[30]

Fanon's cases oblige us to recognize that the private haunts the public. Case

No. 5 concerns a European police inspector. "The thing that kills me most," he tells Fanon, "is the torture. You don't know what that is, do you? Sometimes I torture people for ten hours at a stretch." He had come to Fanon because he was bothered by what he called "fits of madness." He had begun to beat his wife and children, and "as soon as someone goes against me I want to hit him. . . . I say to myself 'If I had you for a few hours my fine fellow you wouldn't look so clever afterwards.'"[31] Such impulses, the inspector reported, were foreign to him. They had come upon him only "since the troubles."[32] The modern distinctions between private and public, person and office, did not hold. The practices of the torturer's profession became the practices of his private life as well. He might leave the interrogation rooms of prison and police station, but he carried the practices proper to those spaces within him. He was haunted by his victims.

Case No. 3, a young soldier of the FLN, was haunted as well. He was visited each night by a woman, "bloodless, pale, and terribly thin," with an open wound in her stomach. Each night she came to him and insisted that he should give her back her spilled blood. The patient, Fanon reports, knew who she was well enough: "it was he who had killed her." She was the wife of "an active colonialist" who had already killed two Algerian civilians. The soldier, whose mother had been killed by a French soldier, watched as she was questioned. "When I looked at her," he told Fanon, "I thought of my mother." He stabbed her, she died, he was taken into custody. "After that," he told Fanon "this woman started coming every night and asking for my blood. But my mother's blood—where's that?"[33]

Who but the son carries the mother's blood?

The soldier's account might be read, as Fanon recognized, as "an unconscious guilt complex following on the death of the mother." One might incline particularly to this reading, as the son had been the support of the family since his father's death some years earlier, and the mother had been killed after the son joined the Maquis.[34] Such a reading, however, too easily reduces a political act to a private revenge. The question "[M]y mother's blood—where's that?" is given several answers in the soldier's account, none complete, none satisfactory. The mother's blood is spilled, the wife of the colonialist carries the mother's blood, the soldier carries the mother's blood. Each night the woman who is and is not the mother reclaims her blood, only to return, pale, bloodless, and demanding, the next night. Like the demand for the proofs of love, the demand for the mother's blood cannot be satisfied.[35] The mother's death cannot be recompensed. The killing of the colonialist's wife supplies a French death by an Algerian hand for an Algerian one by a French hand. Yet "when I looked at that woman I thought of my mother."[36] It was "a manifold repetition of the same woman."[37] Having taken the French woman for the mother and given her the mother's death, the soldier finds that he has indeed taken her for the mother, and his blood is hers. The economy of exchange that exacted the French woman's death established an equivalence between French and Algerian, and in doing so made the Algerian soldier his own enemy. The assumption of the power and authority—the capacity for final judgment—claimed by the colonizer entailed the assumption of bloodguilt as well.

Perhaps the most profound of the cases Fanon discusses is "a borderline case" that serves as a prologue to "Colonial War and Mental Disorders." Here Fanon

writes of "a patriot who had been in the resistance" in one of the newly independent African countries. He had found himself suffering from insomnia, anxiety, and
suicidal obsessions, at the same time each year. "The critical date was that when on
instructions from his organization he had placed a bomb somewhere. Ten people
had been killed as a result." In the period immediately after the event, the revolutionary had not been troubled by these symptoms. They emerged when, after independence had been achieved, he encountered some former colonists and found
he liked them. The revolutionary had, he observes, "never for a single moment
thought of repudiating his past action." Fanon does not encourage him to do so.
What interests Fanon, and should interest us about this case, is that the revolutionary "realized very clearly the manner in which he himself had to pay the price of
national independence." "In other words," Fanon writes,

> we are forever pursued by our actions. Their ordering, their circumstances, and
> their motivation may perfectly well come to be profoundly modified a posteriori.
> This is merely one of the snares that history and its various influences sets for us.
> But can we escape becoming dizzy? And who can affirm that vertigo does not
> haunt the whole of existence?[38]

In Fanon's account, murderer and murdered, the executed and the executioner, oscillate continually. The woman who cries for blood is mother and enemy,
murdered and murdering. Torture of the alien colonized becomes beating of the
coloniser's domestics. The revolutionaries bind themselves psychically, irrevocably,
to those they kill. Vertigo haunts the whole of existence. In this understanding of
politics, action on behalf of the sovereign can offer no absolution. That which enables the one who kills to kill on behalf of another ensures the identification of the
killer with the killed. The elision of the boundaries that divide one from another,
on which politics and ethics depend, does not shelter the executioner or the revolutionary. The individual who kills for the revolution takes the responsibility for those
deaths. The revolutionary's willingness to do this, and the effects of that submission
upon him, sends us back in a dizzying spiral, through the French and English revolutionaries, to the covenant with Abraham and the sacrifice of Isaac.

For Abraham, as for the revolutionaries, innocent death is the price of political
power. "I have made you the father of a multitude of nations," God says to Abraham, "I will make you exceedingly fruitful, and I will make nations of you, and
kings shall come forth from you. And I will establish my covenant between me and
you and your descendants."[39] Abraham's right to make promises follows his willingness to offer up an innocent death. For Derrida, "[I]t is as if Abraham had *already*
killed Isaac" in the instant in which he raised his hand.[40] God, in Derrida's account, takes the intention for the act. Abraham has understood and acted upon his
duty to God. He has assumed absolute responsibility. He is willing to kill, he "had
the courage to behave like a murderer in the eyes of the world . . . in the eyes of
morality and politics."[41] This is the demand revolution makes.

Perhaps this is the demand politics makes. Derrida would have us read the
story of Abraham as one which is reproduced, reenacted, endlessly in the quotidian.
"Day and night, at every instant, on all the Mount Moriahs of this world, I am
doing that, raising my knife over what I love and must love, over those to whom I

owe absolute fidelity, incommensurably." Each commitment to another entails the neglect, the refusal, of an obligation to all others.[42] Absolute duty, each duty, involves the sacrifice of others.

Derrida's account has the divinity demanding the proofs of love. "The command requests, like a prayer from God, a declaration of love that implores: tell me that you love me, that you turn towards me, towards the unique one, towards the other as unique and, above all, over everything else, unconditionally, and in order to do that, make a gift of death, give death to your only son and give me the death I ask for."[43]

The demand for the proofs of love is the demand that cannot be finally satisfied, that renews itself inevitably in the moment of its satisfaction. Yet God's demand does not renew itself. Isaac is not sacrificed. Abraham's covenant with God is sealed not by bloodshed, but by the evasion of bloodshed. This is the contract that does not depend on fulfillment for its authority.

For Abraham, Derrida writes, this "absolute duty" entails no burden of guilt or regret. "Without being so, then, he nevertheless feels absolved of his duty towards his family, towards the human species [le genre humaine] and the generality of the ethical, absolved by the absolute of a unique duty that binds him to God the one."[44] In Derrida's account, Abraham feels himself absolved without being so. Fanon's cases tend to undermine one's faith in this aspect of the scriptural. The scriptural narrative, does, however, join founding with violence, politics with guilt, more insistently than Derrida's account implies. It is not Abraham, but Cain with whom the deity first contracts. Cain has killed. The murder of Abel, and the desire of other men to murder him in turn, prompts God to contract with him, to mark him, to send him into the world. It is the descendants of Cain who build the first cities. The scriptural account reminds us, more forcefully than Derrida, that foundings are never innocent, that pardons may be fruitful, and that politics is the practice of the guilty.

This recognition echoes in the thought of Nietzsche and Freud, Foucault and Althusser. In *The Psychic Life of Power*, Judith Butler marks that echoing insistence and links it to the vertigo that Fanon remarked in his all-too-historical subjects. The founding moment of the subject (of subjection) is, Butler writes, "relentlessly marked by a figure of turning, a turning back upon oneself or even a turning on oneself."[45] Nietzsche's account of the founding of the moral subject in the infliction of pain recognizes that the pleasure of pain visited on another depends perversely on the recognition of likeness to the one punished. His account, Butler writes, is that of "a body in recoil upon itself."[46] Freud "describes conscience as the force of a desire—although sometimes a force of aggression—as it turns back on itself, and he understands prohibition not as a law external to desire, but as the very operation of desire as it turns on its own possibility."[47] The most compelling account of this turning, and the most poignant in its later enactment and inversion, is Althusser's doctrine of interpellation. The subject finds itself in turning guiltily toward the law. "The call itself is figured as a demand to align oneself with the law, a turning around (to face the law, to find a face for the law?) and an entrance into the language of self-ascription—"Here I am"—through the appropriation of guilt."[48]

The subject of capital punishment, like Fanon's subject, is subject to the vertiginous imperatives of politics. When we question the killing of the murderers, we find ourselves in the place of the murderer, obliged to consider ourselves guilty of murder. The question of how we punish the guilty becomes the question of our own guilt, in the quotidian practices as well as the theoretical justifications, of capital punishment.

Though we might wish, like Dr. Guillotin, to fashion a technology of death that approaches painlessness in its application, and achieves indifference to the status of the condemned, we (like him) will find it difficult to fashion a machine that requires no one to set it in motion. What becomes of the executioner? Is office so powerful a purgative that is washes away not only guilt but the myriad effects attendant on becoming the agent of another's death? Those whose faith in the separation of public and private is less than perfect may question the exaction that the state makes from the executioner.

The executioner escapes responsibility only by acting as the impersonal representative of the state, yet the physical presence of the executioner will be necessary to carry out the sentence. Efforts have been made—technically and technologically—to separate the executioner from the execution. The machinery, after the manner of Dr. Guillotin's machine, has been made as impersonal and mechanical—as automatic—as possible. In these collective acts, the willful action of the executioner has been steadily diminished, responsibility steadily diffused. Yet those who are obliged to do the public work of execution may find themselves—like Fanon's Case No. 5, the European police inspector—privately damaged by it.

Fanon's work obliges us to recognize that those who kill, whether they do so on their own behalf, on behalf of the nation, as a refusal of injustice, or in pursuit of justice; whether they do so with their own hands, or through the state, will nevertheless remain (whether they wish to be or not) responsible for their actions.

Fanon (along with Freud and Nietzsche) also suggests, that the assumption of this responsibility enables the once-animal to make themselves human, and citizens. They acquire the right to make promises, they become self-governing, they band together, they restore their lost humanity. The historic role of capital punishment in the origins of democratic government should make us reluctant to dismiss it out of hand.

Responsibility may argue for the retention of capital punishment not only from the perspective of the executing nation and its citizens, but from the perspective of the condemned as well. The notion that capital punishment reduces the dignity and humanity of the condemned is not altogether persuasive. Capital punishment, after all, construes the condemned as having the will and capacities proper to human beings. The gravity of the penalty acknowledges the gravity of the action.

Liberalism has its ambivalent roots in Hobbes, with his intense regard for preserving the integrity of the individual body. Hobbes, who argued that equality rested on the recognition that anyone could kill anyone else, devated himself to preventing the exercise of that ability. The recognition of the power of one person to kill another contains within it a comprehensive claim. The power of the will, the desire to extend that will in the world, the claim that one might have—in the final sense—dominion over others. This power is common to all, marking an equality founded not only in subjection but in a common capacity for dominion.

These considerations, and the histories of democratic revolution suggest that capital punishment may commend itself to us in those instances when it is directed at the powerful. The founding regicides of the English and French Revolutions, the Reign of Terror, and the violence of anticolonial revolutions are all instances in which the ordinary relations of capital punishment are inverted and the state, the privileged, and the powerful become the condemned.

The killing of colonists and kings ended regimes. These deaths cast not only monarchs but monarchy, not only colonists but colonialism, into oblivion. They seem to give us closure, to remove us from the power of claims to power in the blood, from the rule of men to the rule of law. We are indebted to that past. "The subject who would oppose violence, even violence to itself, is itself the effect of a prior violence without which the subject could not have emerged."[49] One need not believe in an afterlife to find oneself haunted in this one. We are left with the specters Nietzsche raised in arguing that violence is necessary to breed an animal with the right to make promises. We are left with the haunting memory of Fanon's revolutionary who believed that he had killed the innocent, bore the guilt, and would not disavow it.

If we are to be haunted, let the ghosts be great ones. But if we find that that which we chose to cast into oblivion returns to make its home in us, then we may decide that the model for capital punishment should be the sacrifice of Isaac. In this myth of covenant, Abraham is called to seal the covenant by executing the innocent. Perhaps it is his willingness to do so that marks him as having the right to make promises. Perhaps it is Abraham's willingness to take upon himself the responsibility for shedding innocent blood that enables him to make a nation. Yet, in the last instant, the power that called for the sacrifice holds him back. "It is not unthinkable," Nietzsche wrote, "that a society might attain such a consciousness of power that it could allow itself the noblest luxury possible to it, letting those who harm it go unpunished."

Notes

1. Friedrich Nietzsche, *On the Genealogy of Morals,* trans. Walter Kaufmann (New York: Vintage Books, 1989), essay 2, sec. 6, p. 65.

2. For an account of the adoption of the guillotine as the instrument of capital punishment in France, see Daniel Arasse, *The Guillotine and the Terror,* trans. Christopher Miller (London: Penguin Press, 1989).

3. Arasse, *The Guillotine,* 16. Verninac's speech was taken from *Le Moniteur,* December 1789.

4. Arasse, *The Guillotine,* 12. Robespierre made this argument in a 1783 essay sponsored by the Academy of Metz on the suppression of ignominious penalties. By 1791 Robespierre had emerged as an opponent of the death penalty, and argued vigorously for its abolition in the May and June 1791 debates in the National Assembly. The Assembly, however, voted against abolition, instead determining that "all persons sentenced to death shall be decapitated."

5. "Louis crachant dans la sac." Cléry, M. *Journal de ce qui s'est passé à la Tourde Temple* (Paris: Mercure de Paris, 1987), p. 42.

6. "Le bourreau est assez bien pour lui." Ibid.

7. "Cela ne me regarde point, je suis ici pour conduire a l'echafaud." Ibid.

8. C. V. Wedgewood, *A Coffin for King Charles* (New York: Time-Life, 1966), 129.

9. In challenging the authority of Parliament to try him, Charles Stuart correctly claimed that "[t]he Commons of England was never a Court of Judicature." In acting as if they were, the Commons literally enacted their claims for the king's subjection to law, and the primacy of their authority. This simulation brought the political order into being.

10. *The Trial of Charles I: A Documentary History*, ed. David Lagomarsino and Charles Wood (Hanover, N.H.: University Press of New England, 1989), 64, 76, 77.

11. Friedrich Nietzsche, *On the Genealogy of Morals*, trans. Walter Kaufmann (New York: Vintage, 1969), essay 2, p. 61, and passim.

12. See Freud, *Totem and Taboo* (New York: W. W. Norton, 19; and Anne Norton, *Reflections on Political Identity* (Baltimore: Johns Hopkins University Press, 1988), ch. 4.

13. Robespierre, Speech before the Convention, December 28, 1792, in Michael Walzer, *Regicide and Revolution* (Cambridge: Cambridge University Press, 1974), 184, my emphasis.

14. De Lally Tollendal, quoted in Edmund Burke, *Reflections on the Revolution in France* (London: Methuen, 1905), 67 n.2.

15. Burke, *Reflections*, 68.

16. Saint Just at the trial of Louis Capet, December 27, 1792, quoted in Walzer, *Regicide*, 76.

17. C. V. Wedgewood, *A Coffin for King Charles* (New York: Time-Life, 1966), 124.

18. "On ne peut point regner innocemment." David Jordan, *The King's Trial* (Berkeley: University of California Press, 1981), vii.

19. Frantz Fanon, *The Wretched of the Earth*, trans. Constance Farrington (New York: Grove Press, 1968), 44–45.

20. Fanon, *Wretched of the Earth*, 37.

21. Jean Paul Sartre's preface to Fanon, *Wretched of the Earth*, 17. This passage prefigures Foucault's suggestion that perhaps we should aim "not to discover who we are, but to refuse who we are." Michel Foucault, "Afterword: The Subject and Power," in Herbert L. Dreyfus and Paul Rabinow, eds., *Michel Foucault: Beyond Structuralism and Hermeneutics* (Chicago: University of Chicago Press, 1982), 216.

22. Ibid.

23. Sartre in Fanon, *Wretched of the Earth*, 30.

24. Fanon, *Wretched of the Earth*, 86, 36–37.

25. Ibid., 93.

26. Ibid., 94.

27. Ibid., 256.

28. Ibid., 257–258.

29. Ibid., 258.

30. Ibid., 257–258.

31. Ibid., 267.

32. Ibid., 268.

33. Ibid., 262–263.

34. Ibid., 262–263.

35. See Jacques Lacan, "The Signification of the Phallus," in *Ecrits* (New York: W. W. Norton, 1977), 289.

36. Fanon, *Wretched of the Earth*, 263.

37. Ibid., 264.

38. Ibid., 253.

39. Genesis 17:5–8. God also gives Abraham land in this passage.

40. Jacques Derrida, *The Gift of Death*, trans. David Wills (Chicago: University of Chicago Press, 1995), 72.

41. Ibid.

42. Ibid., 68–69.

43. Ibid., 72.

44. Ibid., 73.

45. Judith Butler, *The Psychic Life of Power* (Stanford: Stanford University Press, 1997), 3. This book is invaluable, not only for questions concerning capital punishment, but for its broader reflections on law, politics, and subjection.

46. Ibid., 66.

47. Ibid., 63.

48. Ibid., 107.

49. Ibid., 64.

· 2 ·

ABOLISHING THE DEATH PENALTY EVEN
FOR THE WORST MURDERERS

HUGO ADAM BEDAU

I

In the wake of the death sentence for Timothy McVeigh, convicted in June 1997 for his role in the murderous bombing of the Federal Building in Oklahoma City two years earlier, it is timely to ask this question: Who has the better of the argument, those who believe that some offenders (such as McVeigh) ought to be punished by being put to death, or those who believe that no one ought to be executed (not even McVeigh) and instead should be sentenced to long-term imprisonment?

To focus the question and keep the discussion relevant to the current scene, we can put aside the status of the death penalty for nonhomicidal crimes, for at least two reasons. First, the paradigm crime punishable by death has always been murder ("a life for a life"). It is also now settled constitutional law that such nonhomicidal crimes as rape and armed robbery are no longer subject to the punishment of death, as they had been only a generation ago.[1] Second, we need not discuss whether the death penalty is the appropriate punishment for *all* homicides. A mandatory death penalty for those convicted of killing another person would require abolishing the distinction between murder and manslaughter and between first- and second-degree murder; it would also require abolishing prosecutorial, judicial, and executive discretion in capital cases. Even if those considerations were not persuasive, the Supreme Court has decreed that mandatory death penalties, even for first-degree murder committed by a person under life sentence for murder, is unconstitutional.[2]

For these reasons it is plausible to argue that the only issue worth discussing is whether the majority of the public (some 75–80 percent at the present time)[3] is right in approving the death penalty for some murderers; or whether the minority (to which I belong) is right in defending absolute, exceptionless abolition.

We must concede from the start that a pick-and-choose death penalty policy has much to recommend it. It is typical of the contingencies acknowledged by modern morality where issues of life and death are concerned to shun principles that admit of no exceptions. (Thus, most of us do not favor laws prohibiting all abortions, or prohibiting all physician-assisted suicides.) But the absolute abolitionist position by definition allows no exceptions, which has a crucial consequence for the overall argument. It requires that we leave aside issues of great practical importance in the contemporary debate over the death penalty, such as the relatively greater economic costs of our current death penalty systems when compared with a system of long-term imprisonment; the unfairness—arbitrariness and discrimination—with which the death penalty is administered; and the risk of convicting, sentencing to death, and executing the innocent. These issues have been discussed elsewhere,[4] and they provide powerful objections to the death penalty in our society (just as they are the primary factors in the recent call for a national moratorium on executions by the House of Delegates of the American Bar Association).[5] Nevertheless, objections on these grounds are largely irrelevant from my current perspective, because it is possible to imagine an ideal world of criminal justice in which such deep-seated flaws and costs would not arise or, if they did, could be remedied without abolishing the death penalty. In that case, we would still be left with the need to explain whether and why we nevertheless oppose all executions.[6]

II

I propose to look first at the most popular moral grounds on which absolute abolitionists rest their case and see whether they can bear the weight placed on them.

The Value of Life[7]

Some abolitionists hold that human life (if not all life) has infinite value or worth[8] and so must be respected and protected accordingly. It follows from this belief that death is the greatest disvalue and murder the gravest wrong. It also follows that even murderers must be treated in light of the value of their lives, a value not erased (even if severely marred) by the harm and injustice their lethal violence has caused the innocent. And that supposedly rules out the death penalty.

But does it? As an empirical claim in any ordinary sense of "value," the value of a murderer's life is often (though by no means always) open to question. How much value, or potentiality for value, can we reasonably assign to the future life of the worst murderers—the sociopathic serial murderer, or the cold-hearted terrorist multiple murderer, or the unreformed and unreformable recidivist murderer—the Hannibal Lectors of fiction (*The Silence of the Lambs*) and the Ted Bundys and Timothy McVeighs of real life? (Henceforth I shall call all such offenders collectively SMR murderers—serial or multiple or recidivist killers—and their crimes SMR murders.) I think it extremely difficult, perhaps impossible, to make a convincing case that *all* such lives have value, based on their history, present condition, and future prospects—and that this value outweighs whatever benefits might be found (or harms avoided) in punishing them with death. The issue here is not whether an SMR murderer finds his or her life worth living; it is rather whether society can reasonably view such a murderer as having a life to live that is on balance more valuable than not.

I do not want to suggest, much less argue (although some might), that all or even most of the more than three thousand persons currently on the death rows of

American prisons[9] are persons whose lives are essentially worthless or valueless (that is, as judged by society). I wouldn't know how to carry out in a responsible manner a systematic measurement of the worth or value of any human life as judged from society's point of view, especially if doing so were to allow for the possibility that some lives turn out to be worthless or valueless. All but the most prejudiced observers will concede that some (perhaps most) murderers retain more than a shred of human dignity and that some can redeem themselves in their own eyes and in ours at least to some extent. But that is not enough for the purposes of the present argument. What must be shown is that this is true of *all* SMR murderers, and I hesitate to endorse any such sweeping empirical claim. Even if one grants (as I do) that convicted murderers do not cease to be persons by virtue of their terrible crimes,[10] this hardly seems enough to establish the value of the life of each such offender.

Of course, the doctrine that even an SMR murderer's life has some value (enough to outweigh all disvalues) may not be an empirical claim at all. Instead, it may be a disguised normative judgment expressing moral disapproval of all executions. In that case, there is only a verbal difference between asserting (1) *every SMR murderer's life has some value* (and enough to outweigh all disvalues), and (2) *we ought not to execute even the worst of the SMR murderers*. To be sure, assertion 2 looks like the conclusion of an argument in which assertion 1 figures as a premise. But if the two assertions differ only verbally, then an appeal to assertion 1 does not advance the argument for assertion 2; instead, it tacitly begs the question. The only way to tell whether there really is a difference in meaning between assertion 2 and assertion 1 is to defend the one without implicitly relying on the other; but that is a task too large to undertake here.

If we regard assertion 2 as a genuine empirical claim, then our task is to establish this claim in a convincing manner on a case-by-case basis. Whether that can be done I do not know.[11] I doubt that it is unreasonable to be cautious, if not skeptical. (Caution is especially recommended in light of what we know about the sociopathy of most SMR murderers, about how they got that way, and what is necessary—albeit not always sufficient—to bring about fundamental change in their lives.)[12]

Pending the completion of that task in a persuasive manner, I suggest that the default position for abolitionists who wish to rely on the value or worth of all human life is to insist that this value—of each and every person's life as judged by that person—puts the burden of argument on those who favor sentencing to death and killing persons without their informed voluntary consent.[13] Imposing the burden of argument in this manner is not only a minimalist strategy for the abolitionist; it is also fair and essential. The friends of the death penalty cannot reasonably reject or even contest this burden. Surely, there is no question that those who favor deliberately killing other persons *always* bear the burden of the argument. A serious discussion of life-and-death issues is impossible on any other assumption. This means that we must start from the somewhat paradoxical proposition that for the purposes of punishment under law, society must assume everyone's life is valuable, and that our lives have equal value, even though some seem to have little or no value.[14]

The Right to Life[15]

Some abolitionists (especially those influenced by Amnesty International and other human rights organizations) would say that we are morally forbidden to take the life of any murderer because even the murderer has an inalienable human right to life and that sentencing to death and executing a person violates that right. This argument has the merit of leaving aside empirical questions of the sort raised by the appeal to the value of human life. Instead, this argument plainly rests on a normative proposition about our rights.

But is the argument sound? Defenders of the death penalty typically reply (as John Locke did three centuries ago)[16] that even if the right to life is "natural" and "inalienable," the murderer *forfeits* his life (or, in some versions of this objection, his right to life), and so putting him to death at most infringes—and does not violate—that right. Most friends of the death penalty will agree that murderers, even if guilty and convicted, do not forfeit every right; they still have rights to due process of law and to equal protection of the law. Hence lynching a convicted guilty murderer is itself a crime, even in a jurisdiction that authorizes the death penalty. But murderers do forfeit the one right that really matters, the right to life. Or so defenders of the death penalty will typically insist.

What reply do absolute abolitionists have to this objection? They cannot attack the general idea that rights can be forfeited, because that idea seems to be a perfectly ordinary even if tacit feature of any theory or doctrine of rights. For example, the Universal Declaration of Human Rights insists that everyone has a "right to liberty"; but it does not follow from this right that it is always wrong to deliberately deprive a person of liberty, as we do when we imprison a convicted offender. This amounts to conceding that under appropriate conditions (to be specified elsewhere) persons can forfeit their right to liberty.[17]

Absolute abolitionists who resist the temptation to reject out of hand the doctrine of forfeiture of rights are likely to yield to the temptation to insist that whatever may be true of rights in general, the right to life cannot be forfeited—because it is an *absolute* right. That is, the right to life prevails over every other moral consideration that might be thought to compete with or override it. But here there is surely a problem. At best, I think, this is true only when we are referring to the right to life of the innocent. Consider the rationale of the use of lethal force in self-defense (or third-party defense).[18] Few abolitionists will deny that we have the right to act in self-defense to avoid becoming an undeserving victim of another's aggression. All but extreme pacifists will go on to grant that if the only way to prevent someone (oneself or another) from being the innocent victim of an unprovoked and uninvited act of apparently lethal intention is to use lethal force first, then in that sort of case one may kill the aggressor. Further, few abolitionists will insist that the police or other custodians of public order must never use lethal violence.

But once the use of lethal force is granted to be acceptable in such cases, the abolitionist is clearly not regarding the right to life as absolute. At most it is the right to life of the innocent that deserves unqualified respect, not the right to life of the guilty. Abolitionists who reason in this way thus cannot consistently use this right as a shield against deliberate and intentional lethal harm in all cases or as a stick with which to beat down claims by death penalty supporters who believe that even this right can be forfeited.[19]

Abolitionists, however, can reply that if there are any universal human rights at all, surely one of them is the right to life (no doubt in need of further specification). And they can go on to insist that, at the very least, this right puts the burden of argument on those who would kill or authorize others to kill persons (including SMR murderers) without their informed voluntary consent. Thus, if there is a right to life, even if it is not an absolute right, part of its function is to locate the burden of argument. This requires the friends of the death penalty to explain why that punishment merely infringes the murderer's right to life but does not violate it.[20] And they should do this without overreliance on the doctrine of forfeiture, because it turns out on closer inspection that forfeiture may be only a weak reed after all.[21]

Some absolute abolitionists currently want to argue that the right to life is too vague or abstract to be of much help in explaining the immorality of the death penalty in any case. They propose to appeal to a different right altogether, the right not to be executed.[22] Is this really an advance in thinking through the relevance of human rights to the death penalty controversy? To be sure, asserting that (3) *everyone has a right not to be executed* seems to be quite different from asserting that (4) *no one ought to be executed*, because invoking someone's rights is often a way of arguing what someone ought (or ought not) to do. Accordingly, assertion 4 looks like the conclusion for which assertion 3 is a plausible premise. I, of course, accept assertion 4, as do all absolute abolitionists. But I am not sure I accept assertion 3, and so I worry that, after all, there may be only a verbal difference between the two claims. In that case assertion 3 adds nothing to assertion 4.

Perhaps at this point some absolute abolitionists will want to shift from relying on rights to relying upon the sanctity of human life. Such a shift not only puts aside any worry about empirical questions concerning the value of human life; it also has the advantage of making it difficult and perhaps impossible to make sense of forfeiting the sanctity of one's life by committing a terrible crime (even a crime that violates the sanctity of the innocent victim's life). In this respect sanctity has the edge on rights. But these advantages are purchased at a price: the sanctity of human life can be explained and defended only within a sectarian religious framework; one cannot appeal to the sanctity of human life in isolation from a whole host of related ideas and beliefs that do not have universal appeal. What is needed, I suggest, is a secular norm of universal application, which is exactly what the value of human life and the right to life attempt to provide.

General Social Utility[23]

Some oppose the death penalty on utilitarian grounds, arguing that the general welfare is better served by adopting and acting on a rule that forbids killing anyone in the name of punishment. All of us, whether or not we are utilitarians, agree that some enforceable rule prohibiting deliberately killing persons is necessary; we all agree that homicide is a crime unless excused or justified; we also agree that the ideal civilized society is one in which all rational persons would live without anyone murdering anyone; and we also agree that government officials and their agents, as well as private citizens, have committed inexcusable and unjustifiable homicide. (Think, respectively, of the federal government's attack on the Waco compound of the Branch Davidians in 1993, and the bombing of the Federal Building in Oklahoma City in 1995.) Can these agreements best be recognized and enforced by utilitarian reasoning?

Perhaps they can, but they fall well short of what is necessary to rule out all recourse to the death penalty. A utilitarian is very likely to consider certain cases, given the facts, as exceptions to any rule that absolutely prohibits killing other human beings in the name of punishment. Even the abolitionist founders of utilitarianism, notably Jeremy Bentham[24] and J. S. Mill,[25] thought that the death penalty was appropriate in a narrow range of cases; so did Cesare Beccaria[26] before them and the American pragmatist Sidney Hook[27] in our own day.

To see how a utilitarian (or a pragmatist) would reason, consider the following kind of case (variations on this argument were voiced by some who favored the death sentence for McVeigh). Terrorist acts causing great loss of innocent life have been committed against a tolerably just government, and the chief offenders have been captured, tried, convicted, and now await sentencing. There is every reason to believe that many of their coideologists remain at large, scattered across the nation, and that the leaders awaiting sentencing will continue to inspire terrorist attacks as long as they remain alive. Doesn't the most plausible reading of the political facts support putting these convicted terrorists to death (perhaps even by public execution), in order to reduce the likelihood of further rebellion and harmful disorder? Why risk society's precarious security just to avoid putting to death dangerous terrorists who are clearly guilty?[28]

Reasoning of this sort is bound to attract utilitarians; it is always just a question of time and circumstances before the utilitarian opponent of the death penalty caves in and agrees that, yes, in this or that special (hypothetical or genuine) case, we can reasonably predict worse overall consequences for society if we do not put convicted felons to death and instead keep them in prison until their natural death. Utilitarians can easily oppose most death penalty laws—and Beccaria, Bentham, Mill, and Sidney Hook did; but I doubt that any utilitarian (or pragmatist) can oppose such laws and their application in *all* cases.

Before moving on, we should notice that violent political radicals, such as Timothy McVeigh, present a very different problem from other kinds of SMR murderers. No one seriously suggests that these other murderers if not executed are likely to become a rallying point for imitation. Thus, utilitarians have less reason to favor execution of the typical SMR murderer, who is a sociopath, than they do the execution of dangerous ideologues, of whom McVeigh seems to be one. J. S. Mill's parliamentary oration of 1868 in opposition to absolute abolition remains an instructive example of just such reasoning.[29] So does the careful review of the deterrent effect of the execution of Irish rebels in 1922 by the contemporary utilitarian philosopher Jonathan Glover.[30]

A minor chord in the theme discussed above emerged as the jury was deliberating McVeigh's sentence. Some in the public voiced their distress over the spectacle of McVeigh behind bars for life, spewing forth his perverse patriotism to the world over the Internet (as it was said the SMR murderer Charles Manson has been doing from his prison cell in California).[31] As an argument for the death penalty, whether on utilitarian or other grounds, however, this worry seems singularly weak. Surely, an abuse of free speech fostered by excessively permissive prison regulations (if that is what Manson's behavior constitutes) does not have its only, much less its best, remedy in recourse to the death penalty.

Cruel and Unusual Punishment[32]

The Eighth Amendment in our Bill of Rights forbids "cruel and unusual punishment," and the Universal Declaration of Human Rights similarly forbids "torture, cruel, inhumane, or degrading punishment." Most abolitionists regard the death penalty as a violation of these principles.[33] This is not the place to argue the point; let us suppose they are correct. Whence do these constitutional principles derive their authority? Why ought we to respect them, especially given the awful and boundlessly cruel nature of many crimes (especially those committed by SMR murderers)?

We can answer these questions in several ways. First, we might say we simply accept as intuitively sound the authority of these principles prohibiting cruelty; they are fundamental, nonderivative moral axioms governing our political thinking and our policy making. This answer will, of course, prove to have no persuasive effect on two groups of death penalty supporters: those who do not share this intuition in the first place; and those who do but who deny that these principles rule out the death penalty in all cases (especially if it is administered humanely and scrupulously).[34] Most of today's friends of the death penalty fall into the latter class. Few of them will seriously deny that we must accept some upper bound to permissible severity in punishment under law. But that still leaves considerable room for disagreement over just where to draw that upper bound—and in particular over which side of that boundary the death penalty falls.

Second, we might say that constitutional principles marking the upper bound of permissible severity in punishment are derived from something more fundamental. But what might that be? The value of human life, the right to life, the principle of greatest net social utility? Any route of derivation of the upper bound by appeal to a principle that rests on such foundations is likely to prove insufficient to protect all those guilty of SMR murder, as we have already seen.

Another strategy that may commend itself here is to consider whether a policy absolutely barring any death penalty on grounds of its cruelty, regardless of how that policy is administered, is one that a reasonably self-interested person would want adopted by society as a rational choice behind a veil of ignorance.[35] To decide this question requires us to take into account certain general facts about our society, chief among which is the fact that the risk for each of us of being convicted (guilty or innocent) of SMR murder, sentenced to death, and executed is almost certainly far less than is the risk of being a victim of SMR murder. But given these facts, this line of argument will prove to be a weapon in the hands of the friends of capital punishment, not of its opponents.

Of course, I have not exhausted all that moral reflection has to offer in defending a policy of absolute prohibition of the death penalty.[36] But perhaps I have said enough to cause some to conclude that absolute abolitionism is a policy insufficiently supported by sound moral principles (such as those reviewed above), reason, and experience. Those who believe this will view abolitionists as in the grip of an obsession against state authority to kill some prisoners and against exercising that authority in their names and on their behalf. This leads us to ask: Is it fair to impute stubborn irrationality and dogmatic sentimentality to those who are absolute abolitionists? I hope not, and I think not. There is another view to take of the prohibition against any killing as punishment, one that fastens on setting the upper bound of severity in punishment by reference to this question: Does the severity of the punishment under discussion exceed what is necessary to achieve whatever legitimate goals a system of punishment under law has in the first place? I think this question reorients the entire discussion in the right direction, and I now turn to the task of elaborating this perspective.

III

The argument I am about to present is not an abstract or a priori argument (nor do I claim any originality for it), because it relies at several points on empirical generalizations about human behavior and our actual experience with abolition of the death penalty. Rather, the argument is consequentialist (without being utilitarian). Formulated in the context of American constitutional law, jurists would call it a "substantive due process" argument.[37] Political theorists will recognize its central principle as a familiar one in classic liberal political theory. The principle in question is that government must use "the least restrictive means to achieve a compelling state interest." In a somewhat fuller statement it can be formulated this way: Society, acting through the authority of its government, must not enact and enforce policies that impose more restrictive—invasive, harmful, violent—interference with human liberty, privacy, and autonomy than are absolutely necessary as the means to achieve legitimate and important social objectives. Anyone who takes this principle seriously, as I shall try to show, ought to oppose the death penalty in all cases because that penalty—at least in a society such as ours—violates this principle.

To reach that conclusion, one must accept the three propositions that constitute the principle. First, one must believe that the punishment of crime is a legitimate social objective, or (as I prefer) at least a necessary condition of achieving legitimate social objectives; otherwise, using severe sanctions and threatening serious deprivations in the name of punishment will not be warranted. Second, one must believe that the death penalty is much more severe, more invasive, less remediable, more violent than the usual alternative punishment, some form of long-term imprisonment. Third, one must believe that the death penalty is never necessary to achieve valid social objectives because other, less severe forms of punishment, such as constraints on an offender's liberty, privacy, and autonomy through long-term imprisonment, are sufficient.

These three propositions are of very different character. On what evidence and reasoning is each based? As to the first (punishment is a valid state objective), even opponents of current systems of imprisonment agree that some form of punishment is appropriate for the government to impose on convicted offenders, that the threat of punishment is an appropriate measure for society to use as a general deterrent, and that grave crimes call for severe punishment. Only the most radically pacific opponents of the death penalty rest their opposition on a general repudiation of punishment under law. So the friends and the enemies of capital punishment ought to be able to agree on the first proposition.

They are likely to divide, however, on a neglected distinction in this context of some importance. Is punishment as such really a valid state objective? Does punishment (including the threat of punishment) for its own sake, quite apart from its consequences, constitute a goal or purpose of society? I suggest that it doesn't. I also suggest that punishment is generally thought to be a valid state objective because advocating punishment as a *means* to certain valid ends is confused with advocating punishment as an *end* in itself. The relevant and valid state objective is a society tolerably free of violent crime; so it is crime reduction, not punishment infliction, that ought to preoccupy our policy makers. If so, then severe punishment (including the threat thereof) is defensible only to the extent that it is necessary to that end. (On this point, utilitarians have always been correct.) Were other measures to suffice or be reasonably believed to suffice to control crime, punishment under law in a tolerably just constitutional democracy would immediately be put into question. It would be vulnerable to the objection that punishment serves no valid purpose and instead has become pointless cruelty.[38]

Retributivists, and especially retributivist friends of the death penalty, are certain to disagree, as their appeal to what they regard as the justly deserved punishment of criminals regardless of its costs testifies. How we are to resolve this disagreement rationally is not entirely clear; at the least, it would require an investigation into the adequacy of the retributive justification of punishment (about which I shall have a bit to say below).[39] As is true at prior stages of my argument, so here: I think the burden of argument falls on those who would defend punishment under law once it has been shown to be either futile or superfluous as an effective and necessary form of social control. At present, however, this issue is moot because society does not have at its disposal fully effective nonpunitive methods of social control, and so one cannot argue that punishment (including especially the credible threat thereof) is unnecessary.

As to the second proposition (death is a more severe punishment than long-term imprisonment), those in the best position to judge—prisoners on death row and prisoners under life sentence who were, or might have been, sentenced to death—show by their behavior that they overwhelmingly believe death is a worse punishment than prison. Very few death row prisoners dismiss their lawyers and reject appeals and clemency hearings;[40] very few death row prisoners try to commit suicide, and fewer still try until they succeed.[41] As for the judgment of others, defenders of capital punishment typically believe both that it is a better deterrent and fitting retribution, because it is the more severe punishment of the two. Abolitionists also agree that death is the more severe punishment; few if any are on record favoring life in prison because the death penalty is not severe enough. So I suggest we agree about the relative severity of the two modes of punishment and accept the second of my three propositions.[42]

The third proposition (punishment by death is never necessary to achieve valid state objectives) is the one that is the most controversial. The argument for it must be an empirical one because the proposition itself is empirical. One source of disagreement here is lack of familiarity with the relevant evidence and unwillingness to accept the necessary inferences. (I shall ignore here the question of which side has the burden of argument and will proceed as if the abolitionist did.) The best version of the argument for this proposition goes like this: Anyone who studies the century and more of experience without the death penalty in American abolitionist jurisdictions must conclude that these jurisdictions have controlled criminal homicide and managed their criminal justice system, including their maximum security prisons with life-term violent offenders, at least as effectively as have neighboring death penalty jurisdictions. The public has not responded to abolition with riot and lynching; the police have not become habituated to excessive use of lethal force; prison guards, staff, and visitors are not at greater risk; surviving victims of murdered friends and loved ones have not found it more difficult to adjust to their grievous loss.[43]

If, in short, there is any argument for restoring the death penalty in America's abolition jurisdictions, it is not an argument from the failures of long-term imprisonment as a general deterrent or incapacitation. It is not an argument from the insufficiency of retribution. It is not an argument from the destructive social behaviors inspired by abolition. And it is not an argument from the unmanageable dangers that a handful of SMR murderers present to public safety. So, what Michigan and Wisconsin did in abolishing the death penalty over a century ago, Ohio and Illinois could have done—and could do tomorrow if they wanted to. So could the rest of the nation.[44]

That completes the sketch of the general structure of the substantive due process argument against the death penalty; I think it carries the day.

IV

Die-hard friends of the death penalty can try to evade this conclusion in several ways. Perhaps the most obvious and attractive is to insist that the substantive due process argument is incomplete, because it ignores the role of revenge and retribution. Let us look more closely at this objection. "Revenge" and "retribution" are not synonyms, nor is the latter merely a euphemism for the former.[45] They can be deployed against my argument by defending either of two theses: (i) vicarious revenge is not only a legitimate motive, it is an essential motive, out of which the government ought to act in punishment generally and especially where the punishment of SMR murderers is in question; and (ii) the death penalty is the appropriate vehical for retribution where murder is concerned and especially where the punishment of SMR murderers is in question. Attractive though some find these two propositions, I believe both ought to be rejected.

As to the second, anyone who is inclined to believe it must confront some unwelcome facts. First, it is worth noting that the criminal justice systems in many countries reject this appeal to retribution; or, if they accept the fittingness of death for murder, they have reasons for overriding this consideration, because they do not use the death penalty to punish any murderers.[46] Second, in our own country the vast majority (well over 90 percent) of all persons convicted of criminal homicide are never sentenced to death and executed.[47] Are we to infer that our prosecutors, juries, and judges are insufficiently retributive? It is more reasonable to infer that other considerations in practice overrule such retribution as only death is thought to provide. Third, on what basis do we attach any moral legitimacy to the idea that death is what murderers deserve, when we do not embrace (except in moments of extreme and thoughtless anger) the obvious parallels under the retributive principle that would require rapists to be raped, torturers to be tortured, and so on through the list of crimes and their matching retaliatory punishments? I suggest that the appeal to desert in order to decide how to punish murderers is largely a delusion; instead of constituting an appeal to a truly independent principle (a principle of retributive justice, presumably), asserting (5) *murderers deserve the death penalty* really differs only verbally from asserting (6) *murderers ought to be executed*, despite the fact that assertion 6 looks like the conclusion derivable from (5) as the premise.

As for the first proposition above (vicarious revenge is a legitimate motive for punishment under law), it too must be rejected. No reasonable liberal theory of constitutional government can accept the proposition that one of society's permanent, constitutional objectives is to punish the guilty by acting out of a motive of revenge.[48] Revenge is simply too untamed and volatile, too indifferent to the claims of justice to play a role in civilized society. The very idea of vicarious revenge as a motive for official punitive policy and its enforcement is frightening in its implications. Revenge may well be a motive out of which individual persons can and do sometimes act; as Nietzsche would have said, the thirst for revenge (and the desire to use punishment as a vehicle for revenge) is "all too human." But permitting, much less encouraging, officials to act out of vicarious revenge on behalf of society and the state is another matter entirely. More than two thousand years ago the *Oresteia* taught us to be wary of acting out of revenge, and so did the book of Genesis.[49]

Defenders of the death penalty might reject revenge as a motive and insist instead that they advocate only retribution.[50] Retribution is the form justice takes in punishment, and it is precisely what the criminal justice system is supposed to achieve. But (so the objection goes) since the substantive due process argument seems to ignore this, that argument is necessarily incomplete and inadequate.

By way of reply, it should be noted that any plausible system of punishment is retributive by its very nature; punishment aims to impose deprivations on all and only guilty convicted offenders because of their wrongdoing. So the proposition that offenders deserve to be punished (whatever else it is) is a truism of retributive justice.[51] But the issue here is what the punishment ought to be for a given offense—death, imprisonment, or something else altogether? Retributivists believe that the death penalty is necessary for retribution because it is the deserved punishment for some crimes. This requires that society can give practical effect to the idea of someone morally deserving to die as a punishment for his or her crimes. I stress moral desert, because retributivists obviously cannot be satisfied with desert as the law specifies it. One might well say that, of course, offenders deserve whatever punishment the law provides for the crime(s) of which they have been found guilty. But this trivializes the idea of desert because it has the consequence that in Michigan

all convicted murderers deserve life imprisonment, whereas in Illinois some convicted murderers deserve death. Yet as soon as we leave the law behind and try to
figure out what punishment a given offender morally deserves, we are out of our
depth and caught in interminable disagreement. Instead, as I suggested earlier, invocation of desert in order to decide what ought to be the punishment for a given
offender is really a delusion. At least in part it is fostered by the failure to keep
clearly distinct the truism *that* offenders morally deserve to be punished from the
unanswerable question of *what* they deserve as their punishment.[52]

I conclude from this brief investigation of revenge, retribution, and desert that
the role of a system of punishment in a modern civilized society really is only as a
means to the legitimate end of a society without criminal violence.

Let me restate some of the foregoing in another way. So long as we do not fool-
ishly use a mere rebuke or a slap on the wrist as our considered punitive response to
the convicted SMR murderer, or employ any other mild sanction that amounts to an
insult to the homicide victim, we are exacting retribution under law. Any suitable
punishment lawfully meted out to those judged guilty is done in part at least as retribution. That is the nature of punishment in a constitutional democracy governed by
liberal principles of justice.[53] But to try to go further and identify stable moral
grounds on which to decide an offender's morally just deserts, seems to me an impossible task. The manifestly arbitrary nature of recent attempts to construct a penalty scale on grounds of moral desert confirms this judgement.[54] Thus, undermining
the substantive due process argument against the death penalty by appeal to the role
of retributive justice and morally deserved punishment seems to me a failure.

Another way to challenge the substantive due process argument is by attacking
the empirical claim it makes, that is, by arguing that incapacitating the SMR murderer by any punishment short of death cannot be reliably done. Here, too, I think
the rebuttal fails. Keep in mind that we can identify a person as an SMR murderer
only *after* he has been arrested, tried, and convicted—and thus only after he has
committed some terrible crime(s). We have no way to identify an SMR murderer
prior to his commiting the crimes that make him a SMR murderers. So we can classify him under that description only when he is (or only after he has been) securely
in our custody and under our control. In principle at that point he is no more dangerous than any other offender behind bars with a history of prior violence.

At this point, the friends of the death penalty must ask themselves whether they
advocate killing some convicted murderers because of the possibility that in the future they will become SMR killers. Does selective defense of the death penalty for
these offenders really amount to endorsing executions as a preventive measure, and
thus executing some convicted murderers not for what they have done but for what
someone predicts they will (or could, or are likely to) do? (As an aside, is it fully appreciated that this is precisely what capital punishment in Texas involves, since
every death sentence there rests on the trial jury's judgment that the convicted murderer constitutes "a continuing threat to society" because he or she would, if not
executed, "commit criminal acts of violence"?)[55] Preventive *detention* (which in
June 1997 received a strong endorsement from the Supreme Court)[56] may have its
justifications. But preventive *execution* is another matter entirely. The argument for
the death penalty for SMR murderers cannot be carried by nothing more than the

bare assertion that incarceration is insufficient for public safety, because it can be made sufficient; the control of convicted SMR murderers in abolition states proves this. Nor can the argument be carried by pointing to existing cases of recidivist murder, since if such offenders could be identified before the fact while still in custody before they became recidivist killers, they could also be disabled in some lawful fashion well short of death and thus would not have become recidivists.

V

But the friends of the death penalty are not ready to throw in the towel, not yet. They will say, never mind that SMR murderers can be safely restrained; never mind that we cannot agree on which murderers deserve to die for their crimes; never mind that we cannot explain why any murderers morally deserve death rather than some lesser punishment. Leave all that to the side, and answer only this question: What possible *good* can come from not putting these offenders to death? What possible good could we obtain by running further risk from them, however slight? Why expend public resources on behalf of such persons when there are so many other productive uses to which those resources could be put?

The boldest way to address the first of these questions is to declare that it is not the right question and so does not need to be answered. Philosophers have argued for centuries that there is a fundamental difference between doing the *right* thing and bringing about *good* (better or best) results.[57] There is, in general, no easy way to connect the two concepts, and in the argument over absolute abolition we have a good example of their disconnection. Throughout, my argument has been that abolishing the death penalty for all offenders is the right policy, quite apart from whatever good it may achieve. On the view I have been defending, absolute abolition rather than any alternative follows from the fundamental principle on which I have relied (offical punishment policy ought to impose the minimal violence necessary to achieve its valid ends) when taken in conjunction with the best account of all the relevant facts. Asking for more than this in the argument against the death penalty is unreasonable.

Nevertheless, there are a few ancillary comments to be made in a last effort to make that argument more convincing.

First, the complaint about the expenditure of public resources on behalf of the worst citizens in our society—a complaint now often expressed in the angriest of language—is a red herring. For one thing, estimates of relative costs show that our current death penalty systems are far more expensive than systems in which long-term imprisonment is the severest sanction.[58] For another, the refusal to expend public resources to imprison SMR murderers for life instead of executing them opens the door to reducing or withdrawing entirely other resources in the criminal justice system because they, too, are spent on the indigent, the guilty, the undeserving. Setting our feet down that path is guaranteed to aggravate social problems rather than alleviate them.

Second, it is important to realize that the SMR killers we are talking about are mostly sociopaths or psychopaths who belong under detention because they are dangerous both to others and to themselves. It may be that the best we can do for such offenders and for us is to imprison them for life, despite the fact that it is doubtful whether any sentence of punishment is morally appropriate in these cases. The picture of such offenders as autonomous rational serial, multiple, or recidivist killers is largely if not entirely a fictional portrait.[59] Timothy McVeigh may be the exception; he appears to be no ordinary sociopath, and his responsibility for his terrorist act (assuming his guilt) seems to be neither diminished nor in doubt.

Third, where recidivist murderers are concerned, the failure of our prison system (a failure that the public seems uninterested in trying to remedy) to tame if not reeducate them when they were in our custody spreads the responsibility onto the rest of society for the harm they later cause. We had them fully in our control, we knew they were dangerous, and we failed to take appropriate measures to protect others from falling prey to their violent intentions. This failure on our part to moralize and socialize them cannot simply be ignored when the time comes to assess their responsibility as recidivists.

Fourth, it is desirable to close the door tightly against state-sanctioned killing of prisoners, including SMR murderers, lest further exceptions worm their way through the crack and into the law. If, as I believe, liberals and conservatives alike accept the principle that government must not use more force than necessary to achieve society's legitimate objectives, then abolishing the death penalty for all crimes ought to have strong appeal. It is impossible to teach respect for human life by acts of unnecessary and to that extent unjustifiable lethal violence. But this is exactly what the death penalty represents. In no other area of government authority is it so easy to bring sanctioned violence to an immediate end as it is by abolishing outright the death penalty without exceptions.

Finally, such good as there is in not executing SMR murderers is the abstract and negative good of not doing the wrong thing—more precisely, not causing (or permitting others to cause) more harm to persons (in this case, offenders) than is necessary to accomplish legitimate social goals. This good is not lessened when it goes unappreciated by a convicted murderer who "volunteers" for execution or who commits suicide while on death row, or by those whose job it is to operate prisons efficiently and humanely, or by the angry and grieving survivors of the murder of a loved one. Nonetheless, as a society we are better when we act better, and we act better whenever we reject unnecessary lethal violence. We need to uproot the mentality of murder, especially when it is clothed in political authority, carried out under official auspices in cool detachment, and known to be unnecessary. As Albert Camus memorably wrote, let us try to live in a world without becoming either anyone's victim or anyone's executioner.[60]

Notes

1. Coker v. Georgia, 433 U.S. 584 (1977) and Eberhard v. Georgia, 433 U.S. 917 (1977). The constitutionality of nonhomicidal capital crimes as defined in the Anti-Terrorism and Effective Death Penalty Act, enacted by Congress in 1995, has yet to be decided.

2. Woodson v. North Carolina, 428 U.S. 280 (1976) and Sumner v. Shuman, 483 U.S. 66 (1987).

3. Phoebe C. Ellsworth and Samuel R. Gross, "Hardening of Attitudes: Americans' Views on the Death Penalty," *Journal of Social Issues* 50 (1994): 19–52, reprinted in

The Death Penalty in America: Current Controversies, ed. H. A. Bedau (New York: Oxford University Press, 1997).

4. See Bedau, supra note 3; also International Commission of Jurists, *Administration of the Death Penalty in the United States* (Geneva: ICJ, 1996); Raymond Paternoster, *Capital Punishment in America* (New York: Lexington Books, 1991); Welsh S. White, *The Death Penalty in the Nineties: An Examination of the Modern System of Capital Punishment* (Ann Arbor: University of Michigan Press, 1991); and Amnesty International, *United States of America: The Death Penalty* (London: AI Publications, 1987).

5. See *New York Times*, February 4, 1997, A20.

6. See David Dolinko, "Foreword: How to Criticize the Death Penalty," *Journal of Criminal Law and Criminology* 77 (1986): 546–601, where this point is forcefully made.

7. For a general discussion of the value of human life, see John Kleinig, *Valuing Life* (Princeton, N.J.: Princeton University Press, 1991). Kleinig does not address the question of differential valuation of human lives or of how to measure the value of a person's life (nor does he dismiss these questions as unanswerable or as nonsense).

8. Immanuel Kant distinguished between the "relative worth" or "price" and the "intrinsic worth" or "dignity" of all persons. The former could vary from person to person and from time to time, but not the latter; all rational creatures were forever equal in dignity. See Kant, *Grounding for the Metaphysics of Morals*, trans. J. W. Ellington (1785; Indianapolis: Hackett, 1981), 40–41. This did not prevent Kant from arguing that murderers must be put to death; for a critical discussion see Marvin Henberg, *Retribution: Evil for Evil in Ethics, Law, and Literature* (Philadelphia, Pa.: Temple University Press, 1990), 158–171.

9. NAACP Legal Defense and Educational Fund, Inc., "Death Row, U.S.A." (Winter 1998), reports 3,365 persons awaiting execution of a death sentence.

10. See my "Thinking about the Death Penalty as a Cruel and Unusual Punishment," *U.C. Davis Law Review* 18 (1985): 873–925, at 921–923, reprinted in my *Death Is Different: Studies in the Morality, Law, and Politics of the Capital Punishment* (Boston: Northeastern University Press, 1987): 126–127.

11. Jeffrey Murphy discusses the possibility of human beings who are not moral persons because of their sociopathy; see his "Moral Death: A Kantian Essay on Psychopathy," *Ethics*, 82 (1972): 284–298, reprinted in his *Retribution, Justice, and Therapy* (Dordrecht: Reidel, 1979): 128–143. Murphy does not confuse clarifying this concept with arguing for its application in actual cases.

12. See in general John Gilligan, *Violence: Our Deadly Epidemic and Its Causes* (New York: Putnams, 1996).

13. I insert this qualification so as to leave open the possibility that forms of euthanasia or assisted suicide may be morally acceptable.

14. The Supreme Court's decision in *Payne v. Tennessee*, 501 U.S. 808 (1991), which permits victim impact–testimony during the sentencing phase of a capital trial, in effect repudiates this assumption of moral equality, because it invites testimony designed to show that the victim is someone exceptional, and so the killer deserves the exceptional punishment of death.

15. The right to life has yet to receive the lengthy treatment that it deserves. For some recent suggestions, see Susan Uniacke, *Permissible Killing: The Self-Defense Justification of Homicide* (Cambridge: Cambridge University Press, 1994), 209–218.

16. John Locke, *Second Treatise of Government* (1690), sec. 23. For an influential modern moralist who takes the same line (without expressly leaning on Locke) see W. D. Ross, *The Right and the Good* (Oxford: Oxford University Press, 1934), 60.

17. Neglect by contemporary defenders of human rights to face the problems raised by traditional and commonplace claims that any right can be forfeited is nothing short of as-

tounding; for further discussion see my article "The Precarious Sovereignty of Rights," 1997–1998 *Philosophic Exchange*, No. 28: 5–16, and Uniacke, supra note 15.

18. For a general discussion of self-defense and related issues, see Uniacke, supra note 15.

19. For fuller discussion of the issues in this paragraph, see Bedau, supra note 17.

20. I borrow from Judith Jarvis Thomson the distinction between infringing a right (failing to act in accordance with someone's right, but for adequate reasons) and violating a right (failing to act in accordance with someone's right, and for inadequate reasons). See her *The Realm of Rights* (Cambridge, Mass.: Harvard University Press, 1990).

21. See Thomson, supra note 20, at 367.

22. See *Routes to Abolition: The Law and Politics of the Death Penalty*, ed. Peter Hodgkinson, William Schabas, and Elisabetta Zamparutti, forthcoming.

23. For representative contemporary utilitarian moral theory, see Geoffrey Scarre, *Utilitarianism* (London: Routledge, 1996); Richard B. Brandt, *Morality, Utilitarianism, and Rights* (Cambridge: Cambridge University Press, 1992); Anthony Quinton, *Utilitarianism*, 2d ed. (La Salle, Ill.: Open Court, 1989); J. J. C. Smart and Bernard Williams, *Utilitarianism: For and Against* (Cambridge: Cambridge University Press, 1973). None of these sources, however, offers any extended discussion of a utilitarian theory of punishment.

24. Jeremy Bentham, *The Rationale of Punishment* (London: Robert Heward, 1830), reprinted in *The Works of Jeremy Bentham*, vol. 1, ed. John Bowring (Edinburgh, 1838), 388–525. See also my "Bentham's Utilitarian Critique of the Death Penalty," *Journal of Criminal Law and Criminology* 74 (1983): 1033–1065, reprinted in my *Death Is Different*, supra note 10, at 64–91.

25. J. S. Mill, "Speech in Favor of Capital Punishment" (1868), reprinted in *Philosophical Perspectives on Punishment*, ed. Gertrude Ezorsky (Albany: SUNY Press, 1972), 271–278.

26. Cesare Beccaria, *On Crimes and Punishments and Other Writings*, ed. Richard Bellamy (Cambridge: Cambridge University Press, 1995). *On Crimes and Punishments* was originally published in 1764.

27. Sidney Hook, "The Death Sentence," in *The Death Penalty in America: An Anthology*, ed. H. A. Bedau (New York: Doubleday, 1964): 146–154.

28. For my part, I reject this argument for reasons well stated by Thomas Perry Thornton, "Terrorism and the Death Penalty," reprinted in *The Death Penalty in America*, 3d ed., ed. H. A. Bedau (New York: Oxford, 1982): 181–185, and by James Corcoran, "McVeigh Gets a Last Chance: To Be a Martyr," *Boston Globe*, June 22, 1997, D4. The position of Catholic Church as set out in the papal encyclical, *Evangelium Vitae* (1995) contemplates the possibility of the need to make a terrorist exception to complete abolition of the death penalty, but implies that in actual fact modern nations do not need to do it.

29. See Mill, supra note 25.

30. Jonathan Glover, *Causing Death and Saving Lives* (New York: Penguin, 1977), 240–242.

31. See Adolphe V. Bernotas, "Expert on Terrorism: McVeigh Must Die," *Valley* [Lebanon, N.H.] *News*, June 8, 1997, B1.

32. Unfortunately, there is no comprehensive study of this clause in the Eighth Amendment. Larry Charles Berkson, *The Concept of Cruel and Unusual Punishment* (Lexington, Mass.: Lexington Books, 1975), provides little more than a digest of cases and statutes, when what is needed is a much deeper and broader theoretical account. For a fuller discussion of Berkson's book, see my review in *Journal of Criminal Law and Criminology* 68 (1977): 167–168.

33. Why the death penalty is a violation of the Eighth Amendment has yet to receive the thorough treatment it needs. Raoul Berger, in his *Death Penalties: The Supreme Court's*

Obstacle Course (Cambridge, Mass.: Harvard University Press, 1982), vigorously argued against that idea and thereby provoked vigorous criticism in most of his reviewers. See, for example, my review in *Michigan Law Review* 81 (March 1983): 1152–1165. See also my "Thinking about the Death Penalty," supra note 10. On the death penalty as a violation of the UDHR and related norms of international law, see William A. Schabas, *The Death Penalty as Cruel Treatment and Torture: Capital Punishment Challenged in the World's Courts* (Boston, Mass.: Northeastern University Press, 1996).

34. Today, lethal injection is widely defended on these grounds; it may well be true that this method of execution is superior to the legal alternatives (lethal gas, hanging, firing squad, electrocution) and yet still open to objection. For a recent discussion, see Schabas, supra note 33, at 197–200.

35. Reasoning from behind a veil of ignorance to establish fair and reasonable fundamental principles of political organization is in the spirit of John Rawls; see his book *A Theory of Justice* (Cambridge, Mass.: Harvard University Press, 1972): 136–142. For an application of such reasoning in the theory of punishment, see Norval Morris, *The Future of Imprisonment* (Chicago: Chicago University Press, 1974), 81–83.

36. For other discussions of the morality (or, rather, the immorality) of capital punishment, see my "Capital Punishment," in *Matters of Life and Death: New Essays in Moral Philosophy*, 3d ed., ed. Tom Regan (New York: McGraw-Hill, 1993), 160–194, and my earlier essay, "Objections to the Death Penalty from the Moral Point of View," *Revue internationale de droit penal* 58 (1987): 557–565. See also Jeffrey Reiman, "Justice, Civilization, and the Death Penalty," *Philosophy and Public Affairs* 14 (1985): 115–148, reprinted in his *Critical Moral Liberalism: Theory and Practice* (Lanham, Md.: Rowman and Littlefield, 1997); Carl Wellman, *Morals and Ethics*, 2d ed. (Englewood Cliffs, N.J.: Prentice Hall, 1988), 244–266; Stephen Nathanson, *An Eye for an Eye: The Morality of Punishing by Death* (Totowa, N.J.: Rowman and Littlefield, 1987); Richard Wasssserstrom, "Capital Punishment as Punishment: Some Theoretical Issues and Objections," *Midwest Studies in Philosophy* 7 (1982): 473–502; Thomas Hurka, "Rights and Capital Punishment," *Dialogue* 21 (1982): 647–660; and H. L. A. Hart, "Murder and the Principles of Punishment: England and the United States," *Northwestern University Law Review* 52 (1957): 433–461, reprinted in his *Punishment and Responsibility: Essays in the Philosophy of Law* (Oxford: Oxford University Press, 1968).

37. Elsewhere, I have suggested that this argument has merit as an interpretation of the Eighth Amendment; see my "Interpreting the Eighth Amendment: Principled vs. Populist Strategies," *Thomas M. Cooley Law Review* 13 (1996): 789–814.

38. Elsewhere I have explored further the issues of this paragraph; see my "Punitive Violence and Its Alternatives," in *Justice, Law, and Violence*, ed. James B. Brady and Newton Garver (Philadelphia: Temple University Press, 1991): 193–209.

39. Elsewhere I have explored and criticized the retributive theory of punishment (without, however, repudiating it entirely); see my "Retribution and the Theory of Punishment," *Journal of Philosophy* 75 (1978): 601–619, and my "Justice and Punishment: Philosophical Basics," in *The Socio-Economics of Crime and Justice*, ed. Brian Forst (Armonk, N.Y.: M. E. Sharpe, 1993): 19–36.

40. NAACP Legal Defense Fund, supra note 9, at 7–15, reporting forty-seven "volunteers" for execution between 1973 and 1997. The total number of persons sentenced to death during these years is not less than five thousand.

41. Ibid., reporting 51 suicides among death row convicts from 1973 through 1997. Attempted suicides are not reported.

42. Elsewhere I have explored in greater detail the reasons why it is rational to regard the death penalty as a more severe punishment than life imprisonment; see my "Imprison-

ment vs. Death: Does Avoiding Schwarzschild's Paradox Lead to Sheleff's Dilemma?" *Albany Law Review* 54 (1990): 481–495.

43. We lack generally available reports and discussions of the prison behavior of life-term convicted murderers in the prisons of American abolition jurisdictions. In taking the position I do in the text, I am relying mainly on the absence of evidence to the contrary. Thus, at the symposium to celebrate 150 years without the death penalty in Michigan, held in May 1996 at the Thomas M. Cooley Law School in Lansing, Michigan, the state officials and local scholars who spoke on the occasion made no mention of problems in prison management that they believed would have been solved if only Michigan had had the death penalty. See especially Eugene G. Wanger, "Historical Reflections on Michigan's Abolition of the Death Penalty," *Thomas M. Cooley Law Review* 13 (1996): 755–774.

44. Is it reasonable to believe that the death penalty could be abolished tomorrow in the Death Belt across the South (from the Carolinas to Arizona) without troubling social repercussions? One might well doubt that it could be. There is no sign in these states of the political leadership needed to make abolition acceptable by the general public as a humane and rational change in punitive policy. The political climate for the past generation, in which the death penalty has received rabid support, makes legislative or judicial abolition (or extensive executive clemency) all but impossible in these jurisdictions. In other death penalty states, it is a different story. In New York, for example, beginning in 1977 gubernatorial vetos of death penalty legislation prevented its revival, and without public disorder, until 1995. Were New York's legislature or highest court tomorrow to repeal the death penalty or declare it unconstitutional under the state constitution (either is highly unlikely), I am confident the return to abolition could be managed without adverse social effects.

45. Retribution is not a motive, whereas revenge is; revenge knows no upper limits, whereas retribution does; revenge is personal, whereas retribution can be impersonal. For the best discussion, to which I am indebted, of the differences between these two concepts, see Robert Nozick, *Philosophical Explanations* (Cambridge, Mass.: Harvard University Press, 1981): 366–370. For a general discussion of retribution and revenge, see Henberg, supra note 8.

46. For a list of abolitionist nations as of 1996, see the report from Amnesty International reprinted in Bedau, supra note 5, at 78–83. I do not pursue here the strategy that allows us to grant that although murderers do *deserve* to die, we *ought not* to execute them.

47. See Bedau, supra note 5, at 30–32.

48. See in particular the liberal theories of constitutional government variously formulated by H. L. A. Hart, *The Concept of Law* (Oxford: Clarendon Press, 1961); John Rawls, supra note 34, and his *Political Liberalism* (New York: Columbia, 1993); Bruce Ackerman, *Social Justice in the Liberal State* (New Haven, Conn.: Yale University Press, 1980); Michael J. Sandel, *Liberalism and the Limits of Justice* (Cambridge: Cambridge University Press, 1982); Ronald Dworkin, *Law's Empire* (Cambridge, Mass.: Harvard University Press, 1986), and his *Freedom's Law: The Moral Reading of the American Constitution* (Cambridge, Mass.: Harvard University Press, 1996); Brian Barry, *Theories of Justice* (Berkeley: University of California Press, 1989), and *Justice as Impartiality* (Oxford: Clarendon Press, 1995).

49. See in general Henberg, supra note 8.

50. Ernest van den Haag, for one, accepts the distinction between retribution and revenge, and argues that both are legitimate; see his "The Death Penalty Once More," *University of California-Davis Law Review* 18 (1985): 957–972, reprinted in Bedau, supra note 8.

51. For representative recent views on the role for retributive considerations in nonretributive theories of punishment, see H. L. A. Hart, *Punishment and Responsibility*, supra note 36, at 230–237; Nigel Walker, *Why Punish?* (Oxford: Oxford University Press, 1991),

67–118; John Braithwaite and Philip Pettit, *Not Just Deserts: A Republican Theory of Criminal Justice* (Oxford: Clarendon Press, 1990), 156–201; Nicola Lacey, *State Punishment: Political Principles and Community Values* (London: Routledge, 1988), 25–27, 53–56; C. L. Ten, *Crime, Guilt, and Punishment: A Philosophical Introduction* (Oxford: Clarendon Press, 1987), 38–65, 150–160; R. A. Duff, *Trials and Punishments* (Cambridge: Cambridge University Press, 1986), 187–204.

52. Thus a recent defense of retribution in punishment fails to make this distinction, with the result that we do not know what the author thinks is the appropriate deserved punishment for any given crime or offender; see Michael S. Moore, "The Moral Worth of Retribution," reprinted in *Philosophy of Law*, 5th ed., ed. Joel Feinberg and Hyman Gross (Belmont, Calif.: Wadsworth, 1995), 632–654.

53. I would say the same of the "expressive function" of punishment, according to which punishment by its nature "expresses" condemnation of the criminal act. It is plausible to assume that the more severe the punishment, the more severe the condemnation warranted, and thus if murder (especially SMR murder) is the gravest crime, then it warrants the strongest condemnation, which only death can provide. Insofar as this is true, it is only because lesser crimes that now are punished by life imprisonment ("Three strikes and you're out!") make it impossible to "express" the greater condemnation appropriate for murder by life imprisonment. (I am indebted to Michael Davis for bringing this point forcefully to my attention.) Second, cruelty in punishment "expresses" other things besides condemnation of crime; it testifies to the willingness of officials to carry out death sentences on prisoners safely in their custody. It is by no means obvious that the greater condemnation of murder conveyed by execution cancels or supersedes the other messages that executions "express."

54. Two detailed but completely different versions of a retributive penalty schedule are to be found in Andrew von Hirsch, *Doing Justice: The Choice of Punishments* (New York: Hill and Wang, 1976); and in Michael Davis, "How to Make the Punishment Fit the Crime," *Ethics* 93 (1983): 726–752, revised and reprinted in his *To Make the Punishment Fit the Crime: Essays in the Theory of Criminal Justice* (Boulder, Colo.: Westview, 1992). Elsewhere I have criticized von Hirsch's theory; see Bedau, "Retribution and the Theory of Punishment," supra note 39, at 613–615, and my "Classificatiion-Based Sentencing: Some Conceptual and Ethical Problems," *New England Journal of Criminal and Civil Confinement* 10 (1984): 1–26. Some of those criticisms apply to Davis's theory as well. For another attempt at a retributive matching of punishments to crimes see George Sher, *Desert* (Princeton, N.J.: Princeton University Press, 1987), 69–90.

Phillip Montague, in his *Punishment as Societal Defense* (Lanham, Md.: Rowman and Littlefield, 1995), does not present and defend a retributive penalty schedule; but he does defend the death penalty by invoking a principle he believes is required to justify individuals in using lethal self-defense. However, his argument relying on this principle (pp. 42, 135) equally well justifies the use of torture, maiming, decapitation, or any other brutal form of punishment. Montague does not defend this alarming consequence, perhaps because he fails to see that it follows from his argument, thus providing us with another example of what happens in a theory of punishment when no upper bound to cruelty or savagery in modes of punishment is recognized.

For other defenses of the death penalty on retributive grounds that fail to do so within the framework of any comprehensive penalty schedule, see Tom Sorell, *Moral Theory and Capital Punishment* (Oxford: Blackwell, 1987), and Igor Primoratz, *Justifying Legal Punishment* (Atlantic Highlands, N.J.: Humanities, 1989).

55. The problem was identifed and discussed years ago by Charles L. Black Jr., *Capital Punishment: The Inevitability of Caprice and Mistake*, 2d ed. (New York: Norton, 1981), 115–121. For a recent discussion of the vicissitudes in trying to predict future dangerousness,

see Robert Menzies et al., "The Dimensions of Dangerousness: Assessing Forensic Predictions about Violence," *Law and Human Behavior* 18 (1994): 1–28.

56. See *Kansas v. Hendricks*, No. 95-1649, decided on June 24, 1997, upholding state statutes that detain predatory sex offenders beyond the expiration of their prison sentences. *New York Times*, June 25, 1997, A20.

57. On the distinction between the right and the good, and the priority of the former, see Rawls, supra note 35, at 30–32, 446–452.

58. On relative costs, see Richard C. Dieter, *Millions Misspent: What Politicians Don't Say about the High Cost of the Death Penalty*, rev. ed. (Washington, D.C.: Death Penalty Information Center, 1994), reprinted in part in Bedau, supra note 8.

59. See in general Gilligan, supra note 12.

60. Albert Camus, *Neither Victims nor Executioners*, trans. Dwight McDonald (1946; Philadelphia, Pa.: New Society Publishers, 1986).

· 3 ·

A JURIDICAL FRANKENSTEIN, OR DEATH IN THE HANDS OF THE STATE

JULIE M. TAYLOR

I. Imaginaries of Violence

Nightmares fill us with dreads so deep that, when they stay in our minds, the fear they provoke seems primordial. Yet imaginaries of violence differ from culture to culture.[1] The different shapes terrors take have not been investigated, possibly because their study takes us back to the nightmares that feel to each of us universal. Neither violence, nor terror, nor even fear can be an identical experience for everyone in the face of highly specific contexts that are culturally and historically defined. Violence comes in different forms; different peoples expect violences to be wielded by different agents in different ways. These pages explore cultural and historical detail in Argentina that feeds and frames dread of violence in the hands of the state.

The issues of the imaginaries of violence and the experience of legal subjects in the face of law are crucial to the study of terror as well as to a jurisprudence of violence. These issues are key to an examination of why and in what manner legal subjects regard and obey the law and those whom they perceive as its agents. Probing this area helps us begin to formulate in what ways and "how pervasively the law's violence constructs . . . self-perception, influences . . . motives and dispositions, and determines what [members of a culture] . . . are disposed or ill disposed to do."[2]

In the mid-1990s in Buenos Aires, I struck up a close friendship with a woman who proved to be, like myself, a single mother of an adolescent boy. We shared the deep anxiety of parents of young men of an age that can put them on the edge of real trouble. One evening we found ourselves confessing our fears of the police. But the fears spelled themselves out quite differently in our lives in different cultures. Marijó had been raised in the provinces of Argentina, where her parents had moved to escape the epicenter of the repression of the violent dictatorship of the late 1970s and early 80s. She was interested in my remark that I always told my son to be particularly careful of his behavior in the city of Buenos Aires because, I would reiterate, as though speaking of a natural hazard, the police in Argentina could send him directly to jail, unlike their counterparts in the United States who had to summon him to court. Marijó wanted to know more, because she said that her teenager thought that she merely harbored old-fashioned fears left over from the Terror. He refused, for example, to cut his hair just in order to avoid being identified by the police as unruly, uneducated, or just plain poor. Was she, she wondered, exaggerated in her worry? I mentioned that for my son my words conveyed a real threat because of an example of a Latino family in our neighborhood in the United States. A store had caught the nine-year-old of the family trying to pinch a comic book and had called the police, who brought the boy home in the back of a police car. When the child had asked where they were going, the police had answered "Straight to jail," leaving him terrorized on the doorstep with his mother, who was home alone for the evening. My son and I happened to visit when the mother had just finished disciplining the youngster. While my son went off with the other boy who was still drying his tears, the mother commented to me that she had been left open-mouthed by the child's comment upon learning that the police had lied to him about going to jail: "Good thing," he remarked, "that I am brown and not black. If I were black, they would REALLY have taken me to jail." Later that night she had called, shaken, to recount that while she had been serving dinner to her son, still alone with him, the police had returned. The officer had swept past her into her dining room, where he accosted the boy again and berated him. The mother hovered, horrified at the presence of an armed stranger in her house while minutes ticked by. "It took me almost ten minutes," she said, "to remember my rights. I told him as steadily as I could, 'Officer, I have already scolded my son. You'll have to excuse us because now we are eating dinner.' But I didn't think to take his badge number—I was too nervous."

Marijó remained thoughtful as she listened. Then she hesitatingly told me a parallel account. Her own son was going through a troubled period and had been taken to the police station. He had been charged in the station with an infraction that had occurred in an entirely different place, a fact of which Marijó was convinced because the younger brother had come home for her help with a story that differed in convincing ways from the accusations of the police. When she arrived alone in the station the police presented her with the charges that she believed to be false. Frightened, she began to refute them, only to be told, "Either you sign here and take him, or he is not coming out." Marijó did not know what her rights in the situation were. She felt she was in dangerous enemy territory and wondered if she had any rights at all. She reluctantly signed and took her son home, only to be haunted over the following months and years by the fear of what her signature might have meant.

Fears of state violence vary among cultures but also within a given group or sector, according to one's position relative to worlds of power. In the anecdotes just recounted, the frightened mothers had no contacts with power in upper echelons of society or in any underworld of crime or corruption. They were middle-class working women in populations that have traditionally been predominantly middle-class, and they expected their children to attain a position in the middle class through mechanisms—such as education, initiative, taste, and work—that coincided with mainstream cultural values. Their imaginaries of violence would have been different had they been situated differently vis à vis different types of power: were they, for example, members of an illiterate working class—rare in either the United States or Argentina—or of an underground or an elite involved in crime or corruption or both, or of a completely excluded minority. Their imaginaries would also have been vastly different had either lived in a society, like Colombia, where state power has been shattered, rendering agents of violence almost entirely unidentifiable.

Argentina, with a tradition of a successful national project due in part to its enormous wealth, has as well a tradition of a monopoly of violence by the state that has often been pushed easily into dictatorial regimes, the most horrible of which was the 1976–83 Process of National Organization, *el Proceso*. The seven-year rule of the Proceso has become synonymous in the international press with modern reigns of terror. Its "Dirty War" of state terrorism against any opposition, or supposed opposition, in guerrilla forces or any other sector of the population, gave Argentina the dubious distinction of adding the word *desaparecido* to the world's vocabulary. The Proceso represented an important ideological presence on the Latin American scene, the National Security Doctrine, as disseminated by the United States (especially through its military assistance from the 1950s onward), based on the idea that the world faced an ultimate war between communist and noncommunist forces and that this battle would be waged through nonconventional warfare with subservice forces within each nation. The junta finally fell in the wake of the ouster of the military resulting from the Malvinas/Falklands debacle.

In this historical setting, as it developed over time, the police grew into a force of extraordinary independence, implementing certain types of violence and planting both the fear of these violences as well as the idea that they might be necessary evils. The following pages will explore the complicated circumstance that allowed certain invasive forms of state order in Argentina to be imagined as normal. The autonomy of the police, and practices derived from it, may have gone far to create particular Argentine nightmares.[3] However, as a culture that has traditionally been predominantly middle-class, white, and derived largely from European immigration, Argentina is comparable not only with other Latin American cultures but also with North Atlantic nations. Thus the case of Argentina may display combinations, recombinations, exaggerations, and emphases of traits found elsewhere in the West.

These pages spell out reactions to a certain combination of violences that are defined differently elsewhere in the West and often assigned distinctly to the police and the armed forces.[4] Because of the enormously dramatic nature of the horror perpetrated by the Proceso, the years under its rule account for much of today's Argentina. Nevertheless, I agree with scholars such as Osvaldo Berreneche, Paul Chevigny, Laura Kalamaniecki, Nicholas Shumway, and Eugenio Raúl Zaffaroni, and ultimately, with the writers Ricardo Piglia and the great Rodolfo Walsh, who suggest that terror in Argentina acquired its specific shape over the course of different historical eras previous to the Proceso.[5] In this view, the increasing police violence in Buenos Aires, and the extreme violence of the Proceso are seen as related with still other events and forces in Argentine history. This might at first glance make the case of Argentina seem more idiosyncratic and therefore more inscrutable. But many of the details that build up to this picture of terror, such as forms of police harassment, are not foreign to other countries. They in fact may help us understand how differing constellations of such familiar practices may lead to more or less exaggerated violence and resistance or acquiescence to it. This kind of detail informs a space occupied by citizens who fear the law in their everyday lives. But theirs is a space that may never be touched directly by the decisions of a judge, or by the pain and bloodshed caused by these decisions, or even by routine coercive law enforcement. They help us to consider both how we and others live with power and the forces of order, and how our lives are informed by imaginaries of violence that differ by cultural and political context and by historical moment.

This discussion proposes working definitions of violence and terror: violence is considered as exclusion; terror, as absolute exclusion. Exclusions can be spelled out as denial of recourse, or as denial of resources, of which recourse is one. Violence, then would be the denial of recourse to the law, or to wealth, or to the state or its representatives. Terror would be the absolute lack of any of these resources or of any resources at all. This kind of exclusion objectifies its victims by defining them as outside society and without access to the resources that society offers its members. In the course of defining victims as outsiders, violences also define them as less than fully human.

In considering violence as this kind of exclusion, we can see the spectacular violences of the Proceso against "subversives" as partaking of the nature of the exclusions perpetrated by the police when they define their victims as "delinquents." The two terms are in fact sometimes interchangeable in Argentine political discourse, and at times become confused with the idea of foreigners or illegal aliens: "Oh, please," answered General Antonio Domingo Bussi of the Proceso when questioned about his refusal to return the corpse of a guerrilla son to an eminent family: "[T]hat fellow was a subversive delinquent, the author of numberless crimes. He went around the province with a backpack on his shoulder just like el Che Guevara."[6] As this notorious quotation shows, such distancing from a community or from humanity in Argentina, although directed at a population that has traditionally been highly literate, largely middle-class, and predominantly white, is done on the basis of essentialist definitions like those that underlie discriminations on the basis of race and gender. These phenomena illuminate each other in different cultures as well as across cultures. When searching for cases in the culture of the United States comparable to the experience of the radical exclusions enacted by power in Argentina, and in particular by the Argentine police, the most fruitful starting point may be experiences of police harassment as well as other violence of the law against peoples of color, especially, but not only, those disadvantaged by class.[7]

Exclusions, then, may be physical, ranging from bodily restraint or segregation to "the suppression of life," to use the term of the Argentine armed forces. Exclusions also come in the form of the denial of rights. In the anecdotes recounted near the beginning of this chapter, my friend and I discussed a similar panic over the possible exclusion of our children from future participation in a white middle class. Although worried about the curtailment of their rights, we were also deeply frightened by the prospect of physical damage or even death by disease or violence in a reformatory or jail. The difference in the imaginaries of terror between our two different cultures was that, after an initial paralysis, the mother in the United States was able to "remember" her rights and invoke them, reinserting herself into her community as a member who, even completely alone, could contest the police officer. Her rights in that case were a crucial resource to which she laid claim. Her child knew from his experience in public schools in the 1990s that his recourse to rights would vary according to his color. The ten minutes that the mother spent confused by the presence in her home of an armed member of the police force opened a window for me on the situation of my Argentine friend. The latter had tried to make her son avoid marking himself for essentialist definitions of class by encouraging him to cut his hair. In the police station in Buenos Aires, burdened with her memories of disappearances under the dictatorship, she did not know what rights they had and was left with the fear that her son could be indelibly marked for exclusion.

In looking at facets of the culture and history of Argentina that seem to have molded the reception of the radically exclusive acts and institutions that constitute terror, one infers that the Proceso may have been facilitated by a familiarity with violences. Of course, the scars left by the Proceso are so profound that they have distinctly marked contemporary Argentine culture. Rather than propose a causal relation, I will suggest that the different factors with which I deal relate to one another in a complex constellation in the Argentine imaginary. Therefore, while any recent act of violence evokes memories of the Proceso, some of these acts have other institutional or cultural pasts, which are also echoed. Multiple layers of history and culture, including the Proceso, make up the strata of an imaginary of violence. They also raise the question of the extent to which such an imaginary may have hemmed in subjectivity in middle- and working-class Argentina, where Argentines may have accustomed themselves to assert a conditioned agency, unable to interpret the violences of the law as invasions or conceive of them as beyond limits.

II. Violences and the Chain of Command

The Argentine experience, because it is so extreme, makes evident the deeply problematic nature of an imaginary of death and violence at the hands of a Western state. In particular, Argentina's everyday police actions bring to light possible parallels between police power and state terror. How has this specific history come about, with its exaggerated characteristics of police violence in Argentine culture, inside and outside the police? Extended police violence in Argentina has been dubbed a "police politics," consisting of an "exaggeratedly summary death penalty" — *pena de muerte sumarísima*.[8]

In fact, three interrelated forms of violence raise the possibility that cultural patterns have made certain violences more familiar and comprehensible in exaggerated forms in Argentina than in many other Western nations. In 1996, all three featured in major controversies concerning different types of violence in Buenos Aires. First, in March 1996, an epidemic of police brutality left Argentines shaken and perplexed at yet another resurgence of the malady known as *gatillo fácil* or itchy trigger finger (literally, the easy trigger), chronic police violence that displays certain traits and that has historically appeared in outbreaks as a plague on the streets of Buenos Aires. Second, the way for the *gatillo fácil* has been prepared by over a century of Argentine law that classifies misdemeanours not only as separate from the Penal Code, but also as outside the judicial system, regulated by the police edict. The winter months of July and August 1996 threw into crisis the venerable institution of the police edict, because of a small number of unusual appeals in the courts together with issues clustering around legal and political problems of the new autonomy of the city of Buenos Aires. Third, both controversies over different but related abuses of power harked back from time to time to the dark memories of the *Proceso*, the military dictatorship of 1976–83.

There are structural similarities as well as other parallels between *gatillo fácil*, the edict, and the intensely brutal form of state terror imposed by the *Proceso*. The fortuitous combination of themes in the public arena allowed me to add informal interviews and impressions to more formal research at a moment that constituted a watershed in the recent history of Argentine violence.[9] Thus the present work is not based on anthropological fieldwork in the strict sense of the word, although it inevitably draws on the ten years I have spent in Argentina. It emphasizes cultural expectations and experiences of violences by victims and potential victims, rather than by those who interpret or theorize rules or laws that permit violence or by the perpetrators of violence themselves.

Both police edict and *gatillo fácil* are chronic forms of Argentine violence. Because they live in a culture that naturalizes some forms of violence, Argentines may have tolerated it in the hands of the state to a degree other cultures find unacceptable. Yet violence in the form of the power exercised by the police poses a danger in other cultures as well. Similar abuses are frequently naturalized in other parts of the West, as noted by Walter Benjamin,[10] haunting other cultures with potential totalitarian violence.

Benjamin and Argentine legal scholars alike view with alarm a vital structural characteristic of police power: the fact that it depends on a combination of different types of power that, in democracy, are defined as separate. And this in turn determines the disturbing degree of autonomy of the police force and of the police agent, which decouples both force and agent from a chain of command. That is, the police occupy a position where they are required to make autonomous decisions concerning the law that must be applied, the relative guilt or innocence of the person apprehended, and often at least part of the punishment to be meted: whether or not to pull the trigger, raise the billy stick, or ratchet up the "interrogation." The police, then, combine legislative, judicial, and executive powers. While this may occur only in an emergency or contingency, it is always a potential. And it has on occasion been institutionalized, as in states of siege and, in Argentina, in the separation of the body of law that deals with misdemeanor (*ley contravencional*) from the law covering felonies (the Penal Code) and judicial power. In this situation, the police respond to virtually no one; the chain of command is broken.

A broken chain of command was also key to a diagnosis of the Proceso that was produced by prosecutors in the historic and unique trials in Argentina of the nation's own military junta. Their document, *La Sentencia*,[11] contains a lengthy analysis of the dictatorship that emerged from the material amassed as evidence for the trials and constitutes one ethnographic description of the Proceso. The prosecution accused the commanders in chief of the armed forces of having established a "delinquent state." Their Sentence documents the junta's fabrication of a criminal and clandestine plan to use the secret and parallel state apparatus for murder. Their criminal state displayed an important characteristic:[12] a loosening of control and hierarchy up and down the chains of [military] command to involve a high degree of autonomy for individual agents. This trait characterized the junta's rule throughout the years of the Proceso:[13]

> In sum, it may be affirmed that the commanders in chief secretly established a criminal mode of fighting against terrorism. [The lower ranks of] the armed forces were given enormous discretionary powers for the deprivation of the liberty of those who appeared, according to Intelligence, to be linked with subversion. [They] were conceded, finally, broad liberty to define the final destiny of the victim: entry into the legal system [at the disposition of the executive power or on trial], freedom, or physical elimination. . . . Permission to loot was also given.[14]

> [M]any of them were only lieutenants or captains, . . . [yet] as in all other places where dirty wars have taken place, members of the *grupos de tareas* [task groups] sometimes had broader powers of life and death than a normal senior military officer.[15]

These descriptions refer to a deployment of power like that of the police in the modern Western state. The Proceso left as an important part of its legacy a spectacular exaggeration of the autonomy that characterizes police power, as well as an extension of the police as institution. The "Frankenstein jurídico"[16] now openly stalks the Argentine streets as the *gatillo fácil*. But it is not exclusively due to the Proceso, and it is not new. The *gatillo fácil* is recognized often by Argentines[17] both as an eerie echo of recent horror or as yet another form of daily terror and thus of social control, exercised traditionally and routinely by the police forces.

III. *Gatillo Fácil*—The Spectral Echo

On February 22, 1996, I arrived in Buenos Aires for a month of sabbatical leave, able for the first time in fifteen years to travel in the summer of the Southern Hemisphere. I had coped with Antarctic winds off the Patagonian steppes for only too many Junes and Julys, muffled in layers of woolen clothing in a city gray with the loss of the leaves of its many trees. This year I was delighted to arrive with only one bag and to make my way through streets with cafés full of people apparently enjoying the sun, the green, and the spectacular orchid-like flowers of the palo borracho trees that I had almost forgotten. But as the days passed, the rumors in the streets and cafés turned to a puzzle that terrorized the populace: voices lowered to ask what was happening to the police. What was behind the *gatillo fácil*, the itchy trigger finger that was dealing out spectacular new deaths every day?

Such questions in Argentina today inevitably echo the military dictatorship of only twenty years back, although the sense of panic in 1996 reached an intensity far less than that provoked by the Proceso. But similar doubts were broached, with a similar hesitation, in a similar tone of voice, and similar prefatory checks were made of the surroundings to detect possible eavesdroppers. Horrified, I wondered at first if I were overreacting to a phenomenon I had somehow missed previously. Yet rumors and conversations continually expressed similar horror and suggested that Argentines were as taken aback as I. One of them summed up the tragic month:

> Towards the end of February, the police of the Province of Buenos Aires repressed a peaceful demonstration of students in the city of La Plata.[18] Police beat and wounded journalists, young people, and Hebe de Bonafina, of the Madres de la Plaza de Mayo. The next day, a teenager who was with friends on a corner in a downtown neighborhood of Buenos Aires was assassinated with a bullet in the neck by a federal police agent in uniform. The following day, a father who was taking his daughter to the hospital was also assassinated by a federal police agent who shot him in the back: since the man would not slow down the car in which he was driving his little girl [who was in convulsions], the policeman figured that he was dealing with a suspicious character. A few days later, a young man was detained by a police patrol, taken to a vacant lot, and assassinated *a mansalva* and the body burned by the same police agents. The same day that this fact was uncovered, a group of middle-class youths charged a gendarme out of uniform with engaging in an argument with them in the street. The officer got out of the car he was driving, headed toward the car belonging to the teenagers, and began to fire at them. Since his weapon malfunctioned [*se trabó*], he only managed to wound two of the young men. The next day, a young woman appeared before television cameras to show her face and body bruised and swollen due to blows she had received in a police station [*comisaría*] upon refusing to engage in prostitution under the protection of the police agents.
>
> None of these occurrences is foreign to the context of things that occur frequently in Buenos Aires. Nevertheless, it is not common that they occur within so short a lapse of time. Generally, when a case of police violence becomes notorious through the mass media, or when charges or reports of violations of human rights receive publicity, for a few months afterward the police lower the level of violence . . . , for example, in 1991, after the death of [teenager] Walter Bulacio [detained when attending a rock concert], in a police station, after which the time allowed for detention by the police for the *averiguación de antecedentes* was cut from twenty-four to ten hours.
>
> But this time, this was not the case. The violence did not cease. . . .
>
> . . . On March 24, almost 100,000 people gathered in the Plaza de Mayo to repudiate the military coup on its twentieth anniversary.[19]

The connection with the memory of the military junta was not unique to this account. At first glance we "knew" that the unfolding police chronicle before us had no connection with the Proceso of two decades ago. Yet the brutality and arbitrariness of the events, and the fear that lowered our voices as we discussed them, were familiar.

Conversations repeatedly went over an inventory of possible explanations. These musings were in themselves inventories of the ingredients of contemporary Argentine imaginings of the inner workings of violence. There had to be, middle-class Argentines often calculated, some eerie connection between what appeared increasingly to be a systematically arbitrary violence and a higher political power. If it was a plan, a plot, who was giving the orders? It was unlikely in people's minds that we were talking about the chief of police. But, though more probable, it was also hard to imagine that the president himself—despite his notorious previous attempts to give orders to the police bypassing justice—was deploying police forces to terrorize the city.[20]

Could the police be connected to the "unemployed labor force"? These "unemployed," members of the armed forces and paramilitary groups under the dictatorship, many of whom had been amnestied, continue to be identified in criminal actions, most scandalously in the "superbands" that have carried out major violent robberies in the last years. Could the police action somehow be in response to one of the major figures of the dictatorship who, as the newspapers constantly reminded us, still roamed the streets of Buenos Aires? Could there be some plot against the youth of the nation, again reminiscent of persecution under the Proceso? Youngsters today respond to this memory in the name of the popular musical group Innocent for Now, advertised in graffiti throughout Buenos Aires. Was there any chance that this assault could be part of the everyday violence of the increasingly harsh economic plan that had left almost 20 percent unemployment in Argentina? Or—since none of the previous explanations quite made sense of the apparently endless headlines of police violence—was it "simply" that the police force in its entirety was *pasado de cocaína*, accelerated by cocaine, thanks to their easy access to drugs in which they and the government, the commentary continued to speculate, probably dealt in to a point completely out of control?

The dread and confusion that obsessed Argentina for weeks on end in the midst of the summer heat and the flowers of 1996 seemed to sow the kind of bewilderment described by Walter Benjamin: "Unlike law, which acknowledges in the 'decision' determined by place and time a metaphysical category that gives it a claim to critical evaluation, a consideration of the police institution encounters nothing essential at all. Its power is formless, like its nowhere tangible, all-pervasive, ghostly presence in the life of civilized states."[21] In Argentina, such a spectral presence caused a moment of shocked déjà vu, dragging to the surface memories— some precise, many blurred—of the Proceso and constituting part of the imaginary of violence that hovered over Buenos Aires twenty years later.

IV. Autonomy and the Agents of the Delinquent State

The commanders in chief who took over the government decided to maintain in force the current legal framework . . . without the declaration of emergency measures. . . . Yet what actually happened was radically different. Although the operative structure continued functioning, the personnel subordinate to the defendents detained a large number of people, they lodged them clandestinely . . . , they kept them in inhuman conditions, . . . and finally, either they put them at the disposition of the courts or the executive power or they physically eliminated them.[22]

Further, an integral part of the system ordered [by the armed forces] was a guarantee of impunity . . . in order to assure that the different forces organized for the prevention of delinquency did not interfere with proceedings. . . . [Abuses included] hiding the truth . . . before the petitions of judges, organizations, families, and foreign governments, pretending to investigate . . . , using state power to influence foreign and local opinion . . . , through illegal deprivation of liberty, torture and murder . . . [and] other crimes that were not directly ordered, but that may be considered the natural consequences of the system that had been adopted.[23]

With these words, the prosecution in the trials of Argentine commanders in chief described the 1976–83 military dictatorship as a "delinquent state." In order to draw this conclusion in the pages of the Sentence, the prosecution painted a detailed portrait of the Proceso according to the evidence assembled in the course of the legal proceedings.

The prosecution offered proof that the guerrilla movement that had been identified as the target of the junta's violence had in fact been defeated before the coup. Therefore the violence of the dictatorship could not have been directed, as the Proceso constantly alleged, toward combating insurrection. The Sentence establishes first the context of the military coup, the existence and exacerbation of terrorism on the Left. They then point out that this phenomenon reached its apogee in the years 1974–75,[24] just before the end of the constitutional government and the *golpe* of March 1976. Under Isabel Perón, the Argentine state, with constitutional limits still in place, had authorized the armed forces to assume the functions of the police, thereby involving the army, navy, and air force in internal domestic security. At this same time, they remark, the forces of the AAA, or the Argentine Anti-Communist Alliance, emerged,[25] under the leadership of the éminence grise of Isabelita's government, López Rega, former police captain. Under the AAA a new form of kidnaping arose, different from the common criminal form of kidnaping, which had other ends. In 1975, the goals and the responsibility of an abduction were no longer clarified, nor were victims ever liberated. For the first time, it was not that they had disappeared, but rather that they *were* disappeared. Kidnapping had given place to disappearance.

The constitutional government had taken legal measures to control the guerrilla groups.[26] The Sentence concludes that these measures were sufficient from the fact that in all major confrontations in 1975 the guerrillas were defeated. Further, they point out that neither the legislation of the constitutional government nor orders to the armed forces were modified, suggesting that measures against the guerrillas were deemed sufficient.

Having established that the Proceso's violence could not have had as its target the already defeated "subversion," the Sentence documents a systematic assault by the armed forces on their own population. It points out that "with the advent of the military government, there was a significant increase all over the nation of the number of disappearances."[27] These disappearances indicated the application of synchronized and highly standardized methods of abductions, detentions, and torture, which were kept carefully secret. It notes an increase of 1,000 percent in denunciations of illegal deprivation of liberty of people who were detained by armed groups.[28] The abductors in these cases identified themselves as security forces; yet after the abduction legal recourses were denied to relatives of the victims. These operations put into effect "free areas," or areas of operation by only one security force, where, for example, the police turned a blind eye to action by the army, or the army could not interrupt an action of the police.[29] Looting accompanied the abductions.

They were carried out with elaborate measures to ensure secrecy: they occurred predominantly at night, despite the facts that the perpetrators identified themselves as part of the forces of order, and the victims were hidden from the sight of onlookers, covered with blankets on the floor of the car or hidden in the trunk.

The destination of those taken away in this manner were detention camps, usually established in installations belonging to the police or the armed forces, but whose existence was hidden from the public.[30] Here torture was universally and systematically carried out, using techniques that were similar in all the camps, by *patotas* or gangs, the names of whose members were kept secret.[31] Equally systematically, the victims were often "physically eliminated."[32] Relatives' requests for information concerning the disappeared were met by the Ministry of the Interior with form letters complete with blanks for the names relevant to the case at hand, denying any knowledge concerning the fate of the victim.[33] However, the Sentence points out the lack of evidence of any investigation whatsoever of these cases or of cases brought forward by international institutions, pointing once again to clandestinity or a double discourse, in which one version of reality was presented to the national and international public, while a different reality was being systematically mounted in a secret world.

The Sentence concludes that "the manner of proceeding, which supposed a secret suspension (*derogación*) of the laws that were in effect (*normas en vigor*), responded to plans that were approved and given as orders to their respective forces by the military commanders.[34] The executors of the orders, the Sentence concludes again and again, operated with an autonomy (*discreción*) that was systematic. It was they who decided who were "subversive delinquents" and who were, therefore, potential targets for repression.[35] It was they who decided the fate of these victims: freedom, "legalization" in prison or under house arrest at the disposition of the executive power (PEN), or disappearance into an extermination camp and death. Finally, in another indication of a planned assault on the population, the methods of repression and torture were uniform throughout Argentina in the extermination camps of the different armed forces.

The court deduced from direct and indirect evidence that the orders that facilitated the "extreme autonomy" (*discrecionalidad*) were verbal, even though, "given their nature, there exists no documentary evidence of such illegal and secret orders." This evidence was crucial in the Argentine context contemporary to the trials in order to refute versions that circulate to this day attributing the 1976–83 reign of terror to the "excesses" of troops somehow "out of control." The prosecution considered this a matter so important that the Sentence reviews fourteen points of evidence that oral orders existed, followed by quotes from the defense making explicit that there had been orders and that these had been oral.[36] The Sentence addresses the ideas of excess and lack of control throughout, emphasizing that no investigations or court martials were carried out internally to deal with such extreme "excesses," nor could such numbers of excesses be committed without a generalized state of insurrection in the armed forces. Therefore, acts that displayed such systematic uniformity had to be in response to orders that in turn responded to a plan. But the orders and the plan were secret.

The Sentence concludes that orders were given that consistently produced actions characterized by a high degree of autonomy on the part of the actors. It describes such autonomy as part of the nature of the system in which the orders are emitted, as characteristic of its chain of command: those who execute orders within the wide bounds of such systematic autonomy have enough power put into their hands to transform themselves into vigilantes of the state—eerily reminiscent of another, later system and the autonomy it gives to other agents acting as virtual vigilantes: the police.

V. Police as Vigilantes of the State

> Homicide of the type referred to as *gatillo fácil* suggests . . . executions at the margins of the law.[37]

The exaggeration of the Argentine *gatillo fácil* that confronted us in March 1996 underscored the paradoxically systematic nature of the apparent lack of control we witnessed. A detail that escaped some observers and obsessed others is the fact that neither in this intense barrage of death nor in previous equally spectacular if more isolated cases were the deeds punished. And in cases within memory that had called down a sanction, the sanction seemed slight or was successfully appealed.[38]

This observation brought discussions back to the fearful or disgusted question posed by bewildered citizens: Could the *gatillo fácil* be due, not to the low level of education of police agents nor to widespread drug addiction, but to a system or plan? And this question interestingly produced another, involving decisions made on all levels in the police force. Could the power given to the agent on the street, the perpetrator of the deeds involving the *gatillo fácil*, be seen as unreasonable, since an agent in action was expected both to judge the case at hand and to carry out his or her own sentence within minutes?

The conundrums surrounding the phenomenon of the *gatillo fácil* echo in turn the tensions of another controversy salient in law schools, newspapers,[39] and academic papers,[40] which concerned the perplexing nature in Argentina of police power in general and police edicts specifically. The autonomy of the police agent on the street is related structurally to the autonomy with which the police issues edicts: both combine executive, legislative, and juridical functions, in the chief of police as well as in the cop or *cana*. Benjamin's analysis of police violence underlines the fact that both the autonomy of the police agent and the nature of the power conferred on him is characteristic of police power in Europe as well. He notes the relation of the veiled confusion of powers of the police in democracy to the explicit mix of powers in an absolute monarchy. This mystified "degeneration of power" is the source of the extreme danger of police violence in democracy: the police are "less devastating where they represent, in absolute monarchy, [the power of a ruler] in which legislative and executive supremacy are united[,] than in democracies where their existence, elevated by no such relation, bears witness to the greatest conceivable degeneration of violence."[41]

Benjamin's general arguments concerning the power of the police in Europe are also made independently by numerous pages of theory in texts of administrative law in Argentina, where the problematic mixed nature of police power is debated at length. Many Argentine texts question the idea that police power in Argentina should be independent from other sources of power in any way. The concept of police power is thought to have been imported from U.S. jurisprudence, and to be inappropriate in the context of the Argentine constitution. The Argentine constitution can be interpreted as anticipating police regulation. Unlike the U.S. Constitution, the Constitution of Argentina (Articles 14 and 28) stipulates that rights are not absolute but limited by law, thereby contemplating police action to regulate individual rights in the interest of the commonweal.[42] The constitution also allows a definition of policing as part of a larger administrative function,[43] subject to all the limits imposed by the balance of executive, judicial, and legislative powers.

This, then, puts into question the chief of police and the agents under him: the abstract police power that they are sometimes described as representing is, contrary to appearances and to frequent practice, not autonomous. Rather, it exists only as part of broader administrative actions that are in turn limited by justice and the law. In their concrete acts, then, the police also must theoretically base their decisions in administrative norms and law. How this is to work for the policeman on his beat is not addressed by the theorists, who seem by implication to believe a separation possible in practice amongst the executive, legislative, and judicial powers. This leads them sometimes to concentrate their criticism on the police edict. The elimination of the edict would remedy the most offensive arrogation by the police of both legislative power (in the emission of the edict) and judicial power (in its application on the beat). The suppression of the edict, it is thought, would be a step toward curing the police of the abuses that have plagued its history in Argentina.

This optimism is shared by the press, for example, in commentary showing surprise that the police defy justice: "To refuse to testify is a right granted by the Constitution, although in the case of the police it is surprising that they refuse to collaborate with justice (la Justicia)."[44] Similarly the police themselves present an optimistic view, holding out the hope that, for example, further education of police agents would change the nature of the police as an institution. In an interview the provincial subsecretary of security was asked, "Would increased education prevent there being delinquents amongst the members of the police [of the province of Buenos Aires]?" The answer was "Of course, the higher their level of training, the better they will know what is a felony and what is not."[45]

According to Benjamin, this confusion of powers is not remediable, but inherent to the police in democracy. Therefore, the power of the police is irremediably degenerate. According to Benjamin, the police are "allowed to rampage . . . blindly in the most vulnerable areas. . . . [T]his ignominy lies in the fact that in this authority the separation of lawmaking and law preserving violence is suspended." The police force exercises "violence for [legal] ends (in the right of disposition), but with the simultaneous authority to decide these ends itself within wide limits (in the right of decree)."[46]

The case of Argentina throws into high relief an exaggerated form of control that works through violent intimidation of large sectors of a population rather than through reinforcing legal limits on specific transgressors of the law. The details and historical idiosyncrasy of the development of the police and law governing misdemeanors (contravenciones) may thus provide a perspective on the more general nature of the power of the police.[47] The history of the police edict in Argentina has been variously traced from colonial edicts [*bandos*] through mayors [*alcaldes*] and rural judges of the peace who were politically appointed.[48] Control exercised by the police was efficient enough, at least in the face of the political turmoil that plagued Argentina, to make a penal code unnecessary until half a century after independence. Projected codes proposed that misdemeanors be under the jurisdiction of a judge. But these codes eventually were swept aside by a final version that assigned misdemeanors to the police in both the city and the province of Buenos Aires.[49]

This led finally to the situation that characterized Buenos Aires until the city's new autonomy in 1996, and which is proving very difficult to change.[50] For a century, due to the independence of the police from justice, it was easier to avoid jail for a felony than for a misdemeanor.[51] Police edicts covered misdemeanors but not felonies (*delitos*). Police agents can detain citizens and give them sentences of up to thirty days for behaviors that vary from drunkenness to celebrating carnaval (a custom no longer practiced in contemporary Argentina) or playing a game involving betting on beans (which today is completely unknown). The misdemeanor "public scandal" covers an unlimited gamut of offenses such as "awkward words," "corruption of decent customs," and "immoral acts."[52] "Vagrancy" possesses special notoriety because of its role in the oppression of the free-ranging gauchos, who were sent to the frontier to combat native tribes. Today the charge is used in cases such as one publicized at the height of the controversy over edicts: a news photograph appeared of a policeman and two arrested suspects with the caption "We saw them loitering [*merodeando*], which is a misdemeanor.[53] There is no necessity for witnesses other than the police agent involved, even in the case of inebriation where no medical opinion is solicited, nor a breathalyzer used. The detainees do not have the right to a lawyer. While they do have a right of appeal, they must appeal within twenty-four hours. This right has been cited repeatedly as the feature linking the edict with the law, since an appeal sends the case to the courts. However, the right to appeal is not widely known and is not cited by the police during the arrest.

In legal venues, the problem is seen to lie in the dubious constitutionality of the edicts. Although the edicts were declared retroactively and en masse laws of the nation by Congress, they had been issued by the police, who were part of the executive power rather than the legislative power. Strictly speaking, then, the edicts were not based on legislation that sanctions the misdemeanors that they define, and therefore there is a question of whether or not punishment could be meted out (Constitution of Argentina, Articles 18 and 19). Since the edicts then became law, controversy centered increasingly on the unconstitutional proceedings involved in detention for the violation of edicts.

Experientially, the puzzle becomes one of what rights a citizen holds in the face of the seemingly constant police practice of detaining civilians for *averiguación de antecedentes*, the investigation of (police) records. This investigation is justified by the violation, or, importantly, the possible violation, of an edict.[54] When Argentine parents attempt to inculcate their children with the dangers that the police represent, many have little or no idea of the differences between an edict and a law. Most have no idea that a sentence is being passed by the police, nor do they realize that such a sentence can be appealed. In 1994 116,000 Argentines were detained for having violated edicts in the city of Buenos Aires alone. In 1994 only 0.1 percent of the sentences were appealed; of these appeals, 95 percent were successful.[55] The idea of being detained has been naturalized as part of the experience of Argentine youth, as I discovered time and again listening to my adolescent son and other young friends. Jocular anecdotes are often recounted, rather in the vein of North American adolescent accounts of car accidents. Like the North American genre, they contain an element of bravura occasioned by the awareness that they involve real danger. Parents' concerns about such incidents, of course, take on a very different tone: as my research in this area progressed I found that mothers in particular took me aside to implore me to clarify what had already happened to them in a police station where their children had been briefly detained. What had they signed to release a child, and what repercussion might it have on his or her future? The answer was that they had put their signature on an acknowledgment that a police trial had taken place, and that the minor child was guilty.

The problem, then, when broached at all, may be phrased in abstract terms of the violation of the separation of executive and legislative powers, or in the more concrete terms of the extraordinary powers granted to the police agent on the street to detain people and pass sentence on them. This may be phrased quite simply as fear of violence in the application of the edict or during the detention: "The majority of the detainees have been subjected to bad treatment [*malos tratos*] and authoritarian and degrading behavior in the course of being kept in the police station [*comisarías*] jails."[56] Further, when the violence reaches the point of the murder of a person being detained or in detention, it is related to, or seen directly as, a case of *gatillo fácil*.

What has remained, in effect, are two relatively independent, parallel penal systems. Although many of the characteristics of the system involving contraventional law are known, nevertheless relative secrecy reigns on the streets of Buenos Aires, since the average person finds it difficult at the outset to obtain information or commentary concerning the edicts. More difficult still is the task of understanding the idiosyncrasies of contraventional law even when the information is available. Contraventional law is not considered to be of comparable significance to penal law; hence the bibliography is scant and the attention given the subject by lawyers minimal.[57] In sum, in Argentina the functioning of a second penal system, parallel to the strict penal code, has been historically institutionalized through the police edict, removing constitutional guarantees that, while never absolute, when in place serve to impede abuses. Citizens confuse the two systems—assuming that the institutional status of both respond to similar democratic frameworks. This confusion is a danger perhaps greater in a democracy that mystifies the mixing of powers believed separate.[58] Argentines may therefore more readily naturalize violence and a context that makes it possible, as they do in the case of categorizing detention by the police as a "normal" Argentine experience.

The problem of the edicts and the police violence occasioned by them as well as related or unrelated cases of *gatillo fácil* are seen in turn, as noted above, as the result of discretionary powers that deposit an enormous degree of autonomy not only in the hands of the chief of police of the vast city of Buenos Aires but in the hands of the police agent on the street as well. At the same time, the chain of command in this parallel system is characterized by the very nature of the power deposited in the chief of police and the agents at different levels under him: at all levels the police legislate and act as judge and executioner, independent of legislative and judicial bodies as well as of their separation. They act in relative clandestinity as de facto vigilantes of the state.[59]

VI. Continuities

Police agents in Argentina resort to a series of well-known, though unofficial, practices in the course of carrying out their duties: the police raid, planted arms, application of the fleeing felon rule, coerced confession or torture, the "free area," and disappearance. With the exception of the last two, these practices also occur, to different degrees, in police forces in the United States and Latin America.[60] Each could be seen as merely an exaggeration of the autonomy of police power. Each makes it possible for actions to be carried out at the discretion of the police or of a police agent without being accountable to anyone, most especially to the law. In Argentina in 1990s these violent practices have become chronic.

In the *razzia*, or police raid,[61] police agents, in relatively large numbers in relation to the population involved, place themselves at crucial points of exit and entry to a particular area (for example, at a central business section of a neighborhood or barrio, or—in what to a foreigner is an amazing show of armed force—at a rock concert). They demand documents and accounts of activities. Sometimes they demand toll for crossing a bridge or artery. Also attributed to the police are false stories of confrontation, used to cover up deaths that may have been errors or summary executions. The application of the *ley de fuga* or law of escape, is another well-known cover-up: a suspect may be shot on the grounds that he or she attempted to escape, assuming that flight may be taken as an admission of guilt. However, in the absence of witnesses, the suspect is executed before guilt—or for that matter flight—has been proven. Abusive methods of interrogation, including systematic torture, have been widespread in police detentions. A less well-known tactic is the practice of establishing a "free area," that is, lifting control from a defined zone in which police activities may then be carried out illegally. Finally, the police have availed themselves of a tactic that earned a tragic fame for Argentina: they managed to hide the bodies of their victims, in the tactic known as disappearance.

In Argentina these police practices, previously relegated in the main to peripheral cases and populations, suddenly exploded center stage under the military dictatorship. Police power, with its mix of judicial, legislative, and executive traits, was this time not only mystified but veiled in clandestinity. The traits of autonomy and clandestinity are those that led the authors of the Sentence of the commanders in chief of the Proceso to conclude that they had before them a case of a parallel and delinquent state. Yet both traits had had their place in everyday life in the routine intervention of the police. And they continued after democracy took the place of the dictatorship. The autonomous practices and the secrecy in which they were wrapped—with the exception of the *razzia*, or raid, which nevertheless was limited to marginalized sectors of the population—do not have as their goal the elimination of specific criminals nor the punishment of specific crimes. Their goal is control through intimidation and fragmentation, through terror—although on the level of police agents the intensity of repression is low enough and the practices culturally recognizable enough to escape recognition as arbitrary violence. In this context deaths are caused, not to eliminate physically the person who has been killed, but to control those that remain alive, mainly through fear, but also at times, through the shattering of social ties and the removal of leadership.[62]

Police sometimes detain citizens for the particular purpose of "making statistics" (*hacer estadística*), that is, augmenting the number of detentions they effect. It is clear to any newspaper reader in Argentina that detaining suspects is crucially important to the image of efficiency that the police forces want to maintain, although this image is frequently mocked by the press. The pressure to "make statistics" is felt both by individual police agents as well as police jurisdictions. It responds in turn to pressures that come from outside the police force, such as, importantly, indications from the political sphere that social control needs to be intensified, or a demand on the part of powerful economic sectors of the society for a remedy to perceived problems of public order.[63] Like the Argentine institution of the police itself, police violence responds to political ends that formulate violence as a solution for problems of social order.

This is further borne out by the fact that over the last few years in the face of increased crime there has been an increase in both police violence and application of edicts. Detentions in 1992 numbered only 35,350[64] as against more than three times that number for 1994. This rise has been accompanied by calls not only for increased police action but also for the reinstallation of the death penalty.[65] This demand, then, becomes one among others for state violence. The two came together in a project launched by minister of justice, Rodolfo Barra (later to resign upon the revelation of his neo-Nazi [Tacuara] past) in which he proposed an increase in the power delegated to the police and stated his support of capital punishment.[66]

Argentine scholars have noted these crucial similarities between police and the Proceso when speaking of "terrorist contraventional legislation"[67] or when comparing the "terrorist state," or the state under the dictatorship, with the "police state," under the rule of the police edict: "[Their] violence shares fundamental characteristics; it is more, the former was a monstrous prolongation of the latter."[68] Tiscornia adds that "our culture of violence recognizes a violence inscribed in the State, but whose marks extend through the acceptance of an infinite number of authoritarian social interactions in the everyday.[69]

The Sentence of the commanders in chief threw into high relief the fact that the dictatorship shared with police power the particular delegation of autonomy that in both cases constitutes a parallel system. Personal responsibility and obedience and therefore chains of command take forms peculiar to a parallel penal system that traditionally permeated and regulated Argentine life alongside the recognized penal code. Similarly, the delinquent state that operated clandestinely parallel to a recognized state apparatus also involved discretionary powers that transformed chains of command.

The parallel systems, then, are characterized by arbitrary and authoritarian power in both cases. Perceived as uncontrolled and as excess or exception, these powers were actually deeply systematic. The trigger-happy policeman does not represent a police force gone out of control; rather, he represents another apparatus of control running parallel to the legal world of the penal code. Conversely, the "ideal" police agent turns out, in the case cited by Taussig[70] to be totally corrupt.

The Proceso, then, was not a military dictatorship in the strict sense of the term. The dictatorship depended on practices and mentalities more representative of the police than of the military, as characterized in these pages by very different chains of command. "Police state" may also be a misleading term because of its association with a secret police for whom spying is a central activity. Perhaps what obtained in Argentina could be better understood as police dictatorship or police terror. Continuities in police violence might make the expanding violence acquire some cultural sense, lowering a threshold of tolerance to practices that could have been more quickly perceived in other societies as unacceptably invasive.

While the police dictatorship in Argentina was based on traits exaggerated by Argentine history, these traits are also present in the institution of the police in other Western societies. This context renders the Argentine case not the spectacular and exotic horror that it has come to exemplify but rather a concrete example of potential danger endemic to Western democracy. In stark contrast with beliefs in a possible cure for police violence, the key to a delinquent state may lie in Benjamin's dire dictum: "The assertion that the ends of police violence are always identical or even connected to those of general law is entirely untrue. Rather, the 'law' of the police really marks the point at which the state, whether from impotence or because of the immanent connections within any legal system, can no longer guarantee through the legal system the empirical ends that it desires at any price to attain.[71]

Could the historical exaggeration of violent traits of an invading state have contributed in Argentina to a pattern of unusually high tolerance for violence and the invasion of liberties? Argentines were shocked in late 1997 to discover in the newspapers that Argentina had roughly twice as many police per citizen as Italy, Israel, the United Kingdom, and the United States.[72] Yet the delinquent state as it obtained in the horrific case of the Argentine dictatorship may have a parallel with a structural element within any Western state, that is, the police, an institution and a power that is inherently delinquent.[73] This element was able to take over in Argentina—and potentially could do so elsewhere in the West—insofar as it was already culturally recognizable and naturalized. It had become part of an imaginary of violence that continues to feed nightmares of increasing police brutality and corruption two decades later.

Notes

1. Dr. Fernando Maresca, friend of long standing has been a crucial inspiration and a patient teacher in the course of the initial conception of this work. Not least, when he immediately grasped my still unformed concerns, he drew my attention to the phrase "Frankenstein jurídico" in Agustín Gordillo, *Estudios de derecho administrativo* (Buenos Aires: Abelard Perrot, 1963), 21. I would also like to thank Gonzalo Sánchez Gómez, Institute of Political Studies and International Relations (EPRI), National University of Colombia, Bogotá, for his thoughts concerning the different imaginaries of violence. Translations from the Spanish throughout are my own.

2. Austin Sarat and Thomas R. Kearns, "A Journey through Forgetting: Toward a Jurisprudence of Violence," in The Fate of Law, Austin Sarat and Thomas Kearns, ed. (Ann Arbor: University of Michigan Press, 1991), 271.

3. José Pablo Feinmann, "Narrativa polícial y realidad politica," Página/ 12, March 14, 1997 (cited on-line in Interlink Headline News, http://www.torres-c.com/Interlink/ilhn.html.

4. Geoffrey Demarest, The Overlap of Military and Police in Latin America (Fort Leavenworth, Ks.: U.S. Army Foreign Military Studies Office, 1996).

5. See also Donna Guy, Sex and Danger in Buenos Aires: Prostitution, Family, and Nation in Argentina (Lincoln: University of Nebraska Press, 1990).

6. Olga Wormat, "Reportaje a Bussi," Revista Gente, 1994.

7. New York Times, March 7, 1997, 35; October 23, 1997, 18.

8. Elías Neuman, El abuso de poder en la Argentina y otros países latinoamericanos (Buenos Aires: Espasa Calpe, 1994), 132; Carlos Dutil and Ricardo Ragendorfer, La bonaerense: Historia criminal de la policía de la Provincia de Buenos Aires (Buenos Aires: Planeta, 1997), 15.

9. Dutil and Ragendorfer, La bonaerense, 15.

10. Walter Benjamin, "Critique of Violence," In Reflections: Essays, Aphorisms: Autobiographical Writings, trans. E. Jephcott (New York: Schocken Books, 1978).

11. Sentencia is variously translated as verdict, accusation, sentence, and opinion. Fallo is also sentence. The Diario del Juicio contained four documents: testimony, accusation, defense, and sentence (la sentencia). La Sentencia was published by the Argentine Congress.

12. This may distinguish the Proceso from the dictatorship in neighboring Chile, as seen, for example, in the famous case of the degollados that resulted in the resignation of the minister of the interior. See for example Ernesto Aguila Zúñiga and Carlos Maldonado Prieto, "Órden público en el Chile del siglo XX: Trayectoria de una policía militarizada," in Justicia en la calle: Ensayos sobre la policía en America Latina, ed. Peter Waldman (Medellín: Biblioteca Juridica Diké, 1966), 73–98.

13. The problem of similar patterns in the guerrilla groups was noted in the trials by the defense. See El diario del juicio (Buenos Aires: Editorial Perfil, 1985/86), 15, col. 4.

14. El diario del juicio, 14, col. 4; 15, col. 4. The problem of autonomy is noted by the Sentence of the commanders in chief but specified at lower levels usually defined as subordinate. This description may correspond to a political decision during the trials, as an effort was made to find a formula of responsibility that might effect a version of justice at the same time that it did not cause an insurrection of the armed forces in their entirety.

15. Carina Perelli, "Settling Accounts with Blood Memory: The Case of Argentina," Social Research 59 (1992): 446.

16. Augustín Gordillo, Estudios de derecho administrativo (Buenos Aires: Abelard Perrot, 1963), 21.

17. Rodolfo Walsh, El violento oficio de escribir: Obra periodistica, 1953–1977 (Buenos Aires: Planeta, 1995), 282–314; Elias Neuman, Clarín November 24, 1991, sec. 2, p. 1.

18. Other interpretations of this demonstration existed, taking into account the presence, along with the students, of members of the hard-line Left from the Repression of 1973–76 and 1976–83.

19. Sofía Tiscornia, "Violencia y cultura en la Argentina," paper presented at meeting "Tendências atuais no estudo do violência," University of Santa Catarina, Florianopolis, Brazil, March 28–29, 1995. See also Dutil and Ragendorfer, La bonaerense, 121–133.

20. In June and July 1993 a scandal erupted when President Menem bypassed justice to give orders directly to the police for the eviction of squatters from buildings in the capital where many had been living for years.

21. Benjamin, "Critique of Violence," 286.

A Juridical Frankenstein, or Death in the Hands of the State • 79

22. *Diario del juicio* January 28, 1986, 14, cols. 2–3.

23. Ibid., 16, col. 4; January 14, 1986, 14, col. 4.

24. Ibid., January 7, 1986, 8, col. 1.

25. Ibid., January 14, 1986, 10, col. 3.

26. Ibid., January 7, 1986, 11, cols. 2, 3, 4; 12, cols. 1, 2.

27. Ibid., 13, col. 1.

28. Ibid., 14.

29. Ibid., 15, col. 4; 16, col. 2.

30. Ibid., 20, col. 4.

31. Ibid., January 14, 1986, 1, col. 4.

32. Ibid., 7, 8, 9.

33. Ibid., 10, col. 4.

34. Ibid., 10, col. 3.

35. Ibid., 14, col. 3.

36. Ibid., 15, col. 2; 16, col. 1.

37. Amnesty International Report, June 1996, quoted in *Página/12*, June 18, 1996, 7; July 19, 1996, 8.

38. E.g., the *masacre de Wilde*, *Página/12*, June 18, 1996; June 20, 1996, 16; August 14, 1996, 10.

39. *Página/12*, July 20, 1996, 15; *Clarín*, November 24, 1991, sec. 2; August 13, 1996, 33.

40. Tiscornia, "Violencia y cultura," 9.

41. Benjamin, "Critique of Violence," 287.

42. Renato Alessi, *Instituciones de derecho administrativo* (Barcelona: Editorial Bosch, 1970), vol. 2, 466 ff.; Benjamín Villegas Basavilbaso, *Derecho administrativo* (Buenos Aires: Tipográfica Editora Argentina, 1949–56), vol. 5, 346.

43. See, for example, Villegas Basavilbaso, p. 90, and Adolf Merkl, *Teoría general del derecho administrativa* (Mexico City: Editoria Nacional, 1975), 346.

44. *Página/12*, July 16, 1996, 7.

45. *Página/12*, August 8, 1996, 14. Literally: "¿Un mayor grado de instrucción evitará que haya delincuentes entre los miembros de la policía boanaerense?—Efectivamente, cuánto más capacitados estén, van a saber en mejor medida qué es delito y qué no."

46. Benjamin, "Critique of Violence," 286.

47. Brazil, Bolivia, Colombia, Mexico, and Panama are other Latin American nations that do not include misdemeanors in their penal codes. However, the regulation of the codes is different in these countries from that of Argentina.

48. Currently the literature on this subject is contradictory. The best sources, which have only recently become available, are the 1997 theses of Osvaldo Berreneche (University of Arizona), who deals with the colonial *bandos* and the power of the *alcaldes*, and Laura Kalamanieki (New School for Social Research), who emphasizes militarization of the police after the fall of Perón (personal communication). For the influence of conservative nationalist traditions particularly in the 1930s, see Paul Chevigny, *Edge of the Knife: Police Violence in the Americas* (New York: New York Press, 1995).

49. Rafael A. Gentilli, *Me va a tener que acompañar: Una visión crítica sobre los edictos policiales* (Buenos Aires: El Naranjo, 1995), 43.

50. International Headline News, September 14, 1996, 603, September 15, 1996, 604; November 25, 1996, 665, October 31, 1997, 1005.

51. E. Raúl Zaffaroni. *Sistemas penales y derechos humanos en América Latina* (Buenos Aires: Depalma, 1984), 82; cf. Neuman, 117.

52. Gentili, "Me va a tener."

53. *Clarín*, August 13, 1996, 33.

54. Gentili, "Me va a tener," 28.

55. Tiscornia, "Violencia y cultura," 10; *Página/12*, July 20, 1996, 15.

56. Tiscornia, "Violencia y cultura," 10.

57. Gentili, "Me va a tener," 26, 30, 38; Zaffaroní, *Sistemas penales*, 81–83, 123.

58. Benjamin, "Critique of violence."

59. *Clarín*, August 13, 1996, 33.

60. Chevigny, *Edge of the Knife.*

61. Centro de Estudios Legales y Sociales (CELS) and Facultad de Filosofía y Letras, National University of Buenos Aires, *Informe sobre la situación de los derechos humanos en la Argentina* (Buenos Aires: Universidad Nacional, 1994). See also Elizabeth Jelín, *Vida cotidiana y control institucional en la Argentina de los '90* (Buenos Aires, Grupo Editor Latinoamericano, 1996), 141.

62. Zaffaroni, *Sistemas penales*; Chevigny, *Edge of the Knife*, 200.

63. Tiscornia, "Violencia y cultura," 12.

64. CELS, *Informe sobre la situación*, 83; *Clarin*, August 13, 1996, 33.

65. Sofia Tiscornia, "¿Peligrosidad política o peligrosidad social? Procesos de construcción de la hegemonía en torno al (des)órden democrático." In *Antropologia sistemática I: Organización social y política* (Buenos Aires: University of Buenos Aires, Facultad de Filosofía y Letras, Departamento de Ciencia Antropológicas, 1995), 64.

66. CELS, *Informe sobre la situación*, 49–50; Neuman, *El abuso del poder*, 132.

67. Zaffaroni, *Sistemas penales*, 82.

68. Tiscornia, "Violencia y cultura," 12–13; Tiscornia, "¿Peligrosidad politica?" 69.

69. Tiscornia, "Violencia y cultura," 14.

70. Michael Taussig, "The Injustice of Policing: Prehistory and Rectitude," in *Justice and Injustice in Law and Legal Theory*, ed. Austin Sarat and Thomas R. Kearns (Ann Arbor: University of Michigan Press 1996). See also Sidney Lumet's film *Prince of the City*.

71. Benjamin, "Critique of violence," 287.

72. *La Nación*, August 4, 1997, 1; *Página/12*, June 29, 1997, 16.

73. Benjamin, "Critique of violence," 286; cf. Rodolfo Walsh, "La secta de la picana" (1968) reprinted in Walsh, *El violento oficio de escribir*, 293.

· 4 ·

TOKENS OF OUR ESTEEM: AGGRAVATING FACTORS IN THE ERA OF DEREGULATED DEATH PENALTIES

JONATHAN SIMON AND CHRISTINA SPAULDING

One legacy of *Furman v. Georgia*[1] and its progeny has been a new species of legal act, the capital aggravating factor, which features in virtually all post-*Furman* capital sentencing systems. Capital aggravating factors operate in two quite distinct fields. In the penalty trial field, capital aggravators define the homicidal behavior of particular individuals as appropriate for capital punishment. The jury's finding that a constitutionally appropriate aggravating factor applies, even a single one, is an essential prerequisite to a constitutional death sentence (and in some states the jury is thereafter free to impose death without further findings). In the legislative field, they provide a kind of currency through which states seek to recognize various concerns and valorize certain kinds of subjects and situations. Aggravating factors have tremendous symbolic capital because they advertize the priorities of a particular political community in the light of the most charged ritual known to ancient or modern societies: the ceremonial sacrifice of a human being.

In the two decades since the death penalty came back into our midst, the relationship between these two fields has become more problematic. In some respects the first generation of post-*Furman* aggravators insisted on a relationship between these two fields. The swing Justices in *Furman* were concerned primarily with the arbitrariness of the few death sentences handed down by the states. Aggravating factors promised to assure a legitimate public justification for the appropriateness of execution in each prisoner's case. The construction of aggravating factors in the legislative field was to eliminate arbitrariness in the penalty trial field. Swing Justices in *Furman* and *Gregg v. Georgia*[2] first insisted and then assumed that the two would have a tightly controlled and rational relationship. Aggravators were to be the channels of discretion or the arms of an extended public will. The power to kill under law would act through the discretion of juries and or judges, but correspond to the values of law. Other agendas that states might have wanted to advance through executions were suppressed in the name of supporting the basic enterprise of sustaining the death penalty (still an open question after *Furman*).

Research on each of these fields has become more sophisticated and more mutually engaged,[3] but virtually all attention has been focused on the basic set of aggravating factors adopted in response to *Furman v. Georgia* and *Gregg v. Georgia*. These were comprised mainly of the Model Penal Code factors[4] and a few additions that were made at the time of the statutes' initial drafting. In the meantime, especially since the mid-1980s, new aggravating circumstances have been added to capital statutes, like Christmas tree ornaments. These new factors reveal a process self-consciously freed from the dictates of substantive Supreme Court review. Some list special victims, denominated by their vulnerability, including the young and the old and the disabled. Others list a set of what amount to recent government- and media-hyped signifiers of America's ever shifting crime problem, including drugs, drive-by shootings, and gang activity. We believe that these new aggravators deserved to be analyzed as distinct from the first generation of responses to *Furman*.

The new generation of aggravators are products of a much freer legislative process. As Zimring and Hawkins point out, *Gregg v. Georgia* gave the states a new category of political acts by moving capital punishment "from a solely symbolic issue into a practical possibility."[5] But only after the Supreme Court made clear that it was not interested in requiring states to guide discretion in a serious way were legislators really free to allocate the political and communicative potential of aggravators.

These new amendments continue to define capital crimes, to be sure, but they increasingly sound beyond the law in the complicated politics of identity and in the endless battle for prestige and power within the state. Capital punishment is a mark of sovereignty[6] and a "miracle play of government."[7] Through the production of capital aggravators the state lends its majesty to the value that the community places in certain victims and certain conduct. It sheds recognition on groups both in and out of government, from cattle brand inspectors in Nevada to groups concerned with satanism in Louisiana. It is in the light of this new function that we call aggravators "tokens of our esteem." The death penalty has always reflected an implicit judgment on the worth of particular victims by whether or not it is sought by the prosecution or imposed by a jury. In the new generation, categories of potential victims now seek validation in advance of any actual murder (and hopefully in its stead).

In some ways this resumes an old theme in the politics of crime. As the work of E. P. Thompson[8] and Douglas Hay[9] on eighteenth-century England shows, capital punishment can be a highly flexible tool of retail politics as well as reflecting broad mentalities of power.[10] Indeed the two were linked as a larger ideology of elite power was consecrated in the deft deployment of terror, magistracy, mercy, and entertainment. But as tokens of our esteem, aggravators function in a new and populist economy of power that would have been unfamiliar to eighteenthth-century gentry.

In addition to analyzing the political logic and effects of the new generation of aggravators, we hope to offer some provisional insights on how they are likely to operate in the penalty trial field where death sentences are actually produced. As the new aggravators enter a penalty trial arena that is already crowded with duplicative aggravators, they may expand the pool of death-eligible defendants. We suspect that they are not likely to change the semiotics of jury reflection. As we shall explore more fully below, many aggravators are practically pictograms or condensed symbols, standing for whole narratives with more or less widespread salience in the population. Drive-by shooters, car jackers, and wife abusers represent contemporary portraits of evil with *Live at Five* images ready to hand for many members of potential jury pools. The presence of those images may alter the dynamic of jury deliberations and, as a consequence, the strategies of both prosecutors and defendants.

No one would mistake our new capital crimes for the Black Act.[11] Then, people could be hung for hunting stags or stealing clothes. While we may in fact be on the threshold of a new expansion of the substantive crimes available for capital sentencing,[12] we are not likely to go back to the eighteenth century's degree of reliance on the casuistry of death to govern.[13] But between the expensive and politically explosive capital trial and appeals process, and the quest for popular legislation in an era where elected national and state government want to downsize everything but their self-importance, aggravating factors must be recognized as a critical site of governance in the United States today. We offer a preliminary mapping of the new additions to that site from the perspective of both the penalty trial and legislative fields.[14]

Section I describes the first generation of capital aggravators, adapted mainly from the Model Penal Code following *Furman* and *Gregg*, in which the problems of equity and limiting juries' sentencing discretion dominated the politics and litigation of aggravating factors. Section II reviews the diminishing role of aggravating factors as legal levers for appellate court control during the 1980s. Section III describes the new aggravating factors and the emergence of a new and much more diffuse set of functions in both law and politics for aggravators.

I. Typical Aggravating Factors in the Era of *Gregg v. Georgia*

Furman v. Georgia generated a rapid backlash in state legislatures. Within two years, twenty-eight states had adopted new death penalty statutes.[15] Ultimately thirty-three of the states with pre-*Furman* death penalty statutes enacted new ones, as did five states that had rejected it prior to *Furman*.[16] As angered as many legislators were with the Court, they drafted statutes aimed at withstanding Supreme Court scrutiny. Capital murder had to be broken into an archipelago of more specific capital crimes. A number of models emerged to circumscribe the "unguided" discretion the Court had disapproved in *Furman*. The most popular model, and the one that has achieved the greatest support from the Supreme Court, drew heavily on the American Law Institute's Model Penal Code, section 210.6.[17]

The Model Penal Code (MPC) retained a broad definition of capital murder but mandated the decision maker to consider a list of aggravating and mitigating factors at a separate proceeding. Under the MPC at least one aggravator must apply for a defendant to be death-eligible. The fact finders must then weigh those aggravators and mitigators that they find applicable to the facts.[18] Two of the types of post-*Furman* capital statutes approved by the Supreme Court drew on the MPC in defining their aggravators. Some statutes, like Georgia's then allowed the jury to "consider" anything in mitigation. Others, like Florida's, specifically required the jury to weigh aggravators against mitigators. A third successful model, adopted in

Texas, Virginia, and Oregon, abandoned altogether the MPC form, but reinvented the aggravators as a series of five capital murder situations that limit eligibility for capital sentencing.[19]

The statutes that survived *Gregg v. Georgia* and its companion cases had effectively adopted a new grammar of capital sentencing. At the heart of this grammar were a series of pictograms of aggravated murders. Despite the range of models provisionally approved in the 1976 term most of these statutes adopted a narrow range of aggravators or narrowing circumstances or questions (which will also be referred to here as aggravators).

Table 4.1 summarizes the aggravating factors enacted by states during the *Gregg* era. It includes the eight aggravating factors from the MPC and a selection of the most widely used additions. Most states adopted this set of factors between 1972 and 1980. Some of these aggravators appear later, as more states and the federal government adopted the new death penalty.[20]

The *Gregg*-era aggravators reflect at least three distinct political imperatives (not to be confused with principles) operating on the legislatures that drafted them.

TABLE 4.1: Aggravating Factors of the *Gregg* Era

---

1. The murder was committed by a convict under sentence of imprisonment.[a]

2. The defendant was previously convicted of another murder or of a felony involving the use or threat of violence to the person.

3. At the time the murder was committed the defendant also committed another murder.

4. The defendant knowingly created a great risk of death to many persons.

5. The murder was committed while the defendant was engaged or was an accomplice in the commission of, or an attempt to commit, or flight after committing or attempting to commit robbery, rape or deviate sexual intercourse by force or threat of force, arson, burglary or kidnapping [aircraft piracy, child abuse].[b]

6. The murder was committed for the purpose of avoiding or preventing a lawful arrest or effecting an escape from lawful custody.

7. The murder was committed for pecuniary gain.[c]

8. The murder was especially heinous, atrocious, or cruel, manifesting exceptional depravity.

9. The murder was committed against any peace officer, corrections employee, or fireman while engaged in the performance of his official duties.

10. The murder was committed to hinder enforcement of laws or government function.

11. The defendant committed the murder by lying in wait.

12. The murder was committed against an elected or appointed public official engaged in the performance of her official duties.

13. The murder was committed against a witness or potential witness in a criminal or civil proceeding because of such proceeding.

14. The existence of a probability that the defendant would commit criminal acts of violence that would constitute a continuing threat to society.

---

a. Most states expanded this to include escaped prisoners.

b. States have frequently added to the list of predicate felonies in the basic felony-murder aggravator. These represent typical additions by states during the *Gregg* era.

c. Many states added an aggravator for the person hiring another to murder.

First, they seek to meet the demands of the Supreme Court (as heard in *Furman* and *Gregg*),[21] and in that sense they are primarily statements that sound in a juridical discourse. They are laws designed to sound lawlike. They provide, in Robert Weisberg's terms, a "metaphor" of rationality—a list of rules and procedures.

The MPC model had been around since the early 1960s, sparking no great interest among states that enthusiastically adopted many of its other provisions.[22] For legislatures looking for models to restore the death penalty in the wake of *Furman*, the MPC stood for instant legal respectability. The MPC, after all, shared with its cousin restatements the imprimatur of the elite of the bar and of academic circles. Moreover, unlike the implicit faith in the common law expressed in the restatements, the MPC's architects set out self-consciously to bring about a process of reform and rationalization of the criminal law.[23] Ironically the capital sentencing provision may have been one of the areas where the code drafters were least successful in establishing a relationship between culpability and punishment. Indeed, the thin official comments reflect a real lack of effort to resolve the question of who should die.[24] Instead the aggravators seem gathered from unsurprising but unanalyzed sources—common law tradition and the sense of public opinion.[25] Factors 1, 3, 5, 7, and 11 all restate traditional forms of aggravated murder but resituate them so that the decision maker must consider them in the context of other factors, both aggravating and mitigating.

Second, those aggravators that are not aimed primarily at establishing legal respectability reflect instead a primary concern with the state itself. Factors 1, 6, 9, 10, 12, 13 all seek to preserve the integrity of the public functions of the states against violence aimed at disrupting them. The public figure most singled out for protection in the *Gregg*-era statutes is the police officer. It is not then the state in itself that is honored (by protecting, for example, the chief magistrate, which only a few did) but those directly engaged in enforcing law and order.

The private fears and rages of the citizenry are a distant third imperative. Two factors, 8 and 14, focus on the private concerns of jurors. Factor 8, which speaks of "heinous, atrocious, and cruel" killing, directs the jury and the citizenry to the horror of the crime from the perspective of the victim. The belief that the "heinous, atrocious, and cruel" factors are nothing less than an invitation for the jury to unleash its private feelings about the crime or criminal has led to many challenges.[26] Factor 14, also focuses on the private citizenry, but now as an aggregate body, civil society, which must face the potential threat of killers not eliminated by the state. Both factors seem to invite jurors to use the state's ultimate power to eliminate those offenders they find the most threatening.

II. Deregulating Death

It is possible to imagine how these imperatives might have developed had the Court stayed the course that it seemed to be charting in *Gregg*. In this alternative present, aggravating factors would have reflected an ongoing trialogue between the state, its juries, and appellate courts, with the goal of wielding the power to execute in a manner both democratic and rational. Disciplined by a Supreme Court willing to call the experiment off at any time, we would expect state legislatures to refine their aggravating factors as court decisions challenged their ability to meaningfully guide juries. This is the vision of capital sentencing jurisprudence that Justice Brennan could still offer as a viable account of past precedent as late as *Lowenfield v. Phelps*:

> Narrowing the class of death eligible offenders is not "an end in itself" any more than aggravating circumstances are. Rather, as our cases have emphasized consistently, the narrowing requirement is meant to channel the discretion of the sentencer. It forces the capital sentencing jury to approach its task in a structured, step-by-step way, first determining whether a defendant is eligible for the death penalty and then determining whether all the circumstances justify its imposition. The only conceivable reason for making narrowing a constitutional requirement is its function in structuring sentencing deliberations. By permitting the removal of the narrowing function from the sentencing process altogether, the Court reduces it to a mechanical formality entirely unrelated to the choice between life and death.[27]

Today, few believe that aggravating factors really serve to legally constrain the sentencing process. As Robert Weisberg termed it in his eloquent and prescient 1983 article, the Court was "deregulating death."[28] The suggestion that aggravating and mitigating factors would be the language of a dialogue between courts and legislatures has been abandoned.

A. Stop Making Sense

On the mitigating side, the Supreme Court has enforced fairly strictly the constitutional requirement that states may not by statute, instruction, or evidentiary ruling prevent a capital sentencer from considering or giving effect to mitigating evidence.[29] On the aggravating side, however, the Supreme Court has, in a series of decisions, demonstrated its unwillingness to impose more than the most minimal regulation. In Zant v. Stephens,[30] the Court explained that the only constitutionally required function of an aggravating circumstance is to "genuinely narrow the class of persons eligible for the death penalty." Aggravating circumstances need not play any further role in guiding the jury's sentencing discretion.

Consequently, apart from the one aggravating circumstance necessary to render a defendant eligible for the death penalty, there is no constitutional requirement that aggravating circumstances be identified and limited by statute.[31] While states may impose other limits on aggravating circumstances, the invalidity of an aggravator under state law alone has no constitutional import.[32] While the Court has said that a statutory aggravating circumstance "must provide a principled basis" for "distinguish[ing] those who deserve capital punishment from those who do not,"[33] it has in practice found aggravating circumstances to run afoul of the Constitution only when they are too vague to provide any guidance to the sentencer[34] or when they are based on erroneous or false evidence.[35]

The "narrowing" requirement is similarly limited. The Supreme Court has held that a death sentence may rest on a single aggravating circumstance that simply duplicates an element of the underlying offense—as long as the state "narrows" the class of death-eligible defendants in its definition of capital murder.[36] The Court has never held an aggravating circumstance to be invalid on the substantive ground that it failed to select "the worst criminals or the criminals who commit the worst crimes."[37] Empirical studies suggest that, applying current lists of aggravating factors, 80–90 percent of defendants who were death-eligible before *Furman* are still death-eligible.[38]

The "deregulation" of the death penalty also extends to the jury's evaluation of aggravating factors against mitigating factors. Once the defendant is deemed death-eligible, the state need not give the jury any further guidance as to how to consider or weigh aggravating and mitigating evidence.[39] In fact, the Court has said that "the sentencer may be given 'unbridled discretion in determining whether the death penalty should be imposed after it has found that the defendant is a member of the class made eligible for that penalty.'"[40]

B. The Relationship between Capital Politics and Capital Penalty Trials

"Regulated" capital punishment, in the years immediately after *Gregg,* had its own quite explicit theory of the relationship between the politics of lawmaking in capital statutes and the battlefield tactics of the capital penalty trial. Statutory elements, especially aggravating factors, would function as the synapses of the capital penalty system, connecting legislatures and the local courts on the one hand, and the legislatures and appellate courts on the other. If the aggravators were guiding discretion, and not simply limiting its scope, then courts would have to review them carefully against the kinds of cases in which they produced capital sentences. Policing the integrity of the system as a whole, state high courts would craft narrowing interpretations of aggravators, and, where necessary, the legislature would amend or replace whole provisions.

In the era of deregulation there is no constitutional theory of a necessary relationship between capital lawmaking in the legislative and the penalty trial fields. The aggravators that the legislature writes may be the door into the inner house of death but, after *Lowenfield,* they do not proscribe what goes on inside.

1. FELONY MURDER AS PARADIGM   Daniel Givelber identifies the heart of the new law of murder in the very old category of felony murder—an anathema to most modern criminal law scholars because of the priority it gives to essentially accidental results (e.g., a police officer killed by friendly fire in a gunfight the felon did not plan on).[41] From this perspective the premeditation ground for capital murder in traditional statutes was the just basis for capital punishment, even though it was often obtusely phrased, because it emphasized the role of the killer's own deliberate choices in bringing about the lethal outcome. The authors of the MPC were generally uncomfortable with the combination of severe crimes and penalties and a strict liability theory of *mens rea.* The felony murder provision of the code is written to diminish the scope of felony murder by making it a rebuttable presumption of extreme reckless *mens rea* (210.3). But surprisingly, the MPC retained a broad version of felony murder in the death penalty provision (210.6).[42]

Like felony murder, many of the MPC aggravators emphasize the existence of some harm other than the killing itself that is not necessarily a deliberate choice of the offender: "an independent felony, a frustration of law enforcement, the killing of an additional person, and the infliction of suffering beyond that necessary to kill."[43] Other aggravators are related to character but only in an implied way (e.g., murder by someone previously convicted of murder or a violent felony). Only three of the eight include a distinct *mens rea* element ("knowingly created a great risk of death to many persons"; "murder was committed for the purpose of avoiding or preventing a lawful arrest"; "the murder was committed for pecuniary gain").

This new law of murder thus stresses behavioral facts over mental facts. In its own way it moves toward a kind of strict liability jurisprudence in which harmful or dangerous actions are the priority. There is little concern in the new law for the difference between those who deliberately do harm and those who fall into it.[44] Nor is the killer with the most "evil" or perverse mental state necessarily selected for capital punishment. In part this reflects the success of academic criticism of traditional premeditation statutes[45] and a desire to make the law more objective. In part it reflects the code drafters' willingness to accord weight to what they perceived as public values.

One implication that Givelber derives from this is a bias toward stranger crimes.[46] Premeditation typically involves people who know each other and thus have some reason to plan a killing. Felony murder is more likely to be a stranger killing and is fraught with racialized fears. Statistics suggest that stranger crimes are committed disproportionately by African American perpetrators. A policy that favors executing felony murderers over executing premeditated murderers may therefore result in the disproportionate execution of African Americans.

2. DISTANCING   Designed to satisfy a judicial audience that the legislature was serious about channeling the decision maker's discretion in capital sentencing, aggravating factors probably do help structure decision making, but in ways that work at cross-purposes to the original vision of ordered deliberation. Most importantly they may allow juries and judges to escape the traditional burden of judgment.[47] Many of the MPC aggravators operate as legal presumptions,[48] allowing juries to arrive at judgments about the appropriateness of capital sanctions in a particular case without having to morally evaluate the offender's conduct.

This might be tolerable, if, for example, the aggravators represented a principled resolution of the state's competing values in executions. But even the ALI, a body designed to produce such resolutions, avoided doing so in formulating of the capital aggravators.[49] Instead, even the code's commentators cited public reaction toward certain types of crime as a primary reason for several of the factors and loosely discussed depravity and dangerousness for the others (MPC comments 210.6 1980).

3. BEHAVIORISM AND THE NEW PENOLOGY   While states did not appear to choose their aggravating factors with any particular penological strategy in mind, the new law of murder, at least in its *Gregg* phase, fits the larger pattern of development in criminal justice institutions that Feeley and Simon describe as the

"new penology."[50] They identify three shifts as characteristic of this pattern: (1) from a concern with individuals to a concern with categories of offenders; (2) from a concern with normalizing criminals and reintegrating them to a concern with managing more efficiently the risks produced by a permanent class of criminals; and (3) from a focus on community priorities (less crime) to a focus on systemic performance.

The *Gregg*-era aggravators, and their felony murder paradigm, parallel these developments. In place of the individualizing judgment about the appropriateness of executing a particular killer, the aggravators shift concern to categories of behavior or harm. In rejecting mandatory death penalties, the Court limited the ability of categories to drive outcomes as a matter of law but not the ability of a jury to use the categorical aggravators to resolve the moral problem of judgment.

In their focus on the dangerousness of the offender, the MPC factors embraced risk management as the core role of penal sanctions, including the death penalty. Incapacitation is becoming a leading element of death penalty support, suggesting that the public views the death penalty as a rational strategy of risk management, perhaps because they do not believe life imprisonment will really mean life imprisonment.[51]

From the start the aggravating factors were an example of systemic thinking (and were only indirectly about defining who should die) used in the decision-making process. The aggravators were supposed to bring about a rational and democratic death penalty. While *Gregg* hinted that aggravating factors might have to meet some substantive standard of penological rationality, it is now clear that the states may pursue any combination of ends that satisfies a minimum rationality standard. Stripped of any pretense to substantively guiding discretion, the aggravators appear as rational only in their systemic role of "narrowing the field" or, in the view of some, "mechanical formality."[52]

Of course the mitigation side of the capital sentencing process works against these tendencies toward categorization, risk management, and mechanical formalism. The mitigation defense seeks to bring the focus back to the offender as an individual, to the particular background that explains his or her lethal actions, and to the conditions of moral judgment necessary to justify a jury in condemning this individual to death. In all these regards the mitigation defense constitutes one of the places in the system where something like the "old penology" still holds sway.

III. Capital Aggravators: The New Generation

In the wake of decisions like *Zant v. Stephens*, *Barclay v. Florida*, and *Lowenfield v. Phelps*, it was made clear to states that their statutory aggravating factors were no longer the site for a constitutionally mandated discussion of justice and fairness. States, however, were not free to simply abandon aggravating factors; they still played a residual role in theoretically narrowing the class of death-eligible persons.[53] Aggravating factors lost their original purpose of policing the rationality of capital sentencing, but remained necessary features of capital sentencing law. As crime has heated up as an issue throughout the 1980s and 1990s,[54] aggravators have been a ready made category of law that legislators could use to serve constituencies interested in capital punishment.

A. Amending Capital Statutes

As might be expected, states amended their aggravating factors from the beginning. In some instances legislatures were responding to appellate court decisions. Many states reshaped their version of the "heinous, atrocious, and cruel" aggravating factor to accord with limiting constructions of their own or some sister state's supreme court to cure the constitutional vagueness problem identified by the U.S. Supreme Court in *Godfrey v. Georgia* and *Maynard v. Cartwright*. Similarly, states sought to stay ahead of emerging court challenges to capital sentencing statutes on the ground that they irrationally selected some forms of aggravated murder while ignoring others long a part of legal doctrine (like premeditation). Thus several states added factors such as that the homicide was committed in a "cold, calculated, and premeditated manner."[55]

States have amended their statutes more rapidly since the Court signaled its lack of interest in policing the content of aggravating factors.[56] This legislation takes a variety of forms:

1. Many states have picked up specific *Gregg*-era factors that for whatever reason were omitted from their original statutes.
2. States have added to the lists of predicate victims or felonies in traditional factors. Thus aggravators for murdering a police officer or fire fighter have frequently been amended to include a growing list of state agents and quasi agents (like informers) with law enforcement–like jobs. Traditional felony murder predicates have also been expanded with offenses that have temporarily captured the public imagination, including car jacking, and home-invasion robberies, as well as perennial concerns like drug trafficking and child abuse.
3. States have also created whole new aggravators aimed at denouncing new forms of conduct or protecting new categories of victims.

In this essay we are primarily interested in the second and third types of amendments. A selection of this new generation[57] of aggravators is listed in table 4.2.

B. Nevada's Adoption of "Hate Crime" and "Peace Officer" Aggravators in 1995: A Case Study of the Legislative Process

Federalism in the United States makes it very difficult to talk about an "American" death penalty.[58] Forty jurisdictions—thirty-eight states, the federal government, and the military—authorize capital punishment. While each state's statute, and the corresponding legislative history of its new aggravating circumstances, is somewhat unique, a more detailed look at one state's recent experiences provides some insight into the politics of lawmaking in the new aggravators.

On May 23, 1995, Nevada's governor signed Senate Bill 139, which amended Nevada's death penalty aggravators in several respects, including adding a hate crime aggravator applicable when "[t]he murder was committed upon a person because of the actual or perceived race, color, religion, national origin or sexual orientation of that person."[59]

Senate Bill 139 began its legislative life almost exactly four months earlier,

TABLE 4.2: Selected Aggravating Factors since 1985

1. The victim was an emergency medical technician . . . employed by a municipality or other government unit, killed in the course of performing his official duties, to prevent the performance of his official duties, and that the defendant knew or should have known that the murdered individual was an emergency medical technician.[a]

2. The victim . . . was listed by the state or known by the defendant to be a witness against the defendant and the defendant committed the murder with the intent to prevent the person from testifying.[b]

3. The victim of the murder was less than twelve years of age.[c]

4. The victim was . . . sixty-five years of age or older.[d]

5. The defendant knew or reasonably should have known that the victim was especially vulnerable due to significant mental or physical disability.[e]

6. At the time of the killing the victim was in her third trimester of pregnancy or the defendant had knowledge of the victim's pregnancy.[f]

7. The murder was committed upon a person because of the actual or perceived race, color, religion, national origin, physical or mental disability, or sexual orientation of the person.[g]

8. The murder was committed for the purpose of interfering with the victim's free exercise or enjoyment of any right, privilege, or immunity protected by the First Amendment to the United States Constitution, or because the victim has exercised or enjoyed said rights.[h]

9. The offender was engaged in the distribution, exchange, sale or purchase, or any attempt thereof, of a controlled dangerous substance.[i]

10. The capital felony was committed by a criminal street gang member.[j]

11. The defendant committed the offense with an assault weapon.[k]

12. The murder was committed during the course of or as a result of a shooting where the discharge of the firearm, . . . is either from a motor vehicle or from the immediate area of a motor vehicle that was used to transport the shooter or the firearm, or both, the scene of the discharge.[l]

a. Illinois.	g. Nevada.
b. Indiana.	h. Delaware.
c. Indiana.	i. Louisiana.
d. Arizona.	j. Florida.
e. Wyoming.	k. Connecticut.
f. Pennsylvania.	l. Washington.

when it was read for the first time and referred to the Committee on Judiciary (hereinafter "the committee"). At that stage it did not include the hate crimes aggravator at all. In its first printing it proposed to do two things. First, the proposed bill amended the existing aggravator for "murder . . . committed upon a peace officer" by expanding the list of law enforcement agents in Nevada qualifying as peace officers for capital-sentencing purposes. The existing statute included "[s]heriffs of counties and their deputies, marshals and policemen of cities and towns, the chief and agents of the investigation division of the department of motor vehicles and public safety, [and] personnel of the Nevada highway patrol."[60]

The version first considered by the committee on March 7 added "special investigators employed by the attorney general, investigators employed by a district attorney, the chief parole and probation officer and his assistant parole and probation officers."

Second, a separate section of the bill proposed to add a new aggravating factor for juvenile victims, which read: "The murder was committed upon a person less than 14 years of age." This provision entered into the final law unchanged and with no mention at all in the legislative history. Perhaps it was uncontroversial in Nevada because child or juvenile victim aggravators have been the most widely adopted in the deregulation era. No objection was raised to any feature of this second provision.

In contrast, the expansion of the peace officer aggravator (a common *Gregg*-era aggravator) generated a number of objections, testimony, and eventual changes. The original initiative for the bill seems to have come from the district attorneys who wanted their investigators to be included in the list of peace officers represented in the aggravator. Senator Washington eventually introduced this amendment after several other peace officer categories were added. The primary objections to it came from two senators on the committee who were specifically concerned about the constitutional consequences of expanding this traditional aggravator:

> Senator Adler stated he believed the original language of the original statute was phrased as it is, because of a concern that the statute be specific as to what the aggravated circumstance is. He said he was concerned about invalidating the provision in the statute, " . . . and not having it apply to anybody if we are not careful." (LCB 9)[61]

> Senator James indicated it might not be wise to "go too far down the slippery slope," and add categories that have no rational basis. He added the definition should include people "who are required by their jobs to deal with very dangerous criminals on a day-to-day basis." (LCB 9)

These senators voiced concerns that few of the witnesses before the committee from either the state or the defense bar shared—a belief that their rationality as legislators was of substantial interest to appellate courts. The testimony was dominated by various groups of peace officers seeking to establish their relevance to the aggravator. Most of this testimony was aimed at establishing a rational basis (in the weak sense that is used in equal protection analysis) for including more law enforcement agents under the provision. A few witnesses candidly invited the committee to exercise its legislative prerogative to award this inexpensive prize to favored groups.

The first of the new categories of peace officers included in SB 139 were parole and probation officers. Typical *Gregg*-era aggravators covered only correctional officers working in prisons, although some covered all "employees of the department of corrections." The case for parole and probation officers was made in large part by showing videotape of a television program produced and aired by a local Reno, Nevada, television station. The program titled "Invisible Cops" described parole and probation officers "doing the same jobs as uniformed officers and placing their lives on the line" (LCB 8). The witness for the Nevada Division of Parole and Probation cited the video in arguing that Nevada's parole and probation officers were no longer managing minor offenders or mostly rehabilitated former prisoners. Instead, parole and probation officers faced "the worst of the worst" and must be considered in as much danger as traditional "first response" agencies (LCB 8).

The next witness was from the district attorney's office of Washoe County, speaking on behalf of the district attorney's investigators. He acknowledged that such investigators were not "first response" agencies, but asserted that they did have to contact "family, friends and close associates of the 'criminal element'" (LCB 8). Furthermore, their duties include delivering warrants for nonsupport: "Which adds to exposure to individuals with a propensity for violence. He said approximately 10 percent of persons served with such warrants are wanted for other criminal charges, with 30 percent of those persons being ex-felons with convictions for violence related offenses" (LCB 8).

David F. Sarnowski, chief criminal deputy attorney general for Nevada, indicated that his office had helped draft the statute for its principal legislative sponsor, Senator Washington. Sarnowski indicated that he had attempted to provide "a very expansive definition" of peace officer. In response to the queries from Senators James and Adler about the constitutional dangers of expanding the category too far (quoted above), Sarnowski somewhat confusingly agreed and advised: "He believed the less expansive and definitive the law is, ". . . the easier it would be to defend against a constitutional challenge" (LCB 9). At the same time, Sarnowski argued that investigators in the attorney general's office should be included in a rational category, noting: "Even persons being investigated for 'white collar crimes' had been found with weapons, although fortunately no escalated incidents had occurred to date. He said investigators involved in death penalty cases could be at risk, and some have been subject to threats as a result of the performance of their duties" (LCB 9).

Discussion of the peace officer issue continued for several more meetings of the committee. The committee was warned by Eric Cooper of the Nevada Sheriffs and Chiefs Association, who had served on a body called to study the proliferation of this legal status in Nevada, that it faced "'[a]n inundation of people requesting to be moved into this category.' He suggested it would be preferable to include 'all peace officers,' unless that would face serious constitutional challenge. Cooper warned that 'the moment you start discussing . . . or attempting to categorize peace officer positions, you raise the hackles on the backs of all peace officers'" (LCB 10). The groups now before the committee might face real hazards, but Cooper predicted that the "laundry list" would certainly grow.

Senator Adler reiterated his constitutional concerns and quoted his colleague Senator James's earlier skepticism that these various peace officer positions warranted the enhanced deterrence of being included in an aggravator: "How could you say the killing of a [cattle] brand inspector in the line of duty warrants the death penalty, when a 7–11 clerk is one of the most dangerous jobs in Nevada?"

On March 14, Senator Washington confirmed the laundry list prediction by proposing to add juvenile probation officers to SB 139. Sergeant Todd Shippley, representing the Peace Officers Research Assocation of Nevada (PORAN), urged the committee to adopt a simplifying amendment, placing all peace officers into the aggravating factor and eliminating the growing list. Senator James once again attacked the breadth of this new, comprehensive peace officer pro-posal: "The purpose of the aggravator is to show the death penalty is imposed only under 'certain, specified circumstances,' he explained, because we want a perpetrator to know, should harm come to an officer when he or she is out there en-forcing the law and facing threats to life and limb, that officer is protected and sup-ported by the state, through the imposition of the highest penalty the law will allow" (LCB 14).

Sergeant Shipley responded by defending the rationality of designating all peace officers as needing such protection: "[He] opined that there is no difference between 'the man in blue' and the sheep inspector (both covered under the statu-tory definition requested by PORAN), because both are 'out there representing government' and they have the responsibility to enforce the laws that are promul-gated by the Legislature. He added that frequently 'sheep inspectors' and game war-dens are faced with life and death situations and they deserve the same protections afforded the metropolitan police officers" (LCB 14).

James Jackson, the state public defender, undermined the position of the skep-tical senators by suggesting that intricate divisions among peace officers would make the statute more vulnerable to constitutional attack than a broader, simpler definition: "He opined, 'the simpler the aggravator the better off you are.' The dis-tinction might actually be what activity the officer was engaged in at the time the killing occurred, he offered, noting if they were engaged in a 'lawful, law enforce-ment activity and fit the definition of the peace officer, . . . it seems that that would probably pass muster'" (LCB 14).

Mr. Sarnowski, appearing again for the attorney general candidly described the amendment's real purpose: "I just think you need to recognize the secondary pur-pose of an aggravating circumstance may be to afford recognition to a class, that being peace officers, it certainly does not afford protection in the sense we think of it. The peace officer at issue is already dead" (LCB 15). Sarnowski quickly reminded the senators, however, of the more orthodox view of aggravators: "What aggravated circumstance statutes are required to do, according to the United States Supreme Court, is to adequately and constitutionally narrow that class of first-degree murders to make them eligible for the death penalty. That is the sole purpose of an aggravat-ing circumstance statute. . . . The more narrowly defined, I believe, the more easily defensible it is" (LCB 15). He concluded by assuring the committee that he could defend the language as Senator Washington proposed it (the laundry list rather than the broad PORAN definition).

On April 10 the committee formally moved to substitute the PORAN language for the original language in Senator Washington's bill. Three days later, they also added prison employees who do not come into direct contact with prisoners as part of their jobs (other prison employees were already covered).

The hate crimes element of the bill was added on April 20. The next day the senate as a whole adopted SB 139 by a vote of nineteen to one. The lone opponent was Senator Neal, who had proposed the hate crimes provision. After very short consideration in committee, the assembly approved the unamended measure forty-two to none. The only member to record his reasons noted that he had earlier op-posed the state's aggravators, but had been moved by recent events: "In light of the recent events in Oklahoma City and the increase in crimes that are indefensible by any known measure, I am going to vote in favor of Senate Bill 139. I know my conscience is not done with me yet, but I also know that an unmistakable message has to be sent that the taking of human life, especially that killing which is motivated solely by unreasoning hate, must stop" (LCB 39).

Shortly after SB 139 became law, the hate crime provision came up for possible revision when the assembly considered a larger hate crimes bill. The new statute, Assembly Bill 606, established a series of measures against persons who "commit certain felonies because of the victim's race, color, religion, national origin, physical or mental disability" (LCB AB606 3). The bill made such offenders eligible for enhanced prison terms and the death penalty if a homicide occurred. The law also created a civil right of action for victims of hate crimes, as well as a mandate and agency to collect data on hate crimes. The language of the proposed aggravator differed from SB 139 in one important respect. The language in SB 139 had emphasized the victim's identity (rather than the perpetrator's motivation) as primary: "The murder was committed upon a person because of the actual or perceived race, color, religion, national origin or sexual orientation of that person" (LCB 139, 31). The new language included in the first drafts of AB 606 emphasized the offender's motivation: "The murder was committed by a person who was motivated by the actual or perceived race, color, religion, national origin, physical or mental disability or sexual orientation of the victim" (LCB 606, 6). Both formulations invite some consideration of the offender's *mens rea* with regard to the selected features of the victim's identity, but the AB 606 version is far more explicit in identifying motive rather than the victim's identity as central.

By the next hearing, the language had been changed to conform to that of SB 139. The state public defender expressed concern that the muted language regarding motive would make death-eligible some defendants who had not formed a definite intention with regard to the victim's protected identity and might therefore extend the law beyond the paradigm hate crimes into a "catch-all" aggravator (LCB 606, 23). Several witnesses for the state emphasized that this aggravator would be rarely applied. Another witness, however, noted that it could apply to several recent cases in Reno where the killing was the result "of a human on human hunting trip," in this instance by skinheads who selected their victims by race. In such cases, the witness opined, it would not be a problem to discover evidence of the motive: "The vast majority of cases involved more than one perpetrator and conspiracies. There generally is discussion beforehand and Lt. Galeoto advised when there are two or more perpetrators, one perpetrator will talk" (LCB 606, 21).

The law was adopted forty-two to none in the assembly on June 20. Eight days later the senate adopted it without dissent. The governor signed it into law on July 7, 1995.

IV. The New Aggravators Considered

The new aggravators speak to a diverse set of interest groups. One important audience is made up of public employee groups, like those representing peace officers, parole agents, and government investigators. A second audience is composed of the victims rights movement. A third audience consists of a variety of specific community constituencies for whom particular forms of crime have become symbolic of their miseries, including drive-by shootings, car jackings, or gang activity.

How do aggravators function in this new economy of power? We believe their primary function is as a currency of recognition. We call them "tokens of our esteem" because they seem to validate a public identity for those they include. But "token" is an ambiguous term. We typically use it to emphasize the emptiness of a sign as when we refer to a "token of our trip to Hawaii" or, even worse, a deceptive effort—as when a lone minority individual in a large organization is described as a "token." But tokens are also private currencies that on the right occasion get redeemed for real goods. Moreover, as narrative elements they can represent the whole.

The aggravating factors of the *Gregg* era were written to survive judicial review of a very substantive kind. The Supreme Court in *Furman* and *Gregg* seemed to articulate substantive goals for capital punishment that it would enforce. As the Nevada legislative hearings suggest, judicial review remains a concern, but not a profound one. Those senators who sought to mobilize opposition based on concern about the substantive constitutional goal of narrowing the field of murderers were rebuffed. The concern with narrow rationales, if it survives as something more than a formal requirement of legislative choice, is countered by other constitutional concerns about inequitable distinctions.

The post-*Furman* aggravators may not have represented a serious effort to reckon with the traditional criminal law principles,[62] but they reflected legislators' desire that they appear to do so. Being a "metaphor of rationality"[63] requires some level of resemblance to a coherent process. The new generation of aggravators, in contrast, embodies an almost total lack of interest in systemic coherence. Since aggravators do not have to produce a consistent set of substantive priorities, they can reflect a pastiche of symbols intended to operate in different and even contradictory ways for different observers.

A. Populist Punitiveness—Crime as Kitsch

If the new aggravators have a master narrative, it is something like "populist punitiveness"[64] or "punitive kitsch."[65] This reflects a kind of democratization of punishment and its privatization. Elite law professors wrote the MPC. It focused on the "capital" interests of the state, the integrity of the criminal process, and the functioning of government itself. Legislatures today are not looking to "neutral," "expert" law professors to write their aggravating factors. The lawyers who do the drafting are unabashedly advocates. The concerns represented in the factors they create are not the stuff of common law doctrine or its critique, but elements defined in popular discourse. The new aggravators are being promoted for a much more popular audience. Their currency is empathy with people "just like me" and vengeance against those who threaten "us."

Perhaps the most stunning example of this is the aggravator for killing a person during a satanic ritual, adopted by Louisiana in 1995. The act criminalized a number of activities including ceremonies involving animal mutilation and the sacrifice or the ingestion of animal or human blood or waste. The act provided for prison terms of up to five years for such acts, or a $5,000 fine, or both. Murder during such a ritual was defined as an aggravating factor. The sponsoring legislator argued that his purpose was combating "satanic activity in central and southwest Louisiana."[66] Representative Cain cited traditional governmental concerns of deterrence. "Law enforcement officials want the legislation to give them a bigger stick in eradicating the activity that is growing in many areas of the state." At the same time he signaled the importance of that law as a measure of public concern and thus valorization for those combating this (literal) evil. "We need to let the public know and the people of this nation know that we are not going to stand for this type of activity in Louisiana."

B. Privatization

The post-*Furman* aggravators recognized victims only in the form of public actors. Indeed, they predominantly reflected a concern with reproducing state power itself. The new factors, in contrast, reflect concern for the situation of private citizens, among them the old and the young, the disabled, and the pregnant. The goal of sanctioning public agents has been replaced by the goal of sanctifying private pain. As the Nevada peace officer provision shows, even the older public function aggravators are increasingly reconceived as matters of personal entitlement or private right rather than public interest and state power. The probation officers, cattle brand inspectors, and others who are not covered by the existing aggravator are being dishonored by exclusion.

Aggravators for car jackings, drive-by shootings, and gang activity target crimes because they have become the subjects of public fear, not because of any intrinsic features of the crimes. Interestingly, these three all focus on the experience primarily associated with the inner-city poor, of a random and violent death. Maryland, for example, adopted an aggravating factor for murder in the course of a car jacking in response to a gruesome car jacking in the summer of 1992: "In the summer of 1992, the murder of a Howard County mother during the commission of a carjacking, brought the seriousness of the crime to everyone's attention. As a result of the face to face confrontation of victim and offender during the commission of a carjacking, the potential for death and injury of the victim increases. Of the 503 reported carjackings, 3 homicides and 91 injuries occurred during the commission of the crime."[67] Face-to-face confrontations, however, define robberies and most felony murders, which were already represented in virtually all post-*Furman* factors. Similarly, there is no mention of whether the car-jacking homicide or injury rate is any higher than that for regular robberies. The foundation for the new aggravator is not objective criteria but rather the public outcry over a publicized and horrific crime. Addressing the same legislation, the Anne Arundel County government pointed directly to the victim perspective: "For the victim, being ordered out of one's vehicle at gunpoint is a frightening experience and one from which society must be protected. Many people have been victimized by this offense, some of which have been seriously wounded or killed as a result of this senseless activity."[68]

It is important to underline here the difference between this imperative and the far more traditional goal of public safety or social defense. The new aggravators reveal not simply a concern with the security of citizens (a foundational concern of modern government) but with the private experience of pain (an emerging concern of postmodern government). The gap left by the courts as the dominant interlocutors for aggravating factors was filled by the importance that victimization now has in establishing the authority to govern. Meanwhile expanding the death penalty, unlike other reforms involving prison sentences, produces marginal and unpredictable costs.[69]

While the old aggravators reflected a common public interest, the new ones invite a veritable auction of public concern. The new aggravators appear to offer additional protection to vulnerable groups, but, in fact, they are not based on any objective evidence that such groups need protection.[70] Instead, they reflect a prioritizing of the private experience of victimization, which is most powerfully symbolized by these subjects. Ultimately they serve to offer public recognition of private feelings rather than to address greater threats to public order. It is in this sense that aggravating factors function as tokens of our esteem, handed out by our representatives in the name of the political community. They say to probation officers, school teachers, medical emergency workers, and cattle brand inspectors, "We may not put you on television and worship you, but we honor you with the most symbolically potent currency we have." They say to senior citizens, parents, and inner-city residents, "We feel your pain."

C. *Governing through Crime*

Symbolic or not, these tokens must be worth something. Otherwise it is difficult to see why public employee organizations, generally no amateurs at political bargaining, would expend staff time on them. We need to know many more stories than Nevada and in more depth. These tokens may have a range of political value to interest groups that acquire them. Here, we can only speculate about what kinds of economies of power might recognize such tokens as valuable capital.

First, they may alter the likelihood of the prosecution seeking the death penalty in the event of another murder involving a member of the favored class. In some cases, the initial impetus to seeking a new aggravating factor is the refusal of a prosecutor to seek the death penalty in such a case. Now that the legislature has spoken, pity the prosecutor or judge who refuses to seek a death sentence in a case to which the new aggravator applies. In an era when even the tenure of state supreme court justices can be threatened by a single concurrence in a death penalty reversal, local elected officials, like judges and prosecutors, are incredibly vulnerable on this issue.[71]

Second, for a public employee, being added to a death penalty aggravator also certifies that the work you do is dangerous. Agents in parole, probation, and various investigator's offices have long sought to redefine themselves as exclusively law enforcers and shed the unfashionable identity of "helpers" and "enablers" of people who are, after all, criminals.[72] An aggravator may also help acquire other political goods, such as special insurance, the right to be armed, and the bargaining leverage of being a recognized part of society's front line against criminal violence.[73]

For actors who are essentially service deliverers it also defines the population serviced as dangerous. The Nevada peace officer advocates reached out to paint as likely murderers white-collar criminals, persons in domestic disputes, and family and friends of capital murder defendants. Being a member of one of these groups is a risk indicator of a "propensity" for violence. The relentless tendency of these testimonies is to characterize whole segments of society as defined by their proximity to the potential for crime and violence.

Third, victims rights groups share with government agents who want to be treated as law enforcement officers an interest in deepening the sense of the criminality around us. The more crime is out of control the more democratic will appropriately concentrates itself around crime. Aggravating factors function to define whole categories of criminals as superenemies of society.

One way to view these agendas is as by-products of our growing commitment to governing through crime.[74] The more government is "authorized" by its crimefighting ability, the more its relevance and popularity depend on a growing supply of serious bad guys that require lots of law men. On a small scale, these peace officers and parole agents are part of the gold rush to redefine all of government as crime-fighting. On a larger scale Bill Clinton has sought to govern through crime more than he has sought to govern through some kind of "center." A little over a decade ago Robert Cover eloquently reminded us that all law is founded in the possibility of violence and death.[75] In their own way, that is the point that Nevada's peace officers sought to establish, except that while Cover was interested in the powerful forces that distance us from this realization, the peace officers sought to trade in its banality.

D. The New Monsters

The first generation of felony murder offenses was a microcosm of the old world of capital felonies, where robbery, burglary, and rape were all capital in their own right. From the start, some states added then current crime obsessions (e.g., hijacking). The new aggravating offenses spread well beyond the traditional list of violent crimes to encompass new hybrids of harm and technology that have been selected by government and media as the most frightening offenses of our time: gang activity, drive-by shootings, car jackings, assault rifles, and drug sales.

Both crack gangsters and skinheads are "monsters" appropriate to our times, against whom Left and Right can find unity in outrage. James Fox and his colleagues found that "[i]ncreased support for the death penalty, therefore, may be more of a reflection of desire for the execution of Ted Bundy and other celebrity criminals than for the execution of more typical and obscure condemned inmates."[76] Perhaps skinheads and crack gangsters supplement the serial killers that have long helped to solidify support for capital punishment itself.

Like the first generation of felony murder aggravators, the new generation is likely to encourage juries to accept the association between crimes and death-warranting dangerousness or depravity without independent moral judgment.[77] But the new ones may be even more effective in this regard. Robbery and kidnapping are already easy to stretch around the facts of quite ordinary homicides. Aggravating factors for drive-by shootings, assault weapons, or gang activity target crimes that are really media hybrids of traditional serious crimes and certain stereotyped features, usually linked to minority populations. Lacking an objective foundation, they are likely to be even more plastic. For example, at a time when "gang" is widely used to define social life among the inner-city minority youth population, an aggravator for homicide in a gang activity context will be easy to apply to minority defendants. The MPC-style felony murder aggravators already invite the jury to execute those they fear, rather than those who are most culpable. The new felony murder categories may be more deadly simply because they are fresher and more relevant than the ancient categories of robbery and kidnapping.

E. Counteracting Mitigation

Many of the new generation of aggravators appear to be aimed at undermining the use of mitigating evidence regarding the defendant's life. Aggravators that focus on the condition of the victim, for example, age or physical disability, may be aimed at matching mitigating features of the defendant. Likewise, many of the new aggravators appear to create strict liability with respect to the protected aspect of the victim's identity. Florida, for example, defines a murder as aggravated when "the victim of the capital felony was particularly vulnerable due to advanced age or disability."[78] There is no statutory requirement that the perpetrator know of these traits let alone a requirement that they influenced his or her decision to kill.

Conclusion

One legacy of *Furman v. Georgia* has been to introduce a new formal grammar of the law of murder, one that speaks in terms of aggravating factors. In the era of deregulating death, these factors no longer operate in a juridical economy of power (or do so only marginally). Increasingly, they seem to have their real audience and their real currency as elements of a populist politics of vengeance and solidarity based on pain and outrage. They now circulate as tokens of our esteem doled out by our representatives to placate or reward special interest groups.

There is every reason to believe that these capital tokens are more than trivial pursuits. The very activity of legislation suggests effective interest groups with strategic agendas. As we move into an era in which the state sloughs more and more of its active governing onto private actors, government has less to give in its own name (execution is one thing unlikely to be privatized), and such tokens inevitably increase in value.

We expect that the new aggravating factors will have their most important practical effect in increasing pressure on the prosecution to seek death in cases where it is not now pursued. More subtle and difficult to observe will be the changes new factors introduce into the deliberation of capital juries. We suspect that aggravators updated to capture the latest media-hyped fears may prove more immune to the mitigation evidence of the defense. To a society more interested in background as a risk factor than an excuse, the linkage between terrible childhoods and terrible weapons and acts may work against defendants.

As punishment becomes a dominant mode of state power, and victimization the dominant form of entitlement eligibility, capital aggravators are powerful evidence that the particular interest groups recognized in aggravators deserve what state benefits there are. If our theory is correct, we should see groups that have traditionally sought positive state interventions being sent away with new aggravating factors. A law, for example, making the fact that the victim was a former welfare beneficiary an aggravating factor would make just such a point. But we need not wait to worry; the existence of hate crime aggravators and ones proposed for domestic violence tell us that constituencies never seen as particularly supportive of capital punishment can be included in this new economy of gestures.

Yet even our image of an interest group politics of the scaffold may be too sanguine. The rise of capital politics and its deliberate appeal to populist emotions has a disturbing history of association with the rise in authoritarian politics. The Black Act in eighteenth-century England has already been mentioned. That society was no democracy to begin with, but the act clearly sought to mobilize support for the government in that limited gentry class that did get to exercise some political responsibility. In the twentieth century, the politics of capital punishment in the crisis of Weimar Germany and the rise of Hitler form a chilling precedent.

Like the United States in the 1970s, Weimar Germany danced close to the edge of abolition, fed by a government with aspirations to govern through welfare and economic reform and media attention to a series of capital cases in which people with substantial cases for innocence or who were otherwise clearly inappropriate subjects of execution were almost executed.[79] In the early 1930s a conservative drift in politics coupled with media attention to a number of horrifying sex-related murders helped collapse the abolition effort and lent support to the growing strength of the Nazis. Hitler took a personal interest in designating new capital offenses, including a special factor of armed robbery on the new "autobahns" that he had constructed (we would call it car jacking today).[80] The Nazis emphasized the populism of capital punishment as reason enough for its practice. The demand for vengeance was defined as a "healthy popular feeling . . . simple, [and] natural."[81] Strong support for executions after an era of ambivalence and delays served the Nazis in distinguishing themselves from opponents who could be painted as reluctant to choose between criminals and the community.

While aggravating factors in the era of *Furman* and *Gregg* once sought to prevent juries from operating on such "natural," "healthy," and racist sentiments, they have now become a currency of just such populism. One need not believe that the execution of convicted murderers is a step down a path that leads to Auschwitz to believe that a politics that makes executions the very stuff of political authority is a clear and present danger to the persistence of the republican form of government.

Appendix 4A: Aggravating Factors by Jurisdiction with Year of Adoption, 1972–1996

STATE	Murder was committed by a convict under sentence of imprisonment	Defendant was previously convicted of another murder, or of felony involving use or threat of violence	Defendant committed another murder at same time	Defendant knowingly created great risk of death to many persons	Felony murder committed in the course of a rape, robbery, arson, burglary, or kidnapping
AL	(81)	(81)		(81)	(81)
AZ	(78)	(73)	(73)	(73)	
AR	(75)	(75)	(95)	(75)	
CA		(78)	(78)		(78)
CO	(84)	(74)	(94)	(74)	
CT		(73)		(73)	(73)
DE	(77)	(77)	(77)		(77)
FL	(72)	(72)		(72)	(72)
GA	(73)	(73)		(73)	(73)
ID		(77)	(77)	(77)	(77)
IL	(77)	(77)			(77)
IN	(77)	(77)			(77)
KS	(90)	(90)		(90)	
KY		(76)	(76)	(76)	(76)
LA	(76)	(76)		(76)	(76)
MD	(78)		(78)		(78)
MS	(77)	(77)		(77)	(77)
MO	(83)	(83)	(83)	(83)	(83)
MT	(77)	(77)		(77)	(89)
NE		(73)	(73)	(73)	
NV	(77)	(77)	(93)	(77)	(77)
NH		(74)		(74)	
NJ		(77)		(78)	(77)
NM	(79)				(79)
NY	(95)				
NC	(77)	(77)	(77)	(77)	(77)
OH	(81)	(81)	(81)		(81)
OK	(76)	(76)		(76)	
OR	(77)	(77)	(81)		
PA	(74)	(86)		(74)	(74)
SC		(77)	(86)	(77)	(77)
SD	(79)			(79)	
TN	(89)	(89)	(89)	(89)	(89)
TX	(73)		(85)		(73)
UT	(73)	(73)	(73)	(73)	(73)
VA					
WA	(81)		(81)		(81)
WY	(82)	(82)		(82)	(82)
Fed		(88)		(88)	(88)

STATE	Murder was committed for purpose of avoiding lawful arrest or effecting escape from custody	Murder was committed for pecuniary gain	Defendant procured murder	Murder was especially heinous, atrocious, cruel, or depraved; murder by torture	Murder committed to hinder enforcement of laws or, government function
AL	(81)	(81)		(81)	(81)
AZ		(73)	(73)	(73)	
AR	(75)	(75)		(75)	(75)
CA	(78)	(78)		(78)	
CO	(74)	(74)	(74)	(74)	
CT	(73)	(73)	(73)	(73)	
DE	(77)	(77)	(77)	(77)	
FL	(72)	(72)		(72)	(72)
GA	(73)	(73)	(73)	(73)	
ID		(77)	(77)	(77)	
IL?			(77)	(82)	
IN		(77)	(77)	(77)	
KS	(90)	(90)	(90)	(90)	
KY		(76)			
LA		(76)	(76)	(76)	
MD?	(78)	(78)			
MS	(77)	(77)		(77)	(77)
MO	(83)	(83)	(83)	(83)	
MT				(77)	
NE	(73)	(73)	(73)	(73)	(73)
NV	(77)	(77)		(77)	
NH	(74)	(74)		(74)	
NJ	(85)	(78)	(78)	(78)	
NM	(79)	(79)			
NY					
NC	(77)	(77)		(77)	(77)
OH	(81)	(81)			
OK	(76)	(76)	(76)	(76)	
OR		(77)	(77)	(77)	
PA		(74)	(74)	(74)	
SC?		(77)	(78)		
SD	(78)	(78)	(78)	(78)	
TN	(89)	(89)		(89)	
TX	(73)	(73)	(73)		
UT?	(73)	(73)	(83)	(83)	(83)
VA				(77)	
WA	(95)	(81)	(81)		
WY	(82)	(82)		(82)	
Fed		(88)	(88)	(88)	

STATE	Victim was peace officer, fire fighter	Victim was prosecutor, or a judicial, legislative, or executive officer	Victim was correctional officer	Victim was witness	Victim was informant
AL					
AZ	(88)				
AR					
CA	(78)	(78)		(78)	
CO	(74)	(84)			
CT					
DE	(77)	(77)		(77)	(94)
FL	(87)	(88)			
GA	(73)	(73)	(73)		
ID	(77)	(77)		(77)	
IL	(77)		(77)?	(86)	
IN	(77)	(77)	(77)	(96)	
KS				(90)	
KY	(76)		(76)		
LA	(76)		(79)	(79)	
MD	(78)				
MS					
MO	(83)	(83)	(83)	(83)	
MT	(77)				
NE			(73)		
NV	(77)		(77)		
NH					
NJ	(77)	(77)			
NM	(79)		(79)	(81)	
NY	(95)		(95)		
NC	(77)	(77)	(77)		
OH	(81)	(81)		(81)	
OK	(81)		(81)		
OR	(77)	(77)	(77)	(77)	
PA	(77)	(89)	(89)	(74)	(89)
SC	(77)	(77)	(77)	(95)	
SD	(79)	(79)			
TN	(89)	(89)	(89)		
TX	(73)		(93)		
UT	(83)	(83)	(83)	(73)	(73)
VA					
WA	(81)	(81)	(81)	(81)	
WY	(82)	(83)		(82)	
Fed					

STATE	Murder occurred during hi-jacking	Murder effected by bomb	Murder effected by poison	Murderer has probability of / propensity for future dangerousness	Murder was premeditated
AL					
AZ					
AR					
CA		(78)	(78)		
CO		(74)			
CT					
DE					(94)
FL	(72)	(72)			(79)
GA	(73)				
ID				(77)	
IL	(77)				(86)
IN		(77)			
KS					
KY					
LA					
MD					
MS	(77)				
MO	(83)				
MT					
NE					
NV					
NH					(74)
NJ					
NM					
NY					
NC		(77)			
OH					
OK				(76)	
OR		(81)			
PA	(77)				
SC					
SD					
TN	(89)	(89)			
TX					
UT	(83)	(83)			
VA				(77)	
WA					
WY	(82)	(82)			
Fed					(88)

STATE	Murderer lay in wait	Victim was hostage or victim of kidnapping	Victim was juror
AL			
AZ			
AR			
CA	(78)		(95)
CO?	(74)	(74)	
CT			
DE		(77)	
FL			
GA			
ID			
IL			
IN	(77)	(88)	
KS			
KY			
LA			
MD			
MS			
MO			
MT	(83)	(77/87)	
NE			
NV			
NH			
NJ			
NM			
NY			
NC			
OH			
OK			
OR?			(77)
PA		(74)	
SC			
SD			
TN			
TX			
UT		(83)	(83)
VA			
WA			(81)
WY			(82)
Fed			

STATE	Victim was EMT	Victim was child	Victim was mentally or physically handicapped	Victim was senior	Victim was exercising First Amendment rights
AL					
AZ		<15 (85)		>70 (85)	
AR					
CA					
CO		<12 (94)			
CT		<16 (96)			
DE		<14 (94)		>62 (77/81)	(95)
FL		<12 (96)	(96)	(96)	
GA					
ID					
IL	(87)	<12 (82)	(96)	(96)	
IN		<12 (87)			
KS					
KY					
LA		<12 (85)		>65 (95)	
MD					
MS		<12 (77)			
MO					
MT		<18 (89)			
NE					
NV		<14 (95)			
NH		(74)	(74)	(74)	
NJ		<14 (94)			
NM					
NY					
NC					
OH					
OK					
OR					
PA		<12 (89)			
SC		<11 (86)			
SD		<13 (95)			
TN	(96)	<12 (89)			
TX		<6 (93)			
UT					
VA					
WA					(81)
WY		<17 (89)	(89)	>65 (89)	
Fed		(88)	(88)	(88)	

STATE	Victim was pregnant	Offense was a "hate crime"	Murder connected with drugs/conspiracy	Murder connected with gangs	Assault weapon or bullet-proof vest used
AL					
AZ		(96)			
AR					
CA		(78)			
CO					
CT					(93)
DE	(77)	(95)			
FL				(96)	
GA					
ID					
IL			(86)	(96)	
IN			(89/86)	(94)	
KS					
KY					
LA			(89)		
MD					
MS					
MO				(93)	
MT					
NE					
NV		(95)			
NH			(77)		
NJ			(93)		
NM					
NY					
NC					
OH					
OK					
OR					
PA	(95)		(89)		
SC?			(90)		
SD			(89)		
TN					
TX					
UT					
VA					
WA				(95)	
WY					
Fed					

STATE	Murder effected by mail bomb	Murder was drive-by shooting	Murder committed during car jacking; home invasion	Murder committed with torture, mutilation, ritual
AL				
AZ				
AR				
CA	(78)	(95)	(95)	
CO				
CT				
DE				
FL				
GA				
ID				
IL		(95)	(89)	
IN		(96)	(93)	
KS				
KY				
LA		(95)		(95)
MD			(95)	
MS				
MO				
MT				
NE				
NV			(89)	(93)
NH				
NJ				
NM				
NY				
NC				
OH				
OK				
OR				(81)
PA				
SC				
SD				
TN				(95)
TX				
UT	(83)			
VA				
WA		(95)		
WY				
Fed				

⸱

(1972).

1976).

⸱t to think through both of these two fields remains. Franklin E. Zim-
̲̲̲̲kins, *Capital Punishment and the American Agenda* (New York: Cambridge University Press, 1986).

4. American Law Institute, Model Penal Code Sec. 210.6, Final Draft 1962, revised commentaries 1980.

5. Zimring and Hawkins, *Capital Punishment*, 46.

6. Austin Sarat, "Violence, Representation, and Responsibility in Capital Trails: The View from the Jury," *Ind. L.J.* 70 (1995): 1103, 1105.

7. Robert Weisberg, "Deregulating Death," *Sup. Ct. Rev.* 1983 (1984): 305, 385.

8. E. P. Thompson, *Whigs and Hunters: The Origin of the Black Act* (New York: Pantheon, 1975).

9. Douglas Hay, "Property, Authority, and the Criminal Law," in *Albion's Fair Tree: Crime and Society in Eighteenth-Century England*, ed. Douglas Hay et al. (New York: Pantheon, 1975).

10. See also Richard R. Evans, *Rituals of Retribution: Capital Punishment in Germany, 1600–1987* (London: Oxford University Press, 1996).

11. Thompson, *Whigs and Hunters.*

12. The long-term ability of Coker v. Georgia, 433 U.S. 584 (1977) to limit the grammar of capital sentencing to the possible variations of homicide may be in doubt. One would predict that some combination of rape, child abuse, and drug dealing will be likely candidates. For a recent state supreme court approval for a capital crime combining rape and child abuse, see *State (Louisiana) v. Wilson*, 685 So. 2d 1063 (La. 1996).

13. If for no other reason than that we have already bought and paid for the expensive and oppressive police and prison system the eighteenth-century gentry were trying to avoid installing.

14. Because the two realms of capital trials and politics happen to define the special interests of the respective authors, this seemed to offer a promising subject for a collaborative effort. We suspect furthermore that a strong interactive field of effects exists between the two.

15. Zimring and Hawkins, *Capital Punishment*, 38.

16. Ibid., 42.

17. See Proffitt v. Florida, 428 U.S. 242 (1976). David Givelber, "The New Law of Murder," *Indiana L.J.* 69 (1994): 375, 391, describes the MPC factors as the core of the *Gregg*-era statutes. According to his analysis, other than the MPC's eight factors, only aggravators against killing police and correctional officers appeared in at least half of the states retaining the death penalty.

18. A related model, adopted by Georgia and a few other states, requires the capital sentencer to determine whether enumerated aggravating circumstances exist and to then decide, after "considering" mitigating circumstances (which are not enumerated) whether death is appropriate. Although the Supreme Court has found the difference between weighing and non-weighing states to be significant with respect to the impact of a invalid aggravator on a capital verdict, the practical differences between these two types of statutes is not clear. See Marcia A. Widder, "Comment, Hanging Life in the Balance: The Supreme Court and the Metaphor of Weighing in the Penalty Phase of the Capital Trial," 68 *Tulane L. Rev.* 1341 (1994).

19. Zimring and Hawkins, "Capital Punishment," 84. The Texas model was approved in Jurek v. Texas (1976) 428 U.S. 262.

20. For the years of adoption of particular aggravating factors see appendix A.

21. Zimring and Hawkins, *Capital Punishment*, 84.

22. See generally, Franklin E. Zimring and Gordon Hawkins, "Murder, the Model Penal Code, and Multiple Agendas of Reform," 19 *Rutgers L.J.* 773 (1988).

23. Charles McClain, "Criminal Law Reform: Historical Development in the United States," *Encyclopedia of Crime and Justice* 2 (1983), 510.

24. Zimring and Hawkins, *Capital Punishment*, 82.

25. Zimring and Hawkins note that in contrast the mitigating factors were carefully developed (ibid.).

26. See Richard A. Rosen, "The 'Especially Heinous' Aggravating Circumstances in Capital Cases—The Standardless Standard," 64 N.C. L.Rev. 941 (1986).

27. Lowenfield v. Phelps, 484 U.S. 231, 257, (1988) Brennan, J., dissenting.

28. Weisberg, "Deregulating Death."

29. Mills v. Maryland, 486 U.S. 367, 375–76 (1988); accord Penry v. Lynaugh, 492 U.S. 302, 328 (1989); Hitchcock v. Dugger, 481 U.S. 393, 398–99 (1987); Lockett v. Ohio, 438 U.S. 586, 605 (1978).

30. Zant v. Stephens, 462 U.S. 862 (1976).

31. *Id.* at 878–879.

32. *Id.* at 887–888.

33. Arave v. Creech, 507 U.S. 463, 474 (1993).

34. Godfrey v. Georgia, 446 U.S. 420 (1980); Maynard v. Cartwright, 486 U.S. 356 (1988).

35. Johnson v. Mississippi, 486 U.S. 578 (1988).

36. Lowenfield v. Phelps, 484 U.S. 231, 243 (1988) (jury relied on single aggravating circumstance that "the offender knowingly created a risk of death or great bodily harm to more than one person" both to render defendant death-eligible and to support ultimate sentence of death). Under Louisiana law, intentional murder and felony murder are second-degree murder, while first-degree murder is defined more narrowly to require proof of additional circumstances. Id. at 241–42.

37. Zant v. Stephens, 462 U.S. at 877 (1976) n.15 (quoting *Furman*, 408 U.S., at 294 (Brennan, J., concurring)).

38. Carol S. Steiker and Jordon M. Steiker, "Sober Second Thoughts: Reflection on Two Decades of Constitutional Regulation of Capital Punishment," 109 *Harv. L. Rev.* 305 (1994): David C. Baldus, George Woodworth, and Charles A. Pulaski Jr., *Equal Justice and the Death Penalty: A Legal and Empirical Analysis* (Boston, Mass.: Northeastern University Press, 1990).

39. Tuilaepa v. California, 114 S. Ct. 2630, 2638–39 (1994).

40. Id. at 2639 (quoting Stephens, 426 U.S. at 875).

41. David Givelber, "The New Law of Murder," 69 *Ind. L.J.* 375, 420 (1994).

42. For a state adopting the whole code, the somewhat tighter definition of felony murder in the guilt phase might make a difference. But most states simply stuck the MPC's felony murder sentencing provision on to their own form of felony murder liability.

43. Givelber, "The New Law of Murder," 392.

44. Ibid., 394.

45. Zimring and Hawkins, *Capital Punishment*.

46. Givelber, "The New Law of Murder."

47. Givelber, "The New Law of Murder," 394.

48. Janet Halley describes a similar process in the formation of the "don't ask, don't tell" policy regarding gay people in the military. Evidence of gay or lesbian identity creates a presumption of propensity to engage in gay or lesbian conduct. See Janet E. Halley, "The Status/Conduct Distinction in the 1993 Revisions to Military Anti-Gay Policy," 3 *GLQ* 159 (1996).

49. Givelber, "The New Law of Murder"; Zimring and Hawkins, *Capital Punishment.*

50. Malcolm Feeley and Jonathan Simon, "The New Penology: Notes on the Emerging Strategy of Corrections and Its Implications," *Criminology* 30 (1992): 449.

51. James A. Fox et al., "Death Penalty Opinion in the Post-*Furman* Years," 18 N.Y.U. *Rev. L. & Soc. Change* 499 (1990–91). See Simmons v. South Carolina, 114 S. Ct. 2191 (1994) (citing poll showing that only 7.1 percent of jury-eligible adults in South Carolina believed an inmate sentenced to life imprisonment would actually be required to spend the rest of his life in prison); William Bowers, "Capital Punishment and Contemporary Values: People's Misgivings and the Court's Misperceptions," 27 *L. & Soc. Rev.* 157, 169–70 (1993); Theodore Eisenberg and Martin T. Wells, "Deadly Confusion: Juror Instructions in Capital Cases," 79 *Cornell L. Rev.* 1, 7–8 (1993); J. Mark Lane, "'Is There Life without Parole?': A Capital Defendants Right to a Meaningful Alternative Sentence," 26 *Loy. L.A. Rev.* 327 (1993); William W. Hood III, "Note, The Meaning of 'Life' for Virginia Jurors and Its Effect on Reliability in Capital Sentencing," 75 *Va. L. Rev.* 1605, 1620–25 (1989); Anthony Paduano and Clive A. Stafford Smith, "Deathly Errors: Juror Misperceptions Concerning Parole in the Imposition of the Death Penalty," 18 *Colum. Hum. Rts. L. Rev.* 211, 221–25 (1987).

52. Lowenfield, 484 U.S. 231, 257, Brennan, J., dissenting.

53. Id. at 244.

54. Jerome G. Miller, *Search and Destroy: African-American Males in the Criminal Justice System* (Cambridge: Cambridge University Press, 1996).

55. Florida adopted the "cold, calculating" language in 1979. New Hampshire included premeditation in its 1977 statute. Several other states followed in the 1980s. Delaware adopted a premeditation factor in 1994. "Lying-in-wait," a subcategory of premeditated murders, was included in several of the immediate post-*Gregg* statutes. See appendix A.

56. Two different processes are difficult to disaggregate here: the Court's deregulation and the rising tide of public interest in crime. Deregulation may be seen as lowering the cost of producing aggravating factors by making it less likely that some nuance of their construction will result in later court reversals. Crime politics may be seen as raising the demand for capital aggravators. Since either trend independently would be expected to entice legislators to produce more capital aggravators, it is hard to draw any conclusion from the increasing production of aggravators which of these is more significant.

57. We recognize that the term "generation" is a problematic one. An examination of appendix A's table of aggravating factors for each state and the United States showing the year of enactment provides some evidence. The aggravators are listed in columns in a rough order of enactment, with the MPC factors first, followed by typical state additions at the time of original enactment, followed by later amendments.

58. Zimring and Hawkins, *Capital Punishment.*

59. Nev. Legislative Counsel Bureau 31 (1995). LCB hereinafter.

60. NRS 200.033 (7).

61. The Nevada Legislative Council Bureau provides summaries of legislative history that include descriptions of the hearings with small excerpts quoted. I am quoting from the LCB including its internal quotes.

62. Zimring and Hawkins, *Capital Punishment,* 83.

63. Weisberg, "Deregulating Death," 354, quoted in Zimring and Hawkins, *Capital Punishment,* 90.

64. Jonathan Simon and Malcolm Feeley, "True Crime: The New Penology and Public Discourse on Crime," in *Punishment and Social Control: Essays in Honor of Sheldon Messinger,* ed. Thomas G. Blomberg and Stanley Cohen (New York: Aldine de Gruyter, 1995); Miller, *Search and Destroy.*

65. Miller, *Search and Destroy.*

66. "Satanic Ritual Bill Passes," *Baton Rouge Morning Advocate*, June 22, 1989, 10A. The concerns apparently arose over reports of ritualistic activities at two abandoned military bases. Given the importance of military bases to local economies, this would be just the kind of situation anthropologists have linked to witchcraft. See Robert Shuler, "House Panel OKs Bill Banning Ritualistic Acts," *Baton Rouge Morning Advocate*, May 26, 1989, 12A.

67. Maryland Department of Public Safety and Correctional Services, "Position on Proposed Legislation," Senate Bill 39 (car jacking) (1993).

68. Anne Arundel County, Position Paper on Senate Bill 339 (1993).

69. It remains unclear to us how much this is driven by the organized lobbying groups that now represent the victims rights movement and how much is driven by politicians. The emergence of the victims rights movement over the last two decades has itself involved a complicated interaction between federal law enforcement initiatives and local grassroots activists. See Paul Rock, "Society's Attitude toward the Victim," in *From Crime Policy to Victim Policy: Reorienting the Justice System*, ed. Ezzat A. Fatteh (New York: St. Martin's Press, 1986).

70. Children, old people, and pregnant women are if anything less likely than others to be the victims of violent crime.

71. Stephen B. Bright, "Political Attacks on the Judiciary: Can Justice Be Done amid Efforts to Intimidate and Remove Judges from Office for Unpopular Decisions?" *N.Y.U. L. Rev.* 72 (1997): 308. Bright suggests that the major problem is the willingness of politicians to engage in populist judge bashing with the aid of modern direct mail campaigning. If judges can be removed from office or prevented from reaching a higher bench because they have concurred in reversals of single death sentences, the independence of the judicial branch is fatally compromised. Bright calls on the bar and academics to challenge the legitimacy of political attacks on judicial independence and on lawyers to seek to disqualify judges who have campaigned on a promise to get tough on criminals or enforce the death penalty (p. 330).

72. Miller, *Search and Destroy*, 128–130.

73. Correctional officers and police unions increasingly find it effective to go to the legislature over the heads of their managers. While death sentences are far removed from most of the issues contested by these unions, establishing an aggravator may help frame the political stature of such public employees for future reference.

74. See Jonathan Simon, "Governing through Crime," in *The Conundrum of Crime: Essays on Criminal Justice*, ed. Lawrence Friedman and George Fischer (Boulder, Colo.: Westview Press, 1997), and a larger manuscript on file with the authors.

75. Robert Cover, "Violence and the Word," 98 *Yale Law Review* 160 (1986).

76. Fox et al., "Death Penalty Opinion," 510.

77. Givelber, "The New Law of Murder."

78. Fla. Stat. s 921.141(5)(m).

79. Richard J. Evans, *Rituals of Retribution*, 548.

80. Ibid., 632.

81. Ibid., 624.

· II ·

CAPITAL PUNISHMENT AND
LEGAL VALUES

· 5 ·

"ALWAYS MORE TO DO": CAPITAL PUNISHMENT AND THE (DE)COMPOSITION OF LAW

PETER FITZPATRICK

The news lived in the air of the courtroom. It was as if there had been one kind of existence in the room, and now there was another: a man was going to be executed. It was real but it was not comprehensible. The man was standing there.

Norman Mailer, *The Executioner's Song*

Introduction

To begin, or even to attempt a beginning, is already to deny the reign of finality. It may be as well to summon such reassurance at a time when progressive, rational utilitarian arguments for punishing and not punishing are very much at bay and retribution seems so conclusively resurgent. That outcome is perhaps nowhere so marked as in the revival of capital punishment in the United States. Not only has the rise of capital punishment put paid to evolutionary optimism about the meliorative history of punishment—an optimism that was hardly dented by those revisionist histories most conspicuously associated with Foucault[1]—but it has also contributed to a sense of the futility of committed intellectual work on capital punishment, to a certain terminal perplexity. Hugo Bedau no less, while "still nursing the unconquerable hope," pessimistically concluded a recent survey of capital punishment in the United States by noting that "more has been investigated, researched, written, litigated, and publicly argued against the death penalty in America . . . than in the rest of the world combined."[2] And Roger Hood begins the new edition of his "world-wide perspective" on the death penalty by noting that "no one can embark upon a study of the death penalty without making the commonplace observation that from a philosophical and policy standpoint there appears to be nothing new to be said."[3]

Our courageous editor has nonetheless gathered our essays together on the assumption that there is something new to be said, something more to be done, and it is this idea, the idea of there always being something new or something more, that will be the leitmotiv of this chapter. This is signaled in the title. It is borrowed from one of Austin Sarat's informants, "a death penalty lawyer," who is talking about the decisions that have to be made in acting for a client—a situation where any decision "could well determine if your client lives or dies."[4] But the lawyer can never, as it were, decide enough. The responsibility cannot be met or matched because it can never be limited. "It doesn't matter if you live from now until eternity, there would always be more to do."[5] In that spirit, my argument will be that law cannot accommodate either the general decision to have capital punishment or the particular decision to kill someone. Death, in this argument, marks a limit of the law.

This gnomic conclusion will now be amplified by looking at the composition and decomposition of law in its relation to death and to the death penalty. Then the abnormality of capital punishment for law and the intrinsic failure of law in its attempting to effect capital punishment will be illustrated by visiting scenes of execution. Finally, I will indicate how this failure of law is revealed yet "resolved" in judicial discourse in the United States on the death penalty and indicate how the reform literature, despite its great virtues, does not inevitably challenge that putative resolution.

Death and the (De)composition of Law

Any argument that law and capital punishment are incompatible must appear quixotic when confronted with those cogent claims that they are, rather, eminently suited. Time and again, law and the death penalty are linked in some supposedly integral relation and joined as components of sovereign power.[6] And the death penalty has been used quite purposively as a mode of marking and effecting sovereign rule.[7] In more modernist terms, "the death penalty, today as in the past, symbolizes the ultimate power of the state, and of the government of society, over the individual citizen."[8] In all this, the etymology is, of course, accommodating: "capital" as *caput* the head and *capitellum*, above.[9] The public execution, in Foucault's terms, brings into play "the dissymmetry between the subject who has dared to violate the law and the all-powerful sovereign who displays his strength. The punishment is carried out in such a way as to give a spectacle not of measure, but of imbalance and excess; in this liturgy of punishment, there must be an emphatic affirmation of power and of its intrinsic superiority."[10] The "excessive" sovereign power can thus assume a secular transcendence, a coming from beyond, in its power over death. This place beyond has been occupied in various ways, obviously—"we owe God a death" for one thing[11]—but with modernity it is law which has sought to occupy it, more or less uneasily.

Locke famously tied the death-dealing sovereign power to law. This power comprised "*a Right* of making Laws with Penalties of Death, and consequently all less Penalties" for certain purposes.[12] And this, in terms of old and new justifications, could be not simply a matter of an excessive sovereign power but one of exact exchange. From antiquity to Durkheim, crime caused a social disequilibrium that was corrected by a punishment balancing out or reciprocating the crime.[13] Law itself had for long and often been conceived in terms of exchange, a righting of the balance. Kant could then readily link "the law of retribution" and law as "legal justice" by placing both at the foundation of society.[14]

We may stay within that tradition but start to move toward its poststructural disruption by invoking Benjamin's "Critique of Violence," along with the pertinence given it in Derrida's "Force of Law." Benjamin, writing of the proponents of capital punishment, felt

> that an attack on capital punishment assails, not legal measure, not laws, but law itself in its origin. For if violence, violence crowned by fate, is the origin of law, then it may be readily supposed that where the highest violence, that over life and death, occurs in the legal system, the origins of law jut manifestly and fearsomely into existence.[15]

This is Derrida's rendition of the sentiment:

> Benjamin seems to think that the arguments against the *droit de punir* and notably against the death penalty are superficial, and not by accident. For they do not admit an axiom essential to the definition of law. Which? Well, when one tackles the death penalty, one doesn't dispute one penalty among others but law itself in its origin, in its very order. If the origin of law is a violent positioning, the latter manifests itself in the purest fashion when violence is absolute, that is to say when it touches on the right to life and to death.[16]

In the definitive elevation by the death penalty of what is absolute—of what is final, certain, and comprehensive—the wonder becomes not that capital punishment is somehow incompatible with the progressive advance of liberal legality but, rather, how such a legality could ever do without it.[17] Indeed, in its reliance on the rule of law, liberal legality embraces law's power of ultimate or final determination—very much a deathly competence. However, as Derrida goes on to indicate, Benjamin's is not a novel argument in philosophy, and we can hardly expect poststructuralism to rest content with any repeated resolution. So, there must be more to be done.

Blanchot introduces a note of disturbance like this: "[T]he law reveals itself for what it is: less the command that has death as its sanction, than death itself wearing the face of the law. . . . The law kills. Death is always the horizon of the law: if you do this, you will die."[18] But the horizon is productively ambivalent. As marking our limit, it is ours. It is of us. So, approaching the horizon from within as it were, we can have some idea, some cognizance of it. Yet we cannot know or experience the horizon fully because it does mark our limit. It borders and connects with what is beyond us. But not utterly beyond, for if the horizon were completely divisive there could be no connection and no relation between what is separated. It would, to continue in a personalist mode, no longer be our horizon. Its two sides would exist in complete difference, not knowing at all of each other. So, with a horizon there must be a subsisting relation and hence some commonality between the two sides. But, obviously, the horizon cannot be purely relational either. In a pure relation, the two sides would simply appear or disappear in each other and there could be no horizon between them. So we are "bound" to a seeming irresolution of the horizon as the condition and quality of our contained identity and the horizon as opening onto all that lies beyond an identity. The elaboration can be taken further, but let me do that now in expanding Blanchot's claim that death is the horizon of the law.

Law's ready correspondence to death has just been copiously instanced, but there is more to it. "The law kills," but in "the possibility of the death penalty" exalting law "above natural and biological life" something more pervasively typical of law is being revealed.[19] Death accommodates law's intrinsic claim to fix, determine, and hold life, to deny its circumstance and possibility. Put more conventionally, the rule of law would provide certainty, an assured stability. But this competence cannot mark law's achieved completeness if law itself is to survive. True, "the imperious law" would in one way seek this outcome, but the static and terminal nature of that outcome corresponds to a comprehensive death.[20] There would be nothing living left for law to rule. We can, then, say that death is the horizon of the law in that death is a horizon belonging to law. Law has an affinity with death or some similarity to it. But the horizon is a relation between law and death as different and separate. Should, or could, law relate purely to death, in the sense of identifying completely with it, or, in Blanchot's terms, if law were only "death itself wearing the face of law," law would be no more.[21]

So, law must be something more than its traditional attributes of determined fixity, assured stability, and so on, and that "more" can also be found in death as the horizon of law—the horizon now where we reach and orient ourselves toward what is beyond us. We cannot know our death or experience it "in" life. What is of ultimate significance to us remains ever beyond us and inclines us always beyond ourselves. Death as the horizon, then, conjoins the determined fixity of identity within the horizon with the opening or the responsiveness to all that lies beyond the identity. There cannot be an isolated fixity, a solitary stasis. Identity, including the identity of law or of a law, depends on a constant responsiveness to all that would, coming from beyond, impinge on and challenge it. We could say, in short, that death is the horizon of the law not just in the standard and simple sense that law kills or that it fixes and positions, but also and conjointly in the sense that death impels a responsiveness to all that is beyond fixity and position.

I will now expand these compressed thoughts on law and death in a way that focuses on the opposition between law and capital punishment, and I shall do this by returning to the jurisprudentially more familiar "Force of Law."[22] I would propose beginning in a helpful equivocation found in Sarat's "Bearing Witness and Writing History."[23] Here "death penalty lawyers" are found "making a record" of their clients and cases "in the struggle against capital punishment"—a record meant to inform and bring about a better future.[24] This is a future hopefully suffused in definitive understanding—a future where, to take an instance provided by one of the lawyers, "maybe 100 years from now . . . someone will look and say 'Oh my God, it was true that the death penalty was really just an engine of discrimination.'"[25] More generally, the lawyers envisage that a fuller picture of social causality, and more particularly a fuller picture of the effects of social deprivation, will finally tell us what the death penalty "was really." Sarat transposes that aspiration in terms derived from Derrida's "Force of Law" to conclude that the lawyers' "struggle against the present reality of law's violence is carried out in the name of a justice deferred."[26] That perception of justice is clearly sufficient for Sarat's account, but if we were to take it further in Derrida's terms, then we would have to question the assumption that justice can be or could ever possibly be achieved. For Derrida, justice is "deferred" in the sense that it can never be attained, it always remains *à venir,* ever to come.[27] Derrida's nonconformism on this score is central to my argument, and I will now say a little more about it.

For Derrida, in "Force of Law," justice imports an unlimited responsiveness to and responsibility for the other. As such, it utterly respects the singularity of the other. The very particularity or finiteness of the other calls for an infinite regard. The illimitable demand of justice without more, or without less, is impossible and even inexpressible. To be effective, to be made possible, justice must be given operative force. But for this, it must, in a sense, be denied. The limitless expanse of justice, that is, must be "cut" into, reduced and rendered expressible. An obvious contradiction now emerges: justice can only be made just in a way that is unjust.

Law is that which cuts into and assures justice (and less than justice). In this, "law is the element of calculation."[28] It imports a stability and regularity. It codifies, prescribes, and determines. It lends its intrinsic force and enforceability to justice. It cannot, however, be accounted for in terms of justice. And justice, in any case, is unlimiting and cannot account for anything. So, Derrida frequently contrasts justice and the just decision with the legal decision, which "simply consists of applying the law," or in which "the judge is a calculating machine," or in which "we placidly apply a good rule to a particular case, to a correctly subsumed example, according to a determinate judgment."[29] Yet, despite Derrida's assertion that these things happen, he must also recognize that law in this guise would be impossible. The element of calculation, the determining cut, in itself is neither legal nor illegal.[30] So, it is not only the case that law is necessary for the enforcement of justice, but justice is also necessary for the enforcement, the existence of law. Each legal decision brings existing laws to bear on it, but it cannot ever do only that. There is "an ordeal of the undecidable," which inhabits and persists in and beyond the legal decision: "the undecidable remains caught, lodged, at least as a ghost—but an essential ghost—in every decision, in every event of decision"; and "each case is other, each decision is different and requires an absolutely unique interpretation, which no existing coded rule can or ought to guarantee absolutely."[31] In all, the legal decision combines law as the calculable with justice as the incalculable response to the "absolutely unique," beyond determined calculation, exchange, or reciprocity.[32] Justice, in its turn, is effected through law as calculable. Each is necessary for the operation of the other, yet each is necessarily distinct from the other. There is a relation of "difference and . . . co-implication" between them.[33]

The distinction between law and justice entails nothing less, and perhaps somewhat more, than the process of deconstruction itself. Deconstruction, variously, "is justice" or is situated "between law and justice."[34] More elaborately, "deconstruction takes place in the interval that separates the undeconstructability of justice from the deconstructability of *droit.*" Justice can be called in aid to convey the "impossible" movement of deconstruction continually beyond all presence. And law could be a figure of determined presence or a figure of its determination. But if both these things are so, "justice" is not a compendious way of describing deconstruction, which, rather, "takes place" between justice and law.[35]

So, justice may "be" deconstruction, but justice operates through law. Deconstruction, it may be said, relies upon law as presence. And that presence, as Derrida recognizes, persists.[36] Its avatars—presences, as against presence, and laws, as opposed to the law—are "deconstructable." But ultimately presence, like justice, is a condition of deconstruction and cannot itself be deconstructed. No matter how illimitable, no matter how "mad" justice or the desire for justice may be, it is held in conjunction with presence.[37] So, "justice exceeds law and calculation," but law is also seen by Derrida as "exceeding" justice.[38] We must, Derrida emphasizes, calculate, and we must negotiate "the relation between the calculable and the incalculable": "This requirement does not properly belong either to justice or law. It only belongs to either of these two domains by exceeding one in the direction of the other."[39] Law, then, as calculation can only "properly belong" to itself, or be itself, by exceeding itself "in the direction of" justice.[40] Calculation, in short, goes to as well as against justice. Or inversely, as we have already seen, justice is operatively integral to law, to the legal decision. The question of how just is the decision, of how far it goes "in the direction of" justice, is another matter. Law sets the decision in relation to justice, in an "inclination" toward the other.[41] As to the other side of the equation, justice exceeding itself in the direction of law, we have also seen that, to have effect, justice depends on law: "incalculable justice *requires* us to calculate."[42] If "I" am to be in a relation of responsibility to the other, to say nothing of relating to a diversity of others, then justice must be delimited in the legal decision. Without a limit, there can be no relation to the other. Giving my-self to the other in the unalloyed demand of justice is inherently unachievable. It could never form or resolve into a relation. Or, in a more apocalyptic vein, once the giving were achieved, there would be a simultaneous dissolution of the very "I" that was to relate to the other. In all, if law is the place where contained presence impossibly combines with uncontained responsiveness, perhaps deconstruction "is" law more than it is justice.

Law then, in my argument, becomes the impossible combination of determination with all that is beyond determination. It cannot be simply or solely the principle of calculation, that which cuts into and renders the responsiveness of justice operative. Justice, responsiveness, responsibility—responsability, to adopt an archaic usage—also renders law operative. The legal decision must "be both regulated and without regulation: it must conserve the law and also destroy it or suspend it enough to have to reinvent it in each case, rejustify it, at least reinvent it in the reaffirmation and the new and free confirmation of its principle."[43] In this openness, the legal decision is not "just" in the sense of conforming to some "ideal" or to "the Good."[44] This justice is, rather, indwelling, something integral to law and as such it "is always very close to the bad, even to the worst for it can always be reappropriated by the most perverse calculation."[45]

Let me now link justice as integral to law with capital punishment and the arguments against capital punishment by looking at the probative foundation of those arguments—that is, by looking at the claim to a truth through knowledge. This is a knowledge of the deterrent impact of capital punishment or the lack of it, a knowledge of the impelling effects of social disadvantage on offenders, and so on. It is, in all, a knowledge of the truth behind capital punishment, of what "was really." A connection, hopefully not too tenuous, can be found here with "Force of Law" in the passing mention there of truth. Truth, for Derrida, seems to share the dual dimensions of justice. If infinite, incalculable justice is to be done, the "determinate knowledge" or "decidable knowledge" of law must be brought to bear on it; truth can then be seen as just or exactly right and apt—truth as *justesse*.[46] But the legal decision, or the cutting into incalculable justice, is also an opening out to that justice. It is in this incalculable dimension of justice that truth itself takes on another dimension, one that is within and needful of justice: "There is nothing more true than justice."[47] Justice, in its infinite going out to the other, takes truth with it. Truth becomes equally infinite, as it were, with justice and equally impossible of realization. But the truth accompanying justice is, like justice, "always very close to the bad even to the worst."[48] In the name of indivisible, complete knowledge, truth can putatively know the other, can "discover" the other and leave no space for an active alterity that would call for a giving response to the other. Such a truth would extinguish justice. Foucault, for one, was adept at discerning the bad and the worst in this truth with his explorations of the regimes of truth in modernity—their pervasion through the totality of social existence, their enactment in universalist "sciences of man and society." In the debate over capital punishment in *Foucault Live*, the knowledge that most concerns him is the psychiatric, with its ability in the trial to be a knowledge made "for cutting."[49] It cuts into the unfathomable complexity of legal judgment and presents itself as having the truth of a person.[50] The seeming exigency of law's truth can provide even more dramatic instances. Because Roger Coleman's appeal was filed three days late as a result of his lawyer's error, a federal court refused to hear his constitutional claim against conviction for murder and he was executed.[51]

It is only the finality imported by death that can produce the ultimately determined or determining decision. As we have already seen, "no existing, coded rule can . . . guarantee absolutely" what will be decided.[52] And what has been decided, judicially or legislatively, cannot stand apart in a determined or determining isolation. The decision cannot "be" in the world if it seeks merely to affirm or be affirmed in itself—if it has no connection, no relation to anything else. To maintain its "place" it must ever go beyond its own bounds and relate to all circumstance and possibility that would impinge on it.[53] Even, or especially, the most conservative, the most self-conserving, law or legal decision is a constant/repeated response to the challenge of difference. To assert invariant sameness in the face of challenging and uncontainable difference requires a responsiveness to all that is ever beyond. This responsiveness itself imports the capacity to change. Hence, law or the legal decision has constantly to destroy itself to stay itself. It has always to decompose in order to be composed. There is always something "rotten" in law—"something decayed or rotten . . . which condemns it or ruins it in advance."[54]

Such a responsiveness "in" law can never, then, be satisfied in terms of what is known. A determination based on knowledge cannot ever be complete in some final isolated resolution. Even if it could, we, being "within" knowledge, could never know it to be complete. Something could always come from beyond, something "more," and reveal our overconfident conclusion to be not so. We could begin to grasp that "more" in its relation to law by looking at it negatively. If determination were adequate or complete, there would be no place for decision or for judgment. Alternatively, there will always be "in" truth, or "in" justice, something beyond any particular or possible determination. There will always and at every moment (that is, at every point of impinging difference) be a demand for "fresh judgment."[55] It is in the very absence of determination, or in the presence of irresolution, that there is a demand for law and for legal judgment. The responsibility, or the responsability, involved in judgment cannot be accommodated within the determined or the known. There is always "in" it a "secret," a mystery, a "madness."[56] Being responsible, we may always judge contrary to what is indicated or suggested by what is known.

In modernity, the locus of this responsibility is taken to be the subject. Subjects, we say, are "free." They are not bound by the determined. They could always have done "more" or done other than what they did. This is the basis on which we as legal subjects can be held legally responsible for another or for what we do to another. To elevate society, the sovereign, the head definitively over the subject in its ability to deal death to the subject is to deny that subjectivity on which responsibility in law is founded. Not surprisingly, if we follow through the implication of this elevation, we arrive at the two notions of community predominant in the Occident. Both, in their insistence on commonality, would ultimately deny any place to the diversity of individual subjects. (It is not uncommon to find arguments about capital punishment being put in terms of the desirability or undesirability of individualism.)[57] With one of the two types of community, there is what we could call a vertical loss of the subject. Here a social totality or an encompassing totalitarianism is affirmed, and all differential subjectivity is absorbed into a sameness symbolized by the head. The other type of community was to deliver us from this. It is a type of liberal community where there is a lateral loss of the subject. Here commonality is secured in a conjoint individuality in which all "individuals" must act or be in the same way. In either situation, as Nancy says, "the fully realized person . . . is the dead person"—a person not having any distinct existence, a non-subject: society, in these renderings, becomes "a work of death."[58] To kill is, therefore, the apt expression of such a society.

In all, law's rottenness assumes a certain duplexity, and complexity. Law is rotten because it is always less than whole. It cannot be complete, fully determined, and fully determining, because it must ever extend beyond determination. It cannot be integral and achieved, because it must always be responsive to what is beyond. Law is also rotten, and less than itself, when it definitively denies this responsibility or responsability "in" itself by dealing death. And to deny this responsibility, as we have just seen, is to deny that subject which founds responsibility in law. The "law" that attends these denials is an impossibility—inanimate, a pure and desolate stasis. I will now follow that dismal and deranged scene into two of its more palpable, if not always palatable, locations—into the crowd at executions and into the rottenness of judicial discourse in the Supreme Court of the United States on the death penalty. The idea in doing this is to illustrate and further identify a lack of law when the putatively legal engages in capital punishment. And the point is, hopefully, reinforced by showing that it can be made in two such disparate locations.

Scenes from the Execution

If it were the case that dealing death is the supreme expression of the law, then we may expect the scene of execution to mark law at its most efficacious and assured. But it does not. Instead of a confident and maximal assertion, the scene of execution shows law as uncertain and vulnerable. The precise expectation that law will pointedly contain death, or manifest an instrumental dominion over it, is always frustrated. At first sight, however, tales of execution would not uniformly support that argument, for there is a relevant dispute among historians about how we may describe and interpret the behavior of crowds at the site of execution. To set this dispute I will take the monumental and in ways contrary accounts of capital punishment provided by Gatrell for England and by Evans for Germany, and I will extract a comparability between the two situations.[59] The disagreement, bluntly, is between the perception of the crowd as awed and orderly and the perception of it as resistant and riotous. My argument will accommodate both perceptions. The place of execution was an unsettled and uncertain zone for the crowd, a place where law's force of affirmation and legitimation no longer pertained. The crowd was transgressive, and to the extent that it was otherwise this was due to the presence of compensating modes of order—modes of the sacred and of official discipline. There is a preliminary problem in that firsthand accounts of the crowd which the historians use are themselves affected by the class, gender, and other positions of the tellers. To rely, for example, on descriptions of the crowd as being like children, women, or savages is not itself to accept that either the crowds or those to whom they are likened are accurately described. What in one view may be "loose and disorderly behaviour" will in another be highly focused and ordered.[60] But what subsists in both views is the transgressive nature of the behavior, and this is all that is needed for my argument. What abounds in the literature are indications that at the site of execution we are entering a place that is qualitatively different to what surrounds it. The ordinary rules somehow no longer apply, and it is uncertain what does. The void could be momentarily filled by a show of official force or by the straining solemnity of religious rituals, but there always remained a pervasion of illigitimacy and unease—a dis-ease. Gibbon Wakefield captured something of this: "Fail not to watch the people; the men, women and children, good, bad and indifferent, who have gathered to behold the sacred majesty of the law. You will see such flashing of eyes and grinding of teeth: you will hear sighs and groans, and words of rage and hatred . . . and then laughter, such as it is, of an unnatural kind, that will make you start; and jests on the dead, to turn you sick."[61] But perhaps what is most telling is the crowd's own perception of pathology. The crowd "seldom unambiguously affirmed [the] legitimacy" of the execution.[62] "Too often that despised crowd denounced justice as murderous in itself ": "Who was the murderer here? It was the crowd's question."[63] The question was posed in some particularly potent ways. The execution and its trappings were to exemplify supremely the law's awesome force but, despite doing this at times very effectively, the crowd also "saw through the law's pretentions more clearly than the polite people did, commenting sardonically on a tableau which they refused to accept as their own."[64] Pointedly, the state had to make its protective presence felt "when the offence had been against the sovereign" and extra precautions had to be taken by officialdom "at politically loaded executions."[65] The execution of an official could be an occasion for cheers but, contrarily, "there was never doubt as to where the crowd's sympathies lay when radicals or protestors were executed."[66]

Those in authority may have taken fleeting consolation in seeing the crowd's exuberance as "primal gratifications," or as "a collection of insensate lusts and hatreds," but, no matter how base the crowd's behavior was taken to be, it still meant that "the 'sordid assemblage of the lowest among the vulgar' mocked 'the awful sentence of the law.'"[67] The very presence of the transgressively uncowed countered law's claim to ultimate affirmation at the very point where it was supposed to be most manifest. Rather than a scene of assured legality, the place of execution was "a summons to all thieves and pickpockets, of both sexes . . . a free mart, where there is an amnesty for outlaws . . . one continued fair, for whores and rogues of the meaner sort."[68] It was an occasion of "low, black-guard merry-making" and a playing out of "quasi-erotic fantasies," and often more than quasi as well.[69] In all, "no sorrow, no salutary terror, no abhorrence, no seriousness; nothing but ribaldry, debauchery, levity, drunkenness, and flaunting vice in fifty other shapes."[70] But the attribution of 'perversion' and 'passions' to the crowd was at times simply a denial of the acuity of its protests.[71]

The sustaining simplicity of the argument so far has now to be made a little more complex. The historians would see the claim that transgression typifies the crowd in the shadow of the scaffold as at least overdone, and Foucault is usually advanced as the major culprit.[72] What happened, instead or as well, is that crowds respectably "consented" to the proceedings and these proceedings, in turn, successfully "implant[ed] the law's presence."[73] No matter what the vagaries of the English situation, where "public hangings . . . were squalid, hasty often chaotic affairs," in Germany and "in other European countries" the execution was a more ordered and acquiescent occasion.[74] But, as Evans tells us, execution riots did occur in Germany, and with increasing frequency from the early nineteenth century.[75] For my purposes, this divergence of perceptions about the crowd is productive rather than insuperable.

There is, I hope to show, little mystery in all this. The uncertainty in the literature is testament to the uncertainty at the scene of execution. It was not simply a matter of the crowd being consensual at one execution and resistant at another. There were also "strange but revealing fluxes in crowd behaviour at the scaffold."[76] "Coarse behaviour" could break out "at a whim."[77] To take another way of looking at it, if the crowd's behavior had been uniformly resistant, the public execution would soon cease to have much attraction for authority. Even in relation to the unruly English, Gatrell pours some scorn on those who would argue that "it was the populace, not the law, that controlled the scaffold arena."[78] My argument will suggest that it was neither and both. With its own infliction of death, the law can present only its naked determining force. Adequacy is the principle of law's operation, and in dealing death law becomes incomplete and inadequate. The crowd thus has a "space" in which to be effective as itself. Since neither the law nor the crowd could provide resolution, the outcome could only be persistently uncertain.

We could approach that outcome in another way by looking at the quality of the "consent" that the public execution was supposed to have secured. What passed for the crowd's support of law could be more volatile and qualified than it seemed. One trigger for the crowd's rebellion was the law's failure to be less than determinative in effecting death—when, for example, the execution was botched or there was a last-minute reprieve.[79] Traitors and "radicals," people whose offenses denied law's conclusiveness, were notably able to excite the crowd's sympathies, as were those bold criminals who exhibited defiance and panache on the scaffold.[80] Law's inhibition in dealing death could also be revealed in the recognition by those in authority that there was a limit to the number of executions "the people would tolerate."[81] And perhaps even more revealing of the limits on law as violence was the fact that "this insubordinate scaffold crowd touched the deepest anxieties of the polite classes."[82] The introduction of the guillotine into Germany initially foundered on élite aversion to its revolutionary association.[83]

The debate over the behavior of the crowd—"carnival or consent," to borrow Gatrell's chapter title[84]—confirms the chronic inadequacy of law when we come to consider a nice historical transition from consent to something more like carnival. Evans shows that the crowd was very much consensual at executions in Germany, and the evidence, he adds, is to the same effect "in other European countries."[85] But this consent was somewhat constrained. Not only was the crowd restricted by the considerable presence of officials and troops buttressing law's violence, but its energies were channeled into "the ritual and ceremonial aspects" of the execution, and especially into religious observances.[86] Decline in these compensatory modes was matched by increase in the rebelliousness of the crowd.[87]

And such modes were clung to by the crowd even after official support for them declined. One of the most influential arguments among the élite for ending public executions was that, even with the spread of post-Enlightenment rationality, executions remained a backwater of religious and folkish superstition. Whenever in Germany there was "a disruption of the symbolic economy of honour, magic, and religion that surrounded the execution," the crowd were "moved to protest."[88] Although Evans contrasts the unbridled English crowd with the German, contained as it was in elaborate ritual, Gatrell observes of English "gallows hanging" that "no ritual was so securely embedded in metropolitan or provincial urban life."[89] In both locations, the execution was saturated in exemplary religious ceremonial, and official religions were a mainstay of capital punishment.[90] Not every reliance on the sacred was for its stabilizing effects. Sometimes it could be purposively exploited in a semiotics of power: "By passing outside the city walls into the world beyond, the execution procession crossed a number of symbolic boundaries . . . between civilization and the wild, between the community and the outer world, between life and death. This symbolism was maintained in rural areas by the erection of scaffolds and gallows at crossroads or on the boundaries of districts or parishes."[91] The crowd itself made its own magico-religious contribution. The places of execution could be endowed by it with a consecrate aura and become a place of miracles and divine intervention.[92] Relics of the executed or of the event were prized—handkerchiefs dipped in the blood, strands unwound from the rope.[93] These relics were often ascribed the power of magical healing, as was stroking afflicted parts of the body with the hands of the executed; "the hanged or about-to-be-hanged were converted into mediators between death and life, and harnessed to good."[94]

But what of an administered world, to borrow the phrase, which admits of no such mediation, no transcendent reference, and tolerates no endemic rebelliousness? How can the law, left now to itself, cope with its own inadequacy and its own decomposition? How can it maintain a semblance of its necessary completeness and coherence? In engaging with these questions, I will look next at the judicial attempt in the United States Supreme Court to accommodate death to law and argue, of course, that the attempt reveals the pathological quality of law's relation to capital punishment that I have already delineated.

Legal Decision and What Death Does

A brief answer to the question of how law maintains its integrity in judicial discourse when dealing death could be that it does not. To put the impossible combination of law's two dimensions, the determinative and the responsive, in an apt setting, we could refer to Dworkin's paen to United States law for its vital ability always to be responsively other than what it "is"—to be incapable of finality.[95] The small problem with this is that such a law could never "be" anything. Law, as we saw, is also that which "is" finally. Roger Coleman's lawyer was three days late in lodging his appeal, and that, for Coleman, proved to be quite final.[96] This irresolution manifestly afflicts the Supreme Court's handling of death penalty cases. As we will see, the Court has become petulant and arbitrary in blocking appeals and reviews concerning the death penalty. In the Court's view, it would, without such drastic action, remain beleaguered by the endless machinations of death penalty lawyers and no case involving the death penalty would ever be resolved. But in other moments, the Court recognizes, at least implicitly, that it is not providing any percipient basis for resolving death penalty cases. The Court has for over twenty years repeatedly formulated the issue in irresolvable terms. These are terms that are well nigh indistinguishable from those encapsulating the earlier discussion of law and death, terms of an integral irresolution "in" law and in death between certain determination and complete responsiveness. So, repeatedly, the Court feels that in deciding on the death penalty there must be a response to "the uniqueness of the individual" or there must be "fundamental fairness." For these things an effective "discretion" must be exercised. But there is also a monotonous accompaniment: "unbridled discretion" produces "arbitrariness," and the sentencing decision must manifest determined "consistency" and "objectivity."[97] In all this we may readily concede that the Supreme Court aptly formulates the irresolution, even if it seems unstilled and at a loss when confronting it. It may, of course, be asking too much for a court of ultimate authority to confront law's ultimate irresolution. But the particular contribution of death here is that the confrontation becomes unavoidable.

Death, then, does make a difference. Law in its determining effect cannot be everything. Obviously it must choose and elevate some modes of existence and suppress or ignore others. So, to be more and aptly specific, law will give recognition to and sustain the mores of one ethnic or racial group and thereby subordinate those of another.[98] But law maintains its appeal to an-other by always being more than determined, by being ever able to be otherwise than what it determinately is. One day to come, *à venir,* law could actually be more and extend to the previously excluded. Death denies that promise. It effects a closure around the already determined and denies it the ability to be otherwise. So, in dealing death, law makes irremediable the exclusions that have gone to make it what it is. These exclusions are now revealed as intrinsically beyond law's reach. The very borders securing law and its domination can no longer be places of expansionary promise. Instead, they are turned around and become a ground challenging the law's rejections. Law's range is thus revealed as epistemically constrained in its truth, ethnocentrically exclusive in its favored populace, and so on. There is, then, point to that litany of complaint directed at capital punishment in its well-documented discriminations against the disadvantaged. Such discriminations are part of numberless other areas of law, but what peculiarly concentrates them in relation to the death penalty is that it has, to borrow a helpful judicial phrase, a "unique finality."[99] When it is not effected in death, law's finality can always be rendered less so. Law can always extend itself differently. But with the "unique finality" of death, law remains fixed and monotonously the same. It is revealed as intrinsically rejecting of the racially oppressed and the impoverished, and its decisions become axiomatically partial.[100]

None of which is, or can be, allowed to disrupt or dissolve the usual course of law. The death penalty is simply taken into law in its usual course, even if the resulting absurdities do indicate persistently that it should not be there. What law operatively does, or tries to do, is to fragment death's force in reifications of the process producing it. The form of judicial judgment, as an instance of the "metaphoric writing of the West," seeks to convey "the immediate vision of the thing, forced from the discourse which accompanied or even encumbered it."[101] So, for instance, law is able to constitute or determine "responsibility"—to determine the indeterminable. This is not only a matter of responsibility for the criminal act. It is also a matter of determining whether the "individual" responsibility of the defendant warrants a sentence of death—all of which takes a particular effrontery in the criminal trial, where responsibility's indetermination is close to manifest in the almost routine conflict in "expert" psychological ascriptions of responsibility and in the infinite vagaries of jury selection and decision making. "No one really knows what happens in the course of a trial."[102] The prospect of death intensifies our awareness that responsibility cannot be ascertained definitively. Rather than that awareness pervading all judging of responsibility, the direction of judicial thought is the reverse: responsibility can be determined generally in the judicial process, and the infliction of death is a particular consequence of such determination.[103] The death penalty then becomes one form of another distinct "thing" called punishment which simply follows the judgment. There are some supplementary tricks that would situate death within a norm of "punishment." One involves the idea of proportionality. There is the judicial requirement in elaborations of the Eighth Amendment that the death penalty not be disproportionate to the crime, or there is the use in many states of "proportionality review" to determine "whether the death penalty is excessive or disproportionate to the penalty imposed in similar cases."[104] This, obviously, is to assume that incomparable death can be brought into a proportionate relation to other forms of punishment— that it becomes generically the same as them. Another trick is to recognize that death is different but not too different by providing that, where there is a sentence of death, there should be something like a further step in the legal process to ensure that the death sentence is appropriate or justified.[105]

There is an even more audacious judicial trick played on death, however. This enfolds death into the "things" that make up the judicial process in such a way as to affirm their integrity. Let us take as an initial instance the idea of fairness, both as a general notion and as it inhabits the constitutional guarantee of the due process of law. I will look first at the invocation of fairness in two notable judicial condemnations of the death penalty. One comes from Justice Brennan in *Sawyer v. Whitley* (1992) where he "expressed" his "ever increasing scepticism that, with each new decision from this court constricting the ability of the Federal Courts to remedy constitutional errors, the death penalty can really ever be imposed fairly."[106] Here there is an implied affirmation: if the courts' ability were not so constricted, the death penalty could "really" be imposed fairly. For the other judicial condemnation, the stakes can be raised by invoking Justice Blackmun's famous dissent in *Callins v. Collins* (1994).[107] His tearing eloquence on that occasion has been much discussed but the basis of his objection is plain enough: error was inevitable, and so some defendants were going to be wrongly killed. But even this potent, if not unusual, point still imports a singular and knowable truth, which can be discovered in the absence of error. The death penalty would still remain apt when there is no error and, of course, more can or should be done to counter error and advance truth.[108] To take a commonly adduced example, there is the constant advocacy of "effective" legal representation in death penalty cases. But how can representation ever "be" fully effective? The constitutional guarantee of the due process of law leaves us in the same problematic. To apply due process to cases involving capital punishment is to say that there is—that there can "be"—a process that ensures all that is due to a person who is to die as a consequence of what that process determines. But such process is incapable of being "due" enough. Something of this inherent inadequacy can be detected in the oxymoron of that "super due process" considered apt for death penalty cases. If all that is "due" has been provided for, how can there be a supersaturated something still owing?

Of course, the imperative of law as determining always stands ready to negate the infinite demands of fairness, or of effective representation, or of what is procedurally due. This imperative tends to be rendered in death penalty cases as law's finality. My argument has been that law cannot be tied to finality and that when it purports to be it is less than law. Or, as it was put somewhat more positively, law is an impossible combination of determination with responsiveness—or, in other words, with nonfinality. The death penalty effects an hiatus between these, elevating an absolute determination over responsiveness. So, in *Herrera v. Collins* (1993): "Under Texas law, post-conviction evidence must be filed within thirty days of the end of the trial, but the evidence Herrera's attorneys believe would have acquitted him *was not available to him* until eight years later."[109] The Supreme Court upheld the determinative effect of the time limit, urging the petitioner instead to seek executive clemency, which he did, and then he was executed. A further and particularly telling example can be found in *Smith v. Kemp* (1983) and *Machetti v. Linham* (1983), both in the Supreme Court: "In a Georgia case two co-defendants were both sentenced to death in separate trials within a few weeks of each other in the same County. The composition of the juries in both of the trials violated constitutional standards. . . . The appellate lawyer for one of the co-defendants challenged the selection process and was granted a new trial, whereas the court appointed counsel for the second defendant was unaware of any basis for challenge and his client was sentenced to death and executed."[110]

Let me continue with what is becoming a conclusion by taking a famous example of finality so as to show how law is decomposed and made inadequate by the death penalty in its denial of law's responsiveness. This is *McCleskey v. Kemp* (1987), a death penalty case coming out of Georgia, like so many others.[111] Here the Supreme Court had to decide whether a death sentence on a black defendant was a violation of the constitutional guarantee of "equal protection of laws." Of course it is a common objection to the death penalty in the United States that it is racially discriminatory in its imposition, and in this case there was cogent evidence showing statistically that in Georgia black defendants were overwhelmingly discriminated against in the imposition of the death penalty. The court held, however, that violation of the constitutional guarantee could not be established unless there had been intentional racial discimination. But it is well known that the Supreme Court accepts a similar type of statistical evidence in proving or correcting racial discimination in other areas such as voting and employment. Doubtless, there are problems in these areas with accommodating such evidence to the law's characterstic modes of determination, but such an accommodation is effected in various ways. Death, however, is not so adjustable, and this kind of responsive possibility can hardly be made available in capital cases. If the evidence were to be allowed cogency in such cases, then the black defendant should never be executed. Comparable evidence would serve also to exempt people denied equal protection for other reasons, such as poverty. The outcome would be that only people not so discriminated against could be executed. An uncomfortable conclusion in itself. But immediately that solution is adopted, black and impoverished defendants are no longer being discriminated against so they could (continue to) be executed. But then the statistical evidence could again be resorted to so as to show they were being discriminated against and should not be executed. And so on. "Finality" thus produces a reductio ad absurdum. Another terminal variation can be found in *Vasquez v. Harris* (1994), where, in manifest desperation at the law's impertinent responsiveness, the Supreme Court proclaimed that "no further stays of Robert Alton Harris' execution shall be entered by the federal courts except upon order of this Court" — a diktat of primal violence aptly described as "lawless."[112]

Discourses of resistance to capital punishment can share these pertinacious judicial assumptions. These discourses can thence become hostages to fortune and be appropriated in the cause of capital punishment. There may be little choice in the matter. A defense lawyer cannot forego the strategy of evoking sympathy or empathy for a client on certain grounds simply because this implies that the death penalty could be apt in other cases where those grounds do not pertain. The literature on reform can also be caught in this discursive embrace. One of the most frequented arguments against the death penalty is that it has been shown in study after study to have no deterrent effect. But this is not an argument against the death penalty itself.

If, or to the extent that, studies were to show it had a deterrent effect, the logic of the objection would require that the death penalty be supported.[113] These difficulties do not only afflict utilitarian arguments but extend to the more humanitarian as well. For example, the American Bar Association would argue against imposing capital punishment on people under eighteen when the crime was committed: "The opposition is based on a recognition of the fact that minors are not fully mature, hence not fully responsible or culpable and are more likely to be capable of reform, thus rendering the death penalty a particularly inhuman punishment in their case."[114] Unless we accept law's necessarily strained truth that responsibility can be uniformly ascribed at a certain age, then the "base" of the opposition would require that those under eighteen at the commission of the crime be executed when it is shown that they were "fully responsible or culpable" and "[un]likely to be capable of reform." Likewise with the advocacy of procedural reform. It could hardly be denied that propensities for "error" in the processes of detection, prosecution and trial should be corrected.[115] But this can be taken as much in support of capital punishment as against: "progress towards a procedurally flawless legal process . . . may best serve the cause of retentionists."[116]

A broadly similar duplexity attends the efforts to legitimate or delegitimate capital punishment in some ultimately resolving way. God and savagery have been two of the main modes. Dismissing the death penalty as a primitive or savage survival manifestly has little effect on those for whom it remains the guarantee of civilization. And the strident assertions that God is for capital punishment could, with some diligence, be matched with revelations that "he" is not.[117] Resort to that contemporary equivalent of the sacred, to society, resolves matters no more successfully. The most cogent research into the social causes and effects of capital punishment coexists with the "expert" and other uses of social factors in ascribing responsibility and liability in capital cases. It coexists also with the general justification of the death penalty as an assertion or affirmation of "society."

All of which accords with my argument that there can be no end to all this, neither an ending nor some end in view. There is an inexorability, then, to the common conclusions that decisions about capital punishment "ultimately rest upon the subjective moral evaluations of prosecutors, juries, and judges" that any issue "concerning the death penalty is ultimately a matter for moral and political judgement."[118] Capital punishment cannot be opposed unambiguously in our knowledge of what it "really" is. It may be opposed more assuredly in our never being able to know.

Notes

Heartfelt thanks to Colin Perrin for making many connections, to Brian Simpson for very apt references at very apt moments, to Mariana Valverde and Hans Mohr for insightful comment, and to Hester Magnuson for a telling point. And particularly poignant thanks to Austin Sarat for the generous invitation to contribute and for insisting that I had something to say about capital punishment when that ability was not conspicuous.

1. Michel Foucault, *Discipline and Punish: The Birth of the Prison*, trans. Alan Sheridan (Harmondsworth: Penguin, 1979).

2. Hugo Adam Bedau, "The United States of America," in *Capital Punishment, Global Issues and Prospects*, ed. Peter Hodgkinson and Andrew Rutherford (Winchester: Waterside Press, 1996). The "unconquerable hope" comes from Arnold's "The Scholar Gypsy."

3. Roger Hood, *The Death Penalty: A World-Wide Perspective* (Oxford: Clarendon Press, 1996).

4. Austin Sarat, "Narrative Strategy and Death Penalty Advocacy," *Harvard Civil Rights–Civil Liberties Law Review* 31 (1996): 353.

5. Ibid.

6. For examples see ibid., 359 n. 28.

7. See, e.g., Richard J. Evans, *Rituals of Retribution: Capital Punishment in Germany 1600–1987* (Oxford: Oxford University Press, 1996), 893–894 and generally.

8. Hugo Adam Bedau as quoted in Larry W. Koch and John F. Galliher, "Michigan's Continuing Abolition of the Death Penalty and the Conceptual Components of Symbolic Legislation," *Social and Legal Studies* 2 (1993): 323, 327.

9. Walter K. Skeat, *A Concise Etymological Dictionary of the English Language* (New York: Capricorn, 1963), 75.

10. Foucault, *Discipline and Punish*, 49.

11. *Henry IV, Part Two* III: 2.

12. John Locke, "The Second Treatise of Government," in *Two Treatises of Government* (New York: New American Library, 1965), 308, para. 3.

13. For the Durkheim half in this perspective see David Garland, *Punishment and Modern Society: A Study in Social Theory* (Oxford: Oxford University Press, 1990), 26, 35, 42–43.

14. Immanuel Kant, *The Metaphysical Elements of Justice*, trans. John Ladd (Indianapolis: Bobbs-Merrill, 1965), 331–333.

15. Walter Benjamin, "Critique of Violence," in *One Way Street and Other Writings*, trans. Edmund Jephcott (London: New Left Books, 1979), 140.

16. Jacques Derrida, "Force of Law: 'The Mystical Foundations of Authority'," trans. Mary Quaintance, in *Deconstruction and the Possibility of Justice*, ed. Drucilla Cornell et al. (New York: Routledge, 1992), 42.

17. The story of capital punishment and of the extent of its use cannot be rendered in terms of progressive advance: see Harry Potter, *Hanging in Judgment: Religion and the Death Penalty in England* (New York: Continuum, 1993), 1, and for a strong "case" see Evans, *Rituals of Retribution*.

18. Maurice Blanchot, *The Step Not Beyond*, trans. L. Davis (Albany: SUNY Press, 1992), 24–25.

19. Derrida, "Force of Law," 42, 45.

20. See Maire Jaanus, "'A Civilization of Hatred': The Other in the Imaginary," in *Reading Seminars I and II: Lacan's Return to Freud*, ed. Richard Felstein et al. (Albany: SUNY Press, 1996), 344–345, 347.

21. Blanchot, *The Step Not Beyond*, 24, for the quotation.

22. Derrida, "The Force of Law."

23. Austin Sarat, "Bearing Witness and Writing History in the Struggle against Capital Punishment," *Yale Journal of Law and the Humanities* 8 (1996): 451.

24. Ibid., 451, 460.

25. Ibid., 461.

26. Ibid., 462.

27. Derrida, "Force of Law," 27.

28. Ibid., 16.

29. Ibid., 16, 23.

30. Derrida says this of the violence originating law but there is, he would add, this originating element in every legal decision: ibid., 14, 43–45.

31. Ibid., 23, 24.

32. Ibid., 7. The implications are considerable. Blanchot, in identifying what flows from "the infinite that comes to me from man as *autrui*," says that "it could engage us in a denunciation . . . of nearly all Western philosophies, at least those that subordinate justice to truth or only take as being just a reciprocity of relations." *The Infinite Conversation*, trans. Susan Hanson (Minneapolis: University of Minnesota Press, 1993), 58.

33. Jacques Derrida, *Specters of Marx*, trans. Peggy Kamuf (New York: Routledge, 1994), 177.

34. Derrida, "Force of Law," 15, 21.

35. Ibid., 15–16.

36. Jacques Derrida, "Limited Inc abc . . . ," *Glyph* 2 (1977): 162.

37. Derrida, "Force of Law," 25–26; and Jacques Derrida, "Cogito and the History of Madness," in *Writing and Difference* (London: Routledge, 1978).

38. Derrida, "Force of Law," 28.

39. Ibid.

40. Ibid.

41. Cf. Jean-Luc Nancy, *The Inoperative Community*, trans. Peter Connor (Minneapolis: University of Minnesota Press, 1991), 42.

42. Derrida, "Force of Law," 28, his emphasis.

43. Ibid., 23.

44. Cf. Sarat, "Narrative Strategy," 356–357; and Sarat, "Bearing Witness," 458.

45. Derrida, "Force of Law," 28.

46. Ibid., 16, 27, 56.

47. Ibid., 27. This is not strictly a quotation but a translation of Derrida's sentence "La justice, y a qu'ça de vrai."

48. Ibid., 28.

49. Michel Foucault, *Foucault Live*, trans. John Johnston (New York: Semiotext(e), 1989); cf. Michel Foucault, *Language, Counter Memory, Practice: Selected Essays and Interviews*, trans. Donald F. Bouchard and Cherry Simon (Ithaca: Cornell University Press, 1977), 154.

50. Foucault, *Foucault Live*, ch. 14.

51. Coleman v. Thompson, 111 S. Ct. 2546 (1991).

52. Derrida, "Force of Law," 26.

53. Ibid., 38, and Derrida, "Limited Inc."

54. Derrida, "Force of Law," 39.

55. Ibid., 26.

56. Ibid.; and Jacques Derrida, *The Gift of Death*, trans. David Wills (Chicago: University of Chicago Press, 1995), ch. 1.

57. See, e.g., Evans, *Rituals of Retribution*, 625–626, 902.

58. Nancy, *Inoperative Community*, 13, 17.

59. V. A. C. Gatrell, *The Hanging Tree: Execution and the English People, 1770–1868* (Oxford: Oxford University Press, 1994); and Evans, *Rituals of Retribution*.

60. Cf. E. P. Thompson, *Customs in Common* (London: Merlin Press, 1991), ch. 4.

61. Gatrell, *Hanging Tree*, 76.

62. Ibid., 99.

63. Ibid., viii, 606, 608.

64. Ibid., 608.

65. Ibid., 98–99.

66. Ibid., 103.

67. Ibid., 32, 603; and Evans, *Rituals of Retribution*, 209–210.

68. Gatrell, *Hanging Tree*, 59.

69. See ibid., 74, 604.

70. See ibid., 60.

71. See ibid., 609.

72. That is Foucault, *Discipline and Punish*.

73. Evans, *Rituals of Retribution*, 876; and Gatrell, *Hanging Tree*, 90.

74. Evans, *Rituals of Retribution*, 106–107.

75. Ibid., 195.

76. Gatrell, *Hanging Tree*, 75.

77. Evans, *Rituals of Retribution*, 263.

78. Gatrell, *Hanging Tree*, 90.

79. Ibid., 50, 68; and Evans, *Rituals of Retribution*, 220.

80. Gatrell, *Hanging Tree*, 30, 98–99, 103.

81. Ibid., 103.

82. Ibid., 56; and see Evans, *Rituals of Retribution*, 202.

83. Evans, *Rituals of Retribution*, 221.

84. Gatrell, *Hanging Tree*, 90.

85. Evans, *Rituals of Retribution*, 106–107.

86. Ibid., 107, 881.

87. E.g. ibid., 209–210.

88. Ibid., 195.

89. Ibid., 107; and Gatrell, *Hanging Tree*, 30.

90. Evans, *Rituals of Retribution*, 902; and Potter, *Hanging in Judgment*.

91. Evans, *Rituals of Retribution*, 78.

92. Gatrell, *Hanging Tree*, 30, 81, 89.

93. Ibid., 69; and Evans, *Rituals of Retribution*, 307.

94. Gatrell, *Hanging Tree*, 80–81 and Evans, *Rituals of Retribution*, 195.

95. Ronald Dworkin, *Taking Rights Seriously* (London: Duckworth, 1977), ch. 8.

96. See Hood, *The Death Penalty*, 23.

97. Justice Blackmun's dissent in Callins v. Collins, 114 S. Ct. 1127 (1994), provides a good coverage in these terms.

98. See e.g. Peter Goodrich, *Languages of Law: From Logics of Memory to Nomadic Masks* (London: Weidenfeld and Nicolson, 1990), ch. 6.

99. See Peter Hodgkinson et al., *Capital Punishment in the United States of America: A Review of the Issues* (London: Parliamentary Human Rights Group, 1996), 18.

100. Cf. ibid., 19, 26; and Norman Mailer, *Executioner's Song* (London: Arrow Books, 1979), 374–375, 399.

101. Jacques Derrida, *Dissemination*, trans. Barbara Johnson (Chicago: Chicago University Press, 1981), 189–190.

102. Foucault, *Foucault Live*, 158.

103. Reversing the dynamic, it could be said that the "absolute immanence" of responsibility or its becoming "fully realized" encompasses the death of those held responsible: cf. Nancy, *Inoperative Community*, 12–13. Yet we seem unable to face the consequences of such an absolute or monadic responsibility. If its inevitable arbitrariness is translated into purely statistical calculations about who should be convicted and executed, the reaction is one of horror: Ian Hacking, *The Taming of Chance* (Cambridge: Cambridge University Press, 1990), ch. 11. Our sentimentality in this is revealed through the ready acceptance of no less arbitrary outcomes in convicting and killing. For example, the psychological sciences in one

age would justify the execution of the "degenerate" criminal, yet in another these sciences would constitute moral unfitness as excuse or mitigation. Another example: we attach execution to responsibility monadically but there is often a sharp diversity of judicial views in a case. Difference is eliminated by voting, and, for good measure, it will not always be a view of the majority of the judges eventually involved in a case that prevails.

104. See Hood, *The Death Penalty*, 152; and Gregg v. Georgia 428 U.S. 153 (1976), at 183. Dastur writes of "the magnitude of death, that respect in which it refuses to be thought, pondered, weighed according to any system of equivalences." It is "incomparable with other kinds of knowledge because it exposes us to the immeasurability of something we can never experience." Françoise Dastur, *Death: An Essay on Finitude*, trans. John Llewelyn (London: Athlone, 1996), 3–4.

105. See Hood, *The Death Penalty*, 199–120, 126.

106. See Hodgkinson et al., *Capital Punishment in the United States*, 25.

107. 114 S. Ct. 1127 (1994).

108. Cf. Hodgkinson et al., *Capital Punishment in the United States*, 14.

109. Michael L. Radelet et al., *In Spite of Innocence, Erroneous Convictions in Capital Cases* (Boston: Northeastern University Press, 1992), xii, their emphasis. This was a stunning addition made to the preface in 1994—while the book was still in press, it would seem. In pointing out the aptness of executive clemency in this case, the Supreme Court had referred to this study, presumably in manuscript. However, as the authors point out, "[T]he Court failed to mention the twenty-three cases we record in which no clemency was granted and a defendant we believe to have been innocent was executed." Ibid.

110. See Hodgkinson et al., *Capital Punishment in the United States*, 12.

111. Ibid., 29–30.

112. See Evan Caminker and Erwin Chermerinsky, "The Lawless Execution of Robert Alton Harris," *Yale Law Journal* 102 (1992): 225, 246–252. Comparable desperation can be found in defences of this draconic prohibition. As Judge Kozinski opined, "[T]he drama had no other possible outcome" and, in the ultimate tautology, "enough is enough": see Alex Kozinski, "Tinkering with Death," *New Yorker*, February 10, 1997: 48, 50–51.

113. Even short of this revelation, reliance on knowledge always leaves scope for contest. Counterinstances can be adduced where deterrence did "work," putatively superior forms of knowledge such as common sense can be advanced, and so on.

114. See Hodgkinson et al., *Capital Punishment in the United States*, 43. The sentiment is, of course, standard. It also serves to impart an invariant responsibility to those over eighteen, or whatever age is chosen, in the absence of cogent evidence to the contrary.

115. Cf. Radelet et al., *In Spite of Innocence*, xii and 280.

116. Hodgkinson and Rutherford, "Introduction," 14, and see Mailer, *The Executioner's Song*, 920.

117. Cf. Koch and Galliher, "Michigan's Continuing Abolition," 328.

118. Hood, *The Death Penalty*, 157–158, 162.

· 6 ·

THE EXECUTIONER'S DISSONANT SONG: ON CAPITAL PUNISHMENT AND AMERICAN LEGAL VALUES

FRANKLIN E. ZIMRING

This essay concerns the implications of the practice of capital punishment on American legal values and procedures. I argue that a conflict between the death penalty and legal values takes place at three levels. First, any death penalty conflicts with substantive principles of human dignity in obvious ways. This is why proponents of the penalty avoid phrasing their arguments as if basic questions of the constitution of government were at issue. Second, attempts to reduce the delays that bog down executions necessarily undermine the integrity of the legal process in death penalty cases. Third, the compromises made to speed up executions threaten respect for due process throughout the criminal justice system in jurisdictions that execute. The conflict about executions in the United States is not, in this view, a temporary phenomenon associated with a transition toward executing prisoners as business-as-usual. Instead, the clash between the operational needs of an execution system and the principles and procedures of American legal culture is fundamental. Either the basic rules and values will change or the practice of execution will remain infrequent, conflict-laden, and problematic. Capital punishment can only come to be regarded as normal state behavior by reimagining fundamental principles of fairness in criminal justice.

The first part of this essay will contrast two ways of characterizing capital punishment—as a discrete subsystem in the criminal justice system or as a system that is an important element of the environment of government. I will argue that only a conception of executions as a central aspect of government can explain recent American legal history. The second section examines two recent cases before the U.S. Supreme Court to illustrate the pressure that facilitating executions places on legal sentiments and values. The third section discusses some ripple effects from the rules made to serve the operational imperatives of capital punishment to the values governing the larger realm of criminal procedure. The precedents, both legal and moral, in the recent judicial and legislative career of capital punishments cast a wide shadow over American legal values.

I. A Question of Principle or of Crime Control?

Listen closely to the debate about the death penalty in the United States and you will discover a disagreement about where the practice is located in a map of American values and practices. Proponents of execution favor a specific and discrete conception of capital punishment: to them it is a question of the appropriate sanction to be imposed on the most serious form of murder, a matter of principal importance to one part of the administration of criminal justice. By contrast, the abolitionists see the impact of executions as a statement of pervasive importance about the relationship between the government and the individual. Abolitionists in the United States view capital punishment as a fundamental political issue; proponents usually assert that the question is neither fundamental nor political.

While this is just one way in which the disputants talk past each other in the capital punishment debate, this particular disagreement helps to explain other aspects of the capital punishment dispute. Proponents of capital punishment speak the language of local option and states' rights not only because this insulates the pro–capital punishment orientation of most state governments from federal review, but also because states and localities are the levels of government that usually hold power over ordinary criminal justice decisions. State legislatures, local prosecutors and judges, and the particular values of specific communities are supposed to shape criminal justice outcomes. National government and constitutional values have little direct influence on most punishment decisions. If the availability of death as a criminal punishment were a garden-variety choice of punishment option, state and local power over them would be consistent with an important American tradition. If, on the other hand, one regards capital punishment as a fundamental moral and political question, the national government and constitutional values are the appropriate vehicles for decisions.

The proper way of characterizing the death penalty may be an important question but it is not a difficult one. Our history, the recent history of other developed nations, and even the importance that the proponents of the penalty attach to it are powerful evidence that the death penalty is an issue of transcendent importance, one that is principally moral and political.

A. A *Singular American History*

In American history, this ultimate penalty has been singled out for special treatment for more than a century. Special procedures ranging from direct appeal to gubernatorial involvement in the clemency process antedate the involvement of federal courts in death cases by many decades. The death penalty has also been a focus of special efforts at abolition since the mid-nineteenth century. A significant number of American states rejected capital punishment by the 1920s, and these states have not reversed course. This creates a long-standing division among American states on the use of a punishment, a division that is absent with the use of other punishments such as fines, probation, and incarceration. There is almost nothing in the American history of the death penalty that supports regarding it as merely a criminal justice policy. Only the fact that individual states retained power to choose their own destinies can be enlisted in support of a parochialist interpretation.

By the 1960s, the U.S. Supreme Court had acknowledged what a considerable history in the several states had long before established: death is different in a qualitative way from other criminal sanctions. The belated entry of the national government and of constitutional standards to the capital punishment controversy built on an extensive history in the culture and in state government that regarded the death penalty as an issue that transcended the normal boundaries of criminal justice.

B. What the Neighbors Are Thinking

A second demonstration of the transcendent nature of the death penalty comes from the recent history of the issue in the other major Western industrial nations. In the first generation after the end of the Second World War, the abolition of the death penalty went from being a minority position to a uniform policy in Western Europe and Scandinavia, as well as the industrial nations of the British Commonwealth.

At every stop along this road, the cavalcade of abolition was a movement based on human rights concerns and limitation of state power, rather than an adjustment in criminal justice policy. Indeed, one of the most remarkable elements of the transition in Europe from execution to abolition was how quickly an abhorrence of the executioner became the moral orthodoxy in nations that had recently endorsed capital punishment as state policy.

The English, for example, imposed a five-year moratorium on executions in 1965 that public opinion opposed and only ended the penalty in 1970. As recently as 1984, the Thatcher government had proposed reintroducing death for terrorist murder. By the late 1980s and early 1990s, however, the obscenity of executions was a British moral dogma deemed fit for export to the United States. The London-based Amnesty International campaign to achieve an end to the death penalty in the United States through moral education was the kind of missionary intervention in domestic American policies that had previously been observed only on issues like slavery and race. The Amnesty program is not regarded as eccentric in the United Kingdom or in Europe. In Italy, both the Pope and Italian public opinion were involved in a campaign to secure a stay of execution for a Virginia prisoner. When a stay was granted, the news "was greeted with applause in the Italian parliament."[1] This shows that the relatively recent abolition of the death penalty has hardened into a broadly supported moral orthodoxy in short order. In the late 1980s, the United States was considered as ripe for missionary labors because the death penalty was regarded as an issue of fundamental political morality and the right answer to the question was by then considered obvious.

From a European perspective, the failure of some Americans to acknowledge the fundamental character of the capital punishment question would be considered a rhetorical version of willful blindness, a perverse refusal to confront the obviously essential quality of the question of whether the state might permissibly use death as the intentional punishment for those who disobey important state commands.

C. The Proponent's Contradiction

That European perspective may be correct. One of the most significant problems encountered by those who would classify the death penalty as an operational criminal justice issue is the way that proponents of the penalty put substantial emphasis on the issue despite its very limited practical effect. Executions in the twentieth century have never reached a level that is even 1 percent of our current rates of criminal homicide, and executions have averaged less than one-fifth of 1 percent of homicides in the 1990s. To expect a punishment so limited to make a major dent in crime would make the miracle of the loaves and fishes seem modest.

Yet this rarely used sanction is a hot button issue for political actors, at least as important as any other issue in crime and justice in any state where change in policy is a real possibility. Does not this inflated emphasis on a little-used sanction show that the important stakes are symbolic, an affirmation of state authority in an ultimate sense? And does not this symbolic importance imply that the center of the debate is the morality of state execution?

The fundamental character of the issue of capital punishment is so obvious that attempts to see this debate as anything other than centered on the proper power and limits of government should cause us to carefully examine the psychological need for denial. One motive for denial is to avoid the jurisdictional consequences of finding the death penalty a fundamental moral issue. Such a characterization favors a national level of government to decide such a basic issue and constitutional principles to be the basis for a decision. But there is also a substantive problem that makes proponents of execution reluctant to discuss fundamental values as first and foremost. This reluctance may be fueled by an intuition that discussing the state's claim to execute as a general instrument of state policy is inconsistent with American skepticism about government and high regard for the value of the individual. If so, the best way to argue for capital punishment is to avoid a context of fundamental value and to focus instead on the operational necessity of executions.

But concentrating on the operational necessity for execution stirs up more trouble. The remaining sections of this essay will explore the conflict between the operational needs for execution and the demands of American legal values about fairness and judicial review by considering two recent cases before the United States Supreme Court and then discussing the way in which the operational needs of a capital punishment system may subvert due process and fairness values broadly throughout the criminal justice system.

II. Two Hard Cases

When the U.S. Supreme Court refused in 1987 to question a disproportionate rate of death sentences when the victim was white as unconstitutional,[2] the difficult and divisive wholesale constitutional challenges to capital punishment were thought to have been exhausted.[3] Eight years of Reagan appointments had created a Court more favorably disposed toward sustaining capital sanctions than had been seen in Washington for a generation. The Bush years produced even more movement toward a Court sympathetic to what had been called "deregulating death."[4] By the early 1990s, all of the *Furman v. Georgia* majority Justices had been replaced, and the balance of the Court had shifted substantially to the right. The conventional wisdom was that the legal challenge to capital punishment lacked both a broad issue to bring before the Court and a judicial constituency on the Court willing to entertain objections to executions. If ever a practice seemed safe from judicial embarrassment, it was capital punishment in the 1990s.

But major threats to the operational efficiency of executions do continue, and the United States Supreme Court has been forced to embrace rather extreme doctrine to protect the execution policies of the states from debilitating legal requirements. After showing why hard cases continue, I shall examine two recent examples of the extremes apparently motivated by the necessity to protect the operation of a capital punishment system.

A. *The Frustrating Impact of Delay*

What makes capital punishment a particular problem for criminal justice is that any pending legal challenge delays the imposition of the punishment. By contrast, a term of imprisonment normally begins right after sentencing, and jail confinement often starts after arrest. Even the most protracted appeal process in such circumstances usually does not postpone punishment. So keeping the legal process involved in the case is costless from the perspective of assuring the imposition of imprisonment. The prisoner is not winning a battle against the state as a function of the appeal.

But no meaningful legal appeal can proceed without delay in the schedule of an execution. Even though the prisoner remains in custody, the punishment provided for the crime will not be imposed as long as any part of the review of the case is not complete. From the district attorney's perspective, then, there may be little cost when the imprisoned offender pursues an appeal, because the penal objective of the state is not frustrated. But when legal processes delay executions, the penal objectives of the state are delayed and even frustrated. From the district attorney's perspective, the condemned prisoner is winning a contest with the state as long as he or she lives.

This situation creates two instrumental incentives in the appellate legal process. First, it encourages any defendant who wishes to avoid execution to do so by prolonging the legal process. Second, it makes the state representatives anxious to bring the legal review process to a close. As long as the appeal process is active, the state's penal purposes are frustrated. This situation produces a special hostility to the judicial review of capital punishment that is not present for imprisonment.

So what is really a tug-of-war about the timing of execution is transformed into a competition between the state and the condemned prisoner to control the timing of judicial review. The defendant desires reversal, or at least delay, while the state is frustrated by any extension of time to facilitate review. This frustrating consequence of delay is at the heart of the competition between capital punishment and legal values. In such circumstances, the objective of a capital punishment regime must be to minimize the scrutiny of the legal system and to make the review process as short as possible.

PENRY   All of this is a necessary introduction to the Supreme Court decision in the case of *Penry v. Lynaugh*, decided in June 1989. Johnny Paul Penry was convicted of rape murder in Texas and sentenced to death. While twenty-two years old at the time of the crime, the defendant "had the mental age of a six-and-a-half year old," which meant that "he has the ability to learn and the learning or the knowledge of the average six-and-a-half year old kid." Penry's social maturity, or ability to function in the world, was that of a nine or ten year old."[5]

The defendant pressed two claims in the Supreme Court. First, he argued that it was unconstitutional to refuse his request for a jury instruction that his mental retardation could be considered as a mitigating circumstance. Second, the defendant asked the Court to rule that it would be cruel and unusual punishment under the Eighth Amendment to execute a mentally retarded person with Penry's level of impaired function.

The *Penry* case split the Court into three camps. Four Justices would have rejected both the need for an instruction and the defendant's per se Eighth Amendment claim. Four of their colleagues would have held that the execution of retarded persons like Penry would violate the Eighth Amendment. Justice O'Connor broke this deadlock by accepting the constitutional need for a mitigation instruction to the jury, but rejecting Penry's Eighth Amendment claim.

The O'Connor opinion is a puzzle. This Justice had earlier led the Court in concluding that the execution of a person for a crime committed when not yet sixteen would be an Eighth Amendment violation. Why not a per se rule for a defendant with abilities and controls less than those of the average ten-year-old? Even though the concept of "mental age" is rather arbitrary, the gap between Johnny Penry and normal seems wide enough for a per se rule. And Justice O'Connor's opinion in *Penry* is not unsympathetic to the arguments for an Eighth Amendment ban. Indeed, Justice Stevens who dissented on this issue saw no need to outline the reason for his conclusion because he believed that Justice O'Connor's opinion (to the opposite result) "adequately and fairly states the competing arguments respecting capital punishment of mentally retarded persons."[6]

What then is the special danger of per se rules on this subject to Justice O'Connor? One answer to this question may be the potential of delays in large numbers of cases if an Eighth Amendment ban on executing the retarded were announced. Reversing in *Penry* because of a trial court's failure to give a requested instruction on mental retardation does not affect the judicial prospects of many capital defendants. Holding that mental deficiencies can bar execution could (and likely would), however, add a new layer of litigation onto a large number of cases where brain damage or subnormal intelligence is present. There are many such cases. Even if the number of cases that eventually met the constitutional standard was small, the volume of cases where more litigation and more delay would result could be much larger. This possibility is nowhere discussed in Justice O'Connor's opinion, but its role as a subtext is one of few plausible explanations for the O'Connor vote.

The potential for delay certainly distinguishes retardation from objectively uncontrovertible factors such as chronological age, where only eligible defendants could benefit from a new legal rule. With no bright line between borderline and profoundly retarded adults and many hundreds of death row inmates who suffer from substantial cognitive deficits, the threat of a per se exemption for the retarded to the operation of a capital punishment system is by no means trivial. Excluding defendants who had not raised the issue at trial would seem morally objectional. Sorting out deserving from nondeserving claims on the merits would take years. So allowing the Eighth Amendment exemption would produce delay and extra litigation. This is one important way in which the rule on chronological age is less troublesome than a rule on mental retardation.

But not allowing such an exemption compromises the substantive claim that this ultimate penalty is reserved for only the most blameworthy criminal defendants. Nowhere in the opinions of the *Penry* case is there any argument to the effect that Johnny Penry is more culpable than a fifteen-year-old who murders, or than a fully competent rapist who is exempted by the Eighth Amendment from the death penalty because no death occurred as a result of his acts.

Penry shows us the two contrasting levels of analysis discussed in section I passing each other in the night. The operational danger of setting up a new categorical target for postconviction litigators to aim for is quite real. The substantive problem of allowing the ultimate penalty for a person profoundly disabled in judgment and cognitive ability is equally severe. A tidy moral system will bog down in the extra hearings many defendants will gain. An operationally efficient capital punishment system will be morally compromised by its failure to protect those undeserving of death. These are the kind of hard choices that produce sharp and close divisions among Justices confronting a dilemma.

HERRERA   The clash between operational necessity and moral legitimacy is even more evident in the 1993 decision of *Herrera v. Collins*.[7] The petitioner in *Herrera* had been convicted of the murder of a police officer and sentenced to death in 1982. Ten years later, after exhausting state remedies and fully prosecuting one federal habeas corpus petition, Herrera brought another federal habeas action alleging that he had proof of his actual innocence of the crime for which he was sentenced to death. He argued that executing a person for a crime he did not commit would constitute cruel and unusual punishment under the Eighth Amendment, and that he was entitled to one evidentiary hearing to establish the existence of his innocence. The federal district court ruled that a hearing was in order on this claim.

The Court's opinion, by the Chief Justice, rejected Herrera's claim without deciding the question of whether the execution of an innocent person would constitute an Eighth Amendment violation: "We may assume, for the sake of argument in deciding this case, that in a capital case a truly persuasive demonstration of 'actual innocence' made after a trial would render the execution of a defendant unconstitutional, and warrant federal habeas corpus relief if there were no state avenue open to process such a claim."[8]

The opinion then holds that the proof offered by the defendant falls short of such a "persuasive demonstration" and therefore does not require the Court to decide whether the assumed constitutional standard should become an actual constitutional rule.

Two concurring opinions joined in by three Justices go further in supporting some constitutional protection against the execution of the probably innocent defendant, so that one might count as many as six of the nine Justices as supporting some form of Eighth Amendment protection in extreme cases.

But why is the concession that executing the innocent might be a constitutional error so grudgingly made by all but the three dissenters? Why are the proper procedural channels and waiver rules so important not only to Justices Scalia and Thomas (who reject any constitutional protection), but also to the Chief Justice, who will only "assume for the sake of argument" that there is some constitutional problem with hanging the wrong man?

What we have here is a head-on collision between the operating needs of the capital punishment system and the sentiments and norms of Anglo-American criminal justice. As a substantive matter, nothing could be worse for a criminal justice system in the United States than the execution of an innocent person. No matter the procedural history that might precede such an event, no set of circumstances would seem to justify or excuse the outcome. But that means the strongest appeal for last-gasp hearings and procedures is to save the innocent from execution.

A rule that provided a right to a fresh hearing when new evidence might cast doubt on guilt would provide a procedural avenue of delay that most death row inmates would try to use. The true measure of the impact of such a new hearing is not the few reversals that will result but the scores of two-year delays that will be tacked on at the end of a long and convoluted process.

In *Herrera*, the Court could not forthrightly endorse a basic sentiment of American justice without placing the efficient performance of the capital punishment system in substantial jeopardy. This is the only plausible explanation for the ambivalent and indecisive analysis of most of the majority justices in *Herrera* on a basic issue of principle.

B. An Inherent Conflict?

Is the conflict between legal values of fairness and certainty and the operational needs of a capital punishment system inevitable? As a logical matter, the answer to this question is no. The primary conflict is between delay and the perceived needs of a system that executes. And there are two ways that the current system's problems might be avoidable, but neither path away from the conflict is likely in the United States.

One path out of the conflict would be to reduce the amount of time necessary to assure just outcomes in capital trials and appeals. Since it is only the passage of time that prejudices the capital punishment system, why not invest resources in excellent lawyers, quick trials, and expeditious appeals in capital cases? With enough resources in place, just outcomes might also be swift enough so that the objectives of the capital punishment system are not compromised.

There are three problems with this formula for faster justice in capital cases. First, the political units that maintain criminal justice systems with capital punishment are unwilling to make the heavy investment in defense services that faster, high-quality justice would require, and this is particularly true of the states where death sentences and executions are most common. Massive investments in the defense at trial and initial appeal of capital cases would be required in states like Texas, Georgia, Virginia, Florida, Arkansas, and Alabama. Nothing could be further from the priorities of most of those who hold executive and legislative power in such places.

Second, the insufficient judicial and lawyer resources available at the state level limit the potential for swift and effective appellate review. In California, finding appellate counsel for direct appeal in capital cases takes four or five years. Even the perfunctory version of appeal that has emerged in California during the last decade takes many years to accomplish and dominates the agenda of the state supreme court. As long as the number of capital cases remains large, the scale of the enterprise will require that careful review of death cases will consume extra time because of the limited resources available for judicial review.

A third impediment to swift but careful justice in capital cases is the lack of quality control capacity in the federal courts. Federal district courts now are discouraged from the kind of scrutiny that could assure the fairness of accelerated state appeal processes.

With more than three thousand persons on death row, limited appellate and judicial review resources would still probably mean that best case trial and appeal systems would produce a ten-year lag between trial and execution if the defendant wishes to delay death. A delay of that length would generate the same frustration and aggression currently on display. So limiting the acceleration of the process to procedures that would assure fairness would not reduce the anger and hostility of prosecutors about judicial review.

There is one other possible method of ending the conflict between the needs of capital punishment systems and the time required to ensure fair trial and review processes. Why not redefine the penal objectives of capital punishment systems so that delay in execution would not be regarded as a fatal flaw? When considering the retributive, incapacitative, or deterrent functions of capital punishment, it is not clear that an execution must quickly follow trial to achieve the effect desired for it. In Japan, where the government controls the timing of executions without aggressive judicial intervention, there are time gaps as great or greater between the start of a criminal trial and the execution of a death sentence. One prisoner received a sentence commutation after spending thirty-five years on the Japanese death row. Why not reorient prosecutors, police, and victims to expect and to accept long delays as part of the capital punishment process? This would relieve the tension between the penal goals of the system and the requirements of fair procedure.

The problem here is a potent mixture of human psychology and the American adversary system. As soon as a capital sentence is sought, the execution of the defendant becomes the ultimate goal of the prosecutor and avoiding that outcome is the defense attorney's goal. Since the timing and outcome of judicial review are beyond the control of the prosecutor, every significant delay produces uncertainty about whether the execution will ever happen. Perhaps the Japanese minister of justice is not upset with delays because of his near-complete control of the outcome. But the adversarial nature of American criminal justice means that every delay in execution is regarded as a victory for the prosecutor's opponent. The type of long-range perspective that would be required to break out of this pattern is more often found in Zen practitioners than among American capital case prosecutors. It is thus likely that those who prosecute cases for death sentences will continue to experience the delay in execution as a personal defeat. Victims' families will be told to experience any delay in execution as personal rejection. This, in turn, will produce the tension between efficiency and due process discussed at the beginning of this section. In theory, the conflict between fairness and efficiency is not necessary. In practice, it is inevitable.

III. The Tail That Wags the Dog

Legal rights for persons accused of crime are never politically popular, and due process is a particular source of contention when fear of crime is a conspicuous part of the urban social landscape. Rules of substantive and procedural legality are cumbersome and inconvenient for those charged with the investigation and prosecution of crime. Francis Allen has recently reviewed the manifold threats to what he calls the Habits of Legality that currently operate in American society and government.[9] In this section, I would like to add to his litany of impediments the potential role of compromises in due process in capital cases as a force that undermines procedural guarantees throughout the criminal justice system. Even though capital cases are infrequent, and even though the special tension between judicial review and punitive closure only occurs in capital cases, the momentum of insensitivity to considerations of legality can carry over from capital cases to the rest of criminal justice.

Insensitivity to matters of legality is, to some extent, contagious no matter where in the justice system it occurs. But compromising principles in capital cases carries more than general contagion. Because death is the system's largest punishment, when rights are forfeited in capital cases, there is an a fortiori momentum that the same compromises can be made when the penal stakes are more modest. If the capital defendant cannot claim a right, who can?

Hostility to the delay produced in capital cases may also result in broad curtailment of legal remedies because capital cases cannot permissibly be singled out for special prejudice. In habeas corpus, for example, while the real target of both legislative and judicial restriction was the death cases, the curtailment of the federal great writ in all state criminal cases was the means employed to achieve the restriction in death cases. This was almost literally a process of letting the tail wag the dog in collateral review of state criminal justice.

The deconstructive influence of capital cases on rights and remedies in other criminal cases is a historical process come full circle. The capital case was always a leading indicator of the direction in which due process guarantees would be extended. The constitutional right to counsel was extended in state capital cases a full generation before it was extended to state felonies. But even with that time gap, the flow from *Powell v. Alabama*[10] in 1935 to *Gideon v. Wainwright*[11] in 1963 was obvious. So there is symmetry if not poetic justice when capital cases now serve as leading indicators of a contraction in defendant's rights and the scope of judicial review.

Hostile reactions to delay are by no means the sole reason for restrictions on due process protections in the criminal justice system. But the contribution of the death penalty cases to the contraction of the scope of judicial review in habeas corpus, the growth of harmless error doctrine, and recent enthusiasm for enforcing procedural default rules is evident and very important. Further, when formalism neutralizes moral claims for procedural protection in capital cases, there can be no persuasive moral claim to protection in lesser cases. The behavior of the Supreme Court in capital cases thus becomes a leading indicator for moral regression in criminal justice generally.

This essay has suggested three ways in which the practice of capital punishment is in tension with fundamental political and moral values. The first section discussed how the claim that this punishment is proper implicates deep moral and political questions. The second section illustrated how frustrating delays in capital punishment can only be avoided by restricting both the moral claims for exemption from execution and procedural avenues for avoiding the execution of the innocent. The death penalty in the United States can only be principled if it is not efficient; it can only be expeditious if it is morally and procedurally arbitrary.

But the momentum toward moral regression cannot be confined to capital cases. If the conflict between efficiency and fairness compromises the principle in capital cases, the whole of the criminal justice system is at risk. In the immediate future, units of government in the United States can have a smoothly functioning system for executing some persons convicted of murder, or these units of government can have criminal court systems with due process guarantees and effective judicial review in criminal cases. They probably cannot have both. The very idea of capital punishment is troublesome for a number of reasons. In practice, the death penalty also corrupts the integrity of the criminal law and the criminal process that seeks its enforcement.

Notes

1. Celeste Bohlen, "Italy Joins Death Row Appeal in Virginia," *New York Times*, December 20, 1996, A5.
2. McClesky v. Kemp, 48 U.S. 279 (1987).
3. Robert Burt, "Disorder in the Court," *Michigan Law Review* 85 (1987): 1741.
4. Robert Weissberg, "Deregulating Death," *Supreme Court Review* (1983): 305.
5. Opinion of Justice O'Connor, 492 U.S. 302 (1989), at 307.
6. 492 U.S. 302, 350 (1989).
7. 506 U.S. 396 (1989).
8. Opinion of Chief Justice Rehnquist, 506 U.S. 396 (1989), at 417.
9. Francis Allen, *The Habits of Legality* (New York: Oxford University Press, 1996).
10. 287 U.S. 45 (1932).
11. 372 U.S. 335 (1963).

· 7 ·

SELLING A QUICK FIX FOR BOOT HILL: THE MYTH OF JUSTICE DELAYED IN DEATH CASES

ANTHONY G. AMSTERDAM

"What is this galoot charged with?" asked the judge.
"Running stolen cattle across the Rio Grande down at Painted Cave."
"Sure this is the man?"
"Caught him in the middle of the ford driving the cattle."
"Then what did you bring him here fer when I am so busy? In a case like that always give the galoot what he deserves. Take him away and string him up."
Then turning to a line of men at the bar who had been listening, [Judge] Roy Bean asked, "Well, boys, what are you going to have?"
— "Necktie Justice"

I want to talk about a body of United States Supreme Court decisions that offend humanity and reason. They forsake fairness, orderly procedure, intelligence, and judicial efficiency for no stated reason and no rational purpose. Insofar as their results are explained in opinions, the opinions are delusory in the double sense of being built upon delusion and promoting it.

Their delusiveness is what I chiefly want to explore. This involves a kind of warping of reality that can allow civilized people to conceal from themselves and others that they are engaging in atrocities. It is a principal ingredient in getting American judges—who, after all, include a great many very decent individuals—to feel and sound self-righteous as they play their necessary, mindless part in killing human beings under the language of obedience to the largely self-made rules of capital punishment jurisprudence.

The specific cases I examine are those in which the Supreme Court vacates a stay of execution that a lower federal court has issued pending judicial consideration of a condemned prisoner's claims that his or her conviction or death sentence violates the Constitution of the United States. The cases come up at various procedural stages, but the basic scenario is this:

A person has been sentenced to death for murder, and his or her date of execution is set. S/he files a petition for habeas corpus in a federal district court, which has jurisdiction to determine whether the conviction or sentence was obtained in disregard of the guarantees of individual rights embodied in the federal Constitution.[1] The federal district judge concludes that he or she cannot practicably give appropriate consideration to the petitioner's claims before the hour set for execution, so s/he issues an order temporarily forbidding ("staying") the execution until the district court has time to deliberate about the merits of the claims.[2] (Or a federal district judge—or a judge or judges of a federal court of appeals—may issue a similar, temporary stay to give the petitioner time to appeal to the court of appeals from an adverse decision on the merits by the district court.[3] Or any of these judges may issue a similar, temporary stay to give the petitioner time to seek the United States Supreme Court's discretionary review of an adverse decision by the court of appeals.[4]) The state's lawyers then ask the Supreme Court to set aside ("vacate") this stay order so that the execution can be carried out without delay. The Court does so, after summary review of the papers filed by the state's lawyers and any response to them that the condemned prisoner's lawyers are able to file quickly.

The first time the Court did this was on August 10, 1982, in the case of a Virginia prisoner named Frank Coppola. A word of historical background will be useful:

In 1965, the NAACP Legal Defense Fund began to coordinate a national effort to challenge the death penalty throughout the United States on federal constitutional grounds.[5] It developed a number of substantive constitutional arguments, embodied them in form pleadings that included applications for a stay of execution, instructed local lawyers on the arguments and the procedures for presenting them, and undertook to represent any condemned inmate for whom no other competent representation could be found. After June 2, 1967, no executions occurred in the United States for almost ten years.

In 1972 a divided Supreme Court invalidated virtually all then extant capital punishment statutes by a series of decisions of uncertain scope.[6] The states enacted new statutes, and in 1976 a divided Supreme Court sustained some kinds of statutes while invalidating others.[7] Again the scope of the Court's decisions was unclear; difficult questions about the constitutionality of various capital trial and sentencing procedures[8] and their applications[9] persisted. These were taken up and decided—some going one way, some another—in dozens of additional Supreme Court rulings and in hundreds of rulings of the lower federal courts on habeas corpus petitions for the next two decades.

The Court's 1972 and 1976 cases marked a new beginning for constitutional analysis of a wide range of issues, including the shape that capital punishment statutes could take,[10] the validity of particular features of such statutes,[11] the nature of the conduct for which a death sentence could be imposed,[12] whether sundry procedures were permissible in the trial of capital cases,[13] and whether sundry other procedures were required.[14] The first person to be executed while this body of issues was shaking down was Gary Gilmore.

Gilmore fired his lawyers and waived his appeals. When his mother instituted proceedings questioning his mental competence, he joined the State of Utah in opposing them.[15] The U.S. Supreme Court sustained his right to die as a volunteer with the constitutionality of his conviction and sentence unresolved;[16] and he was killed by a firing squad on January 17, 1977.[17]

Five and a half years later, by midsummer 1982, only three additional people had been executed—two of them, like Gilmore, volunteers.[18]

At this time there were about 1,050 prisoners on death row in thirty-one states.[19] Perhaps a third of them had exhausted their direct appeals and were in various stages of state and federal postconviction proceedings. Many had received stays of execution from state and federal courts. In the cases of the four prisoners who had been executed, all lower courts had eventually denied stays (sought in one case by the prisoner, in two cases by family members or former attorneys of the prisoner who asserted that the prisoner was mentally incompetent to waive available judicial review, and in one case by another death row inmate); and the Supreme Court had thereafter been asked and refused to stay the executions.[20]

Frank Coppola was another volunteer for the chair, but a latecomer. For three and a half years after his conviction and death sentence, he had challenged their constitutionality in a series of proceedings in which he was represented by a lawyer named J. Gray Lawrence Jr. and associates. While housed in the Mecklenburg Correctional Center, Virginia's maximum-security prison, Coppola also became a plaintiff in a lawsuit filed by the ACLU National Prison Project, which contended that conditions at Mecklenburg were inhumane and psychologically brutalizing. Then, in April of 1982, while still protesting his innocence, Coppola discharged his lawyers and withdrew the federal habeas corpus petition that they had filed on his behalf.

A psychologist who had served as an expert witness in the prison conditions lawsuit told Coppola's lawyers that he believed that Coppola's decision to quit was the product of suicidal tendencies exacerbated by protracted solitary confinement under Mecklenburg conditions. Coppola's execution was set for 11:00 P.M. on August 10, 1982, after he was examined by a state-employed forensic psychiatrist and psychologist and found competent. He was slated to be transferred from Mecklenburg to the Virginia State Penitentiary in Richmond in late July, and there appeared to be a chance that he would change his mind under less oppressive conditions of confinement.

As it turned out, he did not. So, on August 9, 1982, J. Gray Lawrence filed a next-friend federal habeas corpus petition challenging Coppola's mental competency, the adequacy of his recent mental evaluation, and the constitutionality of his conviction and sentence. This petition and an application for a stay of execution were denied by the federal district court on the same day. Lawrence then filed a stay application with the federal court of appeals. On August 10, eight hours and twenty minutes before the scheduled execution, a judge of the court of appeals granted a stay to permit Lawrence's claims to be heard.

After an unsuccessful motion for reconsideration, the attorney general of Virginia applied to Chief Justice Warren Burger, in his capacity as circuit justice for the region that includes Virginia, to vacate the stay. What happened next was reported in an order issued by the Supreme Court on Coppola's execution day. The Chief Justice referred . . . [the application] to the Court. There being only four members of the Court available in Washington, a conference call was arranged to include those outside Washington except Justice O'Connor who was outside the United States. After consideration of the matters presented . . . , the application is granted and the stay entered by Circuit Judge John D. Butzner, Jr., of the . . . Court of Appeals . . . is hereby vacated. Justice Brennan and Justice Marshall would deny the application. Justice Stevens would call for a response from J. Gray Lawrence, Jr. . . . Justice O'Connor took no part in the consideration or decision of this application.[21]

When the order was released, I remember I was working twenty-hour days on habeas proceedings for a dozen other condemned inmates, but I stopped for one long minute to ask myself what in hell was going on. I had conferred briefly with the lawyers for Mr. Lawrence but was not deeply into the Coppola case, as I had been into three of the four earlier cases of executions. By this time I had my hands full with clients who wanted to live. Still, I couldn't help but wonder what the Supreme Court was up to.

Forget about the nationwide conference call razzle-dazzle, although in 1982 that was not only legally a solecism but technologically an import from Star Wars. Forget about setting aside an order issued by a circuit judge without offering the beneficiary of the order any opportunity to defend it. Forget about respect for Judge Butzner—let alone respect for human life—that might have cautioned against vacating his stay summarily, without a single word explaining what was wrong with it or why. Forget, too, about the time-honored Anglo-American tradition of judicial circumspection *in favorem vitae* and the manifest impossibility of correcting any mistakes made while killing people expeditiously.

Forget about all these things and still the basic question stood unanswered: Why had the Supreme Court bothered to review Judge Butzner's stay order in the first place? The Court's jurisdiction to review orders of the lower federal courts in habeas corpus cases is entirely discretionary, like most of the Court's docket. Even in matters presented for the Court's consideration in the ordinary course of business, with no need for overtime or special efforts, the Supreme Court Justices decline to review all but a very small fraction of the lower-court decisions they are asked to review; and they almost never review a lower-court decision unless it involves some legal issue of general significance. At that, the Court is deplorably overburdened by its caseload; and Chief Justice Burger was incessant in deploring it.[22] So why had he and his colleagues entertained an application by Virginia's attorney general that they must have known would soon be emulated by impatient attorneys general of other states—a kind of application that was bound to draw the Court into a whole new set of harried, hasty reviews conducted under the deadline of a scheduled execution date?

To be sure, the Justices were already being drawn into the preexecution millrace in cases in which all lower courts had *denied* a stay, and a Justice was asked to *grant* one. But it had always been supposed that the Justices' reason for entertaining a condemned inmate's last prayer for a stay was the irremediability of an executed execution.[23] What was the comparable exigency that compelled the Court to multiply its most stressful labors by reviewing lower courts' grants as well as their denials of stays?

Why did it matter much to the Commonwealth of Virginia whether Frank Coppola was executed in August or a couple of months later? Coppola was going nowhere in the meantime; he was locked up firmly in a maximum-security prison. Even if Judge Butzner's stay of his execution was unwarranted, it would terminate upon the resolution of the case on the merits; and Coppola would still be there, waiting for Virginia to kill. Deterrence, retribution, the forestalling of private violent vengeance—all of the justifications that the Supreme Court had accepted for the death penalty—would seem to be as well and fully served by killing Coppola a bit later rather than a bit sooner.[24]

Perhaps there was some other special reason why immediate Supreme Court action to avoid any delay of Coppola's execution was believed by five Justices to be imperative. But since they didn't say what that reason was, their action was a standing invitation to other attorneys general to seek Supreme Court review of lower-court stays with no need to assert or demonstrate anything more than that the stay was improvident.

Thus besought, the Court proceeded to its task. In 1983 and the first half of 1984, it vacated four stays of execution issued by lower federal courts.[25] Arithmetically, this may not strike you as a lot of Supreme Court activity or a lot of extinction of human life. But consider that, during this period, the total number of executions carried out in the United States was fourteen.[26] Beginning with Frank Coppola's case, the United States Supreme Court set aside stays of execution in the cases of exactly one-third of the persons put to death in this country during the next twenty-one months. The Court was unmistakably about the work of whipping the lower federal courts into line to speed the lagging rate of executions.[27]

So what, you may ask, do I find inappropriate about that? You have just heard me say that a stay will necessarily come to an end sooner or later. Why not terminate it sooner? If that is the way the Supreme Court chooses to spend its time and energy, the result may be inefficient but it is not unfair or unjust, is it?

I have three answers, apart from the obvious answer that all of us—the murderer, the murderer's victim, the Justices of the Supreme Court, you, and me—are living our entire lives under a stay of the sentence of death; and that, in all our cases, the issue is not whether the stay will terminate but when, at whose choice, for what reasons other than mortality, and with what meaning the time and manner of our dying will be invested.

In shorthand, my three points can be captioned *pace*, *pass*, and *piss*. Let me begin with:

PACE   Fast-paced adjudication is conducive to mistakes; and mistakes made in vacating a stay will ordinarily be fatal.

Mistakes can occur even in the class of case in which you would think them least likely. Take, for example, the case in which a lower court has rejected a condemned prisoner's constitutional claims on the merits but grants a stay of execution to permit the prisoner to petition the Supreme Court of the United States for discretionary review by writ of certiorari. Before the petition is filed, the state's lawyers ask the Supreme Court to vacate the stay and it does so, saying (1) that a stay pending certiorari should not be granted unless "there exists '"a reasonable probability that four members of the [Supreme] Court would consider the underlying issue sufficiently meritorious for the grant of certiorari"'";[28] (2) that the prisoner's claims "are amply evident from his opposition to the motion to vacate the stay, his voluminous filings in the lower courts, and the opinions and proceedings in . . . [those courts]"; and (3) that "[n]one of these claims warrant certiorari and plenary consideration."[29] Surely, you will say, there can be no mistake here. If anybody is in a position to assert authoritatively that four Justices of the Supreme Court will probably not vote to grant certiorari, it is the Justices of the Supreme Court. Yet . . .

Consider the case of Alvin Bernard Ford in Florida. Ford went mad on death row; the governor decided he was nonetheless sane enough to execute; Ford filed a federal habeas corpus petition challenging the fairness of the governor's decision and its accuracy. A district judge denied the petition but, one day before Ford's scheduled execution, the court of appeals gave him a stay by a vote of two to one. Florida asked the Supreme Court to vacate the stay; the Supreme Court refused to do so; but three Justices—Chief Justice Burger, then-Justice Rehnquist, and Justice O'Connor—did vote to vacate.[30] When the court of appeals rejected Ford's claims on the merits, the Supreme Court of the United States granted certiorari and reversed, agreeing with Ford that his execution without a fair and reliable determination of his mental competency would be unconstitutional.[31] Chief Justice Burger and Justice Rehnquist again dissented, but Justice O'Connor concurred in the result. She had apparently proved to be a poor predicter of her own informed views on the merits, let alone her colleagues'; and Chief Justice Burger and Justice Rehnquist differed from her only in persistence, not in prescience.

Similar predictive errors have apparently occurred in other cases.[32] Worse yet, there is reason to suspect that sometimes they have been avoided only by tailoring the Court's ultimate decision on the merits to fit the outcome predicted by those Justices who had voted to let the prisoner die without first reading briefs, hearing arguments, or studying the record.[33] And if this has been the level of the Justices' performance at the relatively easy task of predicting their own voting behavior, how much confidence can they or anybody have in the accuracy of their predictions when they undertake to vacate a stay issued by a lower court to allow the lower court time for careful study and deliberate decision of a condemned prisoner's constitutional claims? Yet the Court has not hesitated to vacate such stays, both by opinions saying that the cases in the lower courts present "no 'substantial grounds' ["'upon which relief might be granted'"]"[34] and in orders unsupported by any reasoning or explanation at all.[35]

The dangers of this practice are the worse for being self-concealing. Few of the mistakes that a hasty Court is bound to make will likely come to light to serve as cautionary warnings for the future, and some of the Court's mistakes will positively propagate themselves. It is simply not possible to take comfort in the belief that a claim which a condemned prisoner was denied the chance to make to the courts before he got executed was a claim that would have been rejected on the merits anyway.[36]

How do we know it would have been rejected? Consider, once again, the case in which our confidence of this appears to be most justified: a case in which the same claim mooted by a prisoner's demise is later presented to the Supreme Court in another prisoner's case and is rejected on the merits.[37] Doesn't this prove that the first prisoner's execution was no mistake? Sure—but only if you think that the first prisoner's execution after the Supreme Court had vacated a stay was not weighing on the Justices' consciences enough to influence their decision in the second prisoner's case. Assume *you* were the second prisoner. How satisfied would you be with the fairness of the hearing that your claim would get before a Supreme Court Justice who has cast a public, lethal vote predicated on the prediction that your claim, once heard, would be found to lack merit?[38]

PASS   Beginning in 1983 and with increasing stridency, the Supreme Court's decisions vacating stays of execution sent an unambiguous signal to the lower federal courts. This was a signal to Pass, in every sense of word: to Pass by on the other side, to Pass on, to Pass up the quest for finding constitutional error in capital cases, to Pass the buck, to just let it all Pass over.

To understand the force of this message, you have to read it in context. Staying executions and adjudicating claims of error in death cases are not easy or congenial labors for the judges of the lower federal courts. The death-sentenced prisoner is a notorious, vicious-looking criminal. All of his or her constitutional claims have been rejected by the state courts already and, in most cases, the United States Supreme Court has declined to review the state court rulings. The momentum for execution is mounting. Whoever stands in its way will appear to be an intermeddler, an obstructionist. If a federal judge issues a stay, the politicians will predictably howl about obstructionism in the public press. The legal issues in death cases are complex, the paper records dauntingly voluminous, the lawyers often frazzled and unhelpful. Tough judgment calls concerning matters of fact and discretion are almost always decisive of the question of life or death, if the judge is willing to confront them. For a judge to undertake serious, conscientious study of a case of this kind is a terrible, crushing responsibility.

Lower federal judges undertake that responsibility only if and because they accept it as a solemn obligation. Crucial to their sense of obligation is the belief that the task which they are being asked to take on is a meaningful one. To subvert their belief that this is meaningful work is to destroy their will to do it. And subversion of that belief is precisely what the Supreme Court decisions vacating stays of execution are about.

The Court's opinions—when the Court deigns to write opinions rather than overruling the lower courts peremptorily with no explanation—portray the federal district and circuit judges as a bunch of blind and blundering boobies, blinkered into injudicious, quirky, or quixotic action by the wiles of crafty death row prisoners and their conniving lawyers. This tale began in *Alabama v. Evans*,[39] the first case after Coppola's.

John Evans was a suicidally disposed, vacillating volunteer for execution. He authorized attorneys to file a federal habeas petition for him in 1979 but then—after the United States Supreme Court had reversed a decision of the Fifth Circuit

Court of Appeals invalidating his conviction—Evans discharged his lawyers and asked the court of appeals to dismiss the case rather than go on to consider its constitutional challenges to his death sentence. The court of appeals dismissed the case on October 19, 1982. Several days later, when the state asked the Alabama Supreme Court to set an execution date for Evans, he changed his mind again and filed a *pro se* motion opposing the setting of a date and requesting a new sentencing hearing. The Alabama Supreme Court denied his request on February 18, 1983, and on April 8 it set his execution for April 22.

Evans permitted new volunteer attorneys to file a petition for certiorari on his behalf in the Supreme Court of the United States on April 19, accompanied by an application for a stay addressed to Circuit Justice Powell. Powell denied the application at about 5:45 P.M. on April 21, saying that he had circulated Evans's papers to the entire Supreme Court and that six other Justices concurred in denying a stay. An hour later, Evans's lawyers filed a second federal habeas corpus petition in the United States District Court. It was assigned to a federal district judge who had not handled Evans's first habeas petition, because the prior judge was temporarily out of the state on business. The new federal district judge stayed Evans's execution, saying that its imminence gave him insufficient time to make a meaningful review or study of the case. The court of appeals refused to upset this stay but the Supreme Court did so in a *per curiam* opinion accompanied by a concurring opinion by Chief Justice Burger and dissents by Justices Brennan and Marshall.

The *per curiam* opinion begins by reciting most of the history of the case that I have just given you, but omits the fact that Evans's first habeas corpus appeal was dismissed on his motion in order to permit his execution to be carried out. It says that "Justice Powell's order of April 21 . . . described the lengthy proceedings that have followed . . . [Evans's] conviction and death sentence" and quotes Powell to the effect that Evans's "'constitutional challenges to Alabama's capital-sentencing procedure have been reviewed exhaustively and repetitively by several courts in both the state and federal systems.'"[40] It notes that Evans's present habeas petition contains only one claim which was not presented in his earlier petition; it grumbles that this claim was not raised "at any time in any of the many prior state and federal proceedings" but was "raised for the first time . . . approximately seven hours before his scheduled execution"; it questions "the justification for raising this issue now"; but then it goes on to decide the new claim and to hold it "without merit."[41] This holding is announced conclusorily, with no supporting reasoning, as though the point were self-evident.[42] Finally, the Court drops a footnote saying:

> In a case of this kind, a district court normally should find and state substantive grounds for granting a stay of execution. In the circumstances of this case, however, we understand the difficult situation in which the District Court found itself. Judge Cox was not the judge who had reviewed this case on the previous habeas corpus petition. Apparently without notice, this second habeas corpus petition and application for a stay of execution, filed by the same counsel who had filed the previous application for a stay in this Court, was not filed until about seven hours prior to the scheduled execution time. No explanation has been offered by counsel for the timing of these applications.[43]

So what the case was all about, the Court was saying, was a stay ignorantly entered by a district judge selected for his ignorance and made a tool and fool by some designing lawyer who had lain in ambush for the opportunity. The Court does not mention Evans's history of four manifest postconviction changes of mind about whether he wanted to contest his death sentence or embrace it—a history that raises obvious questions about how free his lawyer was to pick his time for filing anything.[44] Nor does the Court face up to the awkward fact that the decision which it is reviewing and undoing is *not* the district judge's decision to issue a stay but the court of appeals's decision that the stay was proper, given the district judge's discretion. If the district judge receives at least the Court's condescending pity as a new camper, the court of appeals is excommunicated entirely from the camp of players to be considered.

Chief Justice Burger filed a concurring opinion in the Evans case that tells essentially the same story of a rube district judge taken for a ride by conniving lawyers, but the Chief Justice's version is more explicit.[45] "This case," says the Chief, "falls within a familiar pattern of literal 'eleventh hour' efforts to frustrate judicial decrees after careful and painstaking judicial consideration over a period of years."[46] I will return shortly to the serial novel of *The Shysters*, of which this is an early volume. For now the more important serial to follow is the *Perils of the Errant Lower-Court Judge*.

There was a limit to how credibly the Supreme Court could continue to tell or believe stories about lower-court judges being misguided through sheer unfamiliarity with the case at hand. Over time, the plot evolved to make them either knaves or fools.[47] Let me give you the entire text of a Supreme Court opinion vacating a stay ten years after Evans's case—in 1993:

> PER CURIAM
> Applying the prevailing legal standard, it is "particularly egregious" to enter a stay on second or subsequent habeas petitions unless "there are substantial grounds upon which relief might be granted." [This is a quotation from Justice O'Connor's concurring opinion in *Herrera v. Collins*, in which the Supreme Court rejected a claim that a prisoner's proffered evidence that he was factually innocent of the crime for which he had been condemned to die required an evidentiary hearing or a stay of execution in federal habeas corpus.[48] I omit only the citation.] No substantial grounds were presented in the present case. The District Court stated that the "facts in *Herrera* mirror those in the present case." [Citation again omitted.] This assessment was not even questioned by the Court of Appeals, and is obviously correct. There is therefore no conceivable need for the Court of Appeals to engage in "more detailed study" over the next five weeks to resolve this claim. [Citation to the Court of Appeals's stay order omitted.]
> It is an abuse of discretion for a federal court to interfere with the orderly process of a state's criminal justice system in a case raising claims that are for all relevant purposes indistinguishable from those we recently rejected in *Herrera*. Accordingly, the Court of Appeals' stay must be vacated.[49]

That's the whole opinion. No legal reasoning. No mention of the fact—emphasized by Justice O'Connor's concurrence in *Herrera*—that *Herrera* was a fact-specific decision which explicitly declined to announce a general rule that could be applied to some other case without a study of the entire record of trial evidence and newly discovered evidence.[50] The Supreme Court did not pretend to have reviewed—or even to have received—the record in the present case before concluding that the court of appeals needed no time to study it. The Supreme Court heeded neither law nor facts but based its ruling solely on unreasoned castigation of the court of appeals.

It has posted the same canards against the lower federal courts in other opinions vacating stays.[51] But its most extraordinary performance in this vein was played in the Robert Alton Harris case. There, the Supreme Court not only set aside several stays of execution issued by the Court of Appeals for the Ninth Circuit but also ordered: "No further stays of Robert Alton Harris' execution shall be entered by the federal courts except upon order of this Court."[52] That constitutes a declaration that the twenty-eight judges of the Ninth Circuit Court of Appeals and the several dozen federal district judges in California are collectively incompetent to administer the law or to protect themselves against seduction by the beguiling impostures of Harris's crafty counsel. Thanks be to God, who has given us the Supreme Court of the United States, which is alone capable of fidelity to duty, of sniffing out the wiles of Satan, and of snuffing out the lives of Satan's minions!

Are decisions of this sort unfair or unjust, you asked? It does seem to me that the minimal condition for the fair administration of justice is an absence of floridly paranoid ideation. Again I ask you to take a homey reality test: If you were required to make a decision having potentially serious consequences for the welfare of another person, and if you doubted your own dispassion in the matter sufficiently to want to get a second opinion from a source whose judgment you could trust, would you consider for one moment consulting anybody who was manifestly talking and acting like the Supreme Court is doing in these cases?

PISS   An omnipresent feature of the Supreme Court's decisions vacating stays of execution is their tone of rage. The supporting opinions are uniformly marked by petulance, impatience, and wrath. The stays to be vacated and the proceedings underlying them are described as threatening and subversive. The dignity and authority of the Court are plainly seen as being on the line. These opinions rattle with the hot breath of offended, balked, beleaguered, but determined and indomitable majesty.[53] The Court is, in three high words, Mightily Pissed Off.

I have already quoted a few of its hot breaths, and I will quote more later. Simply to read them is to wonder whether justice is at all likely to be done by people so enraged. The question deepens if you comb this body of opinions for some nonconclusionary legal reasoning or explanation of their results. Customarily, they offer none or almost none. Taken all together, the Court's opinions in stay cases show a higher ratio of fulmination to reason than any other body of writings by the Justices.

But, you may object, perhaps that ratio is justified. Perhaps there is simply nothing to reason about in these cases. Perhaps they are simply easy cases.

They are not easy cases. They are hard cases made to seem easy. And in that invented seeming lies their culminant injustice, their descent from mere unfairness into evil. For it is not necessarily an evil thing for judges to choose an outcome that they know will injure other human beings unfairly, even when they might have chosen otherwise. As Martha Nussbaum has noted, fairness is not always the order of the universe; and people who are charged with making decisions about the course of human events are sometimes left with no other options than to choose that either a greater wrong or a lesser wrong must happen.[54] To make that choice is necessary, although painful. What is evil is to deny that one is choosing between wrongs, or that one has a choice, so that one avoids the pain and comes to do wrong easily and with the pious faith that it is right. That way lies atrocity. It is because the Supreme Court has acted in that way in this body of cases that I accuse it of atrocity.

I have said that the stay cases are hard cases that are made to look easy. Let us now examine how this is done, and to what effect.

Two basic processes are involved: metaphoric coding and the creation of a conspiracy myth.

Metaphoric coding is the use of language that has the peculiar double meaning which is the essence of metaphor. Metaphor is not simply polysemy, the use of a word with two distinct definitions. It is the use of language that conveys two meanings simultaneously in a way that forges their relationship while making it impervious to logical analysis.[55] In Paul Ricoeur's compendious phrase, "[M]etaphor is the rhetorical process by which discourse unleashes the power that certain fictions have to redescribe reality."[56] It lets you deal with one thing while thinking all the thoughts and feeling all the feelings evoked by another; and so it is a potent tool in both propaganda[57] and self-deception.[58]

Creation of a conspiracy myth is another rhetorical device for shaping one's own and other people's conception of the nature of things. It combines a couple of the common cognitive processes that are sometimes lumped under the heading of "fundamental attribution error"—the postulations that an actor's behavior is deliberate rather than unintended, and that it is rooted in the actor's character rather than in the actor's circumstances[59]—with the plot device of demonification[60] to produce convenient excuses for doing violence under the righteous illusion of self-defense.

The two devices are used jointly in the stay cases: they are interwoven in the fabric of most of the Court's opinions vacating stays. But they can be teased apart, to some extent, to facilitate analysis. I begin with metaphoric coding, and with one particular example of it, the use of the phrase "abuse of the writ [of habeas corpus]" or its equivalents.

The phrase recurs with rattling regularity. Take, for example, the 1984 case of *Woodard v. Hutchins*,[61] in which the Supreme Court vacated a stay issued by a federal circuit judge pending the district court's consideration of a condemned prisoner's second federal habeas corpus petition. Justice Powell's opinion for five Justices says the following: "This is another capital case in which a last-minute application for a stay of execution and a new petition for habeas corpus relief have been filed with no explanation as to why the claims were not raised earlier or why they were not all raised in one petition. It is another example of abuse of the writ."[62]

Those are the second and third sentences of the opinion and sound its clarion. The rest of it is little more than a refrain.[63] Or take the 1990 case of *Delo v. Stokes*,[64] in which a federal district judge saw enough merit in a fourth habeas petition to warrant granting a stay, the state's motions to vacate the stay were denied both by a panel of the court of appeals and by the court of appeals *en banc*, but the Supreme Court vacated the stay by a five-to-four vote, quoting *Hutchins*'s language that this "'is another example of abuse of the writ.'"[65]

Now, the term "abuse of the writ" has both a technical legal denotation and a rich rhetorical connotation. The word "abuse" itself commonly means *misuse* in every sense, ranging from simply overusing something (as in "he abused my patience") to using it perversely (as in "alcohol abuse" or "drug abuse") to using it perfidiously or viciously (as in "abuse of confidence," "abuse of trust," or "child abuse"). In the history of the writ of habeas corpus, the phrase "abuse of the writ" has long been used both doctrinally—to define the circumstances in which a second or successive application for the writ did not have to be entertained on the merits despite the inapplicability of ordinary *res judicata* rules to habeas corpus[66]—and deprecatingly, to complain that the writ was being put to uses that the writer wanted to disparage.[67] Both usages were current when the Supreme Court and then Congress adopted the terminology of "abuse of the writ" to govern issues raised by repeater petitions in federal practice;[68] the terminology was applied compendiously to "needless, piecemeal litigation *or* . . . collateral proceedings whose only purpose is to vex, harass, or delay";[69] and this compound signification had not been disentangled[70] at the time the Court began to talk about abuse of the writ in *Hutchins* and other cases involving stays of execution[71] in the mid-1980s.

In 1991, the Court did undertake to "define the doctrine of abuse of the writ with more precision."[72] It held that "[a]buse of the writ is not confined to instances of deliberate abandonment" of claims[73]—let alone deliberate manipulation of the judicial process—but extends to situations in which a prisoner's lawyer has failed to exercise appropriate diligence in raising claims available at the time of an earlier habeas petition.[74] This result was explained on the ground that the interests of the states in the finality of their criminal judgments and the dignity of their courts, together with the interests of the federal judiciary in using its limited resources most efficiently, had to be balanced against the importance of keeping the writ of habeas corpus available "when a petitioner raises a meritorious constitutional claim in a proper manner. . . ."[75] Thus it was necessary and proper to "impose on petitioners a burden of reasonable compliance with procedures designed to discourage baseless claims and to keep the system open for valid ones";[76] and if a death-sentenced prisoner's lawyer failed to comply with the procedure of raising all available claims in a first habeas petition, the unraised claims would be deemed *abusive* and would not be entertained on a second or successive petition, whatever their merit, except under narrowly defined circumstances.[77] Since this holding, the word "abusive" has been used in federal habeas corpus practice as a shorthand summary for any situation in which a second or successive petition raises new claims and the state calls upon the courts to determine whether the narrow circumstances permitting the hearing of "abusive" claims exist.[78]

You see, of course, where the power of metaphor to redescribe reality comes in. Although the only thing that a condemned prisoner has done wrong is to have a negligent or overstretched court-appointed lawyer, the Court has been able to talk about this prisoner as an *abuser* of legal process when it elects to cut the process and the prisoner short.[79] Consider: You are a judge with the authority to terminate a stay of execution. Would you find that easier to do if you could begin your opinion with the declaration "This is another case of abuse of the writ," instead of saying what that phrase actually means, namely: "This is another case in which a bum lawyer or some equally bad break has brought a criminal defendant to the brink of execution with no serious judicial consideration of constitutional errors that would otherwise invalidate the death sentence"? Or "This is another case in which the importance of according finality to criminal judgments and of keeping the work-load of the judiciary within bounds requires that a human being should be killed with possibly meritorious constitutional claims unheard because his lawyer goofed"?[80]

Conversely, would you find it easier to vacate a stay if you could say and believe that what you were doing was "to enable criminal processes to operate without undue interference from the federal courts"?[81] That's the typical metaphor for telling an execution squad to hold off stuffing somebody into the electric chair or sticking a needle full of poisons into somebody's vein.[82] I've never seen the words "kill" or "killing" in an opinion vacating a stay. What all these stays are stopping, if the Court's rhetoric is taken for reality, is "the orderly process of a state's criminal justice system."[83]

Other metaphors teem in these opinions: the metaphor of "abuse of discretion" (by which lower-court judges are convicted as accomplices to the condemned prisoner's abuse of the writ),[84] the metaphor of "delay" (which depicts any lateness as contrived),[85] the metaphor of "eleventh-hour" or "last-minute" filings (which describe a merely temporal phenomenon but imply both tricksiness and triviality),[86] and so forth.[87] They drive the opinions from beginning to end. Most of the opinions consist of little more than a summary of facts refracted into a narrative by these metaphors, a conclusionary statement that the events so narrated "clearly"[88] call for no further judicial consideration, and an order vacating the stay.

For the most part, the narrative is a tale of conspiracy, with the condemned prisoner and his or her lawyers as the villains. I have already mentioned Chief Justice Burger's announcement of the conspiracy theory in his *Evans* opinion in April 1983. There he discerned that three cases, in each of which there were circumstances that might have made the filing of a new legal proceeding shortly before a scheduled execution date unavoidable,[89] added up to "a familiar pattern" of "efforts to frustrate judicial decrees" by eleventh-hour filings.[90] Two weeks later, Justice Powell, speaking at the annual Eleventh Circuit Conference, similarly described the Evans case as one that he believed to be an example of a lawyer "taking every advantage of a system that irrationally permits the now familiar abuse of process."[91] Justice Powell's progressive immersion in this *noir* tale is itself an interesting story.[92]

In September of 1983, Justice Powell denied a motion to vacate a stay of execution that the Court of Appeals for the Eleventh Circuit had granted to John Eldon Smith, but encouraged the court of appeals to expedite its consideration of the case. He inserted a footnote saying "this case has now been reviewed 16 times by state and federal courts" and adding "I cannot say whether the judicial process has been abused deliberately."[93] Students of classic rhetoric and fans of Antony's speech burying Caesar will recognize the figure that Justice Powell is using here. It is called *occultatio* or *paralipsis*[94] and consists of protesting your inability to prove some-thing that would not otherwise have been imagined to be true, in order to insinuate that it is true when you haven't got a shred of evidence to back up the insinuation.

Four months later, in January 1984, Justice Powell delivered his *Hutchins* opin-ion, which I have already mentioned.[95] Now he is able to write in the text: "Succes-sive petitions for habeas corpus that raise claims *deliberately withheld* from prior pe-titions constitute an abuse of the writ."[96] From this sentence, he drops a footnote saying: "There is no affirmative evidence that the claims were deliberately with-held. But Hutchins has had counsel through the various phases of this case, and no explanation has been made as to why they were not raised until the very eve of the execution date."[97] Since the classic rhetors had no term for this extraordinary fig-ure, I propose we call it *vacuum pedicurat*—which means that, having made an empty charge in text, he tried to back it up with a lesser one in footnote. Hutchins's lawyers filed a second federal habeas petition shortly before execution and failed to explain why the claims in it were not raised earlier. Does this permit—let alone compel—the inference that the claims were deliberately withheld earlier?

Not unless you assume a world in which the most likely explanation for a con-demned prisoner's arrival at the verge of execution with constitutional claims un-raised is that he or his lawyers deliberately saved them for the last minute, and that any alternative explanation would have been pleaded. Let us take the second as-sumption first. Why would alternative explanations have been pleaded if they ex-isted? Presumably because they would have helped Hutchins's case on his repeater petition and the lawyers knew it. But if the alternative explanations were that the lawyers or earlier lawyers for Hutchins had screwed up, then pleading those expla-nations would *not* have helped Hutchins's case.[98] So, while the lack of explanation might support an inference that no legally sufficient explanation existed, it could not support an inference of deliberate withholding. Justice Powell was, in other words, entitled to hold that the federal judiciary had discretion (which the lower courts had not yet exercised) to deny Hutchins's petition as an unexcused repeater; but he was not entitled to displace or prejudge the exercise of that discretion by re-sorting to the bogus, bloated rhetoric of deliberate manipulation.[99]

Now let us look at the first assumption. Deliberate withholding has never been the most likely explanation for why so many condemned prisoners come close to execution with legal issues in their cases that have not been properly presented. Justice Powell himself began to acknowledge the alternative possibilities several years after Hutchins's demise. In June 1988, shortly after his retirement from the Supreme Court, he was appointed by Chief Justice Rehnquist to chair an Ad Hoc Committee on Federal Habeas Corpus in Capital Cases. The committee's report recommended changes in the federal habeas corpus statutes to reduce the number of postconviction reviews available to death-sentenced prisoners, speed up the re-maining reviews, and improve their quality by assuring that the prisoner had ade-quate legal representation and an automatic stay of execution throughout the process.[100] "Under current procedures," it said, "a prisoner has no incentive to move the collateral review process forward until an execution date is set, and at this point additional litigation over a request for a stay of execution is inevitable."[101] "Adding to the problem," it observed, "is the fact that prisoners often cannot obtain qualified counsel until execution is imminent."[102] But if this is so, what does it do to Justice Powell's comfortable assertion that the claims filed on Hutchins's behalf after his execution became imminent had theretofore been deliberately withheld?[103]

Actually, the Ad Hoc Committee itself seriously understates the problem of inadequate legal representation of condemned prisoners.[104] It appears to think that the "qualified counsel" who entered death cases at the last minute emerged from some deep pool out of which they could be dredged or baited in sufficient numbers to represent one inmate with no resulting scarcity of representation to others. In fact, these qualified counsel almost always and everywhere were, or depended critically for backup upon, a tiny group of volunteer lawyers or staff attorneys for underfunded *pro bono* agencies. The committee's recognition that there was "no incentive" to move cases until an execution date was set is a half-truth: there were also no capable lawyers to move cases before an execution date was set. The few attorneys willing and able to handle death cases in federal habeas proceedings had to give priority to the inmates whose executions were most imminent. This is why "eleventh-hour" filings were common, why the cases in which they were presented had sometimes been through earlier stages at which slapdash postconviction pleadings had been tossed together without investigation of all potentially valid claims, and why there wasn't time to review and demonstrate the insufficiency of the prior proceedings unless a stay of execution was obtained.[105] Moreover, the attribution of sinister significance to "waiting until the eleventh hour" overlooks the point that "[i]n a system of review that employs artificial execution dates as a catalyst, there are *many* eleventh hours . . . because . . . the petitioner . . . [must] seek a stay of execution at virtually every level."[106]

But even the Ad Hoc Committee's limited awareness of the scarcity of qualified habeas corpus counsel for death row inmates was sufficient to undermine the only possible reasoning that could have supported an inferential leap from the fact of late filing to the construct of deliberate withholding. Did this make Justice Powell and the other members of the committee (who were lower federal court judges) any less confident of the construct? Not at all. "In some cases," they wrote, "last-minute habeas corpus petitions have resulted from the unavailability of counsel at any earlier time. But in other cases attorneys appear to have intentionally delayed filing until time pressures were severe. In most cases, successive petitions are meritless, and we believe many are filed at the eleventh hour seeking nothing more than delay."[107] Here, undocumented *appearance* and *belief* survive the failure of their factual premises: a conspiracy myth, once it has seized the imagination, will not let go.[108]

And that is particularly true in the dialogic process of advocacy and adjudication, in which lawyers trying to avoid unnecessary crossing of a judge's preconceptions will say things that can be heard as confirming them. Back in 1983, a case called *Barefoot v. Estelle*[109] came before the Supreme Court, raising the question whether a federal court of appeals could dispose of a condemned prisoner's case by denying him a stay of execution pending appeal without following the ordinary procedures of appellate deliberation. The NAACP Legal Defense Fund, which at that time was attempting to provide legal assistance to hundreds of death row inmates, filed an amicus curiae brief arguing that such a truncated appellate process was improvident, as least in a first federal habeas corpus case like Barefoot's. Concerned because the Supreme Court, in denying a stay of execution only two months earlier, had telegraphed in a terse order that it was suspicious of "'the eleventh-hour presentation of new issues,'"[110] the Legal Defense Fund included in its brief a concession that repeater petitions could involve different considerations. The Court's *Barefoot* opinion then quoted a sentence out of this passage of the brief, prefixed with a sentence of its own that effectively translated the Legal Defense Fund's statement from the subjunctive mood into the declarative: "Second and successive federal habeas corpus petitions present a different issue. 'To the extent that these involve the danger that a condemned inmate might attempt to use repeated petitions and appeals as a mere delaying tactic, the State has a quite legitimate interest in preventing such abuses of the writ.' Brief for NAACP Legal Defense Fund."[111] And so, more than a dozen years later, the *Barefoot* quotation could itself be requoted by the Court, with its appearance of factuality intensified as follows:

"*Barefoot* indicated that stays in '[s]econd and successive federal habeas corpus petitions present a different issue,' since in such cases it is more likely that '"a condemned inmate might attempt to use repeated petitions and appeals as a mere delaying tactic."'"[112] Thus does a hypothesis, offered to propitiate prejudgment, become a prophesy and thence a probability.

Out of such gossamer strands was the great web of conspiracy woven. By the time of the Robert Alton Harris case in 1992, the Supreme Court had no trouble seeing Harris's repeated efforts to develop claims of constitutional error in his conviction and death sentence as an "obvious attempt at manipulation."[113] Two months after Harris's execution, Chief Justice Rehnquist wrote an opinion for the Court in a case setting new, more stringent standards for a second or successive habeas petition which contends that a constitutional error has produced a miscarriage of justice in the imposition of a death sentence. The Chief Justice said in his text that the pleading rules for such claims had to be particularly clear because "[i]n the every day context of capital penalty proceedings, a federal district judge typically will be presented with a successive or abusive habeas petition a few days before, or even on the day of, a scheduled execution."[114] He added a footnote saying:

> While we recognize this as a fact on the basis of our own experience with applications for stays of execution in capital cases, we regard it as a regrettable fact. We of course do not in the least condone, but instead condemn, any efforts on the part of habeas petitioners to delay their filings until the last minute with a view to obtaining a stay because the district court will lack time to give them the necessary consideration before the scheduled execution.[115]

This slides by smoothly until you read it twice and realize that Chief Justice Rehnquist is asserting that he has direct personal "experience" of other people's motives. Only psychotics and omniscient authors of the worlds they inhabit have that.

In a world of abused judges and abusive, scheming lawyers, it was easy for the Court to deliver a succession of decisions making postconviction relief from a death sentence very difficult to obtain. It progressed from authorizing federal judges to decide capital habeas cases on a rushed schedule (in *Barefoot*)[116] to admonishing them to do so, with threats of monitoring if they did not.[117] It developed doctrines limiting the scope of claims that could be raised in federal habeas proceedings,[118] expanding the scope of procedural bars to those claims,[119] and, at the same time, retracting the substantive constitutional protections afforded to capital defendants in sentencing,[120] and even in the trial of guilt or innocence.[121] Chief Justice Rehnquist and Justice Powell had advocated legislative "reform" of the "system" of federal habeas corpus in death cases as well;[122] and the Chief Justice literally did an end-run around the Judicial Conference of the United States in order to send Congress an unapproved copy of the Powell Committee report recommending abbreviated proceedings in capital habeas cases.[123] Meanwhile, prosecutors and politicians were pounding similar-sounding drums, and the voters of the United States were electing a law-and-order Congress. After the Oklahoma City bombing, the pressures on congresspersons to make a show of support for the death penalty built still higher, and in April of 1996, Congress enacted the so-called Antiterrorism and Effective Death Penalty Act,[124] which, among other things, imposed even more stringent limitations upon the federal courts' powers to review constitutional errors in state death-penalty cases.[125]

I am not, of course, suggesting that the Supreme Court's rulings and rhetoric in the stay-of-execution cases were the necessary or sufficient condition for all of these changes in the law. Powerful political and social forces were in play, and their interaction was complex. But the rulings and the rhetoric in the stay cases created the discourse for an imaginative universe in which the changes could be depicted and accepted as more *right* and *just* than they would otherwise have seemed. Stern repression was the obvious denouement of a narrative[126] featuring a sleazy lawyers' plot to thwart the Nation's Will, weaken its Sovereign Powers of Self-Protection,[127] bamboozle its inferior judges, and thereby nullify the solemn judgments of its Highest Court.[128]

More immediately, this imaginative universe was one in which the Justices could develop a comfortable habit of killing. The habit itself was bound to harden. For once a judge has sent some people to their deaths after struggling with uncertain questions whether that is constitutional, the judge must kill and kill again—first to insist that his or her struggle be taken seriously, then to ratify that those already dead died rightly. But *comfort* with the habit also had to be achieved.

And the myth of the Death Penalty Defense Lawyers' Conspiracy provided that comfort, in three important ways.

First, it gave the Justices somebody to be mad at. Killing is easier if you are angry.[129] These lawyers really are insufferable. They won't allow the Justices to do the work of justice at a decent distance from the stench of death.[130] They insist on dragging the courts into the very countdown. They are always filing pleadings with labels like: DEATH CASE—EXECUTION IMMINENT.[131] And even when a Justice thinks that he or she has finally managed to kill a particular prisoner once, here it is to do all over again. These cruel and unusual lawyers are imposing double jeopardy on the Justices.[132] So damn them anyway—they and their damned clients.

Second, the Lawyers' Conspiracy made it possible for the Justices to deny that many of the issues which they and the lower courts were deciding in death cases were close judgment calls. Close judgment calls are discomforting reminders of one's fallibility. But even seemingly plausible lawyer's arguments can be dismissed without accepting the risk of deciding them wrong if they can be viewed as mere delaying tactics, ruses, wiles—doubtless all the more specious for being ingenious, since they are the instruments of deliberate deceivers.[133]

Third, the Conspiracy explained why so few death sentences were being carried out in a nation that supposedly embraced the death penalty as a fit and proper punishment for crime. Even after the Supreme Court had taken on itself the task of flogging the lower federal courts into speeding executions, an embarrassingly small number of people were getting killed.[134] Why? Because a tiny but immensely powerful cabal of schemers had succeeded in bringing this country of 240 million people to its knees.[135] That *had* to be the explanation, because otherwise the explanation might be that this country of 240 million people is so conflicted and agonized about the death penalty that—unlike any other criminal penalty on the books—we almost never can enforce it in the concrete, however much we may swear by it in the abstract. But this latter explanation would mean that, when the Supreme Court sustained capital punishment as consistent with contemporary standards of decency in 1976,[136] the Justices got those standards wrong. And *that* would mean that maybe—just maybe—they have killed and killed again to buy themselves false comfort.[137]

Notes

1. The jurisdiction is conferred and regulated by statute, 28 U.S.C. §§ 2241–2254 (1994). The circumstances under which federal judges may grant relief to state prisoners in the exercise of this jurisdiction were restricted by the Antiterrorism and Effective Death Penalty Act of 1996, which was signed into law on April 24 of that year. See Larry Yackle, "A Primer on the New Habeas Corpus Statute," *Buffalo Law Review* 44 (1996): 381. Virtually all of the cases I discuss arose before the 1996 enactment. For a thorough treatment of the doctrines governing federal habeas corpus during this period, see James S. Liebman and Randy Hertz, *Federal Habeas Corpus Practice and Procedure* (Charlottesville, Va.: Michie, 2d ed. 1994).

2. Judicial orders staying execution of a death sentence to permit the court's consideration of the condemned prisoner's claims are no modern phenomenon, nor is controversy over them. See United States v. Shipp, 203 U.S. 563 (1906). A federal statute, 28 U.S.C. § 2251 (1994), expressly authorizes any federal judge or justice "before whom a habeas corpus proceeding is pending . . . , before final judgment . . . or pending appeal, [to] stay any proceeding . . . in any State court or . . . under the authority of any State for any matter involved in the habeas corpus proceeding," including execution of a death sentence, see McFarland v. Scott, 512 U.S. 849, 857–858 (1994).

3. In a habeas corpus proceeding brought in a federal district court, an appeal may be taken to the federal court of appeals for the region if, but only if, the district judge or a federal appellate judge, justice, or court issues a certificate of probable cause. 28 U.S.C. § 2253 (1994). See In re Burwell, 350 U.S. 521 (1956). The current standard for issuance of a certificate is described in Barefoot v. Estelle, 463 U.S. 880, 893 (1983): the prisoner must "make a 'substantial showing of the denial of [a] federal right'" (bracket in originial).

4. The jurisdiction of the Supreme Court of the United States to review the decisions of lower federal courts in habeas corpus matters is, for all practical purposes, limited to the discretionary writ of certiorari, principally under 28 U.S.C. § 1254(1) (1994), secondarily—in rare cases—under the all-writs statute, 28 U.S.C. § 1651 (1994).

5. See, e.g., Michael Meltsner, *Cruel and Unusual: The Supreme Court and Capital*

Punishment (New York: Random House, 1973); Burton H. Wolfe, *Pileup on Death Row* (Garden City, N.Y.: Doubleday, 1973); Jack Greenberg, *Crusaders in the Courts* 440–456 (New York: Basic Books, 1994).

6. Furman v. Georgia, 408 U.S. 238 (1972); Moore v. Illinois, 408 U.S. 786, 800 (1972); Stewart v. Massachusetts, 408 U.S. 845 (1972) (order with no supporting opinion), and companion cases, 408 U.S. at 932–941 (1972).

7. Gregg v. Georgia, 428 U.S. 153 (1976); Proffit v. Florida, 428 U.S. 242 (1976); Jurek v. Texas, 428 U.S. 262 (1976); Woodson v. North Carolina, 428 U.S. 280 (1976); [Stanislaus] Roberts v. Louisiana, 428 U.S. 325 (1976); Green v. Oklahoma, 428 U.S. 907 (1976) (order with no supporting opinion).

8. See, e.g., Beck v. Alabama, 447 U.S. 625 (1980), and Hopper v. Evans, 456 U.S. 605 (1982); Estelle v. Smith, 451 U.S. 454 (1981); Eddings v. Oklahoma, 455 U.S. 104 (1982), and Hitchcock v. Dugger, 481 U.S. 393 (1987); Booth v. Maryland, 482 U.S. 496 (1987), and Payne v. Tennessee, 501 U.S. 808 (1991); Mills v. Maryland, 486 U.S. 367 (1988), and McKoy v. North Carolina, 494 U.S. 433 (1990); Penry v. Lynaugh, 492 U.S. 302 (1989), and Johnson v. Texas, 509 U.S. 350 (1993); Simmons v. South Carolina, 512 U.S. 154 (1994). See also the cases cited in notes 10, 13 and 14 infra.

9. See, e.g., Coker v. Georgia, 433 U.S. 584 (1977); Dobbert v. Florida, 432 U.S. 282 (1977); Godfrey v. Georgia, 446 U.S. 420 (1980); McCleskey v. Kemp, 481 U.S. 279 (1987); Thompson v. Oklahoma, 487 U.S. 815 (1988), and Stanford v. Kentucky, 492 U.S. 361 (1989); Sochor v. Florida, 504 U.S. 527 (1992). See also the cases cited in note 12 infra.

10. See, e.g., [Harry] Roberts v. Louisiana, 431 U.S. 633 (1977); Lockett v. Ohio, 438 U.S. 586 (1978); Zant v. Stephens, 462 U.S. 862 (1983); Pulley v. Harris, 465 U.S. 37 (1984); Spaziano v. Florida, 468 U.S. 447 (1984); Sumner v. Shuman, 483 U.S. 66 (1987); Lowenfield v. Phelps, 484 U.S. 231 (1988); Walton v. Arizona, 497 U.S. 639 (1990).

11. See, e.g., Maynard v. Cartwright, 486 U.S. 356 (1988); Lewis v. Jeffers, 497 U.S. 764 (1990); Shell v. Mississippi, 498 U.S. 1 (1990) (order with no supporting opinion); Stringer v. Black, 503 U.S. 222 (1992); Espinosa v. Florida, 505 U.S. 1079 (1992); Arave v. Creech, 507 U.S. 463 (1993); Tuilaepa v. California, 512 U.S. 967 (1994).

12. See, e.g., Enmund v. Florida, 458 U.S. 782 (1982); Cabana v. Bullock, 474 U.S. 376 (1986); Tison v. Arizona, 481 U.S. 137 (1987).

13. See, e.g.., Gardner v. Florida, 430 U.S. 349 (1977); Adams v. Texas, 448 U.S. 38 (1980), and Lockhart v. McCree, 476 U.S. 162 (1986), and Wainwright v. Witt, 469 U.S. 412 (1985), and Gray v. Mississippi, 481 U.S. 648 (1987), and Greene v. Georgia, 117 S. Ct. 578 (1996); California v. Brown, 479 U.S. 538 (1987); Bullington v. Missouri, 451 U.S. 430 (1981), and Arizona v. Rumsey, 467 U.S. 203 (1984), and Poland v. Arizona, 476 U.S. 147 (1986); Dawson v. Delaware, 503 U.S. 159 (1992).

14. See, e.g., Ake v. Oklahoma, 470 U.S. 68 (1985); Skipper v. South Carolina, 476 U.S. 1 (1986); Turner v. Murray, 476 U.S. 28 (1986); Lankford v. Idaho, 500 U.S. 110 (1991); Morgan v. Illinois, 504 U.S. 719 (1992).

15. The story is told in Norman Mailer, *The Executioner's Song* (Boston: Little Brown, 1979).

16. Gilmore v. Utah, 429 U.S. 1012 (December 13, 1976).

17. The dates of this execution and of others to which I later refer are found in the comprehensive listing provided by NAACP Legal Defense Fund, Inc., *Death Row, U.S.A.* (Summer 1996 ed.), at 3–9.

18. The volunteers were Jesse Bishop (Nevada), executed October 22, 1979, and Steven Judy (Indiana), executed March 9, 1981. The nonvolunteer was John Spenkelink, consistently misspelled Spinkellink by the State of Florida, which killed him on May 25, 1979.

19. NAACP Legal Defense Fund, Inc., *Death Row, U.S.A.* (August 20, 1982 ed.), 1–17.

20. Spenkelink v. Wainwright, 442 U.S. 901 and 906 (May 24 and 25, 1979) (orders with no supporting opinion); Gilmore v. Utah, 429 U.S. 1012 (December 13, 1976); Lenhard v. Wolff, 444 U.S. 807 (October 1, 1979) (order with no supporting opinion); Williams v. Indiana, 450 U.S. 971 (March 6, 1981) (order with no supporting opinion).

21. Mitchell v. Lawrence, 458 U.S. 1123 (August 10, 1982) (order with no supporting opinion).

22. E.g., Warren E. Burger, "The Time Is Now for the Intercircuit Panel," *American Bar Association Journal* 71 (April 1985): 86 (the State of the Judiciary address); Remarks of Chief Justice Burger, in "Proceedings of the Forty-Fifth Judicial Conference of the District of Columbia Circuit," *Federal Rules Decisions* 105 (1985): 251, 257 (date of remarks: May 21, 1984); see also Justice Powell's 1983 Eleventh Circuit Conference speech, cited and discussed in note 91 infra, at 1–2.

23. See Robert L. Stern, Eugene Gressman, Stephen M. Shapiro & Kenneth S. Geller, *Supreme Court Practice* 690, 698 (Washington, D.C.: Bureau of National Affairs, 7th ed. 1993); Wainwright v. Booker, 473 U.S. 935 n. 1 (September 24, 1985) (concurring opinion of Justice Powell). Cf. O'Connor v. Board of Education, 449 U.S. 1301, 1306 (1980) (opinion of Circuit Justice Stevens in Chambers) ("[I]n deciding whether to vacate the stay, I have a duty to consider the potential of irreparable harm to the respective parties."); Holtzman v. Schlesinger, 414 U.S. 1304, 1308–1309 (1973) (opinion of Circuit Justice Marshall in Chambers) ("There are, of course, many cases suggesting that a Circuit Justice should 'balance the equities' when ruling on stay applications and determine on which side the risk of irreparable injury weighs most heavily.").

24. See Franklin E. Zimring, "The Executioner's Dissonant Song: Of Capital Punishment and American Legal Values," chapter 6 of this volume.

25. Alabama v. Evans, 461 U.S. 230 (April 22, 1983); Maggio v. Williams, 464 U.S. 46 (November 7, 1983); Woodard v. Hutchins, 464 U.S. 377 (January 13, 1984) (order with no supporting opinion of the Court; concurring opinion by Justice Powell, joined by Chief Justice Burger and Justices Blackmun, Rehnquist, and O'Connor); Wainwright v. Adams, 466 U.S. 964 (May 9, 1984) (order with no supporting opinion).

26. Charlie Brooks in Texas, 12/7/82; John Evans in Alabama, 4/22/83; Jimmy Lee Gray in Mississippi, 9/2/83; Robert Sullivan in Florida, 11/30/83; Robert Williams in Louisiana, 12/14/83; John Eldon Smith in Georgia, 12/15/83; Anthony Antone in Florida, 1/26/84; John Taylor in Louisiana, 2/29/84; James Autry in Texas, 3/14/84; James Hutchins in North Carolina, 3/16/84; Ronald O'Bryan in Texas, 3/31/84; Arthur Goode in Florida, 4/5/84; Elmo Sonnier in Louisiana, 4/5/84; and James Adams in Florida, 5/10/84.

27. The goal of getting executions going (although by a somewhat different means) had been announced by then-Justice Rehnquist in his opinion dissenting from the denial of certiorari in Coleman v. Balkcom, 451 U.S. 949, 956 (1981). He wrote that

> Although this Court has determined that capital punishment statutes do not violate the Constitution . . . , and although 30-odd States have enacted such statutes, apparently in the belief that they constitute sound social policy, the existence of the death penalty in this country is virtually an illusion. Since 1976, hundreds of juries have sentenced hundreds of persons to death, presumably in the belief that the death penalty in those circumstances is warranted, yet virtually nothing happens except endlessly drawn out legal proceedings.

Id. at 957–958. "The 5-year history of death sentences, as opposed to execution of those sentences, is a matter with respect to which no Member of this Court can be unaware." Id. at 963. "I do not think that this Court can continue to evade some responsibility for this mockery of our criminal justice system." Id. at 958. "What troubles me is that this Court, by constantly tinkering with the principles laid down in the five death penalty cases decided in 1976, together with the natural reluctance of state and federal habeas judges to rule against an inmate on death row, has made it virtually impossible for States to enforce with reasonable promptness their constitutionally valid capital punishment statutes." Id. at 959. "There can be little doubt that delay in the enforcement of capital punishment frustrates the purpose of retribution." Id. at 960. To speed executions, Justice Rehnquist urged that the Supreme Court adopt a policy of granting certiorari to review denials of state postconviction relief in death cases so as to forestall federal habeas corpus proceedings.

Justice Rehnquist did not hesitate to express the view that the condemned inmate in this case, Wayne Carl Coleman, "has had a full opportunity to have his claims considered on direct review by both the Supreme Court of Georgia and this Court and on collateral review by the state courts of Georgia, and . . . [that] the issues presented are not substantial." Id. at 957. Embarrassingly, in the subsequent federal habeas corpus proceedings that Justice Rehnquist was seeking to foreclose, the courts found that Coleman's conviction was unconstitutional because it had been obtained in an atmosphere poisoned by prejudicial publicity. Coleman v. Kemp, 778 F.2d 1487 (11th Cir. 1985), rehearing denied, 782 F.2d 896 (11th Cir. 1986), cert. denied, 476 U.S. 1164 (1986), rehearing denied, 478 U.S. 1014 (1986).

28. In cases within the Supreme Court's discretionary certiorari jurisdiction, it is the Supreme Court's standard practice to grant review—technically, to grant certiorari—if four of its nine members vote to do so.

29. These were the Court's stated grounds for vacating a stay pending certiorari in Maggio v. Williams, 464 U.S. 46, 48 (November 7, 1983). Similar grounds (with the addition of the prediction that even if certiorari were granted, there was no "significant possibility that this Court will reverse the decision below") were given by Justice Powell for his vote to vacate a stay pending certiorari in Wainwright v. Booker, 473 U.S. 935 (September 24, 1985). The Court vacated the stay in *Booker* by a vote of five to four on September 23, 1985, with no supporting opinion of the Court. Justice Powell's double-barreled standard for the validity of stays pending certiorari was derived from Barefoot v. Estelle, 463 U.S. 880, 895–896 (1983).

30. Wainwright v. Ford, 467 U.S. 1220 (May 31, 1984) (order with no supporting opinion).

31. Ford v. Wainwright, 477 U.S. 399 (1986).

32. In Selvage v. Lynaugh, 485 U.S. 983 (March 29, 1988) (order with no supporting opinion), Chief Justice Rehnquist, Justice White, and Justice O'Connor dissented from the Court's *granting* of a stay of execution pending a petition for certiorari. In Selvage v. Lynaugh, 493 U.S. 888 (1989) (order with no supporting opinion), certiorari was granted in the wake of Penry v. Lynaugh, 492 U.S. 302 (1989), to determine whether Selvage's *Penry* claim was procedurally defaulted. After briefing and oral argument, the Court concluded that the question was too complicated to decide without additional guidance from the court of appeals, so the case was remanded to that court for further proceedings. Selvage v. Collins, 494 U.S. 108 (1990).

In Netherland v. Tuggle, 515 U.S. 951 (September 1 [*sic*: actually September 14], 1995), the Court granted an application by the attorney general of Virginia to vacate a stay of execution that had been issued by the Court of Appeals for the Fourth Circuit pending the filing of a petition for certiorari. The Court's *per curiam* opinion, speaking for five Justices, noted that the court of appeals had issued no opinion in granting its stay; thus, "[t]here is no hint that the court found that 'four Members of th[is] Court would consider the underlying issue sufficiently meritorious for the grant of certiorari' or that 'a significant possibility of reversal' existed. *Barefoot*, . . . [see note 29 supra]. We think the inescapable conclusion is that the Court of Appeals mistakenly believed that a capital defendant was entitled to a stay of execution until he has filed a petition for certiorari in due course." Id. at 952. Justices Stevens, Souter, Ginsburg, and Breyer voted to deny the application to vacate the stay. Fortunately, counsel for the condemned prisoner did not give up but manged to file a rushed petition for certiorari, together with a renewed application for a stay, before the execution date. After reading them, the Court granted the stay, Tuggle v. Netherland, 515 U.S. 1188 (September 21, 1995); and then granted certiorari and held—nine votes to zero—that the Virginia Supreme Court's affirmance of the prisoner's death sentence was constitutionally infirm. Tuggle v. Netherland, 516 U.S. 10 (1995).

33. In Darden v. Wainwright, 473 U.S. 927 (September 3, 1985), the Supreme Court, by a vote of five to four, denied an application for a stay of execution pending the filing of a petition for certiorari. There was no Court opinion on the order denying a stay, but Chief Justice Berger filed a concurring opinion saying that Darden's claims had been repeatedly reviewed in earlier proceedings and deserved no more consideration. Realizing that four votes for certiorari is ordinarily enough to grant the writ (see note 28 supra), Darden's lawyers then asked the Court to treat the stay application as a certiorari petition. This time, the Court granted certiorari and a stay, while Justice Burger filed a dissenting opinion (saying, among other things, that Darden's claims "have been considered by this Court four times . . . and have been passed upon no fewer than 95 times by federal and state court judges," 473 U.S. 928, 929) and Justices White, Rehnquist and O'Connor dissented without opinion. After briefing and argument, the Court rejected Darden's claims on the merits by a vote of five to four, Darden v. Wainwright, 477 U.S. 168 (1986), the same five-to-four lineup as at first. So perhaps one might conclude that the five-Justice majority had been astute (if venturesome) predicters of the outcome on the merits, although not of the cert. grant (see note 29 supra). The trouble with this conclusion is that the converse hypothesis is at least as plausible: that the five Justices who ended up voting against Darden on the merits had to do so to avoid looking like idiots and barbarians for voting against a stay earlier without briefing, argument, or even a certiorari petition in front of them. Justice Blackmun's dissenting opinion hints at this hypothesis, 477 U.S. 188, 204–205 and n. 9, and draws a defensive response from Chief Justice Burger that plainly doth protest too much, 477 U.S. at 187–188.

Another troubling case is Leonel Herrera's. Herrera's claim, like Darden's, was fact-specific, so we will never know whether its ultimate rejection was influenced by self-fulfilling prophesies or how the case would have been decided in their absence. A federal district judge had stayed Herrera's execution to allow Herrera time to present evidence that he was innocent of the crime for which he stood condemned. The court of appeals vacated this stay. The Supreme Court granted certiorari—implying that four Justices believed Herrera's claims deserving of review—but the Court also voted, five to four, to deny Herrera's application for a stay of execution pending briefing and argument. Herrera v. Collins, 502 U.S. 1085 (February 19, 1992). Herrera would have been put to death after the certiorari grant but before briefing if a judge of the Texas Court of Criminal Appeals had not seen the absurdity of this situation and granted a stay. There was little surprise when the Supreme Court subsequently rejected Herrera's claims on the merits. Herrera v. Collins, 506 U.S. 390 (1993). It could not have done otherwise without convicting five of its members of criminal negligence at the least.

34. Delo v. Stokes, 495 U.S. 320, 321 (May 11, 1990); see, e.g., Delo v. Blair, 509 U.S. 823 (July 21, 1993); Bowersox v. Williams, 517 U.S. 345 (April 9, 1996).

35. E.g., Wainwright v. Adams, 466 U.S. 964 (May 9, 1984) (order with no supporting opinion); Angelone v. Bennett, 117 S. Ct. 381 (November 4, 1996) (order with no supporting opinion).

36. I have been in this game for a third of a century now, and I am repeatedly surprised at the rulings that courts make in real cases, after they have studied the issues thoroughly, and how different those rulings are from one's predictions of them or even one's after-the-fact speculations about what might have been. I have lost cases that I was absolutely sure I would

win; I have won cases I was absolutely sure I would lose; and I doubt that there are many liti-gators of experience who would not say the same thing. Are judges, even Supreme Court Jus-tices, any better guessers or second-guessers? If there is a virtue to Teague v. Lane, 489 U.S. 288 (1989), it is that *Teague* has given us a laboratory test of this question. For the issue which *Teague* has required the Supreme Court to decide in case after case is whether "reasonable jurists hearing . . . [a particular] claim at . . . [a particular] time . . . 'would have felt compelled by existing precedent' to rule [in a particular way]." Graham v. Collins, 506 U.S. 461, 467 (1993). And in case after case the Court has found the issue impossible to decide without dramatic division. See, e.g., Gray v. Netherland, 518 U.S. 152 (1996); Graham v. Collins, supra.

37. This is the atypically comforting case. The typically discomforting case is one in which the prisoner's claims, being fact-specific to his or her circumstances, die with the prisoner, because no one has any motivation to revisit or vindicate them after s/he has been executed.

38. For example, on November 7, 1983, by a vote of six to three, the Court vacated a stay that had been issued by a court of appeals pending the filing and disposition of a petition for certiorari by Robert Wayne Williams, a Louisiana prisoner. Maggio v. Williams, 464 U.S. 46 (November 7, 1983). One of the issues presented in Williams's case was similar to the principal issue on which the Court was scheduled to hear oral argument later the same day, November 7, 1983, in the case of a California inmate, Robert Alton Harris. A *per curiam* opinion in *Williams* seemed to say that the two cases were distinguishable and that the Harris case was not being prejudged; but the very distinction offered by this opinion necessarily de-pended upon implicit reasoning that undermined one of Harris's major constitutional argu-ments. The Court subsequently rejected this argument and upheld Harris's death sentence in Pulley v. Harris, 465 U.S. 37 (1984).

In giving you this example, I should inform you that I was the lawyer who presented the losing argument for Robert Alton Harris before the Supreme Court on November 7, 1983. I am probably biased in my assessment of the fairness of the procedure followed by the Court in *Williams*. However, the three dissenting Justices also thought the procedure unfair. Justice Brennan, joined by Justice Marshall, wrote:

> By vacating the stay granted by the Court of Appeals and allowing the execu-tion of Williams to proceed, the Court is implicitly choosing to adopt one of two wholly unacceptable alternatives. Either the Court, prior to its full consideration of Pulley, is pre-empting any conclusion that the Constitution mandates statewide proportionality review, or the Court is announcing that someone may be executed using appellate procedures that might imminently be declared unconstitutional.

464 U.S. at 65. Justice Blackmun wrote:

> By vacating the stay, the Court today summarily decides the issue against Williams and, to that extent, pre-empts Pulley.
> It seems to me that standards of orderly procedure require that the stay of exe-cution granted by the Fifth Circuit remain in effect until Pulley is decided. I there-fore dissent from what appears to be an untoward rush to judgment in a capital case.

464 U.S. at 65–66.

39. 461 U.S. 230 (April 22, 1983). The plot had been foreshadowed in Justice Rehnquist's solo opinion dissenting from an order denying a motion to vacate a stay in Wainwright v. Spenkelink, 442 U.S. 901 (May 24, 1979) (order with no supporting opinion). Justice Rehn-quist there suggested that lawyers for condemned prisoners were engaged in a tactic of filing

last-minute stay applications in order to gull judges into enjoining each execution order during the period for which it was valid, thereby requiring the setting of a new execution date that they could frustrate in turn. "Considering . . . that there are several hundred federal judges in the United States who have authority to issue stays . . . , [the states' power to impose death sentences] could turn out, as a practical matter, to be entirely closed to them." 442 U.S. at 903. Although the story line of this opinion features Pied Piper lawyers of exceptional musical talent, its emphasis seems rather to be on the foolishness of the hundreds of judgemice swarming in the Piper's wake: "I respectfully suggest that there may be a tendency on the part of individual judges or courts . . . not merely to resolve all constitutional questions fairly admitting of doubt in favor of a . . . petitioner under sentence of death, but to create or assume such doubts where in fact there are none." 442 U.S. at 902. See also Coleman v. Balkcom, 451 U.S. 949, 956, 957 (1981) (opinion of Justice Rehnquist, dissenting from the denial of certiorari): "And throughout this exhaustive appeal process, any single judge having jurisdiction over the case may of course stay the execution of the penalty pending further review. . . . Given so many bites at the apple, the odds favor petitioner finding some court willing to vacate his death sentence because in its view his trial or sentence was not free from constitutional error."

40. 461 U.S. at 231.

41. 461 U.S. at 232–233.

42. 461 U.S. at 233. The point was nowise self-evident. Evans's claim was that a statutory aggravating circumstance used to support his death sentence had been construed by the Alabama courts in such a vague and limitless manner as to make it unconstitutional under the rule of Godfrey v. Georgia, 446 U.S. 420 (1980). The statutory aggravating circumstance was that the defendant had knowingly created a great risk of death to persons in addition to the murder victim. The trial judge found this circumstance established by the facts that Evans had committed numerous armed robberies and kidnappings *on other occasions than the present murder.* The Supreme Court declared, without explaining, that "[o]n the facts of . . . [Evans's] case, there was no violation of the Godfrey principle in finding this particular aggravating circumstance." But to the extent that this declaration depended on its introductory clause, the relevance of "the facts of . . . [Evans's] case" demanded explanation (see Maynard v. Cartwright, 486 U.S. 356 (1988), holding that *Godfrey* claims are *not* to be resolved on the facts of the particular case); while to the extent that it depended on the assumption that armed robberies and kidnappings generically endanger human life, the use of such an assumption for the purpose of assessing a death sentence required reasoned examination (especially in the year immediately following Enmund v. Florida, 458 U.S. 782 (1982)).

43. 461 U.S. at 233 n. *.

44. The Court was well aware of this history. See Evans v. Bennett, 440 U.S. 1301 (April 5, 1979) (opinion of Circuit Justice Rehnquist in Chambers); Lenhard v. Wolff, 443 U.S. 1306, 1307 n. *, 1308 (September 7, 1979) (opinion of Circuit Justice Rehnquist in Chambers); Evans v. Alabama, 461 U.S. 1301 (April 21, 1983) (opinion of Circuit Justice Powell in Chambers).

45. "For more than six months prior to April 21 the courts were open to consider the petition presented to Judge Cox at or about 5:30 P.M. . . . April 21, but counsel failed to present any application for relief during that period. At that late hour a petition that could have been presented long before was thrust upon a judge who had no previous contact with the case." 461 U.S. at 234.

46. Id. The Chief Justice supports this statement with a footnote that consists entirely of the citation to two cases. One is the Supreme Court's order in the Coppola case, which I have previously discussed (text at notes 20–24). The other is the Supreme Court's order in

Brooks v. Estelle, 459 U.S. 1061 (December 6, 1982), denying a stay of execution without opinion but with a preambulatory recitation quoting the court of appeals's opinion below to the effect that "'[d]espite the eleventh-hour presentation of new issues [in a case which "'by this time [has] been reviewed by 23 judges, state and federal'"], we have reviewed each of the new issues carefully and again reviewed each of the issues previously presented . . . [and] we find no substantial question presented.'" The Supreme Court had previously denied Brooks's petition for certiorari on direct appeal on June 29, 1981, and denied rehearing on September 29, 1981. Brooks v. Texas, 453 U.S. 913, 950 (orders with no supporting opinion). His single federal habeas petition was filed on December 2, 1981, and denied by a district judge on October 28, 1982. On November 9, 1982, the district judge granted Brooks's application for a certificate of probable cause to appeal but denied a stay of execution (set for December 7, 1982) pending appeal. Brooks applied to the court of appeals for a stay on November 12. The court of appeals ordered oral argument on the stay application to be heard on November 26 and denied the stay that day. After Brooks filed a motion for rehearing with the court of appeals and a stay application with Justice White—both complaining that the court of appeals had consigned him to execution without deciding his appeal on the merits despite the district court's issuance of a certificate of probable cause to appeal, in apparent violation of the rule of Nowakowski v. Maroney, 386 U.S. 542 (1967)—the court of appeals issued (on December 6) the opinion quoted by the Supreme Court (also on December 6) in denying a stay (with Justices Brennan, Marshall, and Stevens dissenting). If the *Coppola* and *Brooks* cases establish any "pattern" at all, it assuredly bears not the most remote resemblance to the pattern described by Chief Justice Burger.

47. See, e.g., Wainwright v. Booker, 473 U.S. 935 (September 23, 1985) (opinion of Justice Powell, concurring in an order of the Court vacating a stay with no supporting Court opinion) ("The Court of Appeals offered no reasons for its decision to grant the stay application, and no plausible reason appeared from the record.") Delo v. Stokes, 495 U.S. 320, 322, 323 (May 11, 1990) (concurring opinion of Justice Kennedy, joined by Chief Justice Rehnquist and Justice Scalia) ("Delay or default by courts in the federal system must not be allowed to deprive parties, including States, of the lawful process to which they are entitled."); Demosthenes v. Baal, 495 U.S. 731, 737 (June 3, 1990) ("We realize that last minute petitions from parents of death row inmates may often be viewed sympathetically. But federal courts are authorized by the federal habeas statutes to interfere with the course of state proceedings only in specified circumstances . . . [where] an adequate basis exists. . . . In this case, that basis was plainly lacking."); In re Blodgett, 502 U.S. 236, 238–241 (1992) ("Neither the [court of appeals's] response [to a state attorney general's petition for mandamus] nor the record reveals any plausible explanation or reason for the panel's delay in resolving the case from June 1989 until July 1990."; "[A]ny further postponements or extensions of time will be subject to a most rigorous scrutiny in this Court.").

48. 506 U.S. 390, 419, 425–426 (1993). See note 33 supra.

49. Delo v. Blair, 509 U.S. 823 (July 21, 1993).

50. 506 U.S. at 417–419. Justice O'Connor's reaffirmation of the point is in 506 U.S. at 420–421, 427.

51. See, e.g., Netherland v. Tuggle, 515 U.S. 951, 952 (September 1 [sic: actually September 14], 1995) ("Nothing indicates that the Court of Appeals even attempted to undertake the . . . inquiry required by our decision in *Barefoot* [see note 29 supra]."; "There is no hint that the court found . . ."; stay vacated five-to-four); Bowersox v. Williams, 517 U.S. 345, 346 (April 9, 1996) (invoking the "particularly egregious" doctrine of *Blair* while vacating a stay, five-to-four).

52. Vasquez v. Harris, 503 U.S. 1000 [No. A-768] (April 21, 1992) (order with no supporting opinion). See also Vasquez v. Harris, 503 U.S. 1000 [No. A-766] (April 21, 1992) (vacating

stay; order with no supporting opinion); Gomez v. United States District Court, 503 U.S. 653 [No. A-767] (April 21, 1992). For the story of the Robert Alton Harris case from the perspective of the lower federal courts, see Judge Stephen Reinhardt, "The Supreme Court, The Death Penalty, and The Harris Case," *Yale Law Journal* 102 (1992): 205, or the earlier version of the same talk, Stephen Reinhardt, "Cruel and Injudicious Process: The Supreme Court, the Death Penalty, and the Harris Case," *Yale Law Report* 38 (no. 2, Spring 1992): 2.

53. See, e.g., notes 127 and 134 infra.

54. Martha C. Nussbaum, *The Fragility of Goodness: Luck and Ethics in Greek Tragedy and Philosophy* (Cambridge: Cambridge University Press, 1986; paperback ed. reprint 1994).

55. See, e.g., Ivor Armstrong Richards, *The Philosophy of Rhetoric* [The Mary Flexner Lectures at Bryn Mawr] (London: Oxford University Press, 1936); Paul Ricoeur, *The Rule of Metaphor: Interdisciplinary Studies of the Creation of Meaning in Language*, trans. Robert Czerny (Toronto: University of Toronto Press, 1977; paperback ed. reprint 1987); George Lakoff and Mark Johnson, *Metaphors We Live By* (Chicago: University of Chicago Press, 1980); George Lakoff and Mark Turner, *More Than Cool Reason: A Field Guide to Poetic Metaphor* (Chicago: University of Chicago Press, 1989).

56. Ricoeur, supra note 55, at 7.

57. See, e.g., Charles Morris, *Writings on the General Theory of Signs* 226 (The Hague: Mouton, 1971); Oliver Thomson, *Mass Persuasion in History: An Historical Analysis of the Development of Propaganda Techniques* 18–19 (New York: Crane, Russak, 1977); Anthony R. Pratkanis and Elliot Aronson, *Age of Propaganda: The Everyday Use and Abuse of Persuasion* 56–60 (New York: W. H. Freeman, 1992). Classic examples are found in Harold D. Lasswell, *Propaganda Technique in World War I* 47–113 (1927; Cambridge, Mass.: MIT Press, paperback ed. 1971); Michael Choukas, *Propaganda Comes of Age* 138–209 (Washington, D.C.: Public Affairs, 1965); and see Richard J. Evans, *Rituals of Retribution: Capital Punishment in Germany, 1600–1987* 627 (Oxford: Oxford University Press, 1996) ("'Nazi propaganda in the Weimar Republic repeatedly portrayed Social Democrats and Communists as murderers, in order to create a climate in which the killing of left-wing paramilitaries, politicians, and trade unionists by the brownshirts could be justified in terms of self-defence."). For a good case study, see Martha Grace Duncan, "In Slime and Darkness: The Metaphor of Filth in Criminal Justice," *Tulane Law Review* 68 (1994): 725.

58. See, e.g., Robert Jay Lifton, *The Nazi Doctors: Medical Killings and the Psychology of Genocide* (New York: Basic Books, 1986), particularly at 15–16, 476–489 ("Pollution imagery is associated with many forms of victimization involving class and caste as well as color and race." Id. at 482); Christian Pross, "Nazi Doctors, German Medicine, and Historical Truth," in *The Nazi Doctors and the Nuremberg Code: Human Rights in Human Experimentation* 32, 33, ed. George J. Annas and Michael Grodin (London: Oxford University Press, 1992) ("'To clean the body of the *Volk* from everything sick, alien, and disturbing was one of the dreams of the German intelligentsia."); Evans, supra note 57, at 629–631, 681–688, 702–709.

59. See, e.g., Lee Ross and Richard E. Nisbett, *The Person and the Situation: Perspectives of Social Psychology* (Philadelphia: Temple University Press, 1991), particularly at 119–144; Richard Nisbett and Lee Ross, *Human Inferences: Strategies and Shortcomings of Social Judgment* (Englewood Cliffs, N.J.: Prentice-Hall, 1980), particularly at 30–31, 113–138, 161–162, 183–186, 199–227.

60. See, e.g., Neil Forsyth, *The Old Enemy: Satan and the Combat Myth* (Princeton: Princeton University Press, 1987), particularly at 266–280, 304–383, 419, 426; Elaine Pagels, *The Origin of Satan* (New York: Random House, 1995), particularly at 37–111; Norman Cohn, *Europe's Inner Demons: An Enquiry Inspired by the Great Witch Hunt* (London: Chatto, 1975); R. Po-Chia Hsia, *The Myth of Ritual Murder: Jews and Magic in Reformation Germany* (New Haven: Yale University Press, 1988).

61. 464 U.S. 377 (January 13, 1984).

62. Id. at 377–378.

63. The *abuse* terminology occurs six times in an opinion that runs less than three pages. E.g., "Successive petitions for habeas corpus that raise claims deliberately withheld from prior petitions constitute an abuse of the writ." 464 U.S. at 379. (See text and notes at notes 95–99 infra.) "This case is a clear example of the abuse of the writ that [28 U.S.C.] § 2244 (b) was intended to eliminate." Id. "Federal courts should not continue to tolerate — even in capital cases — this type of abuse of the writ of habeas corpus." 464 U.S. at 380.

64. 495 U.S. 320 (May 11, 1990).

65. Id. at 322.

66. "The doctrine of abuse of the writ defines the circumstances in which federal courts decline to entertain a claim presented for the first time in a second or subsequent petition for a writ of habeas corpus." McCleskey v. Zant, 499 U.S. 467, 470 (1991). The history of this usage is chronicled in the opinions in *McCleskey* and in Sanders v. United States, 373 U.S. 1 (1963).

67. See, e.g., Seymour Thompson, "Abuses of the Writ of Habeas Corpus," *American Law Review* 18 (1884): 1; Louis E. Goodman, "Use and Abuse of the Writ of Habeas Corpus," *Federal Rules Decisions* 7 (1948): 313; John J. Parker, "Limiting the Abuse of Habeas Corpus," *Federal Rules Decisions* 8 (1949): 171.

68. The Court adopted the terminology in Price v. Johnston, 334 U.S. 266, 292–293 (1948), to refer to principles that had been discussed in other terms in Salinger v. Loisel, 265 U.S. 224 (1924), and Wong Doo v. United States, 265 U.S. 239 (1924). Congress adopted it from the courts in a 1966 amendment to provisions of the judicial code dealing with repeater habeas petitions. Public Law 89-711, 80 Stat. 1104 (1966), 28 U.S.C. § 2244 (b) (1994).

69. Sanders v. United States, 373 U.S. 1, 18 (1963) (emphasis added).

70. See McCleskey v. Zant, 499 U.S. 467, 477, 489 (1991); id. at 507–510 (dissenting opinion of Justice Marshall, joined by Justices Blackmun and Stevens).

71. E.g., Stephens v. Kemp, 464 U.S. 1027, 1029 (December 13, 1983) (opinion of Justice Powell, joined by Chief Justice Burger and Justices Rehnquist and O'Connor, dissenting from an order staying an execution with no supporting opinion) ("We should now be concerned . . . with whether . . . Stephens is guilty of having abused the writ of habeas corpus."); Antone v. Dugger, 465 U.S. 200, 204–206 (January 25, 1984) (denying a petition for certiorari and a stay); Straight v. Wainwright, 476 U.S. 1132, 1133 (May 20, 1986) (opinion of Justice Powell, joined by Chief Justice Burger and Justices Rehnquist and O'Connor, concurring in an order denying a stay with no supporting opinion of the Court); cf. Kemp v. Smith, 463 U.S. 1344, 1345 n. 2 (September 17, 1983) (opinion of Circuit Justice Powell in Chambers, denying an application to vacate a stay).

72. McCleskey v. Zant, 499 U.S. 467, 489 (1991).

73. Id.

74. Id. at 489–496.

75. Id. at 492–493.

76. Id. at 493.

77. The circumstances are defined by the doctrines of "cause" and "prejudice" (explicated in *McCleskey*) and "miscarriage of justice" (explicated in *Schlup v. Delo*, infra note 78, and cases cited). Notably, "[a]ttorney error short of ineffective assistance of counsel . . . does not constitute cause and will not excuse a procedural default." McCleskey v. Zant, 499 U.S. 467, 494 (1991). See also Coleman v. Thompson, 501 U.S. 722 (1991).

78. See, e.g., Schlup v. Delo, 513 U.S. 298, 318 and n. 34 (1995) (in *McCleskey*, supra note 66, and cognate cases, "the Court held that a habeas court may not ordinarily reach the merits of successive claims . . . or abusive claims . . . absent a showing of cause and

prejudice"); id. at 334, 338, 341 (dissenting opinion of Chief Justice Rehnquist, joined by Justices Kennedy and Thomas); id. at 342, 344 (dissenting opinion of Justice Scalia, joined by Justice Thomas). Cf. Sawyer v. Whitley, 505 U.S. 333, 335–341 (1992).

79. E.g., Bowersox v. Williams, 517 U.S. 345 (April 9, 1996), twice reciting that the distict court had found the condemned prisoner's claims "abusive, successive, . . . procedurally defaulted [or meritless]," while invalidating, by a five-to-four vote, a stay issued by the court of appeals. Id. at 345–346.

80. Or *this is another case in which "the individual interest in avoiding injustice" must yield to the societal interests in finality, comity, and conservation of "scarce judicial resources"?* (See Schlup v. Delo, 513 U.S. 298, 324 (1995); see also id. at 324, describing an aspect of abuse-of-the-writ doctrine as "seek[ing] to balance the societal interests in finality, comity, and conservation of scarce judicial resources with the individual interest in justice.") Or *this is another case in which the highest safeguard of liberty must be withdrawn in order to avoid undue delay, expense, complexity and interference with the "finality" of state legal processes?* (Lonchar v. Thomas, 517 U.S. 314, 322–323 (1996): "As the writ has evolved into an instrument that now demands not only conviction by a court of competent jurisdiction . . . but also application of basic constitutional doctrines of fairness . . . Congress, the Rule writers, and the courts have developed more complex procedural principles that . . . seek to maintain the courts' freedom to issue the writ, aptly described as the 'highest safeguard of liberty,' . . . while at the same time avoiding serious, improper delay, expense, complexity, and interference with a State's interest in the 'finality' of its own legal processes.")

81. Delo v. Stokes, 495 U.S. 320, 322, 323 (May 11, 1990) (concurring opinion of Justice Kennedy, joined by Chief Justice Rehnquist and Justice Scalia).

82. See, e.g., Demosthenes v. Baal, 495 U.S. 731, 737 (June 3, 1990) ("interfere with the course of state proceedings").

83. Delo v. Blair, 509 U.S. 823 (July 21, 1993). See also Wainwright v. Booker, 473 U.S. 935, 937 (September 23, 1985) (opinion of Justice Powell, concurring in an order of the Court vacating a stay with no supporting Court opinion) ("[f]or our system of justice to function effectively"); Barefoot v. Estelle, 463 U.S. 880, 888 (1983) ("'[T]he administration of justice ought not to be interfered with on mere pretexts.'" Quoting Lambert v. Barrett, 159 U.S. 660, 662 (1895)).

84. See, e.g., Delo v. Stokes, 495 U.S. 320, 322 (May 11, 1990); Delo v. Blair, 509 U.S. 823 (July 21, 1993); Bowersox v. Williams, 517 U.S. 345, 346 (April 9, 1996).

85. See, e.g., Gomez v. United States District Court, 503 U.S. 653, 654 (April 21, 1992) ("this abusive delay"); Wainwright v. Booker, 473 U.S. 935, 936 (September 23, 1985) (opinion of Justice Powell, concurring in an order of the Court vacating a stay with no supporting Court opinion) ("Only a generalized preference for delay in capital punishment cases would justify affirming."); cf. In re Blodgett, 502 U.S. 236, 238–241 (1992); Herrera v. Collins, 506 U.S. 390, 419, 423, 426 (1993) (concurring opinion of Justice O'Connor, joined by Justice Kennedy); Coleman v. Balkcom, 451 U.S. 949, 956, 960 (1981) (opinion of Justice Rehnquist, dissenting from the denial of certiorari) ("increasing tendency to postpone or delay the enforcement of . . . constitutionally valid statutes"; "all but prevents the States from imposing a death sentence on a defendant who has been fairly tried by a jury of peers"); see also note 27 supra. Taking Justice Rehnquist's cue, Justice White sent the *delay* metaphor into hyperbolic orbit in his opinion for the Court approving expedited appeal procedures in capital habeas cases in Barefoot v. Estelle, 463 U.S. 880, 887 (1983) ("Even less is federal habeas a means by which a defendant is entitled to delay an execution *indefinitely*.") (emphasis added); and it has remained in that orbit ever since. See, e.g., Autry v. Estelle, 464 U.S. 1, 3 (October 3, 1983) ("'delay . . . indefinitely'"); McFarland v. Scott, 512 U.S. 849, 859, 861 (1994) (Justice O'Connor, concurring and dissenting) ("'delay . . . indefinitely'"). "[D]ila-

tory" (see Bowersox v. Williams, 517 U.S. 345, 346 (April 9, 1996)) is a cognate word with a technical legal meaning that does not require a factual finding of the manipulativeness with which it oozes metaphorically.

86. Woodard v. Hutchins, 464 U.S. 377, 379 n. 3 (January 13, 1984) (opinion of Justice Powell speaking for five Justices) ("until the very eve of the execution date"); id. at 380 (opinion of Justice Rehnquist, joined by Justice O'Connor) (stating that a district court is not "obligated to rule on every 11th-hour petition for habeas corpus before it denies a stay"); Delo v. Stokes, 495 U.S. 320, 322 (May 11, 1990) ("this last minute application for a stay"); Demosthenes v. Baal, 495 U.S. 731, 737 (June 3, 1990) ("last minute petitions"); Gomez v. United States District Court, 503 U.S. 653, 654 (April 21, 1992) ("last-minute attempts to manipulate the judicial process"; "last-minute nature of an application to stay execution") see also text at notes 41, 43, 46, and 62 supra and at note 115 infra; note 45 supra; cf. Herrera v. Collins, 506 U.S. 390, 417–418 (1993); id. at 419, 423 (concurring opinion of Justice O'Connor, joined by Justice Kennedy); Stephens v. Kemp, 464 U.S. 1027, 1028, 1032 (December 13, 1983) (opinion of Justice Powell, joined by Chief Justice Burger and Justices Rehnquist and O'Connor, dissenting from an order staying an execution with no supporting opinion) ("now familiar process in which an application for a stay is filed here within the shadow of the date and time set for execution"; "a typically 'last minute' flurry of activity is resulting in additional delay"); Justice Powell's 1983 Eleventh Circuit Conference speech, cited and discussed in note 91 infra, at 6, 7.

87. Bowersox v. Williams, 517 U.S. 345 (April 9, 1996), is a good example of an opinion which constructs reality almost entirely out of metaphors. It uses the abuse-of-the-writ metaphor (note 79 supra), the abuse-of-discretion metaphor (note 84 supra), the dilatoriness metaphor (note 85 supra), and—four times in a one-and-a-half-page opinion—the metaphor of describing the court of appeals's stay order as a "summary order." The latter term (whose legal meaning is simply an order issued without supporting reasoning, although its metaphoric entailments include rash, peremptory, and baseless action) is peculiarly ironic, inasmuch as the Supreme Court's own *Bowersox* opinion, issued five to four, does not offer a scintilla of nonconclusionary reasoning to support its only nonmetaphoric grounds of decision, which are that "the District Court's careful treatment of . . . [the condemned prisoner's] claims and the surface implausibility of those claims persuade us that the stay should not have been granted." Id. at 346.

88. See, e.g., Woodard v. Hutchins, 464 U.S. 377, 379 (January 13, 1984) (opinion of Justice Powell speaking for five Justices) ("This case is a clear example of the abuse of the writ."); Delo v. Stokes, 495 U.S. 320, 321 (May 11, 1990) ("petition clearly constitutes an abuse of the writ"); Demosthenes v. Baal, 495 U.S. 731, 737 (June 3, 1990) (basis for a stay "was plainly lacking"); Gomez v. United States District Court, 503 U.S. 653, 653–654 (April 21, 1992) ("obvious attempt" [twice within two paragraphs]); Delo v. Blair, 509 U.S. 823 (July 21, 1993) ("obviously correct"; "no conceivable need" for more study).

89. See the discussion of the Coppola case in text at note 21 supra, of the Evans case in text at notes 39–46 supra, and of the Brooks case in note 46.

90. See text and note at note 46 supra. See also Gray v. Lucas, 463 U.S. 1237, 1240 (September 1, 1983) (opinion of Chief Justice Burger, concurring in an order denying a stay with no supporting Court opinion) ("This case illustrates a recent pattern of calculated efforts to frustrate valid judgments after painstaking judicial review over a number of years."); Sullivan v. Wainwright, 464 U.S. 109, 112 (November 29, 1983) (opinion of Chief Justice Burger, concurring in an order denying a stay) ("The argument so often advanced by the dissenters that capital punishment is cruel and unusual is dwarfed by the cruelty of 10 years on death row inflicted upon this guilty defendant by lawyers seeking to turn the administration of justice into the sporting contest that Roscoe Pound denounced three-quarters of a century ago."); cf.

Lenhard v. Wolff, 443 U.S. 1306, 1312 (September 7, 1979) (opinion of Circuit Justice Rehnquist in Chambers); Wainwright v. Spenkelink, 442 U.S. 901 (May 24, 1979) (opinion of Justice Rehnquist dissenting from an order denying a motion to vacate a stay with no supporting
opinion), discussed in note 39 supra.

91. Remarks of Lewis F. Powell Jr., Associate Justice, at the Eleventh Circuit Conference in Savannah, Georgia, May 9–10, 1983, page 7. This accusation was accompanied by a
profession of understanding that had the dual rhetorical effect of (a) relieving the accuser of
the need to prove the accusation because he appeared to be extenuating it, and (b) treating it
as proved because the very assumption of *understandable temptation* which he generously offered in extenuation implied both that such temptation actually existed and that counsel actually succumbed to it. Justice Powell began by saying that "[r]esourceful counsel, six
months after federal habeas seemed to have been exhausted, sought a stay of execution from
me as Circuit Justice"; that "[w]ith the concurrence of six other members of the Court, I denied it"; that about twenty minutes later, "the same counsel" filed a second federal habeas
petition; that "[t]his belated filing occurred less than seven hours before scheduled execution time"; and that "[c]ounsel offered no explanation for the timing of these applications."
Id. at 6. (Justice Powell did not say why he believed that counsel was obliged to offer explanations or would have been aware of any such obligation; later, at the end of his speech, Justice Powell suggests that hereafter it "may be desirable [for courts] to require counsel" to sub-
mit sworn explanations for belated filings and to include them in the record for appeal. Id. at
8.) Then Justice Powell generalizes: "Perhaps counsel should not be criticized *for taking
every advantage of a system* that irrationally permits the now familiar abuse of process. The
primary fault lies with our permissive system, that both Congress and the courts tolerate." Id.
at 7 (emphasis added). This last passage, together with the no-explanation passage, was duly
reported in the *Times* coverage of the speech. Linda Greenhouse, "Justice Powell Assails
Delay in Carrying Out Executions," New York Times, May 10, 1983 (late City final edition),
A 16. Other aspects of Justice Powell's historic speech are discussed in Anthony G. Amsterdam, "In Favorem Mortis: The Supreme Court and Capital Punishment," *Human Rights* 14
(Winter 1987): 14. See also Stephens v. Kemp, 464 U.S. 1027, 1028 (December 13, 1983) (opinion of Justice Powell, joined by Chief Justice Burger and Justices Rehnquist and O'Connor,
dissenting from an order staying an execution with no supporting opinion) ("[t]his is another
capital case in the now familiar process . . .").

92. Justice—later Chief Justice—Rehnquist also played an interesting part in the creation of the tale. He was the first Justice to see a world of trickster lawyers leading troops of
stupid judges by the nose, see note 39 supra, but his early tellings were more concerned with
the stupidity of the judges than with the trickiness of the lawyers. See id. and note 27 supra.
When bashing dumb judges failed to rouse his colleagues sufficiently, he turned to lawyer-
bashing. See, e.g., text at note 115 infra.

93. Kemp v. Smith, 463 U.S. 1344, 1345 n. 2 (September 17, 1983) (opinion of Circuit
Justice Powell in Chambers). A fuller story of the John Eldon Smith case than Justice Powell
told is found in Steven M. Goldstein, "Chipping Away at the Great Writ: Will Death Sentenced Federal Habeas Corpus Petitioners Be Able to Seek and Utilize Changes in the
Law?," New York University Review of Law & Social Change 18 (1990–1991): 357, 395 n. 210.

94. See, e.g., [Cicero], *Rhetorica ad Herennium* 320–321 [Book 4, ch. 27.37], with trans.
by Harry Caplan, vol. 1 of the twenty-eight-volume Loeb Classical Library Cicero (Cambridge, Mass.: Harvard University Press, 1989 reprint); Cicero, Orator 410–411 [ch. 40.137],
with trans. by H. M. Hubbell, vol. 5 of id. [*Brutus/Orator*] (Cambridge, Mass.: Harvard University Press, 1988 reprint); III Quintilian, *Institutio Oratoria* 399–405 [Book 9, ch. 2.44–51],
with trans. by H. E. Butler, Loeb Classical Library (Cambridge, Mass.: Harvard University
Press, 1986 reprint).

95. See text at notes 61–63 supra.

96. Woodard v. Hutchins, 464 U.S. 377, 379 (January 13, 1984) (opinion of Justice Powell speaking for five Justices) (emphasis added). See also id. at 380: "A pattern seems to be developing in capital cases of multiple review in which claims that could have been presented years ago are brought forward—often in a piecemeal fashion—only after the execution date is set or becomes imminent." Cf. text at note 90 supra.

97. Id. at 379 n. 3.

98. The statute cited by Justice Powell as the basis for holding that Hutchins's repeater petition constituted an abuse of the writ provided that a successive habeas petition need not be entertained unless "'the applicant has not on the earlier application deliberately withheld the newly asserted ground *or otherwise* abused the writ.'" 28 U.S.C., § 2244 (b), quoted in Woodard v. Hutchins, 464 U.S. 377, 379 (January 13, 1984) (opinion of Justice Powell speaking for five Justices) (emphasis added). See also McCleskey v. Zant, 499 U.S. 467, 489 (1991), finding that decisions in 1963 had established "with clarity" that "[a]buse of the writ is not confined to instances of deliberate abandonment."

99. Both the statute cited by Justice Powell in *Hutchins* (28 U.S.C. § 2244 (b)), and the controlling caselaw in 1984 (Sanders v. United States, 373 U.S. 1, 18–19 (1963)) gave the federal courts discretion to entertain an unexcused repeater petition on the merits.

100. Judicial Conference of the United States, Committee Report and Proposal of the Ad Hoc Committee on Federal Habeas Corpus in Capital Cases, August 23, 1989 (Agenda E-22), reprinted as "Report on Habeas Corpus in Capital Cases," *Criminal Law Reporter* 45 (September 27, 1989): 3239. I will cite the latter version hereafter.

101. Id. at 3239.

102. Id. at 3239. The report elaborated at 3240:

> Capital inmates almost uniformly are indigent, and often illiterate or uneducated. Capital habeas litigation may be difficult and complex. Prisoners acting *pro se* rarely present promptly or properly exhaust their constitutional challenges in the state forum. This results in delayed or ineffective federal collateral procedures. The end result is often appointment of qualified counsel only when an execution is imminent. But at this stage, serious constitutional claims may have been waived. The belated entry of a lawyer, under severe time pressure, does not do enough to ensure fairness. In sum, the Committee believes that provision of competent counsel for prisoners under capital sentence throughout *both* state and federal collateral review is crucial to ensuring fairness and protecting the constitutional rights of capital litigants.

103. Justice Powell did observe that Hutchins had "had counsel through the various phases of this case" (see text at note 97 supra) but he did not undertake to evaluate the quality of counsel's representation or the pressures on counsel, nor was he in a position to do so. Cf. Ad Hoc Committee Report and Proposal, supra note 100, at 3243: "Many state prisoners under capital sentence have struggled to secure a stay of execution—often against the vigorous opposition of the State—before availing themselves of even one chance to pursue state and federal post-conviction review. Stay of execution litigation often has been subject to tight deadlines, and places unrealistic demands on judges, lawyers, and the prisoner."

104. At about the same time that the Ad Hoc Committee was preparing its report on federal habeas corpus procedures in capital cases, a task force of the American Bar Association was studying the same subject. The task force received and considered a far broader range of evidence than the Ad Hoc Committee, and its report is manifestly better informed and documented. Vivian Berger, "Justice Delayed or Justice Denied?—A Comment on Recent Proposals to Reform Death Penalty Habeas Corpus," *Columbia Law Review* 90

(1990): 1665. The sections of the report dealing with the problems of inadequate legal representation in death cases (American Bar Association Task Force on Death Penalty Habeas Corpus, *Report and Recommendations: Toward a More Just and Effective System of Review in State Death Penalty Cases* 45–123 (October 1989)), stays of execution (id. at 219–266), and repeater petitions (id. at 267–344) illuminate these problems and their interrelationship. See also Michael Mello, "Facing Death Alone: The Post-Conviction Attorney Crisis on Death Row," *American University Law Review* 37 (1988): 513.

105. See Justice Thurgood Marshall, "Remarks on the Death Penalty Made at the Judicial Conference of the Second Circuit," *Columbia Law Review* 86 (1986): 1, 4–7; American Bar Association, *Guidelines for the Appointment and Performance of Counsel in Death Penalty Cases*, Commentaries to Guidelines 1.1, 2.1, and 11.9.3 at 34–35, 43, 143 (February 1989). The Ad Hoc Committee shows no awareness of the amount of investigation and preparation necessary to identify and develop the issues at the postconviction stage of a death case. See Michael Mello and Donna Duffy, "Suspending Justice: The Unconstitutionality of the Proposed Six-Month Time Limit on the Filing of Habeas Corpus Petitions by State Death Row Inmates," *New York University Review of Law & Social Change* 18 (1990–91): 451, 487–496.

106. ABA Task Force Report, supra note 104, at 265.

107. Ad Hoc Committee Report and Proposal, supra note 100, at 3240.

108. Consider also Justice Powell's speech to the Criminal Justice Section of the American Bar Association at the Association's annual meeting in August 1988, two months after the Ad Hoc Committee had begun its work. Powell, "Commentary: Capital Punishment," *Harvard Law Review* 102 (1989): 1035, 1038; see id. at 1041. (This is a revised version of the original August 7, 1988, speech, which was excerpted in the *Legal Times* under the headline "Death Penalty? Society Has Ruled," August 15, *Verbatim* sec., p. 12, and published in Powell, "Review of Capital Convictions Isn't Working," *Criminal Justice* (Winter 1989): 10. I will cite the *Harvard Law Review* version hereafter.) Justice Powell criticizes the fact that, although the Supreme Court had sustained the constitutionality of the death penalty in 1976 and although "2110 convicted murderers" had since been sent to death row, "there had been only 100 executions." Id. at 1038, repeated at 1040. "However this delay may be characterized, it hardly inspires public confidence in our criminal justice system." Id. at 1040–1041. "A fundamental reason for delay is our unique system of dual collateral review of criminal convictions," id. at 1038, a "system [that] permits—perhaps even encourages—the filing of last-minute stay applications," id. at 1040. "It is only fair to add that a significant part of the delay has been attributable to the difficulty of obtaining counsel for collateral review. . . . When counsel are not involved in collateral proceedings from the start, both the prisoner and the court are less able to ensure that all meritorious claims are addressed. The end result may be the belated entry of a lawyer in the case only under the pressure of an impending execution." Id. Note that the problem of inadequate legal representation is treated as an *addition* accounting for *part* of the delay (which, in this context, refers to last-minute stay applications). What's the other part? See id. at 1039–1040: "Resourceful counsel will advance a new ground for claiming constitutional error, and make a plausible argument for having failed to rely on the ground previously." Here, the rhetorical conjunction of "resourceful" and "plausible" makes the first word mean *crafty* and the second word mean *deceiving*; without this device and the cognitive frame in which it is set, the information stated would be that counsel for condemned inmates, through assiduity, will discover grounds of constitutional error which there are valid justifications for not having raised earlier.

109. 463 U.S. 880 (1983).

110. Brooks v. Estelle, 459 U.S. 1061 (December 6, 1982). See note 46 supra.

111. 463 U.S. at 895.

112. Lonchar v. Thomas, 517 U.S. 314, 321 (1996). There is nothing sinister or surprising in this evolution of the quotation. It is a normal incident of the American convention of composing opinions out of quotations from earlier ones. The *Lonchar* decision is, in the main, both realistically and thoughtfully reasoned, with relatively little reliance on the conspiracy myth. So is the opinion in McFarland v. Scott, 512 U.S. 849 (1994), although it contains a sentence reminiscent of the propitiatory hypothesis in *Barefoot*: "[I]f a dilatory capital defendant inexcusably ignores this opportunity [to obtain counsel who can file a habeas petition before a scheduled execution] and flouts the available processes, a federal court presumably would not abuse its discretion in denying a stay of execution." Id. at 858.

113. Gomez v. United States District Court, 503 U.S. 653, 654 (April 21, 1992). (The phrase "obvious attempt" is used twice in a two-paragraph opinion; the phrase "last-minute attempts to manipulate" is then added, and "last-minute" is repeated.) See also Lonchar v. Thomas, 517 U.S. 314, 334, 337–340 (1996) (Chief Justice Rehnquist, joined by Justices Scalia, Kennedy, and Thomas) (seven references to "manipulation" or its equivalent).

114. Sawyer v. Whitley, 505 U.S. 333, 341 (1992).

115. Id. at 341 n. 7. Cf. Herrera v. Collins, 506 U.S. 390, 419, 423 (1993) (opinion of Justice O'Connor, joined by Justice Kennedy): Affidavits obtained shortly before an execution attesting to information showing the condemned prisoner's innocence "are not uncommon. . . . They are an unfortunate although understandable occurrence. It seems that, when a prisoner's life is at stake, he often can find someone new to vouch for him. Experience has shown, however, that such affidavits are to be treated with a fair degree of skepticism." Since it is the judges with the skepticism who decree the outcome constituting this "experience," the conformity between Justice O'Connor's expectations and experience of the world is not surprising. There is, however, cause for entertaining very different expectations. See Samuel R. Gross, "The Risks of Death: Why Erroneous Convictions Are Common in Capital Cases," *Buffalo Law Review* 44 (1996): 469.

116. 463 U.S. at 887–896. See text and notes at notes 109–111 supra.

117. In re Blodgett, 502 U.S. 236 (1992). See also Delo v. Stokes, 495 U.S. 320, 322–323 (May 11, 1990) (concurring opinion of Justice Kennedy, joined by Chief Justice Rehnquist and Justice Scalia).

118. See, e.g., Teague v. Lane, 489 U.S. 288 (1989); Butler v. McKellar, 494 U.S. 407 (1990); Saffle v. Parks, 494 U.S. 484 (1990); Gray v. Netherland, 518 U.S. 152 (1996).

119. See, e.g., Smith v. Murray, 477 U.S. 527 (1986); McCleskey v. Zant, 499 U.S. 467 (1991) (discussed in text at notes 72–77 supra); Coleman v. Thompson, 501 U.S. 722 (1992).

120. See, e.g., Wainwright v. Witt, 469 U.S. 412 (1985); Payne v. Tennessee, 501 U.S. 808 (1991); Johnson v. Texas, 509 U.S. 350 (1993); Tuilaepa v. California, 512 U.S. 967 (1994). See Susan Raeker-Jordan, "A Pro-Death, Self-Fulfilling Constitutional Construct: The Supreme Court's Evolving Standard of Decency for the Death Penalty," *Hastings Constitutional Law Quarterly* 23 (1996): 455.

121. See, e.g., Mu'min v. Virginia, 500 U.S. 415 (191); Victor v. Nebraska, 511 U.S. 1 (1994).

122. "Remarks of the Chief Justice of the United States, William H. Rehnquist," at the American Law Institute Annual Meeting, May 15, 1990, printed in America Law Institute, *Proceedings* (1990) *of the 67th Annual Meeting* 4, 10 (1991); "Text of Chief Justice Rehnquist's Remarks to ABA," *Chicago Daily Law Bulletin* 135 (no. 1, February 14, 1989): 2, 5; see also Ad Hoc Committee Report and Proposal, supra note 100; Remarks of Lewis F. Powell Jr., supra note 91, at pp. 4, 7; Powell, "Commentary: Capital Punishment," supra note 108, at 1045–1046. For rhetoric of "delay" and "abuse," see, e.g., id. at 1035, 1040–1041, 1046. Justice Powell was frequently cited as an authority because, "[a]s 'Circuit Justice' for the 11th Circuit, Justice Powell has supervisory authority over the Federal Courts . . . [in] states that . . . have far

more prisoners on death row than the states of any other circuit . . . [, so] Justice Powell is confronted more often than any other member of the Supreme Court with last-minute appeals in death penalty cases." Greenhouse, supra note 91, at A16.

123. See Ronald J. Tabak and J. Mark Lane, "Judicial Activism and Legislative 'Reform' of Federal Habeas Corpus: A Critical Analysis of Recent Developments and Current Proposals," *Albany Law Review* 55 (1991): 1, 56–62.

124. Pub. L. No. 104-132, 110 Stat. 1214 (1996).

125. See Yackle, supra note 1.

126. This is the stock script of the Return to Power of the Petrified or Dispossessed King and His Revenge upon the Evil Enchanters Who So Long Held Him in Thrall. See, e.g., "The Twenty-First Night" through "The Twenty-Seventh Night," in *The Arabian Nights* 54–65, trans. Husain Haddawy (New York: W. W. Norton, 1990); "The Two Brothers," in Jacob and Wilhelm Grimm, *The Complete Grimm's Fairy Tales* 290, 306–310, trans. Margaret Hunt and James Stern (New York: Pantheon paperback ed., 1972), which is a representative of tale type 303 in Antti Aarne, *The Types of the Folktale: A Classification and Bibliography* 95–97, trans. Stith Thompson (Helsinki: Academia Scientarum Fennica, 2d rev., 2d printing 1964) [FF Communications No. 184]; Terry Brooks, *The Druid of Shannara* (New York: Ballantine, paperback ed. 1992). For a contemporary version with a plot that parallels the Supreme Court's, see *The Life and Times of Judge Roy Bean*, starring Paul Newman and Victoria Principal, directed by John Huston, produced by John Foreman, screenplay by John Milius (First Artists, 1972).

127. See In re Blodgett, 502 U.S. 236, 239 (1992), where, in threatening a court of appeals with mandamus if it did not proceed more promptly in a federal habeas case in which it had issued a stay of execution, the Court wrote: "None of the reasons offered . . . [by the court of appeals for not moving more quickly] dispels our concern that the State of Washington has sustained severe prejudice by the 2-1/2 year stay of execution. The stay has prevented Washington from exercising its sovereign power to enforce the criminal law." This image—of the entire machinery of the sovereign State of Washington, from the piers of Seattle to the pines of its deepest forests, *immobilized* and required to allow murder and rapine to run rampant for two and a half years because one prisoner's execution has been stayed—suggests the need for an occasional reality check. Cf. McCleskey v. Zant, 499 U.S. 467, 491 (1991) (discussed in text at notes 72–77 supra) ("Our federal system recognizes the independent power of a State to articulate societal norms through criminal law; but the power of a State to pass laws means little if the State cannot enforce them.") (come again?); Lonchar v. Thomas, 517 U.S. 314, 334, 339 (1996) (Chief Justice Rehnquist, joined by Justices Scalia, Kennedy, and Thomas) ("[P]etitioner is frustrating the State's attempts to execute its judgement by exploiting the fact that ordinary principles of res judicata do not apply in habeas corpus.") (huh? does this really say that petitioner is frustrating the State by taking advantage of the fact that there are no legal rules forbidding him to challenge his death sentence?).

128. See Maggio v. Williams, 464 U.S. 46, 51–52 (November 7, 1983) ("We were, of course, fully aware" when we denied review earlier; "[o]ur prior actions are ample evidence"); Delo v. Blair, 509 U.S. 823 (July 21, 1993) ("abuse of discretion for a federal court to interfere with the orderly process of a state's criminal justice system in a case raising claims that are for all relevant purposes indistinguishable from those we recently rejected"); cf. Evans v. Bennett, 440 U.S. 1301, 1303 (April 5, 1979) (opinion of Circuit Justice Rehnquist in Chambers) ("If the holdings of our Court in . . . [names and citation of three 1976 cases upholding capital punishment statutes] are to be anything but dead letters, capital punishment when imposed pursuant to the standards laid down in those cases is constitutional; and when the standards expounded in those cases and in subsequent decisions of this Court bearing on those procedures have been complied with, the State is entitled to carry out the death

sentence."); Coleman v. Balkcom, 451 U.S. 949, 956, 957–960 (1981) (opinion of Justice Rehnquist, dissenting from the denial of certiorari), quoted in note 27 supra; Stephens v. Kemp, 464 U.S. 1027, 1032 (December 13, 1983) (opinion of Justice Powell, joined by Chief Justice Burger and Justices Rehnquist and O'Connor, dissenting from an order staying an execution with no supporting opinion) ("This is a contest over the application of capital punishment—a punishment repeatedly declared to be constitutional by this Court."); Wainwright v. Spenkelink, 442 U.S. 901, 902–903 (May 24, 1979) (opinion of Justice Rehnquist dissenting from an order denying a motion to vacate a stay with no supporting opinion); see also Amsterdam, supra note 91, at 52.

129. As Markus Dubber has recently observed, "There is no reason to believe that Supreme Court justices differ so dramatically from other human beings that they do not share our inhibition against inflicting fatal violence on another person." Markus Dirk Dubber, "The Pain of Punishment," *Buffalo Law Review* 44 (1996): 545, 581.

130. Or, as Austin Sarat and Thomas Kearns put it quintessentially (with an assist from Robert Cover), "to impose pain and death while remaining aloof and unstained by the deeds themselves." Austin Sarat and Thomas R. Kearns, "A Journey through Forgetting: Toward a Jurisprudence of Violence," in *The Fate of Law* 209, 211, ed. Austin Sarat and Thomas R. Kearns (Ann Arbor: University of Michigan Press, 1991).

131. This makes it very difficult for the Justices to keep up the process of distancing which plays a large part in the mechanisms through which "cultural inhibitions against the infliction of pain can be turned into cultural support for such projects [as inflicting death sentences] by otherwise decent persons." Austin Sarat, "Violence, Representation, and Responsibility in Capital Trials: The View from the Jury," *Indiana Law Journal* 70 (1995): 1103, 1104. See, e.g., Sarat and Kearns, supra note 130, particularly at 235–236; Michel Foucault, *Discipline and Punish: The Birth of the Prison*, trans. Alan Sheridan (New York: Vintage Books, 2d ed. 1995); Robert M. Cover, "Violence and the Word," *Yale Law Journal* 95 (1986): 1601; Dubber, supra note 129; cf. William J. Bowers, "The Capital Jury Project: Rationale, Design, and Preview of Early Findings," *Indiana Law Journal* 70 (1995): 1043, 1093–1098. Compare Coleman v. Balkcom, 451 U.S. 949, 956, 962 n. 3 (1981) (opinion of Justice Rehnquist, dissenting from the denial of certiorari) (quoting with approval "'hanging judge'" Parker: "'I never hanged a man. . . . I never hanged a man. It is the law.'") Frank Zimring has noted the second arm of the pincer that comes into play when the Court is drawn into the immediate preexecution drama: The forging of "an intimate link . . . between the Court and the execution process . . . creates a no-win public relations dilemma. If executions are halted, the Court is frustrating the operation of other governmental activities. If executions proceed, blood is on the hands of the justices." Franklin E. Zimring, "Inheriting the Wind: The Supreme Court and Capital Punishment in the 1990's," *Florida State Law Review* 20 (1992): 7, 16.

132. Self-pity can be a powerful anesthetic against guilt feelings. Robert Lifton observed, for example, that "[f]or the most part, doctors raised objections not to the project [of making "selections" at the ramps of Auschwitz] but to being themselves victimized by violations of what they considered fair play: 'For instance, . . . one had to be on duty three nights in a row, . . . because another was shirking.'" Lifton, supra note 58, at 179: and see id. at 178–179, 193–194, 198–199.

133. See Nathan Leites, "Interaction: The Third International on Its Changes of Policy," in Harold D. Lasswell, Nathan Leites and Associates, *Language of Politics: Studies in Quantitative Semantics* 298, 303–304 (1949; Cambridge, Mass.: MIT Press, 3d printing 1966). A good example is Justice Powell's statement about "[r]esourceful counsel" making "a plausible argument," discussed in note 108 supra. Conversely, to take a trickster's arguments seriously is to encourage the trickster to try again to deceive you. See the statement of Circuit Judge Alvin B.

Rubin reported in ABA Task Force Report, supra note 104 at 221: "Moreover, in many in-stances, the panel is of the opinion that granting a stay 'this time,' will lead only to another eve-of-execution application on some other ground at a later time."

134. As Justice Powell often complained, the lagging pace of executions "seriously undercuts public confidence in and respect for the law." Powell, "Commentary: Capital Punishment," supra note 108, at 1044; see also id. at 1035, 1040–1041; Remarks of Lewis F. Powell Jr., supra note 91, at 8 ("undermines public confidence in our system of justice and the will and ability of the courts to administer it"); Ad Hoc Committee Report and Proposal, supra note 100, at 3239, 3241; cf. Stephens v. Kemp, 464 U.S. 1027, 1032 (December 13, 1983) (opinion of Justice Powell, joined by Chief Justice Burger and Justices Rehnquist and O'Connor, dissenting from an order staying an execution with no supporting opinion) ("un-dermines public confidence in the courts and in the laws we are required to follow"); Coleman v. Balkcom, 451 U.S. 949, 956, 959 (1981) (opinion of Justice Rehnquist, dissenting from the denial of certiorari) ("When society promises to punish by death certain criminal conduct, and then the courts fail to do so, the courts not only lessen the deterrent effect of the threat of capital punishment, they undermine the integrity of the entire criminal justice system.").

135. This might appear too silly to believe. But the attribution of superhuman power to a cabal is an old story. See, e.g., Cohn, supra note 60; Hsia, supra note 60; Rene Girard, "Generative Scapegoating," in Walter Burkert, Rene Girard, and Jonathan Z. Smith, *Violent Origins: Ritual Killing and Cultural Formation* 73, ed. Robert G. Hammerton-Kelly (Stan-ford: Stanford University Press, 1987); David Riesman, "The Politics of Persecution," *Public Opinion Quarterly* 6 (Spring 1942): 41; and see Evans, supra note 57, at 625: "As far as the Nazis were concerned, . . . the abolitionist movement of the Weimar years was a wicked conspiracy led by a clique of Jewish lawyers."

136. See Gregg v. Georgia, 428 U.S. 153, 179–182 (1976) (opinion of Justices Stewart, Powell, and Stevens); see also Powell, "Commentary: Capital Punishment," supra note 108, at 1037–1038.

137. Several essays in this volume suggest through complementary insights that the death penalty serves to let mere mortals in democracies play the Divine King, dispensing godlike powers of life and death, although they haven't really got the stomach for it. If this is right, the delusive jurisprudence studied in the present essay may perform a necessary func-tion of covering up—while simultaneously reflecting—the shame-provoking, intense am-bivalence of American popular and political culture toward capital punishment. The Toy King thesis would also help us understand why some Supreme Court Justices get so upset when executions are postponed: if capital punishment is fundamentally about strutting away one's insecurities, then the experience of being thwarted in the carrying out of death sen-tences is an especially humiliating threat. In the Amherst Conference discussion of Franklin Zimring's paper, "The Executioner's Dissonant Song: Capital Punishment and American Legal Values," chapter 6 of this volume, Frank made the telling point that the reason why Japan can tolerate decades-long delays in executing a death sentence is that the Japanese minister of justice is "in control of the whole [post-sentencing] process" and feels no need to prove the Toy King's potency because it's never challenged. These ideas resonate with my essay but go beyond its narrow ambitions.

· III ·

THE DEATH PENALTY AND THE
CULTURE OF RESPONSIBILITY

· 8 ·

THE WILL, CAPITAL PUNISHMENT, AND CULTURAL WAR

WILLIAM E. CONNOLLY

A Brief History of Forgetfulness

The will, we are told, forms a hinge of Western civilization because it is so crucial to our practice of individual responsibility. And murder is often said to deserve capital punishment because it is a *willful* act. But what if the very hinge upon which these judgments turn has always been creaky and unstable? What if the highest moral case for capital punishment rests upon cultural *forgetfulness* of instability in this category itself? Let us, then, review a forgotten history, condensing long stretches of time into brief summaries so that the shifting terms of instability persistently stalking Western conceptions of the will can stand out vividly.

1. "Father, forgive them, for they know not what they do." (Luke 23:34) It is uncertain, according to scholars, whether Jesus said this on the cross or it was attributed to him later by others. Part of the case for the latter judgment is that the statement asserts a difference between Son and Father that Jesus did not express intensely elsewhere. Either way the sentence prefigures an interminable struggle within Christianity. The father, on this reading, is a vengeful god with a soft spot in his heart, while the son is a gentle soul whose forgiveness expresses appreciation for the uncertainty and ambiguity in which violent action occurs. The son's sentiment, however, is not entirely independent of the father's passion: forgiveness becomes appropriate only after an injustice has been recognized. The language of will, in relation to responsibility, desert, and punishment is not highly developed in the Gospels. The killers of Jesus, for instance, are deemed by the one who uttered that sentence to act as much out of ignorance as out of willfulness. For four centuries, before the will became crafted into a cultural instrument of punishment, many Christians opposed the death penalty. The exemplary sacrifice of Jesus on the cross spoke against such a spirit of revenge.

2. "Why should it be? Mind commands body, and it obeys forthwith. Mind gives orders to itself, and it is resisted. . . . Mind commands mind to will . . . , but it does not do so. Whence comes this monstrous state? Why should it be?"[1] Augustinian

(and Pauline) Christianity places the will front and center, setting the stage for the displacement of Jesus/Christianity by a more punitive Christianity. It demands the will, first, to create conceptual space between its omnipotent, benevolent god and responsibility for evil in the world, second, to deepen human responsibility for vice while on earth (virtue, at this stage, is due solely to the grace of God and not to the will of the do-gooder), and, third, to connect the image of humanity itself to the God who willed the world into being. The divided will performs these three historical functions for Augustine. It appears in the world only after Adam, who was initially endowed with a pure, undivided will, disobeyed a divine command willfully. Henceforth, the "monstrous state" of the will arises recurrently when "mind give orders to itself and it is resisted"—by itself. This volatility of the will is part of the punishment visited upon humanity for that first, free, and original sin. Division is both constitutive of the Augustinian will and extremely problematical to it. So Augustine introduces grace to soften the experience of injustice haunting this very instrument of justice.

The theme of division, necessary to Augustinianism for some reasons, also threatens to throw it back into the arms of those devils and heretics, the Manicheans. The latter treat monstrosity in the will to be a manifestation of the cosmic contest between the forces of good and evil. They dismantle the omnipotence of God to make sense of evil. Augustine must thus retain the division while doing whatever is necessary to ward off the loss of divine omnipotence that threatens to accompany it. He responds to this internal uncertainty in a punitive way:

> Let them perish from before your face, O God, even as vain talkers and seducers of men's minds perish who detect in the act of deliberation two wills at work, and then assert that in us there are two natures or two minds, one good, the other evil. They themselves are truly evil, when they think such evil things. . . . Thus they are made into a deeper darkness, for in horrid pride they have turned back further from you, from you who are "the true light which enlightens every man that comes into this world."[2]

"Let them perish before your face. . . ." The Augustinian will is grounded in equal parts on, first, its role in protecting an omnipotent god from evil, second, its indispensability to individual responsibility *and*, third, the bullying of opponents (such as Manicheans and pagans) who point to paradoxes in the very projection of it. Might it have been possible for Augustine to appreciate the indispensability of the will to his faith and then to soften its role in life by emphasizing its uncertain character? Perhaps. But Augustine refuses such a combination. He emphasizes the mysterious character of the will while also asserting its primacy with fervor. He eventually lands on a mix of ecclesiastical discipline and divine grace to civilize a will that is otherwise unruly in its very constitution. The severity of the divine punishments he imagines—including the threat of an eternal "second" death for those who wilfully rebel against faith in his god—reveals how precarious and militant the idea of free will is at the inception of organized Christianity.

3. In Augustinian Christianity, disciplinary practices and the exercise of the will coalesce in an uncertain mixture. By the time of the Enlightenment—to abbreviate radically—disciplinary practices and the exercise of the will become separated

more actively, partly because of uncertainty about the stability of the will itself. Beccaria, for example, first elevates the will above a level susceptible to human knowledge of it; and then he becomes an advocate of disciplinary punishment for crime. Since the god who created the human will is the only one qualified to read its tangled text, the intentions and motives of offenders are to be judged by him alone:

> If He has established eternal punishments for anyone who disobeys His omnipotence, what insect will dare to supplement divine justice? What insect will wish to avenge the Being who is sufficient unto Himself . . . , Who alone among all beings acts without being acted upon? The one Who cannot receive impressions of pleasure and pain from objects. . . ? The seriousness of sin depends upon the unfathomable malice of the human heart, and finite beings cannot know this without revelation. How, then, can a standard for punishing crimes be drawn from this?[3]

Beccaria thus puts the will on ice. Human punishment for crimes of the will is now translated into disciplines of the body designed to subdue the perpetrator and deter others from copying him. Capital punishment now becomes out of the question. It does not deter either those who kill out of momentary rage or those who do so out of a persistent disposition to revenge. And it hardens the hearts of those already disaffected from society by demonstrating to them how profoundly the law is founded on a "war" of the well-connected against the deeply aggrieved. Besides, the attempt to punish in proportion to the degree of evil in the will is futile.

Beccaria is not, however, a gentle soul like Jesus. He applies closely monitored punishments to the body and mind of the offender by apportioning punctual and sustained disciplines to the seriousness of the crime.

> The most powerful restraint against crime is not the terrible but fleeting spectacle of a villain's death, but the faint and prolonged example of a man, who deprived of his liberty, has become a beast of burden, repaying the society he has offended with his labors. Each of us reflects, "I myself shall be reduced to such a condition of prolonged wretchedness if I commit similar misdeeds." This thought is effective because it occurs quite frequently, and it is more powerful than the idea of death, which men always see in the hazy distance.[4]

Beccaria's focus upon the effects of repetitive discipline on the mind takes him to the edge of concluding that the will itself is not a supersensible, master faculty, but a complex corporeal/cultural formation that always bears the specific imprint of the particular experiences from which it is crafted. His disciplinary conception of society points toward such an insight, while the confidence with which he apportions penalties to crimes in the interests of deterrence and reform expresses a scientific image of conduct verging on the fantastic. In general, those who place a timeless will at the center of freedom, responsibility, and punishment are inclined to assert an overweening confidence in their ability to ascertain the right proportion between offense and penalty in the practice of retribution; and those who elevate social causality above attributions of willful responsibility express a corresponding confidence in the ability to devise disciplinary systems geared to the degree of protection, deterrence and reform needed. Each party joins confidence in the precision of its own perspective to a dismissal of the other's ability to establish the proportionality it seeks. Each, therefore, is insightful about the other and blind about itself.

4. The will and capital punishment soon combine in a new way within the Enlightenment. To act morally, according to the moral purist Kant, is to *obey* "autonomously" a moral law each recognizes in itself. A crime thus *deserves* punishment because it is willed against the moral law that anyone is able to recognize and to obey; and the level of punishment must be proportioned to the degree the will's disobedience contradicts its own essence. Punishment is something the will brings upon itself by contradicting its own essence.

> Accordingly, whatever undeserved evil you inflict upon another within the people, that you inflict upon yourself. If you insult him, you insult yourself; if you steal from him, you steal from yourself; if you strike him, you strike yourself; if you kill him, you kill yourself. . . . If . . . he has committed murder he must *die*. Here there is no substitute that will satisfy justice. There is no *similarity* between life, however wretched it may be, and death, hence no likeness between the crime and the retribution unless death is judicially carried out upon the wrongdoer, although it must still be freed from any mistreatment that could make the humanity in the person suffering it into something abominable.[5]

A miracle has occurred. The will, previously uncertain, divided and opaque, has now become pure and rational. Now human punishment can be proportioned to the evil of the offense. Retribution becomes a moral obligation. And note how gentle and painless the image of capital punishment has become by comparison to the judgment of Beccaria. The offender is to be killed by the state only because he brings death upon himself; but this dead man with a beating heart is to be treated decently right up to the point of gentle termination because he also remains a *person*, a rational agent of free will. Punishment now becomes pure and purged of that drive to spectacular revenge the sovereign had only recently invested in it. Augustinian cruelty is surpassed while the will is redeemed. Bells chime and trumpets sound. Freedom, desert, and punishment now fuse together through the medium of the will.

But wait a minute. How does this pure will so often develop a "propensity" to will evil maxims, anyway? How could "radical evil" (consenting to sensual desires that go against the moral law) be such a *regular* effect of action emanating from "the will"? Could the eruption of violence sometimes be an aftereffect *within the will itself* of childhood terrors and abuses experienced before the will matured? Kant almost concedes such a possibility but recovers in time to reconcentrate all responsibility within the will. For to accept that dangerous thesis would be to admit worldly, sensuous elements into the very formation of the will. It would be to jeopardize again the purity, universality, and supersensibility Kant had just worked so hard to install within the will. And retribution in the name of the will would now look too much like a form of cultural revenge. Kantian morality itself would begin to take on the appearance of immorality. And yet . . . , for Kant, the source within the will of the will's own perversion eventually becomes a profound and unanswerable question. We cannot answer it with confidence "within the limits of reason alone," even though our inability to do so threatens to recoil back upon the confidence we invest in our own conception of the will. Let us pray.

> Now if a propensity to this does lie in human nature, there is in man a natural propensity to evil; and since this very propensity must in the end be sought in a will which is free, and can therefore be imputed, it is morally evil. This evil is *radical* because it corrupts the ground of all maxims; it is, moreover, as natural propensity, *inextirpable* by human powers, since extirpation could occur only through good maxims, and cannot take place when the ultimate subjective ground of all maxims is postulated as corrupt; yet at the same time it must be possible to overcome it, since it is found in man, a being whose actions are free.[6]

Man is a free being, but it now becomes less certain just how this freedom is exercised and what impels it so often to compromise itself. Augustinian mystery and division return to haunt the will through the back door. For a "propensity" to evil must reside within the will itself, or the will sacrifices its independent standing in a world where evil is so common. Moreover, the propensity to evil of the will is often not "extirpable" by willpower alone. The source of this propensity is "inscrutable" to the agent, and "yet at the same time it must be possible to overcome it" in a being "whose actions are free." Thus speaks Kant, the pure defender of the pure will.

To escape this impasse Kant is moved to reinvoke—but this time around merely as a "hope"—a divine grace that might enter the will and help to drive its evil maxims away. Such help cannot be assumed or presupposed "within the limits of reason alone," and yet the integrity of the will depends upon the hope that such a supplement will be forthcoming. Grace is both necessary to the integrity of the Kantian conception of freedom and problematical within it. Even as mere hope it creates unwelcome paradoxes. Suppose grace were forthcoming for some and not for others. Must those who murder without the help of grace be spared capital punishment while those who did so despite its aid deserve it? Indeed, what becomes of the human capacity to judge what retribution requires after grace returns to secure and haunt Kantian morality from the inside?

The Kantian recourse to grace corrupts the autonomy of the person. And the Kantian will, as we see in *Religion within the Limits of Reason Alone* eventually stumbles upon those paradoxes that introduced perplexity into the Augustinian conception. But Augustine, recall, offered a less definitive doctrine of human punishment than Kant advances. How do Kantians retain confidence in the morality of retribution, just measure, and capital punishment after they have (re)encountered difficulties internal to the will? Kant does not return to this issue. But, to put the point as bluntly as Kant presents the imperative to capital punishment, after these complexities are introduced you are pressed either to *forget* the complexities of the will to justify capital punishment or to relinquish a *Kantian* justification of capital punishment.

5. The attribution of free will is an uncertain projection, often infused with a drive to revenge that its proponents seldom acknowledge. Neither the free will *nor* scientific determinism, according to Nietzsche, can stabilize itself in the domain of human action, crime, and punishment. Nor with respect to nature for that matter. Every preceding perspective now becomes confounded.

Our usual imprecise mode of observation takes a group of phenomena as one and calls it a fact: between this fact and another fact it imagines in addition an empty space, it *isolates* every fact. In reality, however, all our doing and knowing is not a succession of facts and empty spaces but a continuous flux. Now, belief in freedom of the will is incompatible precisely with the idea of a continuous, homogeneous, undivided, indivisible flowing: it presupposes that *every individual act is isolate and divisible*. . . . Through words and concepts we are still continually misled into imagining things being simpler than they are, separate from one another, indivisible, each existing in and for itself. A philosophical mythology lies concealed in *language* which breaks out again every moment, however careful one may be otherwise. Belief in freedom of the will—that is to say in *identical* facts and in *isolated* facts—has in language its constant evangelist and advocate.[7]

Kant and Beccaria are both unconscious evangelists of language, the first on behalf of purity of will and the second on behalf of the transparency of causal relations. The rest of us, including Nietzsche, are its evangelists as well, though we do have some capacity to tame those evangelical tendencies. Forgive us, for we know not what we do in the realm of punishment. Nietzsche has a grudging respect for Jesus who, he thinks, died on the cross too early to develop the implications of his own thinking. Nietzsche himself struggles to find ways to loosen the hold of these two dominant models of punishment. Such is the ethical task of the immoralist. He does eventually *recover* another, corporeal conception of the will. But this will is implicated in the messiness of the world itself rather than elevated above it. The Nietzschean will becomes a complex cultural/corporeal formation; the cultural elements that enter into its formation turn out to be too disparate, variable, and finely grained to be captured entirely either by the crude categories of explanation or the purity of a free will. Responsibility now becomes a social practice that is both indispensable and inherently problematical. An element of tragedy attaches to it. Punishment may be necessary to protect some from the violent dispositions of others, to deter potential criminals, and even occasionally to restore to the commmunity those who have committed crimes against it. But since the question of desert is fraught with uncertainty, since judgments about the will of others and oneself is haunted by undecidability, the territory of criminal responsibility is now recognized to be one in which "necessary injustice" contaminates the practice of justice. For a culture generally participates in engendering the violences it opposes. Nor can justice and punishment confidently be left to a god; for it is Nietzsche's subtraction of a god from his picture of the self and the world that encourages him to engage the labyrinth of the will and the cruelties attaching to the morality of retribution. Our hallowed conceptions of agency and explanation are themselves human, all too human. So says Nietzsche—while acknowledging the contestability of the assumptions through which *this* judgment is formed.

If you suspect that a drive to revenge enters into the very conceptions of will, freedom, responsibility, and punishment that define your own culture, you may be in a better position to fish more of that revenge out when called upon to judge in concrete cases. Generosity and forgiveness now become invested with new energy. To overcome resentment against the absence of fit between the clarity justice demands and the opacity of the actual cases before us is to fold *generosity* into assessments of the responsibility of others, *hesitation* into cultural explanations of violent conduct, and *forbearance* into the practice of punishment. As I read Nietzsche in writings subsequent to *Human, All Too Human*, the practice of judgment cannot be eliminated. But it might be rendered a little less all too human by those who experimentally apply Beccarian-like tactics *to themselves* to subdue the *ressentiment* in which the most pure and hallowed conceptions of will, freedom, explanation, and punishment are set. With such "arts of the self" we step onto the stage of a post-Nietzschean ethic. It may be because the very Nietzsche who fights against purification of our fundamental moral categories is also so forbearing and subtle when it comes to punishment that so many carriers of cultural forgetfulness are eager to label *him* the consummate agent of nihilism.

Capital Punishment and Forgetting

With the advent of *Dead Man Walking*,[8] first a book and then a 1996 film by the same title, capital punishment returns as an intense topic of cultural debate. The recent upsurge of state executions excites horror in some, a sense of vindication in others, a strange recollection of uncertainty in many, and a differential mix of these feelings in most. But, for the most part, the labyrinthine history of the will, responsibility, and punishment we have reviewed is squeezed out of the discussion. Most parties treat these to be the pillars of "our Judeo-Christian tradition" rather than sites of uncertainty and persistent instability within it.

Dead Man Walking offers a cultural barometer of sorts in this domain. Do "we" have the right to kill those who murder? Sister Helen Prejean's book brings out superbly the awful suffering on death row, and it effectively dramatizes several considerations against state execution. Thus: (1) this ultimate act of finality might (and often does) condemn innocent men (yes, mostly men) to death, and the mistake cannot be taken back if new evidence of innocence is found; (2) we never know for certain whether even a hardened criminal might not reform in the future; (3) if murder is wrong, so is killing by the state, which sends a message of revenge to hardened criminals and hardens the hearts of citizens; (4) many condemned killers have life histories filled with abuse, violence, deprivation, and neglect, and these "mitigating" factors cry out against the death penalty; (5) relatives of the deceased, who (often) press for execution to gain relief from the loss they have suffered, seldom actually experience that much relief after the execution. During a time when the feelings of the aggrieved play such a prominent role in the sentencing of murderers this last experience is particularly pertinent.

Consider Vernon Harvey, who could not wait for his daughter's ruthless murderer to "fry." He is talking to Sister Prejean, the "sob sister" who opposes capital punishment and has nonetheless become a confidante of sorts a few years after the execution of "Willie":

> "Know what they should've done with Willie?" he says. "They should've strapped him in that chair, counted to ten, then at the count of nine taken him out of the chair and let him sit in his cell for a day or two and then strapped him in the chair again. It was too easy for him. He went too quick." He says he's been thinking of a much more effective way. . . . "What we do is fry the bastards on prime-time TV,

that's what we oughta do. Show them dying in the electric chair, say, at eight at night, and see if that doesn't give second thoughts to anybody thinking of murder. . . . [W]e really oughta do to them exactly what they did to their victim. Willie should've been stabbed seventeen times, that's what we oughta do to them."[9]

Harvey's rage has not diminished; "this chapter" has not been "closed" by Willie's execution as he had anticipated. So he fumbles for an act of revenge proportionate to the pain he suffers. And the language of "oughta" suggests that he seeks to enclose these feelings in a moral perspective. His rage and his morality become mixed together, understandably so.

Prejean summarizes her conversation with Harvey on another occasion while he is convalescing in a hospital: "He just can't get over Faith's death, he says. It happened six years ago but for him it's like yesterday, and I realize that now, with Robert (Willie) dead, he doesn't have an object for his rage. He's been deprived of that too."[10] Harvey is not unique. The promise of relief through revenge generally exceeds the experience of it after the unrepeatable deed has been done. If only murderers could be executed several times, or, lacking that, if only the single act of execution were rendered more slow, agonizing, and public. Would crucifixion work? What about burning in oil? In the current political context the public demand to vindicate grieving family members through punishment combines with the unstated impossibility of satisfying that desire fully to place opponents of the death penalty in a position of permanent defensiveness. Their very act of opposition seems to reveal that they do not care that much about mothers, children, lovers, and spouses devastated by the murder of their loved ones.

Sister Prejean poses these issues effectively, then. But a couple of counterdispositions also infiltrate quietly into the book and the film. First, the basic categories through which we judge murderers and assess penalties are themselves treated as stable and untouchable. The harsh childhood of a killer, for instance, is taken to "mitigate" the crime or to provide "extenuating" circumstances; these experiences are not treated as violences that enter into the very crystallization of the perpetrator's will. Such a reflection would throw our most cherished concepts of crime and punishment into uncertainty. It would insinuate culture, with its global divisions along the lines of class, race, and gender and its more finely grained variations in the life of each particular inidividual, into the very practices of action, judgment, and punishment. Many supporters of the death penalty would rather sacrifice the lives of killers than sacrifice the purity of the concepts through which they are judged and sentenced. And even opponents are hesitant to subject the categories to critical review.

Second, as the film reveals, the suspense intensifies pressure upon the condemned man, his loved ones and supporters, the family of the victim, and engaged spectators as the execution clock ticks away and pleas for reversal or delay are rejected. At the end, when the penalty is executed, a certain relief or release accompanies its finality, even among many who resist the death penalty. A decision has been executed as well as a human. An unstated element of authority attaches itself to the act through its very irreversibility. The uncertainty surrounding the right of the state to kill a killer—an uncertainty circulating within many of us as well as between us—becomes muted. We can now turn to other things. At least, those not intimately involved in that particular case can. And the suffering of those most closely connected to the executed man? Or those who have just witnessed the execution of one who killed someone they love? These both recede from the public eye. Two elements deposited in the authoritative background of capital punishment—cultural forgetting of the instability haunting categories of punishment and the strange sense of release attending the finality of execution—work upon one another, each adding a note of silence to the other.

Forgetfulness with respect to the unstable history of the will is lodged in the tangled relations among social science, court decisions, journalistic reporting, electoral campaigns, jury selection, and jury deliberations. These practices form a set of intertexts. Consider the domain of social science. In *Crime and Human Nature: The Definitive Study of the Causes of Crime*,[11] James Q. Wilson and Richard J. Herrnstein work hard to align the dominant cultural mood with respect to punishment with their empirical findings as social scientists. To accomplish this feat the social *explanation* of crime in the interests of deterrence and prevention must be rendered compatible with *retribution* in punishment. For Wilson and Herrnstein, in accord with most members of the culture in which their research is set, explicitly support both. To accomplish this effect they adopt a compatibilist account of social causation and will formation.

> Scientific explanations of criminal behavior do, in fact, undermine a view of criminal responsibility based on freedom of action. And . . . this book has taken pains to show that much, if not all, criminal behavior can be traced to antecedent conditions. Yet we view legal punishment as essential, a virtual corollary of the theory of criminal behavior upon which the book is built. . . . An act deserves punishment, according to the principle of equity, if it was committed without certain explicit *excusing conditions*. . . . For the purposes of the law behavior is considered "free" if not subject to those excusing conditions. One such condition is insanity, but there are others, such as duress, provocation, entrapment, mistake and accident. . . . By proving that excusing conditions are absent and then punishing, the criminal justice system sharply outlines for its citizens the choice between crime and non crime. . . . To the extent such excusing conditions can be demonstrated, punishment should be mitigated or totally suspended.[12]

That's it! The definitive 639-page study on crime and punishment condenses the most momentous and perplexing issue into one fuzzy paragraph. Though people's lives hang in the balance, no uncertainty is allowed to find explicit expression. These guys force Beccaria and Kant together while forgetting the troubles that haunt each theory on its own terms. Deterrence and retribution are both legitimate because, somehow, the people demand the compatibility of will and social causation. How is this sleight of hand accomplished? In a society riven by class and race divisions "the will" is first moved from a position above culture to a place within it (the site of "free" acts). But then deadly dispositions within culture that deviate from an accepted standard of normal conduct are judged to be deserving of retribution by quietly treating them *as if* they were the product of the free will of the agent prior to acculturation. That relieves the culture of apparent implication in the acts it punishes. The authors can count on most readers sliding over this shift because they never truly endorsed the relocation of the will inside culture in the first place.

The authors were the ones pressed to do that, in the interests of fostering a science of criminality.

But what has retribution now become? If the difference between "will" and "excuse" has now become the difference between motives "society" places beyond appeal and those "it" allows to excuse, ameliorate, or attenuate responsibility, retribution now slides from an act of equitable compensation tied to an unstable doctrine of the will to an act of revenge tied to the level of outrage felt by normal people. Can Wilson and Herrnstein, for instance, reiterate Kant's claim that the killer has willed his own execution by murdering another? They cannot. They can only draw implicit sustenance from a broader cultural belief in a model of retribution their own theory calls into question. They get away with this ruse to the extent that the earlier model of the will and retribution was itself fueled by a drive to revenge. A compatibilist doctrine of will and causality now becomes translated into compatibility between the level of punitive action and the vengeful mood of dominant constituencies. Execution no longer punishes murderers according to a standard they themselves are reputed to have willed (the Kantian ideal of retribution); it enacts the desire for revenge, which, understandably enough, follows acts of murder. The pretense to give a definitive *account* of the compatibility between deterrence and retribution devolves into repetition of a cultural *demand* that they be brought into correspondence at whatever cost. In the world of Wilson and Herrnstein, no perplexity or uncertainty is allowed to surface with respect to the most fundamental issues, even though the signs of both keep seeping through their prose.

The Supreme Court joins the cultural cascade of forgetting in the way it front-loads murder cases. The most consequential way it does so, perhaps, is its determination that only those who are "death-qualified" can serve as jurors in murder cases where the death penalty is at issue. This injunction disqualifies at least 20 percent of potential jurors from the start simply because they do not endorse execution as a punishment. It also affects the way the prosecution and the defense proceed in making their cases before a death-qualified jury. For death-qualified juries are demographically distinctive. "They are more likely to be male, to be white, to be well off financially, to be Republican, and to be Protestant or Catholic"[13] than the general population. With such a jury in place a defense lawyer would be foolish to pose difficult questions about attributions of the will. No juror is apt to pick such a theme up during jury deliberation, and most will be hostile to its articulation. A prosecutor, on the other hand, is encouraged to use problematic conceptions of responsibility and the will as a whip to beat down the defense during the sentencing hearing. In such constrained contexts—repeatedly set before the public as a trial by peers who embody "the conscience of the community"—cultural immunity against public excavation of self-doubts about the relations among will, action, responsibility, and retribution is assured from the start. The following interrogation by a prosecutor against a social worker who has presented mitigating considerations in a murder case is doubtless repeated in capital sentencing hearings daily.

Q: Do you believe in the Christian principle of free moral agency? Do you believe that God gave us the capacity to choose right from wrong?

A: Yes, that can happen if one has a nurturing environment that would support that capacity and allow it to be used.

Q: Do you believe that Almighty God gave us the capacity to know right from wrong?

A: Almighty God gave us the potential. . . .

Q: How do you explain why some people who come from bad homes do well in life?

A: We all have different innate endowments and ability to tolerate frustration. One can't just look at people and know who will turn out good and who will turn out bad. . . .

Q: Are you saying that people are not responsible for what they do?

A: What William Brooks did was the product of interaction between himself and his environment. . . .

Q: Can someone be just plain mean?

A: No, not without reason. Children aren't born mean. Children are responsive to their environment.[14]

Austin Sarat shows how the hegemony of this legal discourse steers public attention away from structural modes of violence not readily reducible to the actions of individuals and toward violences that appear to be so reducible. Those who die through the systemic denial of effective health care are ignored, and the limited resources of public attention are focused on those who die through individual acts of murder. I would underline another element within this general politics of displacement. In such a predetermined context of legal argument, the prosecutor appears to be a clear thinker with coherent categories while the social worker emerges as a fuzzy idealist trying to force two opposing conceptions of the world into one story line. The first agent appears to embody the clarity of "our culture" while the second struggles to twist that clarity to save the life of a defendant. But in fact *our* culture is marked by fundamental instability in its basic categories of responsibility and punishment, and it is administered by legal/political practices that translate this instability into a vengeful model of responsibility. To say some people are "just plain mean" is to infantilize the judgment of criminal cases by purging the image of the will of the mysteries and ambiguities that haunt it. Dominant practices of social science, court decision, jury selection and deliberation, prosecutorial presentation, media reporting, and citizen predisposition coalesce to organize this politics of displacement. Capital punishment sacrifices the lives of killers to reassure a culture that would otherwise be perplexed and troubled by the constitutive uncertainty haunting some of its most cherished categories of self-interpretation.

The Death Penalty and the Forgetfulness of Death

Powerful cultural demands for categorical integrity foster political pressure for the death penalty, even when a politics of cultural forgetting is needed to meet those demands. That is the thesis so far. These demands set an authoritative set of intertexts in which legal practice, journalism, social science, and public opinion support one another. And they infiltrate into the judgment of opponents of the death penalty as well as the supporters. But how could this be? The categories, according to my story, have been unstable since their inception; and yet sentiment about the death penalty changes century by century and decade by decade. It seems to me that two major shifts in contemporary life combine with a couple more specific changes to intensify support for the death penalty. The profound shifts include the *globalization* of so many aspects of life in a world organized politically around the presumption of sovereign nation-states and the radical acceleration of *tempo* in several domains of life. The specific changes revolve around the concentration of an African American underclass in inner cities where the most visible acts of violence occur.

The globalization of economic life compromises the nation-state as the highest site of citizen sovereignty. According to the logic of democratic sovereignty *I* am free when I can choose among several life options in a variety of domains; *we* are free when the state formally accountable to us through elections can act to protect both its standing in the world and the institutional conditions of nationhood. But the globalization of economic life deflates the experience of a sovereign, democratic state by imposing a variety of visible effects upon it that the state is compelled to adjust to in one way or another. The state can most easily respond to many of these by shifting their most onerous burdens to its least powerful constituencies. The tendency to shift burdens to the most vulnerable constitutencies is accentuated by the widespread tendency to blame the state for the limits it faces while celebrating the market as a potential site of freedom. That combination, in turn, further depletes the sense of efficacy attributed to the one agency whose actions are accountable in principle to citizens. It deflates again our *sense* of collective freedom. A compensatory site of efficacy and accountability is thereby needed. Perhaps the state will restore its image as a site of effective accountability if it displays awesome power in the single domain everyone cedes to it as its own: criminal punishment. Under these circumstances, signs of general state inadequacy become translated into dramatic displays of state power in the realm of criminal punishment. "We" are free because the state can act impressively in the domain of crime without interfering with the market. Once the state has been constrained from two sides in its effort to address the social conditions of extensive criminality, spectacular acts of state vengeance are wheeled in to compensate for that deficit. That is why the most fervent defenders of the death penalty are typically also defenders of absolute state sovereignty in international life and the minimization of state regulation of the economy. The appearance of collective freedom is now fomented by construing crime as the single most important impediment to it and spectacular punishment by the state as the only viable response. The state becomes a theater of punitive power to retain its appearance of sovereignty and accountability under otherwise unfavorable conditions.

The capacity to execute is a visible and awesome public power, one able to divert attention from the state's limited efficacy in other domains. The "failure" of capital punishment, from the vantage point of deterrence, then, is trumped by its success in symbolizing the state as a potent agent of public revenge in a world of high anxiety. The perverse equation is that *we* feel free as a public under unfavorable conditions of citizen confidence and state efficacy when the primary unit of democratic accountability displays the power to wreak revenge against those who it targets as the most visible threats to personal freedom. These internal and external limits to state power, then, work in rough coordination with the refusal by suburban dwellers to address the conditions of life in the inner cities. The high visibility of black violence in the inner city adds another potent element to the mix, making capital punishment the one act that can represent the power of the state while retaining collective unwillingness to invest in extensive programs of job creation, education, and urban renewal in the cities. We now feel free as a people when the state captures, tries, and kills the internal enemies it helps to render most visible to us.

These pressures combine with the accentuation of tempo in population migration, cultural communication, military mobility, tourism, and entertainment. With the sharp acceleration of tempo in so many domains of life, more people more often encounter ideas and relationships that call into question cherished aspects of their own identities heretofore treated as fundamental, immoveable, natural, or sanctified. Christians encounter diverse theistic and nontheistic faiths; established ethnic groups encounter strange new ethnicities; heterosexuals encounter gays and lesbians who have come out of the closet; males encounter feminists who call into question traits of masculinity previously marked as natural; and so on. The acceleration of tempo renders it more difficult to confirm the natural or transcendental character of what you are; and the tactical advantage such confirmation traditionally carries with it in the domain of moral judgment now becomes jeopardized. What you *are* in the domains of gender, ethnicity, religion, sensuality, and so on, no longer becomes translated so easily into a set of moral commands you and everyone else are obligated to *obey*. You are placed under pressure to desanctify elements of your own subjectivity even as they help to define who you are.

The unstable practice of individual responsibility becomes even more difficult to fix under these conditions; for now the persistent instabilities inside are activated by contact with alternative interpretations outside. This categorical insecurity presses a variety of constituencies to insist more fervently upon fundamentalizing traditional dictates of morality, responsibility, normality, and punishment. For how can those constituencies on the margin of the economy and educational system receive recognition for their insecure achievements and self-restraint unless those who break the code are held entirely responsible for their failures?[15] This may be why it is common to find many in this culture who support the death penalty aggressively to insist with equal fervency about the naturalness of heterosexuality, the moral superiority of Christianity, the irresponsibility of welfare recipients, the vacuity of liberalism, and the nihilism of deconstruction.

Under such conditions the death penalty performs a set of intercoded functions. It first confirms through its rhetoric of retribution a conception of will and responsibility through which a variety of insecure constituencies ratify desert for the precarious social standing they have attained and the difficult self-restraint they exercise at work, in the home, and on the street. It then allows selective release from this difficult logic of self-restraint by allowing vicarious participation in the legal killing of murderers. Finally, it deflects attention from the state's failure to respond to other grievances of those same constituencies and to the larger contexts in which both their grievances and criminal violence are set. Execution becomes simultaneously a theatrical demonstration of state power (amidst a general sense of state inefficacy), a violent vindication of individual responsibility (amidst life in interdependent institutional complexes subjected to feeble coordination), a momentary release from the dictates of self restraint (in a world where its practice elsewhere is demanded), and an opportunity to express strains of fascination and secret identification with outcasts whose acts of violence might be taken to symbolize repudiation of this entire complex of power, responsibility, and restraint. The very aura of finality that accompanies state executions helps to silence questions about the categories of will and responsibility that vindicate the actions.

Capital punishment thus becomes a major front in cultural war. It mobilizes political divisions between one set of partisans, who seek to return to a fictive world in which the responsible individual, retributive punishment, the market economy, the sovereign state, and the nation coalesced, and another set, who seek to respond in more generous ways to new experiences of the cultural contingency of identity, the pluralization of culture, the problematical character of traditional conceptions of agency and responsibility, and the role of the state in a new world order.

The propagators of cultural war augment the first set of dispositions by attacking carriers of the second set of questions. The politics of forgetting is crucial to their success. William Bennett in *The Devaluing of America: The Fight for our Culture and our Children* connects a variety of right-wing campaigns in education, media programming, and drug wars to a more general "fight for our culture and our children." And his celebration of a virulent form of capital punishment forms a key part of that campaign. Bennett himself summarizes a piece of his CNN interview on *Larry King Live* when a listener calls in to press him to up the ante against drug dealers: "Why build prisons?" the caller asks. "Get tough like (Saudi) Arabia. Behead the damned drug dealers. We're just too damned soft." Bennett:

> "One of the things that I think is a problem is that we are not doing enough that is morally proportional to the nature of the offense. I mean, what the caller suggests is morally plausible. Legally, it's difficult."
> I could see King's eyes light up. He asked for a clarification. "Behead?"
> "Yeah. Morally, I don't have anything wrong with it," I said.
> "You would behead . . ." King began again.
> "Somebody selling drugs to a kid?" I said. "Morally I don't have any problem with that at all. I mean, ask most Americans if they saw somebody out on the streets selling drugs to their kid what they would feel morally justified in doing—tear them limb from limb. . . . What we need to do is find some constitutional and legally permissible way to do what this caller suggests, not literally to behead, but to make the punishment fit the crime. And the crime is horrible." During the program I strongly rejected calls for drug legalization and endorsed capital punishment for major drug dealers.[16]

Bennett's rhetoric is potent. He unites in one act of identification forgetfulness of instability in a culture's own categories of will and punishment, the theatricality of the state power to kill, and the promise to make state punishment "morally proportional" to the act. The enunciations of "morally proportional," "morally plausible," and "feel morally justified" do much of the work. They invest intense feelings of outrage and vengeance in the blue-chip stock of morality, covertly debasing the latter until it becomes a container into which selective energies of revenge can be poured. Moral proportionality retains the appearance of equivalence between responsibility and punishment, but that uneasy equation is now translated into proportionality between the intensity of public outrage and the amount of agony to be endured by the targets of public punishment. The Bennett synthesis of beheading and moral proportionality both drowns out liberal questions about the morality of capital punishment and recruits new soldiers to a cultural war in the name of morality.

Once the recruitment pitch is delivered, Bennett moderates the message just enough to paint a veneer of deniability between him and those who fret about the constitutionality or barbarism of beheading. The veneer must be thin because Bennett, as he himself indicates, *seeks to incite* liberal elites to outrage against his virulent proposals in order to make them the primary targets of cultural war. Bennett binds his image of morality to a harsh form of capital punishment to insist that what is truly moral is also hard, efficacious, and satisfying to its perpetrators. Morality is severe and simple; if your brand lacks either quality it falls into the class of subjectivism or relativism. Public objections by liberals miss the point unless we are able to challenge the line of associations between morality, simplicity, revenge and death. Until we do, the agents of cultural war will succeed in using our opposition to associate us with moral softness toward murderers, drug dealers, welfare cheats, and pornographers.

Bennett *converts* the liberal ripostes he calls forth into energies of cultural war against liberalism. Thus: "Many of the elites ridiculed my opinion. But it resonated with the American people because they knew what drugs were doing, and they wanted a morally proportionate response."[17] Why must these "elites" be targets? Because so many hold "our Judeo-Christian tradition" in "contempt" and are "so riven with relativism that they doubt the preferability of civilization to savagery."[18] What is the "morally proportionate" response? One that meets every act of criminal violence with an awesome act of state violence. *That* proportionality preserves the state as an instrument of punitive power and covers its depletion as an instrument of social welfare and education.

I imagine that those people most intensely committed to the death penalty also oppose the right of the terminally ill to doctor-assisted suicide. While I admire Jack Kervorkian as a (marred) hero, they would call him "the Doctor of Death." Why? Perhaps because to endorse the right to die (with procedural protections to ensure against misuses) is to bring one's own death too close. The very thought of making such a *decision for oneself* about the timing of death may be too disturbing to allow others *the right to decide* on the bases of their fundamental conceptions of life and death. For if others are allowed to ponder such a possibility, and sometimes decide for it, your refusal to do so begins to look like a decision too. But where does the death penalty fit into this scenario? Fervent support for the death *penalty* conjoined to intense opposition to the *right* to die draws the thought of death away from oneself and toward the agent of violence. Perhaps when you construe death as a penalty for others while concentrating on your own innocence by comparison to them, state repetition of the "death penalty" inspires on some register the dim sense that *you* do not deserve to die. By binding death to desert through support for the death penalty you push the difficult thought about that inevitable event a little further away from yourself. The linkage between death and penalty is closer to a thought behind one's thoughts than an enunciated thought. But its attribution helps to explain an otherwise odd combination. For now, either the state's introduction of the right to die or its refusal of the death penalty becomes very disturbing. And its adoption of both practices together would rattle you immensely. State refusal of the right to die and state execution of murderers and drug dealers may thereby help to obscure the character of death as an inevitable *event* in favor of its interpretation as a *penalty*. Certainly, there are currents in the Christian tradition supportive of that combination. Augustine himself concluded that the first two humans deserved to die. But this covert linkage between death and penalty means that fostering support for "the right to die" and against the "death penalty" requires work on the same complex of thoughts.

Does such an intense combination also express covert resentment against a Creator who would allow death in the first place? Lurking inside the most fervent demands for execution by the state may be a floating resentment against the obdurate fact of mortality in search of an acceptable outlet. To blame God would be too disturbing. To blame the world would be pointless. So concentrate on those who "deserve to die." This gives the semblance of control over an element in the human condition unsusceptible to evasion in the last instance. The pronouncement of radical difference between you and them obscures, if only partially and temporarily, a more profound similarity of condition. Part of the profound cultural resentment against liberal and secular elites may involve resentment against those whose perspective on the right to die and the death penalty challenges this unstated equation between death and penalty.

My interpretation, as with others of its type, has no certainty attached to it. It tries to read subterranean currents of anxiety and desire at work in those who oppose the right to die and affirm the death penalty with the greatest intensity. Doing so to think about the registers of being that must be engaged by those who oppose capital punishment and support the right to die with procedural protections. The interpretation is limited in its application. It may fit some of the most urgent activists in favor of capital punishment well enough, while it misses others who support capital punishment less urgently, out of frustration with high rates of crime. Or what about Sister Prejean? She opposes the death penalty, but she may well oppose doctor-assisted death, too, on the grounds that only God has sufficient wisdom to make the most fundamental decisions of life and death. I am willing to wager, however, that if she resists doctor-assisted death, she would not insist upon a law forbidding that decision by others once procedural protections were secured. She has too much respect for the value of life and the contestability of every fundamental faith, including her own, for that. And the person who demands capital punishment and the right to die with equal fervor? It would be interesting to meet her.

Capital punishment has become a weapon of cultural war on several levels: it coarsens broad sections of the population, preparing them to accept punitive campaigns against a variety of disturbing constituencies; it foments political divisions favorable to the Right by associating liberal "relativism" and "weakness" with the "savagery" of implacable killers; it fosters the politics of forgetting by translating "moral proportionality" from an uncertain attempt to match penalty to crime into a politically potent equation between the level of social resentment felt by disaffected constituencies and the level of violence taken by the state against convicted murderers; it displays the state as an awesome theater of force in one domain during a time when its effective accountability is otherwise shaky; and it organizes a set of cultural anxieties about the place of death in life.

Sister Prejean and Albert Camus have faith that if only more people saw what actually happens on death row and at executions they would reconsider their abstract commitments to capital punishment. Camus dramatizes how the death penalty, often represented publicly as a brief, surgical event, actually involves a long, arduous "premeditation" and "organization . . . which is in itself a source of moral sufferings more terrible than death"; how it engenders a "devastating, degrading fear that is imposed on the condemned for months or years"; how futile appeals for official reprieve create a "horror parcelled out to the man who is condemned to death." So, by the time a captive of the state has reached the time of execution, "[h]e is no longer a man but a thing waiting to be handled by the executioners. He is kept as if he were inert matter, but still has a consciousness which is his chief enemy"; and "he travels along in the intricate machinery that determines his very gesture and eventually hands him over to those will lay him down of the killing machine."[19] Sister Prejean exhibits the essence of this state utopia of violence in a phrase: "I can hear the words San Quenton guards used to yell when a death-row inmate was let out of his cell: 'Dead man walkin.'"[20]

In the light of evidence from Vernon Harvey and William Bennett, though, the situation appears to be more divided. It may well be that capital punishment— exalted by some as "noble" in public rhetoric and hidden behind closed doors in practice—both diverts the eyes of humanists from its degrading effects and feeds the passions of those who celebrate the state's role in inflicting degradation upon available targets. To satisfy *this* latter demand for "proportionality" between the drive to revenge and state action is what it takes to save "our" culture, according to some. The imagination of an absolute power delivering a defeated and silenced enemy to a vengeful public focuses upon the long-term suffering of "mad dog" killers who await their own execution. But it also includes somewhere in its compass a punitive fantasy about liberals, secularists, and deconstructionists. The immediate prey of state execution pay a heavy price for their second status as surrogates for a larger enemy that cannot be reached so easily. But then the stakes in the war for "our culture" are high. Liberal and deconstructive elites (these two warring factions within the democratic Left are treated as the same by many on the right) might play into the game of supporters of capital punishment by focusing merely on its cruelties. They themselves are targets because they expose things too disturbing to hear by members of the execution brigade. Liberal elites function as imaginary targets of the capital punishment regime because their "moral nihilism" is already associated by cultural warriors with the savagery of murder.

Under these circumstances, familiar critiques of capital punishment, taken alone, are insufficient. They may even contribute something to the politics of resentment they strive to surmount. That, anyway, is the hypothesis entertained here.

204 • *The Death Penalty and the Culture of Responsibility*

To the extent it is true, it remains pertinent to show the least intense devotees of capital punishment how the politics of cultural forgetting proceeds in this domain, how support for capital punishment grows out of that politics, how such a practice imposes immense degradations on its prey while they are on death row and during the moments of execution, and how it diverts the state from other projects needed to sustain the general conditions of democratic pluralism. But these engagements are insufficient, and even liable to backfire, unless they are linked to a broader, more difficult agenda. To engage capital punishment at its cultural source we require interpretations that expose cultural sources of the intense social resentment in circulation today, and we need to probe more carefully the politics by which it so readily becomes shifted onto a selective set of targets. It then becomes incumbent upon us, first, to teach each other how to translate *existential* dimensions of resentment (including resentment over the fact of mortality) into a reaffirmation of life itself. And, second, to join political movements that speak to those economic, educational, and social circumstances that encourage so many to resent their place in a democratic culture. When we address each of these dimensions in relation to the others, we might begin to reduce the huge fund of cultural resentment invested in capital punishment.[21]

Notes

1. *The Confessions of St. Augustine*, trans. John K. Ryan (New York: Image Books, 1960), bk. 8, ch. 9, pp. 196–197.

2. *The Confessions*, 197.

3. Cesare Beccaria, *On Crimes and Punishments*, trans. David Young (New York: Hackett Publishing, 1986), 17.

4. Beccaria, *On Crimes and Punishments*, 49.

5. Immanuel Kant, *The Metaphysics of Morals*, trans. Mary Gregor (Cambridge: Cambridge University Press: 1991), 141–142.

6. Kant, *Religion within the Limits of Reason Alone*, trans. Theodore Greene and Hoyt Hudson (New York: Harper Torchbooks, 1960), 32.

7. Friedrich Nietzsche, *Human All Too Human*, trans. R. J. Hollinger (New York: Cambridge University Press, 1986), 306.

8. Sister Helen Prejean, *Dead Man Walking: An Eyewitness Account of the Death Penalty in the United States* (New York: Random House, 1993).

9. Prejean, *Dead Man Walking*, 236–237.

10. Prejean, *Dead Man Walking*, 226.

11. James Q. Wilson, and Richard J Herrnstein, *Crime and Human Nature* (New York: Touchstone Book, 1985).

12. Wilson and Herrnstein, *Crime and Human Nature*, 505–506.

13. Quoted from V. P. Hans, "Death by Jury" in *Commonsense Justice: Juror's Notions of the Law*, ed Norman J. Finkel (Cambridge, Mass.: Harvard University Press, 1995), 184.

14. Austin Sarat, "Speaking of Death: Narratives of Violence in Capital Trials," 168–169, in *The Rhetoric of Law*, ed. Austin Sarat and Thomas R. Kearns (Ann Arbor: University of Michigan Press, 1994), 135–184.

15. Wendy Brown, in a superb chapter of *States of Injury: Power and Freedom in Late-Modernity* (Princeton: Princeton University Press, 1995), entitled "Wounded Attachments," explores how the attachments people form to destructive modes of their own subjection can foster profound resentments seeking legitimate outlets. "Insofar as what Nietzsche calls slave

morality produces identity in relation to power, insofar as identity rooted in this reaction achieves its moral superiority by reproaching power and action themselves as evil, identity . . . becomes deeply invested in its own impotence, even while it seeks to assuage the pain of its powerlessness through its vengeful moralizing. . . . Indeed, it is more likely to punish and reproach—'punishment is what revenge calls itself— . . .' than to find venues of self-affirming action" (p. 71). This book, and in particular this chapter, explores more deeply and persistently the psychology and social mechanisms I am engaging here with respect to capital punishment.

16. Bennett, *The Devaluing of America: The Fight for Our Culture and Our Children* (New York: Summit Book, 1992), 116.

17. Bennett, *The Devaluing of America*, 116.

18. Bennett, *The Devaluing of America*, 173.

19. The quotations occur between pages 199 and 202 of Camus's "Reflection on the Guillotine," in Albert Camus, *Resistance, Rebellion and Death*, trans. Justice O'Brien (New York: Vintage Books, 1960).

20. *Dead Man Walking*, 156.

21. I suppose that Nietzsche can help on the first front while thinkers like Arendt and Foucault might help on the second. The problem, for starters, is that few of us are now prepared to show how each front is entangled in the other and not too many are prepared to listen even if we made progress in the diagnosis. But it remains important to keep trying.

· 9 ·

BEYOND INTENTION: A CRITIQUE OF THE "NORMAL" CRIMINAL AGENCY, RESPONSIBILITY, AND PUNISHMENT IN AMERICAN DEATH PENALTY JURISPRUDENCE

JENNIFER L. CULBERT

As the United States Constitution is interpreted by the Supreme Court, there is a heightened obligation to determine as accurately as possible the culpability of a defendant who may be sentenced to death for participation in a crime.[1] However, in a "deregulated" political and legal environment, just how such determinations are to be made in a court of law is not clear. As Robert Weisberg has argued, the Supreme Court has failed in its efforts to articulate formal criteria by which to determine responsibility at law. Consequently, lower courts have to rely on the discretion of judges and jurors to make "reliable" sentencing decisions.[2] As a result, defendants are sentenced to death when they violate deeply held though not necessarily articulated assumptions about socially acceptable behavior. In other words, when the Supreme Court fails to define formal criteria for judgment, the legitimacy of legal decisions about punishment and responsibility hinges on moral norms instead of formal principles.

For the purposes of the legal system, norms can serve as meaningful and yet relatively flexible standards for judgment because they are derived from patterns of behavior taken to be typical of a particular group. Indeed, it might be argued that when individuals are judged with reference to patterns of behavior typical of the group to which they belong, verdicts and sentencing decisions will more accurately reflect the uniqueness of individuals and the particularity of their circumstances without compromising the principle of equal treatment. From a perspective within the group, the individual appears to be treated like any other; from a perspective outside of the group, that treatment seems to reflect the individual's unique situation.

In this essay, I consider the legal turn to norms in death penalty decisions. Specifically, I examine how norms serve as formal criteria to determine capital liability at law. In my analysis, I focus on *Tison v. Arizona* (1987), a United States Supreme Court case in which the Court rules that a person may be sentenced to death for a crime he or she neither committed nor intended to commit.[3] I focus on this case for several reasons. First, in *Tison* the Court announces a new standard of capital liability, specifically, a new culpable mental state, "reckless indifference to the value of human life." According to the Court, this mental state—when accompanied by major participation in a felony murder—is so heinous as to warrant punishment with death.4 In so ruling, the Court expresses crucial assumptions about how "normal persons" act, how they ought to act, and the grounds upon which they may be held legally responsible for the consequences of their actions. Second, I analyze *Tison v. Arizona* because the Court's ruling is motivated, at least in part, by a need to protect the practice of using norms to legitimate legal decisions. In the course of such practice, I suggest, the Court exploits the polysemy of the "normal." As Georges Canguilhem points out, "normal" has two different meanings: "(1) normal is that which is such that it ought to be; (2) normal, in the most usual sense of the word, is that which is met with in the majority of cases of a determined kind, or that which constitutes either the average or standard of a measurable characteristic."5 I argue that in the wake of the deregulation of the death penalty, the Court tries to use norms in their "factual" sense as normative principles. Consequently, when the idea of the so-called normal person is undermined by work in psychology and philosophy, the Court's ability to make decisions in its most difficult cases is threatened. Finally, in my analysis of *Tison*, I demonstrate how the Court's efforts to safeguard the "normal person" reveal the limitations of its approach to judgment in a modern, pluralist society. As Hannah Arendt has already argued in her account of the trial of Adolph Eichmann, the legal system must confront the fact that "an average, 'normal' person, neither feeble-minded nor indoctrinated nor cynical, could be perfectly incapable of telling right from wrong."6

Tison v. Arizona: Defining the Sins of the Sons

In 1978, carrying out a plan devised by their mother and other members of their family, Ricky, Raymond, and Donald Tison walked into the Arizona State Prison with an ice chest full of guns and, without firing a shot, managed to break out with their father, Gary Tison, and his cellmate, Randy Greenawalt. The plan continued to go smoothly until, some days later, the group's getaway car was rendered useless by a flat tire. Improvising, they decided to steal another car by flagging down a passing motorist. John Lyons, his wife, Donnelda, their two-year-old son, Christopher, and Lyons's fifteen-year-old niece, Theresa Tyson, stopped when they saw Raymond Tison waving. The men immediately dragged the family from their vehicle and put them in the car with the flat tire. In this car, they were driven out into the desert, where Gary Tison and Randy Greenawalt shot them. Tison's sons were surprised and upset by the killings—they had been fetching water for their captives when the shooting began—but nevertheless, they made no attempt to get away from the two and did not turn them in. Not long after the shooting, however, the group ran into a roadblock and a shootout with police ensued. Donald Tison was killed and Gary Tison escaped into the desert, where he died of exposure. Ricky and Raymond Tison were captured with Greenawalt.

Tried individually for capital murder and a variety of other offenses under Arizona accomplice liability and felony murder statutes, all three were convicted of the murders and a judge sentenced them to death. However, after the Supreme Court ruled in *Enmund v. Florida* (1982) that persons cannot be sentenced to death unless it has been proven beyond a reasonable doubt that they committed or intended to commit murder, Ricky and Raymond Tison appealed their sentences.7 In its ruling on this appeal, the Supreme Court recognizes that neither Ricky nor Raymond Tison intended to kill the victims, nor did they inflict the fatal wounds (137). However, rather than commuting their sentences to life in prison, the Court remanded the case after articulating a new culpable mental state that may be used to support a capital sentencing judgment. This new culpable mental state is "reckless indifference to human life" (151).

The Court's opinion in *Tison v. Arizona* is remarkable because the case under consideration could easily have been decided in terms of either one of two existing felony murder categories the Court had at its disposal. "Felony murder" refers to the legal doctrine derived from a common law rule that one whose conduct brings about a death in the commission or the attempted commission of a felony is guilty of murder. This doctrine is controversial, as it entitles a court to sentence a defendant to death for a homicide he may have had no intention of committing. Indeed, in *Enmund*, the Court finds that capital punishment is disproportional in cases where the defendant is a "minor actor in an armed robbery, not on the scene, who neither intended to kill nor was found to have had any culpable mental state" (149). At the same time, in that case the Court also asserts that capital punishment is not disproportional in cases where the defendant is a felony murderer who actually killed, attempted to kill, or intended to kill (150). Writing for the majority in *Tison*, O'Connor observes that the Tison brothers fall somewhere in between these two extremes.

However, depending on how the Justices chose to delineate the crime for which the Tisons were sentenced to death, the Court could easily have justified a decision either affirming or overturning the judgment. If the Court had limited the crime to the immediate circumstances surrounding the killings, *Enmund* could have governed and the Tisons' death sentences would have been overturned. The Court could have emphasized the fact that when Gary Tison and Randy Greenawalt opened fire on the Lyons family, Ricky and Raymond Tison were fetching water for their captives so that they would not die of thirst in the desert while they waited to be rescued. The Court could also have noted that Gary Tison had already taken the precaution of disabling the car so that the Lyonses would not be able to drive away after he and his sons left. The obvious conclusion to draw from these facts is that Gary Tison intended to leave the Lyons family alive in the desert—indeed, this is precisely the conclusion that his sons drew. Thus, in addition to the fact that Ricky and Raymond Tison did not intend to harm the Lyonses, the Court could have argued that under the circumstances, they had no reason to believe that their captives would be harmed by anyone else.

On the other hand, if the Court had defined the crime as beginning at the prison where both Ricky and Raymond Tison admitted they had been willing to take lives to defend themselves, the Court could have based its decision on felony murder doctrine. As the Court itself notes in detail, both of the brothers brought guns into the Arizona State Prison and armed known killers. In addition, they stole a car and entrusted the lives of the car's occupants to the killers. When their father shot these people, they failed to intervene. What is more, they continued to help their father and his cellmate run from the law.

Yet the Court claims that *Tison v. Arizona* doesn't fit either category and that some other grounds for determining the capital liability of the defendants needs to be articulated. What is it about the *Tison* case that makes another category of such liability necessary?

The simple answer to this question is that while the Supreme Court considers the defendants' participation in the murders "substantial," it also takes seriously their lack of intention in committing the crime. However, in the end, this simple answer amounts to something much more complicated. I suggest that it amounts to what Hannah Arendt in her account of the trial of Adolf Eichmann calls "the banality of evil." Arendt identifies this condition after observing the difficulty with which Eichmann was prosecuted, defended, and judged. While the question of his guilt was never at issue, she sees the court struggling to understand how a man who was neither a monster nor a clown could be responsible for such extraordinary crimes. Arendt concludes:

> The trouble with Eichmann was precisely that so many were like him, and that the many were neither perverted nor sadistic, that they were, and still are, terribly and terrifyingly normal. From the viewpoint of our legal institutions and of our moral standards of judgment, this normality was much more terrifying than all the atrocities put together, for it implied . . . that this new type of criminal, who is in actual fact *hostis generis humani*, commits his crimes under circumstances that make it well-nigh impossible for him to know or to feel that he is doing wrong. (276)

Such is the banality of evil. Under circumstances in which their actions are commonplace and they do not directly hurt others, normal persons have no cause to realize they are doing wrong. Even as they participate in some of the most horrible crimes ever imagined, they have no intention of doing "harm." Similarly, in the *Tison* case, I suggest, the Court confronts the bleak fact that most horrific acts committed by one person against another occur as small thoughtless gestures under mundane, if not trite, circumstances.

In *Eichmann in Jerusalem*, Arendt concludes that modern legal systems may no longer assume that intent is necessary to the commission of a crime (277). *Hostis generis humani* act without imagining or meaning any criminal effect; alternative grounds for judgment must be found. Arendt herself embraces Yosal Rogat's proposition that "a great crime offends against nature, so that the very earth cries out for vengeance" (277). I think that the decision to establish a new standard of capital liability in *Tison v. Arizona* represents a similar gesture on the part of the Supreme Court.[8] In his dissent, Justice William Brennan says as much when he remarks, "[T]he decision to execute these petitioners . . . appears responsive less to reason than to other, more visceral, demands" (183–184). Indeed, he suggests that the Court articulates a new standard of capital liability in this case because the actual murderer is beyond human grasp (184).

Brennan claims that cries for vengeance are anachronistic to a society governed by the Court, but his words are explicitly contradicted by statements made by other justices. In *Furman v. Georgia* (1972), for example, Justice Potter Stewart writes: "The instinct for retribution is part of the nature of man, and channeling that instinct in the administration of criminal justice serves an important purpose in promoting the stability of a society governed by law. When people begin to believe that organized society is unwilling or unable to impose upon criminal offenders the punishment they "deserve," then there are sown the seeds of anarchy—of self-help, vigilante justice, and lynch law."[9] Contrary to Brennan, Stewart believes that the desire for retribution is characteristic both of the timeless nature of man and of the contemporary administration of justice. In addition, as his selective use of quotation marks suggests, Stewart thinks that retribution is not concerned with what a criminal offender *actually* deserves as punishment for a particular crime—that is, determined, at least in part, by the offender's intent in committing a particular crime—but rather with what people in society *believe* is deserved.

And yet, I will argue, the Court's decision in *Tison* is not ultimately motivated by a desire for revenge. The Court articulates a new culpable mental state in this case for a more abstruse but more jurisprudentially significant reason: to reinforce the rapidly deteriorating figure of the "normal person" at law.

The "Normal Person"

Although not technically a term at law, the "normal person" embodies the kind of criteria that make it possible to identify blameworthy individuals when other, more formal criteria of judgment may not be brought to bear. I take the term "normal person" from the work of the legal philosopher H. L. A. Hart.[10] In an essay on punishment and responsibility, Hart argues that a morally acceptable theory of punishment must be able to explain why punishment should be restricted to the perpetrator of a particular crime, and why the severity of the perpetrator's punishment should reflect his intention in committing that crime:

> [A] good reason for administering a less severe penalty is made out if the situation or mental state of the convicted criminal is such that he was exposed to an unusual or specially great temptation, or his ability to control his actions is thought to have been impaired or weakened otherwise than by his action, so that conformity to the law which he has broken was a matter of special difficulty for him as compared with normal persons normally placed. (15)

In fact, the figure of the normal person appears not only in texts of legal philosophy but also in court opinions that determine how the law is actually interpreted and practiced. For example, when the U.S. Court of Appeals for the District of Columbia recognizes the validity of an insanity defense at law, it warns: "Our recognition of an insanity defense for those who lack the essential, threshold free will possessed by those in the normal range is not to be twisted, directly or indirectly, into a device for exculpation of those without an abnormal condition of the mind."[11] "Those in the normal range" are precisely those to whom Hart refers as "normal persons."

Neither Hart nor the court of appeals finds it necessary to describe these persons in any detail: consequently, their shared assumption that the normal person is an autonomous, rational, self-determining agent is only indirectly revealed. Hart, for example, contrasts individuals who may be mentally impaired or unable to control themselves with "normal persons," thus implicitly defining normal persons as those in full possession of their faculties and who act only as they intend. Meanwhile, the Court states that persons who lack "an essential, threshold free will" have an abnormal condition of the mind, implying that normal persons have a basic capacity to choose and to exercise discretion in their choices.

Furthermore, the fact that these claims are made only implicitly suggests that both Hart and the court of appeals assume that the features they attribute to the normal person are familiar to their respective audiences. Indeed, without instructions to the contrary, these audiences are encouraged to think of the "normal person" invoked within a legal context as identical to the "normal person" they themselves might employ in everyday speech.[12] In short, when Hart and the Court refer to the normal person, they refer neither to a formal legal or political category, nor to a figure defined and studied by social science, but rather only to a customary or conventional standard of behavior. The open but still discriminating character of this standard is reiterated in the court of appeals's invocation of "the essential, threshold free will" that it attributes to people in the "normal range." A threshold delineates a space, simultaneously marking an "inside" and an "outside." While it may seem a simple matter to move from one side of a threshold to the other, strictly speaking there is no formal or empirical way to determine when exactly the threshold is crossed. As the Court suggests with this image, what makes a person a "normal person" depends upon a common habit or tradition of interpretation.[13]

The "normal person" serves as the standard by which responsible or blameworthy agents are identified at law: as Hart and the district court imply, only "normal persons" who fail to conform to the law can offer me "good reason" for a less severe penalty.[14] Conversely, only autonomous, rational, self-determining agents may be held fully accountable for the consequences of their actions. Sir William Blackstone offers an early explanation of why this must be the case. According to Blackstone, "[A]n involuntary act[,] as it has no claim to merit, so neither can it induce any guilt.[15] Blackstone says that only the concurrence of the will renders human actions worthy of praise or blame because human actions that are informed by will may reflect or express something in addition to or other than what is accomplished by the act itself, something calling for moral consideration.[16] Of course, Blackstone concedes, the quality of a person's will can only be examined after he has expressed that will in deed. Nevertheless, "to constitute a crime against human laws, there must be, first, a vicious will, and, secondly, an unlawful act consequent upon such vicious will" (2175). In other words, a criminal act alone is insufficient to establish the commission of a crime. The person charged with committing a crime must also have willed the consequences of his or her actions.

This logic is generally reflected in U.S. criminal law. In the United States, in order to find someone guilty of committing a crime the state must establish that the person committed a "guilty act" or wrongful deed (*actus reus*) with criminal intent or a "guilty mind" (*mens rea*). Consequently, defendants may argue that they did not commit a crime even when it is established that they did commit a "wrongful deed." In such cases, defendants excuse themselves: they argue that their "guilty act" was not accompanied by the requisite "guilty mind." As an excuse, they might claim that they did not know what they were doing at the time, or they might show that they knew what they were doing but that they were powerless to stop themselves.[17] Thus, for example, a defendant might argue that although she shot someone, she was being held at gunpoint, and if she had not pulled the trigger, she would have been killed herself. As she did not will the murder she committed, she would argue, she is not responsible for committing it. And indeed, in such a case, according to the law, the person who ordered the defendant to shoot is the guilty party, not the person who actually pulled the trigger.

Even when persons are found to have possessed the will to commit a crime, however, it is still possible to argue that they were not in full possession of their faculties at the time of the criminal act. The law recognizes that at that moment the defendant may have confronted some external conditions or internal limitations that made it particularly difficult for him or her to stay in control.[18] Should there be any evidence of such "mitigating circumstances," the defendant is still held legally responsible for the crime but is not necessarily punished as severely as the law allows. So criminal intent may be a factor not only in the decision that a particular person committed a crime, but also in the decision about what that person deserves for having committed the crime. In presenting arguments to this effect during the penalty phase of the trial, the defendant hopes that the court will decide that he or she does not deserve as much punishment as a "normal" person.

The "Dangerous Individual"

In *Tison v. Arizona*, the Supreme Court announces a new standard for capital liability; however, it does not officially rule on the question of whether Ricky and Raymond Tison are, in fact, culpable under this new standard. Thus, the Supreme Court does not officially consider whether the Tisons themselves are "normal" and therefore deserve as much punishment as the law allows. In dictum, however, the Court observes that the Tisons were major participants in the crimes committed by their father and that "the record would support a finding of the culpable mental state of reckless indifference to human life" (151). Indeed, only a few paragraphs later, the Court states again that the facts of the case "would clearly support a finding that [the Tison brothers] both subjectively appreciated that their acts were likely to result in the taking of innocent life" (152). Despite the fact that the Court is not in a formal position to do so, the Court insists that the Tisons may be held fully accountable for the murders committed by their father and Randy Greenawalt. That is to say, in addition to announcing a new standard of capital liability, the Court identifies no excuses or mitigating circumstances that would provide a "good reason for administering a less severe penalty" in this case. According to the Supreme Court, Ricky and Raymond Tison are "normal."

However, such a conclusion leaves the Court in a quandary, for how can it account for the fact that "normal persons" may thus be the unwitting perpetrators of heinous crimes, crimes apparently beyond the pale of normality?[19] What is more, how can the Court justify punishing such perpetrators with death when, as O'Connor herself writes in the majority opinion, "Deeply ingrained in our legal tradition is the idea that the more purposeful is the criminal conduct, the more serious is the offense, and therefore, the more severely it ought to be punished" (156)? According to O'Connor, death should be reserved for criminals whose offenses are the result of the most purposeful conduct.

The Court does not resolve this problem but obscures it with a single, powerful, but cryptic observation: "[S]ome nonintentional murderers may be among the most dangerous and inhumane of all" (157). According to the Court, individuals who engage in risky behavior can be more harmful to society than individuals who intentionally kill their victims. It argues that such individuals ought not to be considered any less criminal than those who intend to kill simply because they lack malice aforethought. Indeed, as the example of the individual who tortures people and accidentally kills them in the process demonstrates, the Court implies that such individuals present a truly terrifying aspect.

In all but name, the Supreme Court recalls the figure of the "dangerous individual" that Michel Foucault describes in his polemical account of the intervention of psychiatry into the field of law in the nineteenth century.[20] In this account, Foucault argues that psychiatry was able to make inroads into law by identifying the presence of an intrinsically dangerous element in the social body, the individual who, "by his very existence . . . is a creator of risk, even if he is not at fault, since he has not of his own free will chosen evil rather than good" (16). By ruling that people may, without choosing to take part in a lethal crime, nevertheless be found to have a culpable mental state at the time, the Court effectively claims that there are some "normal persons" who are intrinsically, though not intentionally, criminal in their actions.

With this claim the Court is able to obscure the rupture between the implicit legal concept of the normal person qua rational actor and the admission that such an actor can commit acts with unintended consequences. What makes particular individuals "dangerous" is the fact that they retain their capacity to act as autonomous, rational, self-determining agents, while at the same time acting without thought or purpose. Thus, a defendant may be sentenced to death because he acts without anticipating or desiring the consequences of his actions and yet otherwise is completely "normal." Only through subterfuge and equivocation can the Court make it possible to condemn individuals on the basis of a mental state of "reckless indifference to the value of human life." Only through such subterfuge and equivocation can the Court account for the fact that people participate in violent crimes with no intention of doing harm without resorting to psychological or medical accounts of human behavior.

Given the suggestive psychological quality of the facts of the *Tison* case, it is significant that little reference is made to the psychology of the defendants in the Court's opinion.[21] In fact, only Brennan in his dissent suggests that psychology plays any role in the Tisons' behavior. And even he makes such suggestions primarily in footnotes to his opinion. Aside from these few remarks, the Court has little time for the subjects of psychology or psychiatry. I suggest that the Court's reluctance to consider these subjects is an expression of its anxiety about the relationship between the usual "normal person" and the person who is "normal" but completely indifferent to the value of (other) human life. More significantly, the Court's reluctance is also an expression of its hostility toward familiar critiques of the "normal person" that threaten the figure upon which law depends.

Displacing the "Normal Person"

The presence or absence of whatever attributes are required to make a person "normal," particularly mental attributes, cannot be verified by simply observing that person.[22] Consequently, to make an informed judgment about the "viciousness" of a defendant's will, courts have sought to understand some "inner facts," such as what the defendant believed herself to be doing and what her motivations were. To determine how blameworthy the defendant is for her actions, the courts examine the defendant closely and try to consider her actions from her own point of view.[23]

In order to better understand this point of view, over the past century American law has turned to psychology and psychiatry, since these sciences take as their object of study the character of the mind and its relationship to behavior. However, by recognizing the relevance of these sciences to questions of responsibility addressed by the legal system, the legal system has risked undermining its own authority in at least two ways. The first and most obvious way is institutional. When psychologists and psychiatrists testify to the mental state of defendants, experts instead of juries tend to determine when someone may be held accountable for a crime. Obviously, judges and, more importantly, jurors, are not trained to recognize the signs of mental illness. Consequently, the law permits mental health professionals to testify in order to point out the signs that are perhaps invisible to the rest of the court.[24] However, expert witnesses do not simply testify that there are signs: they also interpret these signs, drawing from the latest psychiatric and social science research to support their interpretations. Thus experts speak with an authority that comes not only from experience, but from science.[25] When the responsibility for the judgment itself weighs heavy, as in cases where the defendant may be executed if found guilty, the likelihood of jurors deferring to expert opinion is greatly increased.[26]

The second threat posed by psychology and psychiatry to law is less obvious but more profound. By allowing mental health experts to testify to the presence of an "abnormal condition of the mind," the legal concept of the normal person risks being displaced, if not replaced, by a medical one. Legal scholars often argue that psychiatry conceives of normal persons as passive emotional subjects whose behavior is manipulated and possibly even predetermined by outside influences, while the law requires that normal persons be understood as the first cause of meaningful change in the world. For example, in a recent law review article entitled "*Mens Rea*: The Impasse of Law and Psychiatry," Pamela Hediger argues that psychiatrists should no longer be relied upon to decide whether defendants are to be held criminally responsible for their actions because psychiatric theories are based on assumptions about normal human behavior incompatible with legal assumptions about normal persons and their capacity to choose.[27] According to Hediger, the fundamental premise of criminal law is that "all persons are free agents confronted with a choice between doing right and wrong and that the person who chooses freely to do wrong is criminal" (614). By contrast, Hediger says psychiatry is based on the assumption that every individual act is the result of emotional forces and counterforces that are themselves shaped by past experience (622).

Arguments like Hediger's express a general concern that when normal persons are understood in psychological or psychiatric terms they can no longer be held accountable at law, for their choices may no longer be assumed to reflect what they *will* but only other factors such as family history or social pressure.[28] Consequently, when persons commit criminal acts they will rarely be found to have "guilty minds."[29] And of course, under such circumstances, capital punishment is particularly difficult to justify.[30]

Replacing the "Normal Person"

In *Tison v. Arizona*, the Court seeks to provide an explanation of the defendants' behavior without giving a psychological or psychiatric account of their actions. Hediger's argument suggests why the Court might want to avoid such an account: Should the Court permit, for instance, a mental health professional to determine how responsible the brothers are for their actions, the Tisons might be found to be blameless for the part they played in their father's crime because of the familial pressures involved in this case. Indeed, according to a psychologist who examined both Ricky and Raymond Tison in prison, while both Tisons believed they were functioning of their own volition when they helped their father escape, "it may have been less of their own volition than as a result of Mr. Tison's 'conditioning' and the rather amoral attitudes within the family home" (167). By ruling that "reckless indifference to the value of human life" is a culpable state of mind, and by suggesting that both of the Tisons experienced this state of mind when they helped their father to escape from prison, steal a car, and kidnap the Lyons family, the Court preserves its jurisdiction over the case and its authority to determine that the brothers deserve to die for their participation in the deaths that occurred. In so doing, the Court also saves the figure of the "normal person" from the threat posed by psychology, as envisioned by Hediger. When the Court in *Tison* claims that "reckless indifference to the value of human life" is so pernicious as to warrant death, this mental state is defined in strictly legal terms; the Court does not suggest that "reckless indifference" is equivalent to any pathological condition. Thus, there is no need to analyze the "inner facts" or emotional forces that may have shaped the defendants' perception of themselves and the quality of their actions. In this way, the Court's ruling is able to safeguard the idea of a "normal person" as being the sole source or primary cause of events in the shared life world of human beings and encourages the legal system to continue acting on the assumption that the "normal person" is a subject rather than an object of causal forces.

Indeed, the Supreme Court suggests that when Ricky and Raymond Tison helped their father escape from prison they both "subjectively" realized that their actions might lead to the death of some blameless person. Even though in *Enmund v. Florida* the Court finds that intent may not be equated with foreseeable harm, in *Tison v. Arizona* the Court claims that the brothers "subjectively appreciated that their acts were likely to result in the taking of innocent life." On the basis of this claim, the Court is able to conclude that when the brothers persisted in their actions they consciously accepted this chance and effectively chose to take praise or blame for the outcome. Thus, in *Tison*, when the Court decides that "reckless indifference" is equivalent to intent, it effectively defines this mental state as a rational assumption of risk. The only thing that distinguishes this assumption from foreseeable harm is that the assumption of risk is apparent only after the fact and only when the gamble is lost.

The Tisons were perfectly rational and law-abiding up until the time of the prison break; as boys, the Court notes, the Tisons had never had a single run-in with the law.[31] Consequently, the Court decides that when they helped their father escape and stayed with him through all that followed, it cannot be imagined how they did not grasp the significance of their actions. In effect, the Court assumes that no normal person could make such poor decisions without appreciating and consciously accepting the "likely" consequences.

The "Act"

While the legal system is well acquainted with the challenge posed by psychology and psychiatry to the "normal person" at law, it is less familiar with a challenge posed by philosophy, one that focuses on the theory of action implicit in the Court's death penalty jurisprudence. As we have just seen, the Court attributes to the figure of the "normal person" not simply the ability to intend an act and to act on that intention, but to realize that intention in the completion of an act. To attribute to a person such control, however, a philosophical critique calls attention to the fact that the Court must suppress its own role in separating out from a myriad of tangled details the events that will come to be recognized as a discrete "act." The Court must also deny what this separating activity betrays: that any "act" is essentially "reckless," for it takes place within a web of conventional and idiosyncratic relationships, a preexisting context that ultimately renders the grandest gesture unrecognizable from the point of view of the person who makes it. Because human actions—among them, criminal actions—take place in such a context, they defy any individual's attempt to control, circumscribe, and determine them.

To see this, consider H. L. A. Hart's attempt to develop a rationale for excusing conditions proper to legal discourse.[32] By examining Hart's effort to reformulate excuses and mitigating circumstances in formal (i.e., legal) rather than substantive (i.e., psychological) terms, we can see how context plays a significant part in the definition of a criminal act as such. In addition, we can see how context undermines the command attributed to a particular kind of actor and ultimately calls into question a theory of punishment and responsibility premised on this command.

Legal scholars such as Hediger follow in Hart's footsteps when they argue that psychological justifications for leniency in criminal trials undermine the assumption at law that human beings are capable of making choices.[33] However, in addition to arguing that laws are established to give legal effect to the choices made by individuals, Hart tries to imagine a rationale of excusing conditions that would not contradict the underlying assumptions of this claim.[34] He uses as a model for such a rationale the civil law and the conditions that are recognized as invalidating certain civil transactions (29). Civil transactions are legally binding arrangements made by private parties for their mutual benefit. These transactions do not refer to relationships or states of affairs that already exist in the world. Instead, they realize individuals' wishes and, in Hart's words, "alter their own and/or others' legal position" (34). Hart cites as examples of such transactions wills, contracts, gifts, and marriage.

Criminal acts, of course, are acts committed in violation of a law forbidding them, to which is annexed, upon conviction, a punishment or combination of punishments. While such acts seem to have little in common with civil transactions, Hart suggests that rather than use psychology or psychiatry to support an argument for mercy in sentencing a person convicted of committing a criminal act, criminal acts may be excused on the same grounds that civil transactions are invalidated. Civil transactions may be invalidated when one of three possible conditions occurs: (1) when one of the parties to a transaction is insane; (2) when one of the parties to a transaction is mistaken about the transaction's legal character; or (3) when one of the parties to a transaction is subject to duress, coercion, or the undue influence of other persons (34). Although these invalidating conditions resemble excusing conditions recognized at law, Hart insists there is a difference: criminal acts are excused by definition and civil transactions are invalidated by (lack of) effect. As we have seen, criminal acts are excused when one of the elements that defines a crime as such is missing. Thus, for example, no matter what harm occurs, when the person who commits this harm does so without a guilty state of mind (because she is insane or because she acts under duress), by definition she does not commit a crime. Hart argues that civil transactions are invalidated when they fail to realize the effect that they set out to accomplish. When the conditions necessary to make a particular transaction effective are not in place—as when one party to a contract signs his name "Julius Caesar," for example—the contract does not "come off" because insane persons cannot make a "real choice" to alter their legal circumstances (49). As a result, the agreement they enter into does not reflect their capacity to will and therefore is without force. Similarly, as these persons are incapable of making a "real choice," if they kill someone their "crime" does not represent an expression of their will and they should be excused.

However, civil transactions can still take place and have force when the conditions Hart has posited as invalidating them are present. Indeed, Hart himself recognizes that there are occasions when a transaction "comes off" even though it is not intended. For example, a person may make a promise assuming that her audience understands that she is joking. However, if the joke is not apparent to everyone, she may find herself bound to a commitment she never intended to make. Acknowledging that some such binding agreements may not be immediately invalidated by the three conditions he describes, Hart suggests that a distinction should be made between transactions that are "wholly invalidated" and those that are "valid until denounced" (35).

While this suggestion may seem like a harmless qualification of Hart's original point, it isn't, for this qualification constitutes an admission that the presence of a "normal person" with free will and intention is not necessary in order for a civil transaction to succeed in altering one's legal position. Recall that the criminality Hart seeks to exculpate is predicated upon as assumption of a self-conscious, self-determining will. By admitting that civil transactions are not immediately invalidated by one of the three conditions he describes, Hart acknowledges that some transactions are honored despite the fact that they are not the result of a particular act of will. By analogy, Hart would be forced to acknowledge that some criminals may be held fully accountable for their actions despite the fact that these actions are not the result of a particular act of will.

While Hart may be compelled to admit that there are limits to the power he attributes to the civil, and by analogy criminal, agent, he does not pause to consider the ramifications of this admission for his theory of action. Although he does make reference at one point to "the transaction's normal form" (35), he does not pay sufficient attention, for example, to the fact that the "success" or "failure" of a transaction is not determined by agents but by preexisting conditions. To elaborate on this point then, I turn to J. L. Austin. Hart's argument—and my reading of it—are informed by work in the philosophy of language, and specifically by Austin's work on performative utterances.35 Like Hart's civil transactions, performative utterances do not point to situations in the world but actually bring them into being.36 Although they are "merely words," such utterances do not reflect reality but rather act in and on it. For example, Austin points out that when the bride and groom say "I do" in a wedding ceremony their words do not refer to some preexisting state of affairs. On the contrary, in the act of saying "I do," the bride and groom introduce into the world a new set of social arrangements.37

According to Austin, successful speech acts, or civil transactions, require that certain established procedures be followed, that these procedures be conducted by individuals or institutions that are recognized as the bearers of a certain authority, and that certain other events may have to take place in order for a transaction to be completed. For example, when a wedding is performed, it is not sufficient for a couple to choose to get married. In order to be wed, the couple has to consist of a man and a woman, they have to procure a marriage license from the state, and the person who performs the ceremony has to be officially authorized to do so, and so on. The point here is that the civil transactions to which Hart refers are acts that take place as a function of the force of conventions and contextual elements that precede the specific circumstances of any particular transaction.38 Consequently, it is possible for persons to find themselves in a legally binding situation after unwittingly invoking the conventions that customarily produce a certain effect. Thus, as in the case of the unintended promise, a valid transaction may "come off" without being attributable to any particular will.

This discussion of Hart's attempt to reformulate excusing conditions in criminal law in formal terms reveals the difficulty with which even "normal persons" may be held accountable for their actions. For, willing or not, it is structurally impossible for a person to fully dominate the field in which actions take place and thus determine their effects.39 Acts, or rather the effects that distinguish them and the consequences that define them, are the product of many forces. Persons may well initiate an act, intentionally or unintentionally, but they may not, in effect, complete it themselves. In Hannah Arendt's terms, this "failure" is due to the fact that any action always falls into an already existing web of human relationships.40 According to Arendt, this web exists wherever men live together and is characterized by innumerable, conflicting wills and intentions. As a result of these tensions, she observes, action almost never achieves its purpose. At the same time, however, it is only within this web of relationships that action is real.

Conclusion

Earlier, I suggested that the Court has not yet taken into account the points raised by a philosophical critique of its theory of action. However, as the significant role circumstances play in the formal definition of a crime is often recognized at law, it may seem that I overstated the case. For example, in cases such as Tison v. Arizona, the Court looks to the larger context in which the murders took place to determine the mental state of the defendants at the time of the killings. As the brothers claim that they had no intention of causing anyone any harm, the Court examines that context in order to reconstruct their state of mind. Specifically, as we have seen, the Court looks to the fact that both Ricky and Raymond Tison broke their father out of prison, assisted him in stealing a car, and entrusted him, a known killer, with the lives of John, Donnelda, and Christopher Lyons, and Theresa Tyson.

However, the Court considers this context only to discover within it clues as to the identity of an agent. That is, in the various details of the incidents surrounding the murders, it seeks and finds a state of mind and series of actions that do not simply set a chain of events into motion but determine the character of these events. Friedrich Nietzsche observes: "If someone hides an object behind a bush, then seeks and finds it there, that seeking and finding is not very laudable; but that is the way it is with the seeking and finding of 'truth' within the rational sphere."[41] I am suggesting here that the Court seeks "truth" in the form of an agent within the legal sphere, initially positing in a series of occurrences what it later discovers as their organizing principle. As we have seen, the legal system depends upon the figure of a "normal person" who is autonomous, rational, and self-determining. In the Tison case, the Court finds this person hidden behind the helter-skelter of ambitious schemes, common mishaps, and chance encounters. Under the rubric of the "normal person," the Court then brings together a series of more or less causally connected events and attributes to this figure the intention to realize what the Court retrospectively identifies as their "natural" result (158). In other words, the Court looks to identify a subject as the agent who does not simply cause but also masters events. And it must do so if it is to identify an individual as the first cause of causality in human affairs, as the ultimate source of any harm that may come to people in a shared life world. In any such pursuit, considerations of context must fall away.

However, the discrete identity of any act is always a retrospective construction or reconstruction out of particular elements in a broader context. In Tison, this is particularly clear. In order to determine the defendants' state of mind at the time of the killings, the majority considers almost everything that happened from the moment that the Tison brothers entered the Arizona State Prison with an ice chest full of guns. By contrast, the minority argues that only the brothers' actions in the immediate context of the murders should be considered relevant to such a determination (165). While the Justices disagree about the moment when the "crime" begins (and thus when the defendants' state of mind becomes an issue of importance), they each make a decision about this moment and locate there the intention that will mark those events that complete and realize this intention. The nature of these decisions is as apparent in what the Justices leave out of their accounts of the Tisons' crime as it is in what they include. For example, they do not dwell on the fact that before the episode at the prison Ricky and Raymond Tison had been law-abiding boys. They also do not discuss the fact that after the brothers were charged with the murders they agreed to plea-bargain until it became apparent that they would have to testify to the planning stages of the crime and therefore testify against their mother. These facts the Justices deem irrelevant to their search for an agent: they do not "fit" the story that they wanted, and needed, to tell.

Obviously, my point here is not to claim that one opinion or the other identifies the Tisons' criminal act correctly, but to observe that that act, as such, is not a self-evident fact—it is a product of interpretation. My discussion of Hart demonstrates how even a formal definition of action reveals that an act is a function of preexisting, iterable elements that make any specific act possible but also carry an act away from the grasp and mastery of any particular actor. And any such critique of the act must also have consequences for the self-evidence of the "agent." As Arendt observes:

> Although everybody started his life by inserting himself into the human world through action and speech, nobody is the author or producer of his own life story. In other words, the stories, the results of action and speech, reveal an agent, but this agent is not an author or producer. . . . The perplexity is that in any series of events that together form a story with a unique meaning we can at best isolate the agent who set the whole process into motion; and although this agent frequently remains the subject, the "hero" of the story, we never can point unequivocally to him as the author of its eventual outcome. (184–185)

In the web of relationships in which human beings appear to one another, we cannot know the consequences of the things we begin. This fact in itself implies that we must think about responsibility at law beyond the category of intention.

This is not an easy task. According to Arendt, the court charged with judging Eichmann was reluctant to admit that an average, "normal" person could be perfectly incapable of telling right from wrong. Thus, the judges proceeded on the assumption that all "normal persons" are somehow aware of the criminal nature of their deeds (26). And indeed, I believe that Arendt herself ultimately condemns Eichmann on the grounds that he failed to grasp the essential character of his actions. While Arendt claims that Eichmann did not commit or even intend to commit harm to anyone, she states that Eichmann had to die because he supported and carried out a policy of not wanting to share the earth with the Jewish people and the people of a number of other nations (279). The fact that Eichmann obeyed the law as it was understood in Nazi Germany did not excuse him. In effect, she assumes that on some level, Eichmann should have known better. Despite the phenomenon of the banality of evil that she herself describes, she argues that Eichmann could be executed for failing to critically concern himself with the nature of the effects he was producing, that is, for failing to master his own context.

I think that the Supreme Court proceeds on a similar premise and for similar reasons. If it is to effectively attack the "danger" it diagnoses in manifestations of violence, the Supreme Court must be able to affirm that individuals are completely responsible for their actions, including their extending consequences. In brief, the Court needs an autonomous, rational, self-determining individual to assume the position of the cause of the events that disrupt the pattern of everyday life in an ordered society. And it must affirm this figure without skepticism, that is, without concern that such individuals could not have known better or the sneaking suspicion that they actually thought they were doing something good. Therefore, the sentencing of the Tisons to death may be understood as more than an expression of society's outrage at the horrible murders that occurred in the Arizona desert. Their sentencing is necessary to uphold the premises of the legal system and to contain the effects of the *real* normal person, a person who participates in horrible acts of violence without knowledge or ill will, and even, like these sons and brothers, with love.

Notes

1. Gregg v. Georgia, 428 U.S. 238 (1976).

2. See Robert Weisberg, "Deregulating Death," *Supreme Court Review* (1984): 305–395.

3. Tison v. Arizona, 481 U.S. 137 (1987).

4. Thus, the kind of evidence by which "reckless indifference" must be accompanied to support a capital sentencing judgment already implies the existence of a culpable state of mind. Insofar as a person participates in any violent crime, robbery for example, he or she demonstrates a "reckless indifference to the value of human life." The Court admits as much in a footnote to its opinion (158).

5. Georges Canguilhem, *The Normal and the Pathological*, trans. Carolyn R. Fawcett and Robert S. Cohen (New York: Zone, 1989), 125.

6. Hannah Arendt, *Eichmann in Jerusalem: A Report on the Banality of Evil* (London: Penguin, 1964), 26.

7. Enmund v. Florida, 458 U.S. 782 (1982).

8. Certainly, the Court could have recognized that the Tison brothers participated in the murder of the Lyons family under circumstances in which it would have been difficult for them to realize the wrong to which they were contributing. For example, according to a psychologist who examined both Ricky and Raymond Tison, the brothers were born into an extremely pathological family and were trained to think of their father as an innocent person being victimized in the state prison (167).

9. Furman v. Georgia, 408 U.S. 238 (1972), 308.

10. H. L. A. Hart, "Prolegomenon to the Principles of Punishment," *Punishment and Responsibility: Essays in the Philosophy of Law* (Oxford: Clarendon Press, 1968), 1–27.

11. United States v. Brawner, 471 F.2d 969 (1972), 995.

12. The absence of a description of the normal person also suggests that Hart and the Court take for a granted a norm of belief in the normal person, and this assumption again subtly reiterates the legitimacy of their use of the term.

13. Indeed, I focus on the figure of the normal person because the common sense upon which its meaning depends is not so apparent in figures such as the "rational agent" or the "sane adult."

14. Ironically, it is only "normal persons" who are thus in a position to be convicted of the most incomprehensible or heinous criminal acts.

15. Sir William Blackstone, *Commentaries on the Laws of England*, vol. 2, ed. William Carey Jones (Baton Rouge: Claitor's Publishing, 1976), 2176.

16. According to legal anthropologist Lawrence Rosen, in order to appreciate a concept of the will persons have to be conceived as having an inner life and a private experience that is not visible or revealed to the external world. Rosen argues that such a conception of the self began emerging in Europe only in the middle of the eleventh century. Consequently, the distinction between the physical and the mental aspect of a crime has not always been meaningful, let alone relevant, in matters of determining criminal responsibility. See Lawrence Rosen, "Intentionality and the Concept of the Person," *Criminal Justice: Nomos 27*, ed. J. Roland Pennock and John W. Chapman (New York: New York University Press, 1985), 52–77.

17. The most familiar example of a legal excuse is insanity. In many U.S. states, insanity at law is still determined along the lines set down in Regina v. M'Naghten, 10 Clark and F. 200, 8 Eng. Rep. 718 (1843), which is often referred to as the "right-and-wrong test" because it predicates responsibility at law on knowledge of the wrongfulness of the act in question. Insofar as M'Naghten is still with us, we continue to assume that a capacity of the mind to distinguish between right and wrong is a significant element in the makeup of a normal person. The fact that the right-and-wrong test has shifted from a moral register to a legal one does not undermine the point. For as court cases and critics contest the nature of a moral distinction between right and wrong and challenge its presumed universality, what we may still assert to be true of all normal persons is the capacity to appreciate and act upon what is right and wrong at law.

Other conditions recognized at law as excuses are duress, intoxication, and addiction.

18. Some mitigating circumstances recognized at law are provocation, mental capacity, and age.

19. In his dissent, Brennan argues that the Court's quandary arises as a result of the fact that the majority improperly insists on treating the choice to act recklessly as equivalent to the choice to kill. According to Brennan, it is essential to distinguish between these two choices, for

[t]he importance of distinguishing between these different choices is rooted in our belief in the "freedom of the human will and a consequent ability and duty of the normal individual to choose between good and evil." To be faithful to this belief, which is "universal and persistent in mature systems of law," the criminal law must ensure that the punishment an individual receives conforms to the choices that individual has made. Differential punishment of reckless and intentional actions is therefore essential if we are to retain "the relation between criminal liability and moral culpability" on which criminal justice depends. (171) [Citations omitted]

20. Michel Foucault, "About the Concept of the 'Dangerous Individual' in 19th-Century Legal Psychiatry," trans. Alain Baudot and Jane Couchman, *International Journal of Law and Psychiatry* 1 (1978): 1–18.

21. Indeed, in Foucault's argument about nineteenth-century psychology, the presence of dangerous individuals in the social body created an opportunity for psychiatrists to offer explanations of otherwise inexplicable behavior. By providing a motive or an intelligible link between an act and an actor, Foucault claims that doctors were able to make sense of a particular crime. In this way, he argues, they were also able to ensure that the most effective punishment for the crime was imposed. However, in my argument, the Court's recovery of the "dangerous individual" is just that: a recuperation of the "dangerous being" as a legal rather than a medical category.

22. Indeed, in *United States v. Brawner* (1972), the Court of Appeals for the District of Columbia expresses a fear that instead of disciplining normal people, law may be manipulated or "twisted" by them since the presence or absence of what locates persons within "the normal range" cannot be verified.

23. Samuel Pillsbury argues that people must be able to identify with those whom they punish, otherwise the criminal's actions and his state of mind are inaccessible to them and they cannot affirm the criteria with which they establish the presence of a crime. What is more, Pillsbury claims: "We punish offenders not because they stand outside of society, not because they are alien enemies, but because they are fundamentally like the rest of us." However, in an analysis of several capital trials, Austin Sarat finds that in practice prosecutors try to demonize the defendant because they believe jurors feel less compunction about sentencing a person to death when that person seems inhuman or alien to them. I suggest that

the prosecution must be careful in this strategy so as not to succeed so well as to place the defendant outside the purview of the court, that is, outside the purview of what is normal. The recent popularity of the verdict "guilty but mentally insane" may be understood as an attempt to make sure that those who are not normal are nevertheless normal enough not to escape punishment. See Austin Sarat, "Speaking of Death: Narratives of Violence in Capital Trials," *Law and Society Review* 27 (1993): 19–58; Samuel H. Pillsbury, "The Meaning of Deserved Punishment: An Essay on Choice, Character, and Responsibility," *Indiana Law Journal* 67 (1992): 719–752.

24. See Spring Co. v. Edgard, 99 U.S. 645 (1878).

25. Despite ongoing debate about the legitimacy of this "science," psychiatrists make compelling claims not only about a defendant's past and present mental condition but also about his or her future state of mind. For a closer look at the role mental health professionals can play in capital trials see Ron Rosenbaum, "Travels with Dr. Death," *Vanity Fair*, May 1990.

26. See George E. Dix, "Expert Prediction Testimony in Capital Sentencing: Evidentiary and Constitutional Considerations," *American Criminal Law Review* 19 (1981): 1–48, 16. Indeed, the American Psychiatric Association (APA) itself has come out against the practice of psychiatrists testifying to an individual's future dangerousness because it is concerned not only that psychiatrists are not qualified to interpret the data from which such determinations are derived, but also that juries are unlikely to put psychiatrists' testimony about future dangerousness in proper perspective. Ironically, the Supreme Court appears unconcerned about the influence of expert opinion on juries. In Barefoot v. Estelle, 463 U.S. 880 (1983), the Court argues that the adversary process can be trusted to sort out reliable from unreliable evidence. To which the Court adds, "Neither petitioner nor the [American Psychiatric Association] suggests that psychiatrists are always wrong with respect to future dangerousness, only most of the time" (465).

27. Pamela Hediger, "Mens Rea: The Impasse of Law and Psychiatry," *Gonzaga Law Review* 26 (1990–91): 613–626.

28. For a compelling argument that this view is based on bad psychiatry and an overblown sense of the threat a psychological subject poses for the law, see Michael S. Moore, *Law and Psychiatry: Rethinking the Relationship* (Cambridge: Cambridge University Press, 1984).

29. For an example of such thinking see Bernard Diamond, "From M'Naghten to Currens, and Beyond," *The Psychiatrist in the Courtroom: Selected Papers of Bernard L. Diamond, M.D.*, ed. Jacques M. Quen (Hillsdale, N.J.: Analytic Press, 1994): 249–266. In this article, the influential professor of law and psychiatry argues that as the overwhelming majority of criminals in prisons are sick, prisons should be transformed into facilities that can treat sick people. What is more, he suggests, "It will not be a coincidence if, in the final analysis, the same humane psychological, medical, and sociological methods that are conducive to the rehabilitation of mentally ill and emotionally disordered criminals turn out to be identical with those required for supposedly normal and fully responsible offenders" (263). By speculating that "normal and fully responsible offenders" would benefit just as much as "mentally ill and emotionally disordered criminals" from a broad therapeutic approach to the modification of their behavior, Diamond suggests that the actions of "normal" people are as influenced by "external" factors as the actions of "abnormal" people. What is more, without fully acknowledging the consequences of this observation, Diamond implies that the division between the normal (responsible) and the abnormal (not responsible) criminal may not be based on scientific fact but rather on customary ways of thinking about human behavior and the will.

30. In Gregg v. Georgia (1976), the Supreme Court rules that the death penalty is war-

ranted on the grounds that it serves two "social purposes": deterrence and retribution. However, when persons do not will their actions, punishing them does not serve either of these purposes. For example, when an act is committed unintentionally, the person who commits it cannot be deterred from repeating it with arguments or examples aimed at reinforcing his or her will. In addition, punishment that seeks to provide an example of the rational consequences of such behavior makes little sense when a person's actions do not always reflect what choices he or she makes. Similarly, punishment cannot serve a retributive function when no ill will is expressed in an act. Retribution is based on the premise that when people choose to violate the law they incur a kind of moral debt that must be repaid with their lives or their liberty. When such violations occur unintentionally however, the "debt" incurred has no particular moral character. Indeed, normal persons who do not will their criminal acts have, as we have already seen, committed no crime *per se* and to punish them despite this fact is itself morally questionable.

31. Similarly, Arendt observes that Eichmann was interviewed by several psychiatrists who certified him as "normal." Indeed, Arendt quotes one of the psychiatrists as saying that Eichmann's whole psychological outlook was "not only normal but most desirable" (25–6).

32. H. L. A. Hart, "Legal Responsibility and Excuses," *Punishment and Responsibility: Essays in the Philosophy of Law* (Oxford: Clarendon Press, 1968): 28–53.

33. According to Hart, when excuses and mitigating circumstances are articulated in psychological terms, judges and jurors are obliged to accept the idea that human behavior may always be determined by influences over which the individual has no control (29). Hart objects to this assumption. He notes, for example, that as long as human conduct is understood as subject to forces over which the individual has no control, there is no reason to distinguish between excusable and inexcusable behavior.

34. Hediger herself advises that we simply acknowledge that both legal and psychological descriptions of the person are correct within their own domains and leave the law to define the criteria of criminal responsibility and punishment on its own and in its own terms.

35. According to Peter Goodrich, Austin is the most proximate source of Hart's linguistic methodology. See Peter Goodrich, *Legal Discourse: Studies in Linguistics, Rhetoric, and Legal Analysis* (New York: St. Martin's Press, 1987).

36. J. L. Austin, *How to Do Things with Words*, ed. J. O. Urmson and Marina Sbisa (Cambridge, Mass.: Harvard University Press, 1975).

37. For an elaboration and critique of Austin's work on performative utterances see Jacques Derrida, "Signature Event Context," *Limited Inc*, trans. Alan Bass (1982), (Evanston, Ill.: Northwestern University Press, 1988): 1–23.

38. Thus, Hart assumes that the legally binding arrangements that normal persons seek to make in their lives correspond with the arrangements that existing or potential legal institutions make possible. The controversy surrounding the topic of gay marriage suggests that this assumption is perhaps not warranted. At the same time however, this controversy also attests to the strength of these conventions in so far as it demonstrates how strongly persons want their desires to be legally recognized as conventional ones.

39. In his critique of Austin, Derrida points out that Austin dismisses from the purview of his theory utterances that are "parasitic" upon the speech acts he is trying to describe. According to Derrida, Austin acknowledges the possibility of failure as inherent to the structure of speech acts, but immediately and simultaneously dismisses this possibility as simply irrelevant. That is to say, Austin dismisses as "parasites" those instances when the iterable structure of language permits unintended speech acts to take place. Austin's language suggests that these instances are perversely related to the fundamental or essential character of the structure of speech acts. Derrida points out, however, that the "parasite" may not be separated from the implied "host" in this manner, for it is only as a function of the iterability of the ele-

ments of a speech act that any one speech act can take place at all. I am suggesting something similar here about Hart.

40. Hannah Arendt, *The Human Condition* (Chicago: University of Chicago Press, 1958), 184.

41. Friedrich Nietzsche, "On Truth and Lying in an Extra-Moral Sense," in *Friedrich Nietzsche on Rhetoric and Language,* ed. and trans. Sander L. Gilman, Carole Blair, and David J. Parent (New York: Oxford University Press, 1989), 246–257, 251.

THE CULTURAL LIFE OF CAPITAL PUNISHMENT: RESPONSIBILITY AND REPRESENTATION IN *DEAD MAN WALKING* AND *LAST DANCE*

AUSTIN SARAT

For death must be somewhere in a society; if it is no longer (or less intensely) in religion, it must be elsewhere; perhaps in this image which produces Death while trying to preserve life.

Roland Barthes

Our own death is indeed unimaginable, and whenever we make the attempt to imagine it we can perceive that we really survive as spectators.

Sigmund Freud

Every death agony expresses a certain truth. . . . Hence the insatiable curiosity that drove spectators to the scaffold to witness the spectacle of sufferings truly endured; there one could decipher crime and innocence, the past and the future, the here below and the eternal. It was a moment of truth that all the spectators questioned: each word, each cry, the duration of the agony, the resisting body, the life that clung desperately to it, all this constituted a sign.

Michel Foucault

Even a theater of fictional murder is not an innocent theater. The point, or one of the points, of the murder story is that there can be no innocence in circumstances that give rise to murderous impulses—even if the impulses are aroused in mere bystanders, witnesses, observers; even if the murder is not real.

Wendy Lesser

I. Introduction

Punishment, as Nietzsche reminds us, makes us who we are and constitutes us as particular kinds of subjects.[1] The subject constituted by punishment is watchful, on guard, fearful, even if never directly subject to the particular pains of state imposed punishment.[2] One of the primary achievements of punishment, to use Nietzsche's vivid phrase, "is to breed an animal with the right to make promises,"[3] that is, to induce in us a sense of responsibility, a desire and an ability to take and properly discharge our responsibilities. Dutiful individuals, guilt-ridden, morally burdened— these are the creatures that punishment demands, creatures worthy of being punished.[4]

Punishment constitutes subjectivity through the complex juridical mechanisms that put it in motion as well as the moral tenets and legal doctrines that legitimate it.[5] Here too we can see the centrality of responsibility.[6] The state will only punish responsible agents, persons whose "deviant" acts can be said to be a product of consciousness and will, persons who "could have done otherwise." As Blackstone put it, "to constitute a crime against human laws, there must be, first, a vicious will, and, secondly, an unlawful act consequent upon such vicious will."[7] Thus the apparatus of punishment depends upon a modernist subject and conceptions of will that represses or forgets its "uncertain, divided, and opaque" character.[8]

In addition, because most citizens are not, and will not be, directly subjected to the state's penal apparatus, punishment creates a challenge for representation that is deepened to the point of crisis when the punishment is death.[9] Punishment is inscribed in both our unconscious and our consciousness. It lives in images conveyed, in lessons taught, in repressed memories, in horrible imaginings. Some of its horror and controlling power is, in fact, a result of its fearful invisibility. "Punishment," Foucault reminds us, "[has] become the most hidden part of the penal process."[10] He argues that "[t]his has several consequences: . . . [punishment] leaves the domain of more or less everyday perception and enters that of abstract consciousness; its effectiveness is seen as resulting from its inevitability, not from its visible intensity; it is the certainty of being punished and not the horrifying spectacle of public punishment that must discourage crime. . . . As a result, justice no longer takes public responsibility for the violence that is bound up with its practice."[11] It may very well be, however, that the more punishment is hidden, the less visible it is, the more power it has to colonize our imaginative life. We watch; we seek to conjure an image of punishment; we become particular kinds of spectators, anticipating a glimpse, at least a partial uncovering of the apparatus of state discipline.

And what is true of all punishment is particularly true when death is a punishment. That the state takes life and how it takes life insinuates itself into the public imagination, even as the moment of this exercise of power is hidden from view.[12] This particular exercise of power helps us understand who we are and what we as a society are capable of doing. And, as Wendy Lesser so skillfully documents, the hidden moment when the state takes the life of one of its citizens precipitates, in an age of the hypervisual, a crisis of representation.[13] This crisis occurs as we confront the boundaries of our representational practices,[14] the question of who decides what can and cannot be seen and the adequacy of particular representations in conveying the "reality" of the pain on which the penal apparatus depends.[15]

The modern execution is carried out behind prison walls. In these semiprivate, sacrificial ceremonies a few selected witnesses are gathered in a carefully controlled situation to see, and in their seeing to sanctify, the state's taking of the life of one of its citizens. As Richard Johnson suggests, "In the modern period (from 1800 on), ceremony gradually gave way to bureaucratic procedure played out behind prison walls, in isolation from the community. Feelings are absent, or at least suppressed, in bureaucratically administered executions. With bureaucratic procedure, there is a functional routine dominated by hierarchy and task. Officials perform mechanistically before a small, silent gathering of authorized witnesses."[16] Capital punishment becomes, at best, a hidden reality. It is known, if it is known at all, by indirection.[17] "The relative privacy of executions nowadays (even photographs of the condemned man dying are almost invariably strictly prohibited)," Hugo Bedau notes, "means that the average American literally does not know what is being done when the government, in his name and presumably on his behalf, executes a criminal."[18]

While executions have been removed from the public eye for more than fifty years, in most states capital punishment still must be witnessed by members of the public in order to be legal. It is this linkage between violence and the visual that Lesser explores when she notes that witnesses are "there not just to ensure that the deed is actually done . . . , but to represent and embody the wider public in whose name the execution is being carried out."[19] Thus the state's power to kill is linked to the imperatives and privileges of spectatorship. Whatever the means chosen, execution is always a visual event.

Historically executions were, in Foucault's words, "[m]ore than an act of justice"; they were a "manifestation of force."[20] They were always centrally about display, in particular the display of the majestic, awesome power of sovereignty as it was materialized on the body of the condemned.[21] Public executions functioned as public theater, but also as a school for citizenship.[22] While the act of execution linked violence to spectatorship, it also helped constitute citizens as subjects. On Foucault's account, the drama of execution produced a sadistic relation between the executioner, the victim, and the audience. Yet it also contained a pedagogy of power. "The public execution," Foucault explained,

> has a juridico-political function. It is a ceremonial by which a momentarily injured sovereignty is reconstituted. It restores sovereignty by manifesting it at its most spectacular. The public execution, however hasty and everyday, belongs to a whole series of great rituals in which power is eclipsed and restored (coronation, entry of the king into a conquered city, the submission of rebellious subjects). . . . There must be an emphatic affirmation of power and its intrinsic superiority. And this superiority is not simply that of right, but that of the physical strength of the sovereign beating down upon the body of his adversary and mastering it.[23]

The pleasure of viewing, as well as the instruction in one's relation to sovereign power, was to be found in witnessing pain inflicted as well as in the hope that seeing the death of another would convey the meaning and character of death itself.

The excesses of execution and the enthusiastic response of the attending crowd created an unembarrassed celebration of violence that knew no law except one person's will materialized on the body of the condemned.[24] The display of violence was designed to create fearful, if not obedient, subjects. Execution without a public audience was, as a result, meaningless. "Not only must the people know," Foucault claimed, "they must see with their own eyes. Because they must be made afraid, but also because they must be witnesses, the guarantors of the punishment, and because they must to a certain extent take part in it."[25] In this understanding of the relationship of punishment and the people, "the role of the people was an ambiguous one."[26] They were, at one and the same time, fearful subjects, authorizing witnesses, and lustful participants.

Yet the public execution was also an occasion for the exercise of popular power, if not popular sovereignty. In Foucault's words, "In the ceremonies of the public execution, the main character was the people."[27] It was an occasion on which people could, and did, mass themselves against the punishment that was to be carried out before their eyes and in their presence. Their presence ensured that the act of execution itself, not just the judgment of death, always could be contested[28] and that execution could not be reduced to a bland routine. "[I]t was on this point," Foucault suggests,

> that the people, drawn to the spectacle intended to terrorize it, could express its rejection of the punitive power and sometimes revolt. Preventing an execution that was regarded as unjust, snatching a condemned man from the hands of the executioner, obtaining his pardon by force, possibly pursuing and assaulting the executioners, in any case abusing the judges and causing an uproar against the sentence — all of this formed part of the popular practices that invested, traversed and often overturned the ritual of public execution. . . . It was evident that the great spectacle of punishment ran the risk of being rejected by the very people to whom it was addressed.[29]

Today the death penalty has been transformed from dramatic spectacle to cool, bureaucratic operation, and the role of the public now is strictly limited and controlled.[30] The chance of either disruption or rejection, as a result, has been minimized. The public has been displaced by a small, select, and carefully controlled group of witnesses, who are provided a fleeting glimpse of the rituals of state-sponsored death as it is turned into a problem of administration. Thus the problem of representation, spectatorship, and the public's role remains.

What we know about the way law does death comes in the most highly mediated way as a rumor, a report, an account of the voiceless expression of the body of the condemned. Or it comes in images and representations made available in popular culture. There it lives in its fictive recreations.

My interest in this essay is to make a particular intervention in scholarship about the death penalty,[31] to turn away from abstract, philosophical questions about the morality or legality of state killing[32] and narrow policy-relevant research[33] toward an analysis of the cultural life of capital punishment.[34] My work builds on David Garland's suggestion that we should attend to the "cultural role" of legal practices, to their ability to "create social meaning and thus shape social worlds," and that among those practices none is more important than how we punish.[35] Punishment, Garland tells us, "helps shape the overarching culture and contribute to the generation and regeneration of its terms."[36] Punishment is a set of signifying practices that "teaches, clarifies, dramatizes and authoritatively enacts some of the most basic moral-political categories and distinctions which help shape our symbolic universe."[37] Punishment lives in culture through its pedagogical effects, and it teaches us how to think about such basic social categories as intention, responsibility, and injury. In addition, it models socially appropriate ways of responding to injuries done to us.

The semiotics of punishment is all around us, not just in the architecture of the prison, or the speech made by a judge as she sends someone to the penal colony, but in both "high" and "popular" culture iconography, in novels, television, and film.[38] Punishment has traditionally been one of the great subjects of cultural production, suggesting the powerful allure of humankind's fall from grace and of our prospects for redemption. But perhaps the word "our" is inaccurate here since Durkheim[39] and Mead,[40] among others, remind us that it is through practices of punishment that cultural boundaries are drawn, that solidarity is created by marking difference between self and other, through disidentification as much as imagined connection. "[M]ass-mediated representations of prisoners function as a public display of the transgression of cultural norms; as such, they are a key site at which one may investigate the relationship of the individual to the culture in general, as well as the cultural articulation of 'proper behavior.'"[41]

This is also true when the punishment is death. Execution is even now an occasion for rich symbolization, for the production of public images of evil or of unruly freedom, and for fictive recreations of the scene of death in popular culture.[42]

I examine the cultural life of capital punishment through a reading of two recent films about capital punishment—*Dead Man Walking* and *Last Dance*.[43] I am interested in the cultural politics of these films and the way they seek to convey knowledge of capital punishment. How is the death penalty represented in these films, and what connections do they forge among death, spectatorship, and the constitution of legal subjectivity? What do they suggest about the legitimacy of state killing?

To answer these questions I analyze the way these films speak to two of the kinds of basic conceptual categories to which Garland directs our attention. The first of these is individual responsibility and its utility in explaining the causes of, as well as directing our responses to, crime. *Dead Man Walking* and *Last Dance* do not explore the social structural factors that some believe must be addressed in responding to crime;[44] instead they are preoccupied with the question of personal responsibility. To the extent they contain an explanation of crime and a justification for punishment it is to located in the autonomous choices of particular agents. While building dramatic tension around the question about whether their hero/ heroine deserves the death penalty, these films convey a powerful double message: first, legal subjects can, and will, be held responsible for their acts; second, they can, and should, internalize and *accept* responsibility.

Last Dance and *Dead Man Walking* depend upon categories—agency, will, and responsibility—the stability and coherence of which are today increasingly called into question,[45] yet they evade rather than engage with those questions. These films are deeply invested in the constitution of a modernist, responsible subject as the proper object of punishment, a subject who, as Nietzsche would have it, has the "right to make promises." They suggest that there can be, and is, a tight linkage between crime and punishment, such that those personally responsible for the former can be legitimately subject to the latter.

The second conceptual category to which this essay speaks involves representation, especially how the death penalty is represented to us, and the cultural politics of those representational gestures. While *Dead Man Walking* and *Last Dance* initially appear to deploy complex representational practices that call attention to the partiality and limits of all representations,[46] in the end they depend on a representational realism that allows their viewers to think that they can know the reality of the crimes for which death is a punishment and of the death penalty itself. Instead of inviting us to imagine the scene of death and its significance,[47] they seek to inspire confidence that their viewers can "know" the truth about capital punishment through their "you are there" representations of execution.

Yet, I contend, the death penalty plays an uncanny role in film, pointing as it does to the limits of representation, to the limits of our ability to "know" death[48] and, as a result, of our inability to be sure whether state killing is an appropriate, proportional response to the acts that appear to justify it. Whenever and however death is present in film, it reminds us that, in this domain, seeing is not, and cannot be, knowing.

Traditionally, the cultural politics of state killing has served to shore up status distinctions and distinguish particular ways of life from others.[49] Thus it is not surprising that today the death penalty and death penalty films sit at an important fault line in our contemporary culture wars.[50] In the way they address questions of responsibility and in the representational practices on which they depend, *Dead Man Walking* and *Last Dance*, whatever the intentions of those who made them, enact and depend upon a conservative cultural politics,[51] a politics in which large political questions about what state killing does to our law, politics, and our culture are bracketed[52] and in which viewers are positioned as jurors deliberating solely on the question of whether a particular person merits death.[53] While they raise questions about the calculus of desert that justifies the death penalty in particular cases, they support the conceptual foundations of capital punishment, and they legitimate its place in America's penal apparatus.

II. The Scene of the Crime and the Construction of Responsibility

Every story about punishment is inevitably a story about crime, about its causes and the process of assigning responsibility for it. How we think about punishment is, in part, a function of what we know and think about the crimes that give rise to it. The prevailing common sense suggests that the severity of punishment should be proportional to the seriousness of the crime and that punishment should only be deployed against responsible agents,[54] against free and moral agents, persons capable of knowing right from wrong and choosing to do one or the other.[55] As former Supreme Court Justice Robert Jackson once explained, "The contention that injury can amount to crime only when inflicted by intention is no provincial or transient notion. It is as universal and persistent in mature systems of law as belief in freedom of the human will and a consequent ability and duty of the normal individual to choose between good and evil."[56]

This understanding of crime and punishment depends on what Stephen Carter calls "bilateral individualism."[57] As Carter explains,

The dominant culture's understanding of victimhood awards the status of victim to someone who loses something . . . because of the predation of someone else. Victimization, then, is the result of concrete, individual acts by identifiable transgressors. . . . [The dominant understanding] invents a reality in which the only victims are those who have suffered at the hands of transgressors, and in which any sanctions should be directed toward deterring or punishing those transgressors. . . . To one who accepts this vision, a world like ours, one in which so many violent crimes occur and go unpunished by the state, must seem a world in which the forces of order have lost control. . . . People are afraid of crime and are afraid of becoming victims. They want to strike back at someone to liberate themselves from fear. . . . [B]ilateral individualism can rationalize the need to strike back only by insisting that . . . transgressors are real, individual people, and other individuals have the right to turn their assaults aside.[58]

In this vision the legitimacy of punishment depends on a relatively precise moral calculus in which punishment is a measured and proportionate response to crime. Linking crime and punishment is the supposed reality of individual responsibility.

A second explanation for crime complicates the calculus of punishment, Carter notes, by altering the bilateral individualist's straightforward story of responsibility. It does so by pointing away from individual agency toward the sweep of history and the differential positions of the social groups from which criminals (and often their victims) come.[59] This "enterprise takes the form of a search for explanations rather than a search for villainous agents and attributions of blame; the remedial enterprise is directed to altering institutions, systems, and incentives rather than to exacting punishment."[60] A structuralist perspective is less intent on carefully reconstructing the crime and assigning personal responsibility; instead, it uses the fact of crime to highlight the need to alter social structures.

In the cultural life of capital punishment, at least as it is exemplified in *Dead Man Walking* and *Last Dance*, Carter's bilateral individualism, I will argue, is the prevailing motif. Because stories of the lives and deeds of particular persons have much more dramatic appeal than stories in which causation is impersonal and diffuse and the source of crime is located in social structure,[61] it is not surprising that these films provide narratives of crime and punishment that focus on describing what a particular person did and on fixing responsibility on a blameworthy agent.[62]

In popular culture the linkage between crime and punishment can be, and regularly is, made visual. This is certainly the case in the films under consideration. They focus on someone already condemned to death, living on death row, about whose legal guilt there is little doubt, someone whose crime is graphically, and repeatedly, presented to us. Both are tales of persons coming to terms with their responsibility for gruesome crimes. In *Dead Man Walking*, Matthew Poncelet (played by Sean Penn) has been sentenced for his part in a double murder in which a classically clean-cut boy and girl are accosted while parking in the woods. They are then led off into a clearing, where the girl is raped and repeatedly stabbed, and both ultimately are shot execution-style. In *Last Dance*, Cindy Liggitt (Sharon Stone) is on death row for killing two people with a crowbar during a burglary of their home.

Last Dance and *Dead Man Walking* ask, How can one human being take the life of another? What forces propel such "evil" deeds? They inquire about the capacity of spectators to recognize a shared humanity, to empathize, and to care for or about the condemned. They do so through the pairing of the condemned with a cinematic "buddy."[63] Each film shows the relationship of one significant other person—a lawyer and a nun—with the condemned who becomes the stand-in for the film's viewers.[64] Can we have as much understanding, compassion, as that person? Should we? Should it matter to us whether either Cindy Liggitt or Matthew Poncelet accept responsibility for crimes for which they have already been found legally responsible?

In *Dead Man Walking* and *Last Dance*, images of the crime play a large role in suggesting how those questions should be answered. The crime is presented in a variety of ways and reenacted repeatedly throughout both films in a duet with the impending execution. Visual equivalences are created, and the viewer alternatively is positioned as crime scene investigator, juror, omnipotent truth seeker, voyeur. Through their preoccupations with the scene of criminality, these films establish the background conditions against which responsibility and blameworthiness can be fixed and punishment ultimately assessed. Both focus in a "who-did-what-to-whom" logic on criminal and victim, bracketing questions about history and structure that would complicate the assignment of responsibility and the assessment of punishment. Additionally, presenting repeated, and incomplete, reenactments of the crime, in which the "truth" of what happened is only gradually unfolded, these films seem to highlight the partiality and problematics of viewing, of seeing and knowing. Yet this suggestion is undone in climatic scenes in which the viewer ultimately is reassured that the whole truth has been revealed.

While the use of the repeated reimagining of the crime puts us at the scene as both potential victim and killer, we see the crime most often from the perspective of the killer, first approaching the hapless victim and then acting out a murderous passion. What Young says about *Psycho* and *Silence of the Lambs* is also true for *Dead Man Walking* and *Last Dance* as well: "[W]hile offered temporarily the experience of identifying with the victim, the spectator is incorporated into the film much more significantly as an accomplice of the killer. . . . This . . . identificatory relation is achieved through an association of the spectator's look with the gaze of the cinematic apparatus."[65] We are powerless to stop the violence that unfolds before us, and cinematically reminded of that powerlessness, since we see crimes already committed for which the murderer is now in the custody of the state. So we are safe; the deed is done; we cannot rewrite history.

In *Last Dance* the crime is presented in various ways—through photographic stills seen by different characters and in moving images presented in flashback. Each of these techniques has particular significance in focusing the viewer's attention on issues of responsibility and representation. Thus, when we first see the crime in the form of crime scene photographs glimpsed over the shoulder of Rick Hayes, lawyer, ne'er-do-well brother of the governor's chief of staff, and new employee of the state clemency board, the camera gives us but a brief view of the bloodied body of a man laying on the floor, a fleeting suggestion of what happened. Then it pans quickly to Rick's face and pauses as his face, now shot in close up, registers the horror of what he sees. This register marks one dimension of the responsible subject, someone who identifies with the victim and knows, at the deepest level, that they are incapable of doing such gruesome deeds.

We see more of the crime scene when Rick's first romantic interest in the film, Jill, knocks over a file in his apartment spilling its contents onto the floor. Again there is a quick shot of the bloody photos now strewn on the floor as if in a photo array presented to a court.[66] This time the camera pans to Jill to catch the same distressed and disgusted look that had marked Rick's first sight of the photographs, the same reminder of the way "respectability" depends on just the right combination of responsibility and inhibition.

The looks on the faces of Rick and Jill are "our" looks. They establish a shared understanding of the horror of a sudden, murderous death,[67] and they represent our reaction to the horrible violence that lurks just beyond law's boundary.[68] Responsible people are repelled by the kind of violence depicted in the photographic representation of Cindy Liggitt's crime.[69]

The baseline of responsibility established by Rick and Jill's innocent gaze does two things. First, it provides a standard for viewers to judge Cindy as she later relives the crime in flashback several times in the film. It also sets up an argument that Rick makes later in the film, namely that those who use capital punishment to respond to murder, and are not repulsed by the violence it does, are no different from those they condemn. As he puts it talking to the governor about Cindy, "We never gave her a chance to become like us. Now we've become like her."[70]

This is a key moment in *Last Dance*. It provides a glimpse of what a structuralist response to crime would look like in popular culture. Moreover, it challenges individualism by presenting subject position as fluid, contingent, and reversible. In Rick's line, responsibility is temporarily shifted from the criminal to those who occupy respectable positions in society; "we" are responsible for not giving Cindy the chance to be respectable. Moreover, those who use capital punishment as their way of responding to murder become murderers themselves.[71]

Yet, as *Last Dance* proceeds, the structuralist critique fades. Rick becomes preoccupied with his own tragic, romantic attraction to Cindy, an attraction signaled by the film's title. More importantly, Cindy herself counters Rick's initial structuralist response by her own insistence on taking responsibility.

At the level of the film's representational practices, the photographic stills through which we first see the crime in *Last Dance* represent it as an evidentiary matter. We see the evidence as a jury would have seen it.[72] The still photographs freeze and partialize the scene of death, allowing us to know the pain of the victim through the most graphic representations of the wounds inflicted.[73] Yet they also serve as a reminder that when we see motion pictures of the crime we are being given a privileged viewing available to us only in our access to the memories of the film's central characters. Motion pictures serve as the revealed truth of the crime; they fix our gaze as coextensive with Cindy's recollection of the crime.

We see the crime through Cindy's eyes twice, once as she looks through an art book at a dark and evocative painting of a woman being tormented for her sins, the other in a dream that disturbs and awakens her. It is in these scenes that her insistence on the appropriateness of the logic of free will, agency, and responsibility becomes clear. The first time we get an abbreviated look as she bludgeons one of her victims—Matt McQuire—and sends him hurtling through a glass door. In this moment of murder she appears to be in a trance, until finally interrupted by her accomplice's call to stop. The second time we get a more complete picture, a picture not available to the crime's victims or the jury, as we see Cindy and her accomplice driving toward the house where the crime will occur, both of them getting high smoking crack cocaine.[74] We watch the entry into the house and helplessly follow Cindy as she goes into the bedroom where Debbie Hunt, the other victim, awakens, recognizes Cindy, and yells, "It's you, you fucking whore. Get out of my house." Cindy silences her with a blow to the skull.

It is in Cindy's deeply troubled reactions to these graphic recollections that the narrative of responsibility unfolds. They both connect her with Rick and Jill, and, through them, to us. They serve as a point of critical engagement with Rick's assertion that "we" are somehow to blame. Though she is a murderer, she is disturbed, indeed haunted, by what she has done. While Rick, the lawyer and clemency investigator, is eager to forgive her crime, or to attribute responsibility to her troubled childhood and the fact that she was high on crack at the time of the killing, Cindy, who has already been found legally responsible, insists on *taking* responsibility. As she explains to Rick, "That night (the night of the killing) is inside me like a giant shadow. I hated everything I didn't have and Debbie Hunt used to rub my nose in it. All that hate blew everything apart. I killed them. I killed myself. I know what I did. I can't change that. I can only change myself. I guess there are some things that can't be forgiven." In an odd foretelling of the drama that would unfold around Karla Faye Tucker,[75] and in a recapitulation of Carter's bilateral individualism, Cindy focuses attention on an "I" who acted; she insists that no one is to blame but herself.[76]

This insistence on taking responsibility marks a change that has already occurred in Cindy, and it reminds us that she, like us, is an agent capable of being held responsible. That she is guilt-ridden and morally burdened makes her an icon of modernist subjectivity, a subjectivity fully embracing the burden of its will put to "evil" purposes.[77] Moreover, it establishes the dramatic question that haunts the film—does she *really* deserve to die for her crime?

In *Dead Man Walking* the drama of responsibility unfolds in a more conventional way. Instead of the criminal resisting the structuralist analysis of his interlocutor, it is the latter who, in this film, speaks the language of responsibility against the evasions and deflections of the condemned. But in this film, as in *Last Dance*, the viewer's attention is fixed on a gradual unfolding of the "truth" of the crime, against which responsibility can be measured and punishment fixed.

The crime is seen primarily through the imagination of the main character, Sister Helen Prejean. As in *Last Dance*, the scene of the crime provides a recurring dramatic frame within which the question of whether Matthew Poncelet deserves to die can be posed. The repeated reenactment of the crime in a series of flashbacks spread throughout the film is key to the construction of Poncelet's subjectivity. It delineates the difference between *being* responsible and *taking* responsibility.

As to the question of innocence and guilt, the law is indifferent to the distinction between *being* responsible and *taking* responsibility. The Fifth Amendment protects the accused from being forced to take responsibility, in part because being

"forced" to take responsibility eviscerates whatever moral significance such a gesture would have.[78] While under current Supreme Court doctrine being an accessory is sufficient to create culpability for first degree murder and eligibility for the
death penalty,[79] the assumption that taking responsibility has enormous significance in constituting the moral quality of the subject is as crucial to the dramatic
unfolding of *Dead Man Walking* as it was in *Last Dance*.

Will Matthew Poncelet confess? Will he admit his true involvement and
genuine culpability for the murders for which he was sentenced? Or will he go to
his death still insisting that he was only an accessory swept up in the evil deeds of
another? These questions, rather than any broader effort to understand the society
of which his crime is a part, or the ongoing political and legal problems with the
death penalty, provide the dramatic framing of the film. As Shapiro contends,
"[T]he confession is, in fact, the pivot on which the movie balances. . . . It might
also be said that without the confession, *Dead Man Walking* would give viewers little reason for opposing the execution since this sympathy is largely dependent upon
the defendant's act of contrition."[80]

Dead Man Walking is more concerned with Sister Helen Prejean's ability to
tame the savage beast in Matthew Poncelet, a heroic effort in the face of death,
than about the question of whether state killing is compatible with our Constitution
and our commitments as a political and legal community.[81] Insisting that legal responsibility is not enough to heal the wounds inflicted, or to mark a soul that is
saved, is the work of Sister Helen, the spiritual counselor to Poncelet, the person
whose story *Dead Man Walking* tells. Thus Sister Helen informs the parents of one
of Poncelet's victims, "I want him to take responsibility for what he did."

Whereas in *Last Dance* the lawyer tries to diminish the responsibility of the
condemned, even as Cindy Liggitt insists that she is a responsible agent, in *Dead
Man Walking* Sister Helen works to constitute Matthew Poncelet as a fully responsible agent. She does so, in part, by imaginatively reconstructing the crime and, in
so doing, trying to figure out exactly what he did, if not why he did it. A chronology
of such imaginative reconstructions provides the site at which responsibility gradually can be assessed as well as a continual reminder to the viewer of the salience of
the "who did what to whom" problematic.

Dead Man Walking begins the visual reconstruction of the crime after Sister
Helen has heard a verbal description of Poncelet's deeds[82] from the jaded prison
chaplain who warns her, "There is no romance here, sister. This ain't no Jimmy
Cagney 'I've been wrongly accused. If only I had someone who believed in me'
nonsense. They [the men on death row] are all con men and they will take advantage of you every way they can."[83] This is a warning to the viewer as well. Be wary.
Don't be taken in. Remember who we are about to meet and why he is on death
row. Unlike in *Last Dance*, where Cindy Liggitt is presented as torturing herself
into responsible subjectivity, Poncelet is the unrepentant con man.

As Sister Helen leaves the chaplain and walks into the prison for her first meeting with Poncelet, the film moves back and forth between her observation of the
strange world she is about to enter and scenes of the crime, set off in black and
white. We approach a car parked in the woods; we see the barrel of a rifle; we see a
shot fired, followed by the legs of someone lying face down, then a twisted and

bruised arm, and finally a knife raised in slow motion in three repeated sequences and one dramatic, *Psycho*-like stabbing gesture. But in none of these scenes do we see the faces of the killers; we know something horrible has happened but we cannot yet fix responsibility. The anonymity of the criminal and the lack of narrative cohesion in this scene serve both to keep our gaze fixed on the horror of the act that is presented to us and to warn us that we, like Sister Helen herself, are not yet in a position to judge or to assign blame.

After each of the images of the unfolding crime in this scene, the camera cuts back to Sister Helen's increasingly disturbed facial expression, a kind of "what am I doing here, what have I got myself into" look. What is left undecided is whether her distress is the register of her image of the crime, or the prospect of meeting the killer face to face, or both. But it is nonetheless important to note that at this point Sister Helen has not yet imagined the actual killing or the bloody bodies.

The camera's move to black and white and slow motion does the job of suggesting that it is a fantasy we are seeing. Yet it is an incomplete fantasy, though one already filled with dread even as it brackets the most visually horrible image of the crime. Without its most graphic detail, the scene of the crime is registered on Sister Helen's face as it would be on ours. Like Rick and Jill in *Last Dance*, hers is the face of the responsible subject responding to horror.

In its gradual and partial reconstructions of the crime *Dead Man Walking* also seems to highlight the problematics of viewing and of representation. Perspective is everything; nothing is complete or certain. Thus we see the crime sometimes only briefly as when, during a hearing of the pardon board, we look over the shoulders of its members as they listen to arguments about whether they should recommend clemency for Poncelet. The prosecutor arguing against clemency hands crime scene photos to each of the board members. We see parts of several of the photos, shown in color to mark their status as representations of the real, as the camera moves behind the row of chairs on which the board members are seated. When the camera moves to the front we see them going through the photos, but the wide angle of the shot makes it hard to discern their facial expressions. Finally, we return to a position behind the pardon board and get a close up of a single photo of the naked body of a young woman bloodied by multiple stab wounds.

This is the very image that Sister Helen was unable or unwilling to conjure as she walked to her first encounter with Poncelet, and it provides a devastating moment in the film, a suggestion that only by refusing, at least initially, to contemplate the full horror of the crime can Sister Helen, or we, muster any compassion for someone who did what Matthew Poncelet did. The photo of the young, dead woman demands a response from the film's viewers, just as the prosecutor hoped it would demand a response from the pardon board. Who did this? More precisely, what kind of person could do such a thing? The photo works to narrow consideration, to keep the question of responsible agency at the center of our consideration. In its vividness and its horror it blots out almost everything else.[84]

A similar effect occurs when, later in the film, the parents of one of the victims, Hope Percy, retell the story of the discovery of their daughter's body to Sister Helen. We see Hope's body with stab wounds clearly visible, again in color, suggesting that what we see is an accurate re-creation, not Sister Helen's incomplete imagining.

"My daughter's body," Hope's mother recounts, "was found nude, spread-eagled.
. . . The police wouldn't let us go down to the morgue to identify the body. They
said it would be too traumatic." Sister Helen listens intently, tears welling up in her
eyes. This time the crime is viewed from the perspective of the surviving, grieving
parents, their pain retold as if in a victim impact statement, recounting the gruesome way their daughter died and the consequences for their life.[85]

Vision threatens; all reconstructions of horrible crimes astonish their viewers.
As Connolly notes, "[T]he desire to punish crystallizes at that point where the
shocking, vicious character of a case blocks inquiry into its conditions."[86] A structuralist explanation, in which the perpetrator is himself portrayed as a kind of victim, seems morally inappropriate when one is confronted with the crime's horror;
only bilateral individualism supplies the stuff out of which blame and punishment
can be forged.

This reconstruction of the crime is based on the Percys' assumption that Sister
Helen has come to share their belief that Poncelet is an "animal" who deserves to
be executed for his crime. Their characterization of Poncelet contains twin and
somewhat contradictory elements. In order to believe that crime merits commensu-
rate punishment they must hold Poncelet responsible, even if he doesn't take responsibility. He must be treated as a free agent who could have and should have
made a different choice. At the same time, the anger that drives retributive punishment expresses itself in the view that Poncelet is unlike us, an animal, a monster.
Here Dead Man Walking captures something close to the heart of the desire that always fuels punishment. Punishment, as Connolly puts it, involves imagining the
object of vengeance to be a responsible agent who deserves whatever he gets, and,
at the same time, a dangerous monster with whom we must deal.[87]

When we next are brought back again to Sister Helen's imagining of the crime
the question of responsible agency begins to emerge ever more clearly. This is signaled through a return to black-and-white footage. Her revisiting of the crime is
sparked as she is driven through the prison grounds to the special holding cell
where inmates are kept in the days immediately before their execution. The crime
is revealed as a series of scenes interspersed with her observations of the prison.

On this occasion her view is somewhat more detailed than in her first imagining.
We see more than weapons and legs and arms; we are now able to identify the as-
sailants and to see what they do. It is from this reconstruction of the crime that a tale
of responsibility can be built. At this point, however, we must be wary because Sister
Helen's reconstruction is based on replaying what she has heard from the Percys.

Yet she adds important details; she imagines Poncelet holding a rifle on Walter
Delacroix while his accomplice rapes Hope Percy. In her image Poncelet is surprised by his accomplice's brutality, scared and spooked when his accomplice
comes over, grabs the rifle, and shoots Walter. This imagining is faithful to the story
that, throughout the film, Poncelet has told to Sister Helen. It is a version of events
that maintains some distance between him and the burden of full moral responsibility. That she believes it is testimony to her willingness to take things on the terms
by which they present themselves, the very trait about which she was warned by the
prison chaplain. As Sister Helen later says to Poncelet, "You watched while two kids
were murdered." Throughout Poncelet insists that he is "innocent," having neither

raped nor murdered anyone. While his claim of innocence is not legally tenable, if it were true it would diminish his moral responsibility and invite a reappraisal of the appropriateness of his impending punishment.

Late in the film, on the day of the execution, we finally get an apparently complete, authoritative, visual reconstruction of the crime. It is a reconstruction that serves to fix responsibility at the same time that it allays any doubt that we can know the truth of the crime. Representational realism underwrites the narration of responsible agency. This double gesture comes in response to Sister Helen's suggestion that Poncelet "talk about what happened. Let's talk about that night." The responding narrative is highlighted in its claim to truth because it is again accompanied by color photography of the crime scene. We follow Poncelet and his accomplice as they come upon Walter and Hope kissing in their car. The criminals get them out of the car by claiming that they are trespassing on private property.[88]

Dead Man Walking fully reveals its modernist sensibility when Sister Helen demands that Poncelet take responsibility for these acts. "What possessed you," she asks, "to be in the woods that night?" "I told you, I was stoned," Poncelet responds. "Don't blame the drugs. You could have walked away," Sister Helen responds, fully embracing the language of agency, will, and bilateral individualism. Echoing themes in the classic individualist tradition,[89] Sister Helen insists that the responsible agent makes choices and must accept responsibility for those choices. "Don't blame [your accomplice]. You blame him. You blame drugs. You blame the government. You blame blacks. You blame the Percys. You blame the kids for being there. What about Matthew Poncelet? Is he just an innocent, a victim?" The language of responsibility directs attention away from the legal and political issues surrounding capital punishment just as it refuses to accept structure, accident, or conspiracy as justifications for actions. It insists that whatever the external factors that made an act possible, it is the choice to act that is crucial.

The ultimate unfolding of responsibility for the crimes in *Dead Man Walking* comes in a telling just before we see the completion of this "truest," and most complete, reenactment of the crime. After his last call to his family, Poncelet says to Sister Helen, "It was something you said. I could have walked away. I didn't. I was a victim. I was a fucking chicken. He was older and tough as hell. I was boozing up trying to be as tough as him. I didn't have the guts to stand up to him. I told my momma I was yellow. She kept saying 'It wasn't you. It wasn't you, Matt' [pause]. The boy, Walter, I killed him." In this moment Poncelet takes responsibility in quite the way Sister Helen has been urging him to do. Ultimately Sister Helen puts the question directly: "Do you take responsibility," she asks, "for both of their deaths [referring to Walter and Hope]?" "Yes, ma'am," Poncelet responds. The construction of the legal subject as the responsible subject is completed as complex, uncertain causation is banished by a narrowly focused question and a simple response.

Sister Helen's question and Poncelet's response play out a "death bed" confession, which sets the stage for an act of contrition. His assumption of responsibility is enacted as religious ritual and the constitution of the responsible subject is only completed through the intervention of spiritual necessity. The admission of guilt that law could not secure is finally obtained. Free will and responsibility are affirmed and agency triumphs over structure. Poncelet's "voluntary" assumption of responsibility reassures *Dead Man Walking*'s viewers of the validity of bilateral individualism and suggests that behind every narrative of shared responsibility for crime, of structure overcoming agency, is a deep, authentic truth about choice and voluntary, if misguided, action.

Assuming responsibility is enacted in *Dead Man Walking* as a journey in which the responsible agent comes to acknowledge that he could have acted differently; he could have "walked away," but he chose not to. "Subjects, we say, are 'free.' They are not bound and determined. They could always have done 'more' or done other than what they did. This is the basis on which we as legal subjects can be held legally responsible."[90] Yet while the discourse of responsibility insists on autonomy, the process through which Poncelet comes to take responsibility emphasizes his relationship to Sister Helen. "It was something you said," he tells her. It is this relationship, with its promise that confession leads to forgiveness, that enables Poncelet to do what law, with its promise of punishment, was unable to get him to do. However, as Peter Brooks has recently argued,

> [t]he problem may be that the very act of confessing will so often be the product of a situation, a set of physical conditions, a psychological state that do not conduce to the fullest expression of human autonomy. . . . [T]he search for the true confession, the moment of the baring of the soul, may uncover that moment as one of human abjection. Telling the shameful truth may reap all sorts of psycho-social benefits . . . but it does not necessarily promote an image of human autonomy and dignity. On the contrary it reveals pathetic dependency and a kind of infantile groveling. . . . Even the most indisputable "voluntary" confession may arise from a state of dependency, shame, and the need for punishment, a condition that casts some doubt of the law's language of autonomy and free choice.[91]

The ultimate product of his confession is Poncelet's public acknowledgment of responsibility in the ritual of the condemned's last words, uttered while strapped to a gurney elevated with Poncelet in a Christ-like pose facing Walter and Hope's families; "I ask your forgiveness. It was a terrible thing I did taking your son away from you. I hope my death gives you some relief."

It is only as Poncelet is himself being executed that the "complete truth" of the crime is presented visually. In this presentation we move from the scene of the execution back and forth to the scene of the crime. This quite literal effort to raise the question of whether execution is a just and proportionate response to murder shows Poncelet raping Hope and shooting Walter. The question is further precipitated by the use of parallel images shot from above of Walter and Hope lying face down, arms and legs spread in the woods, and then of Poncelet lying face up, as if crucified. Are these the same acts, the film seems to ask? Or, as Justice Scalia recently argued, does "death-by-injection . . . look pretty desirable next to [the murder of a man ripped by a bullet suddenly and unexpectedly]. . . . How enviable a quiet death by lethal injection compared with that."[92] Does *Dead Man Walking* condemn capital punishment, as Poncelet does when he says at the time of his execution, "I think killing is wrong no matter who does it, whether it is me, or y'all, or your government," or does it provide the strongest justification for it by refusing to let us forget both the nature and brutality of the crime to which it is a response? The film is rigorously indeterminate in its answers to these questions.[93]

It is not, however, indeterminate in its presentation of agency, will, and responsibility. Like *Last Dance*, it affirms the perspective of bilateral individualism against a more structural account of crime. As Connolly suggests, this "formula politely conveys a general cultural disposition to sacrifice socially defined others to protect the appearance of integrity and cleanliness in the messy cultural categories of agency and responsibility. Save the categories; waste those whose conduct or subject position disturbs them."[94] Both *Last Dance* and *Dead Man Walking* provide cultural affirmation of the social indispensability of responsibility against those who would blur the distinction between criminals and victims. They refute broad narratives of responsibility that would implicate us all in the contingencies that produce crime and would undermine the moral and legal scaffolding on which the apparatus of punishment is built.

III. Fetishizing the Technique and the Representation of Death

At first glance, *Last Dance* and *Dead Man Walking* seem to destabilize certain critical representational assumptions about the knowability of crime. They do so through the series of visual reenactments, set off by particular markers to suggest their partiality or incompleteness. Yet eventually both films give us views of the crime that are identified as complete and accurate through the use of specific visual techniques. However, no such movement from doubt to certainty, from the partial to the complete, afflicts their presentation of the scene of punishment. Indeed, both films are unusually preoccupied with the techniques and technologies of execution, showing, often in minute detail, how those technologies work and what their effects are on the body of the condemned. Nothing is left to the imagination as the camera zeroes in on the apparatus of death.[95]

Both films play off contemporary legal prohibitions surrounding the sight (and the site) of execution.[96] They respond by playing out a kind of representational realism.[97] It is as if they are not just providing a rendering of reality but a rendering of a reality "made more real by the use of aesthetic device."[98] For the realist, "the central nature of artistic activity becomes the presentation of a reality more real than that which could be achieved by a simple recording."[99] Yet this realist epistemology is, at least in part, rendered problematic by the presence in the films of witnesses to the executions. These films remind us of what it means to see an execution by letting us watch others watch, by alternatively merging our gaze with the witnesses depicted in the films and then separating the gaze of the viewer from that of the witnesses.

The presence of witnesses marks a difference the films insist on, namely the difference between those who "really" see an execution and those who have access only to its representations. Both do this by giving the viewer a greater visual prerogative than is available to the witnesses. We get behind the scenes views of the "death work" that precedes an execution, close-up, slow motion views of the technology—lethal injection—in action. We see switches being thrown, vials of lethal chemicals methodically emptying, fluid passing through tubes into the veins of the condemned. We are close-up spectators to something that few are "privileged" to see.

We are made aware of our privilege because we see the witnesses in their tightly controlling, more limited viewing. We watch them; we are, if you will, voyeurs at someone else's voyeurism. The act of witnessing is then held up as a kind of mirror in which the viewer is herself captured.[100] As Lesser says, referring to the prospect of televising executions, "It creates a new kind of voyeurism. We, from the invisibility of our private living rooms, are given the opportunity to peer into the most intimate event in someone else's life: his death."[101] Unlike the witnesses to an execution who are there to be seen by the condemned just as they are to see him,[102] the viewer of death penalty films sits at a safe remove, hidden from the condemned's gaze, "real or fictive." That gaze is, of course, the gaze of death itself; we escape it, and, as such, we can imagine ourselves not being implicated in the fictive death that takes place before our eyes.

But perhaps the distinction between witness and viewer is less stark than might at first seem apparent. As Steffey says about his own witnessing of an actual electrocution, "This has to be a Charles Bronson movie. . . . My thoughts even have trouble distinguishing whether tonight was another Bronson movie or reality."[103] The real unreality of death at the hands of the state in a liberal democracy marks the experience of witnessing and viewing.

Nonetheless, we are invited through the detailed, close-up images that *Last Dance* and *Dead Man Walking* present to believe that we have seen what an execution is "really like."[104] Catherine Russell suggests that, "[a]s a symbolic act, the representation of death in film upholds the law of the text: the believability of the image. Insofar as this belief depends on the denial of the film's celluloid status, its twenty-four-frames-a-second 'mortal' state, the illusion of reality sustains itself through a strict censorship of this reminder."[105] In *Last Dance*, there is a deep and unambiguous investment in the believability of the image of the execution. *Dead Man Walking*, in contrast, plays out a somewhat more complicated representational strategy.

In *Dead Man Walking*, as I have already suggested, the scene of execution is interspersed with flashbacks to the crime, and, at the moment when Poncelet dies we see the faces of Walter and Hope reflected in the glass window that separates the witnesses from the death chamber. These devices partially undercut the film's representational realism. They do so by proliferating images and specters of death, showing how Poncelet's death is inseparable from the deaths that he caused, and by bringing Hope and Walter to the site of the execution itself.

In *Last Dance* our witnessing begins as Cindy Liggitt is transported from the women's prison to the death house in the state's male correctional institution. From the high-tech, modern, clean confines of the former she descends into the archaic, fortress-like place where death is done by the law. There we wait with her as the time set for her execution approaches. As in many death penalty films, this one is quite literally preoccupied with time, using scenes of clocks on the wall to mark the inexorable process of life's march toward death. Lesser notes that "[t]he very techniques on which the telling of a murder tale relies—the foreshadowing, delay, irony, surprise, a sense of determinism, the theatrical immortalization of the main character—are techniques that play with the notion of time."[106]

But juxtaposed against the seemingly inexorable movement of time—the clock on the wall—is the prospect of last-minute legal, or executive, intervention. Set against time is law itself, death-doing but also potentially life-saving. "Death," Fitzpatrick says, "marks law's determinate being, its completeness distinct from what is beyond, but death is a relating of law to all that is beyond."[107] Thus for every clock, there is a telephone, the silence of which affirms the stillness of death, but which may, at any moment, come alive to end that stillness.

As Cindy waits in the special holding cell, caught between the clock and the telephone, the visual fetishizing of the technology of death and the marking off of the difference between the thing itself and its representations begin. We see the backstage work of filling vials with lethal substances and close-ups of the vials being fitted into the machinery that will mechanically do the job that no human is authorized to do, of delivering those lethal substances to the body of the condemned. When she is "escorted" into the room where she will be put to death, we again see what the witnesses cannot see, namely the condemned managed with military-like precision, strapped down, IV inserted into outstretched arm. Through these close-ups and backstage scenes, viewers are invited to believe that this is what an execution is "really like," even as we are reminded that it is not a real execution that we will see. We are brought behind the scenes so we can see, and in our seeing know, what the death penalty is and how it operates.[108]

It is only as the curtain separating the room where the witnesses sit from the death chamber is opened that our view is merged with the view of the witnesses. But our view is quickly concentrated on the exchange of looks between Cindy and Rick. The privileged, almost omniscient view of a moment earlier dissolves and is replaced by the gaze of intimacy, the gaze of love. Can that look be our look? Can the viewer move from engagement with the bureaucratic and technological details of state-administered death to embrace and identify the look of love? *Last Dance* works visually to move us from one register of spectatorship to another, from almost clinical detachment, to loving engagement. In this move there is no other visual space allowed. There is no possibility that we can view the execution neither as bureaucrats nor as intimates. The space of citizenship, the juridical posture that this film otherwise seeks to cultivate, is evaporated in the moment of execution.

In *Last Dance*, however, the phone does ring, and in hurried response the execution is halted, as the warden shouts "Stand down! Stand down!" In this moment two things are brought together. First, is a lesson about the difference between the death penalty and murder, namely that the former is subject to the continuing normative standards and control of the community. As Cover notes, the last-minute stay of execution reminds us that "the violence of the warden and the execution . . . [is] linked to the judge's deliberative act of understanding. The stay of execution, the special line open, permits, or more accurately, requires the inference to be drawn from the failure of the stay of execution. . . . In short, it is the stay, the drama of the possibility of the stay, that renders the execution constitutional violence."[109]

Second, the intervention of law ends the privilege of viewing, but only for the witnesses. Quickly the curtains are closed, but our gaze is neither terminated nor averted. We see Cindy, once unstrapped and removed from the table, collapse and scream, as if in a rage against her reprieve. The responsible subject, having taken responsibility, is turned into the victim of a legal process whose obsession with technical legalisms obscures issues of responsibility, justice, and punishment.[110] Cindy becomes the shrieking stand-in for a judiciary and public increasingly outraged by such obsessions.[111] Having been ready to die in the consolation of Rick's gaze, she is wrenched back into life by a legal process that neither she, nor we, respect.

It is, of course, Rick's last-minute, frantic efforts to find the one sympathetic judge who might grant a stay that led to that excruciating agony of Cindy's last-minute rescue. She screams because she knows what the ultimate outcome will be, that she and we will return to the death chamber. But before her return, before the stay is lifted, Cindy talks about the redeeming power of the gaze, of a certain form of spectatorship. "I saw you," she says to Rick, "I could feel your eyes on me. I wasn't scared." After the stay is lifted she says, "You have got to let me go now. Please. . . . Don't take your eyes off of me." What redeems is that the spectator can himself be seen, that his gaze can be returned. Such a redeeming power is not available to us. We are reminded, as if we need reminding, of our distance, our safe disengagement, of the limits of our power and role as spectators.[112]

When Cindy is subsequently returned to the death chamber, there is no last-minute reprieve. The execution resumes, as does our encounter with the machinery of death. We are given another extreme close-up as the procedure for dispensing the lethal chemicals proceeds. First one vial, then another is emptied in a slow-motion sequence that echoes the slow motion of our two views of the scene of the crime. But unlike the violence that Cindy dispensed, the violence done to her is bloodless, antiseptic, accompanied by no shouted obscenities.[113] No human hand is seen. Death comes through the automatic operation of a machine. We are again brought to a scene of death, given the illusion of seeing what is generally forbidden, and through that seeing of knowing death.

In this scene viewers are positioned as seekers of knowledge that we can never attain, knowledge of death itself. What Lesser says about the desire to see an execution is the desire that *Last Dance's* fetishizing of the technique seeks to satisfy. "We want . . . [the condemned] to enact something *for* us; we want to live the terror of death through him [or her], and then be able to leave it safely behind."[114] Yet the representational realism of the execution promises a knowledge it cannot produce. "Death remains ever beyond us."[115] Seeing an image of the technology in action cannot produce for us the experience of the death that technology produces.

Like *Last Dance*, *Dead Man Walking* fetishizes the technology of death. It too uses the extreme close-up of the machinery of death in action to bring us behind the scenes at an execution. But, unlike *Last Dance*, its representational strategy is more unsettling to the viewer, who is brought to and then away from the execution and who is, through that gesture, not allowed to forget the fictive quality of what he sees. Unlike *Last Dance*, however, what we see of the preparations for the execution initially is seen only through Sister Helen's eyes; we get no privileged preview. We watch as she catches a glimpse of the death squad practicing its drill, later asks about the witness forms, and sees preparations being made to feed the witnesses before the execution. We see the distress on her face later when she sees them eating, distress that registers the cruel juxtaposition of their preoccupation with life's necessities even as they are about to see the end of life. We follow as she is led into the witness room. It is only then that our gaze is separated from hers.

In this moment of separation the privileged position of the film's viewer is re-asserted. We see Poncelet strapped to the table and a nurse searching for a vein into which she inserts the IV tube that will soon carry the substances that will end his life. Over her shoulder we catch a brief sight of the vials containing those sub-stances. But from here our gaze is now fixed on the witnesses, as the camera pans from Sister Helen to the faces of the families of the victims. For a moment it seems as if our choice is to see the scene of execution through one or another of these sets of eyes. But in the back row we can see an unidentified, impassive female face. In her anonymity and distance the viewer is reminded of his or her position, poised looking at the execution from further away than either Sister Helen, Mr. Delacroix, or the Percys. We are again made aware of the fact that executions are today, as they always have been, about a particular form of spectatorship. We are again invited to believe that we will see and, through our seeing, come to know more than those whose witnessing is so tightly controlled.

But the camera shifts, fixing its gaze on the eyes first of Poncelet and then of Sister Helen. They stare into each others eyes; their truest connection is expressed in what they see. But his gaze is also fixed on us. He watches and in his look seems to ask how we will see him.

Finally, as in *Last Dance*, we are given first one close-up, and then an even more intense view, of the vials. The camera follows the lethal substances as they leave the vials, travel through the tube into Poncelet's arm, and to his head. We fol-low as if we too could enter his consciousness and know in the last minutes in which knowing is possible what it is like to lose consciousness forever. The visual device is quite stark in its invitation to exchange positions, if only for a minute, with the condemned in order to possess and bring back a knowledge forbidden to the liv-ing. Like Cindy Liggitt, Poncelet dies quietly, as if falling gently to sleep. Only in this moment is his gaze ended and ours released.

In both *Last Dance* and *Dead Man Walking* the scenes of execution, of an exe-cution presented as if the act of a machine, are stripped of grandeur. How far have we come, these films seem to say, from the awe-inspiring majesty of the scaffold? There is, in fact, now almost nothing to see. Death comes quickly; it leaves no visi-ble signature on the body of the condemned. We are invited to see that there is nothing to see in the bureaucratization and medicalization of death.[116]

Yet the sight of execution is, in this age, always a moment of transgression. In this transgression there is a mixture of fear and pleasure, of what we know and what we cannot know. This is especially true of the seeing that exceeds the carefully con-trolled visual field of the witnesses; such sight is a fleeting refusal to acquiesce in the state's definition of the death that it dispenses and in its determined effort to regulate the privilege of seeing. In addition, the representation of death in films like *Last Dance* and *Dead Man Walking* is "a harbinger of mortality. . . . But it is also, at the same time, a means of disavowing this recognition."[117] We are reminded that we too will die and that our death may be as untimely and gruesome as the deaths we are shown, yet because as film viewers we confront death from a distance, we are allowed to walk away unscathed.

As in *Last Dance*, the preoccupation with the act of witnessing and the focus on the gaze in *Dead Man Walking* suggest that even a bureaucratized, medicalized execution "is—as Foucault already implies—more of a show, spectacle, and theater than a closed structure."[118] Show, spectacle, theater, these representational media are central to the rituals of execution. But by focusing on the act of watching and by fetishizing the technologies of death, both *Last Dance* and *Dead Man Walking* play out the limits of representation itself, limits imposed by law (the prohibition of televising executions) and life (the unknowability of death). "The ability to produce the spectacle of death," Russell argues, "is both a discourse of control and of transgression. An uncanny conjunction of crisis and possibility, narrative mortality delineates the threshold of the representable."[119] These films want to give us what life itself will not allow. In so doing they domesticate the death penalty and allow us to believe that we can know what the state does in our name, that we can measure the effects of capital punishment and in that act precisely fix the balance of pains necessary to make the punishment fit the crime.

IV. Conclusion

Last Dance and *Dead Man Walking*, I have argued, are meditations on responsibility and representation. They juxtapose crime and punishment as a figuration of law's commitment to proportionality and, in so doing, affirm bilateral individualism against more radical, structuralist accounts of crime. They make clear the distinction between *being* legally responsible and *taking* responsibility. In this distinction they chart a space in which the modern legal subject can be said to reside, a space of individual autonomy, choice, and desert, a space in which those who take responsibility are accorded "the right to make promises." Despite their "transgressive" efforts to visually represent the site and processes of execution, they redeem their central characters—Liggitt and Poncelet—through the high moralist discourse of a believing world, a world not yet willing or able to come to terms with its disenchantment. In this sense they embody a conservative cultural politics, one quite unwilling to explore the instability of the very categories on which the modern apparatus of punishment depends.

The films, and the cultural politics in which they participate, resist the developments and possibilities of postmodernity that fragment identities, expose contingencies, and open up new possibilities of human connection.[120] Punishment, as represented in *Last Dance* and *Dead Man Walking*, demands that we know who the criminals and the victims are, and that we know the difference between them. It refuses contingency and interdependence and insists that the conditions of failure that accompany brutality are irrelevant to the question of responsibility. These films show, without critiquing, the ways in which those whose identity is jeopardized by the play of difference and contingency in postmodernity construct objects of resentment to protect the identities thus jeopardized.[121] Contingency in identity, Connolly claims, requires that we "acknowledge tragic possibilities in the life of the individual. To take one instance, one might have violent, destructive dispositions inscribed in oneself, dispositions neither chosen in the past nor susceptible to reconstruction now. . . . Typically it is unclear in such cases whether failure [to control those dispositions] represents a refusal, an inability, or a complex un-amenable to these fixed categories."[122] Neither *Last Dance* nor *Dead Man Walking* engages the tragic possibilities Connolly describes or the instabilities that lie at the heart of modern conceptions of responsibility.

What I am calling the conservative cultural politics of these films is also re-flected in the way they position the viewer and in the consequences of that posi-tioning. While viewers are positioned in several different ways in both films—as investigators, truth seekers, voyeurs—the basic structure of viewing is juridical. Though neither film takes us into a courtroom, they invite the spectator to judge as if they were making a life-and-death judgment. As Carol Clover notes, "Anglo-American movies are already trial like to begin with. . . . [T]he plot structures and narrative procedures . . . of a broad stripe of American popular culture are derived from the structure and procedures of the Anglo-American trial; . . . [T]his structure and these procedures are so deeply embedded in our narrative tra-dition that they shape plots that never step into a courtroom."[123] The juridical role offered to the spectator of these films is, however, not the role of adjudicator of guilt or innocence; instead, we sit as if on a jury in the penalty phase of a capital trial.

The films' brief reconstructions of the lives of the condemned and the reasons for their acts play out as evidence in mitigation. Through their extensive focus on the brutality of the crime and the suffering of those left behind, we are presented with the aggravating factors. If Liggitt and Poncelet take responsibility for their bru-tal acts, then, the films seem to ask, are they worthy of mercy? Or is the only mercy that can and should be provided God's mercy, not ours?

The consequence of this juridical role is to bracket, or to derogate, broader questions about the legitimacy and meaning of capital punishment and to focus our attention on the particularities of a single case. This bracketing of these questions is recognizable in certain silences in both films as well as in the way they portray the political and legal controversy surrounding capital punishment. Toward the end of *Last Dance* the political controversy surrounding the legality/morality of capital punishment appears in a series of scenes focusing on the gathering of pro– and anti–capital punishment groups outside the prison where Cindy Liggitt is to be exe-cuted. Those scenes suggest the simultaneous routinization and irrationality that lies at the heart of all such gatherings, routinization in the sense that they are part of the ritual and "ceremony" surrounding every execution and irrationality when they erupt into angry shouting.[124]

In *Dead Man Walking* the gathering of demonstrators plays a smaller role as a figure for the controversy surrounding capital punishment. We are shown a brief scene of Sister Helen in a candlelight vigil at the execution immediately preceding Poncelet's; there we also see the parents of his victims strongly defending the right of the state to use the death penalty. "It is the only way we can insure that they won't kill again," says Mr. Delacroix during a TV interview outside the prison. "These people are mad dogs, maniacs," adds Hope's father. The clearest political message against capital punishment is delivered in *Dead Man Walking* by the least credible speaker, Matthew Poncelet, when, as his last words, he says, "I think killing is wrong no matter who does it, me, y'all, or your government."

Each of these scenes seems jarring, out of place in films that focus so intently on the question of whether a single person deserves to die for his or her crimes. That biographical focus invites the viewer to accept, in a spirit of resignation if not celebration, the legal and political status quo. Thus cultural conservatism ends up serving the cause of legal and political conservatism. In both films, "the basic categories through which we judge murderers and assess penalties are themselves treated as stable and unshakable. The harsh childhood of the killer, for instance, is taken to 'mitigate' the crime or to provide 'extenuating' circumstances; but these experiences are not treated as elements that may enter into the very formation of the perpetrator's will itself."[125] *Last Dance* and *Dead Man Walking* legitimate capital punishment by insisting that all that counts is the question of responsibility and by deploying representational strategies designed to convince their viewers that they can know the reality of the death penalty and, as a result, assess its proportionality.

The cultural conservativism of these films also is seen in the way they depend on a representational realism about execution and in their confidence in the possibility of conveying, through sight, its meaning. *Last Dance* and *Dead Man Walking* use a model of sight/vision in which the visual is rendered reliable and stable, in which vision is privileged in its access to the truth of things, and in which visual connections have the power to soothe and redeem.

Yet there are at least two suggestions to the contrary that call into question the representational realism on which the films depend. First, as I have already noted, is the juxtaposition of the past and present, the embodied and the spectral in the execution scenes of *Dead Man Walking*. Second, is the description that Poncelet provides to Sister Helen of the way lethal injection works, with the first chemical designed to tranquilize, such that the horrible physical effects of the remaining chemicals are not registered on the body of the condemned.

In this description we are reminded that the visual field of the modern execution, the fact that there is "nothing to see," depends on a technologically induced condition. Yet it is another such condition, film itself, with its angles, pans, and close-ups, that produces the illusion that seeing is knowing,[126] that to see an execution enacted in film is to know the meaning of death at the hands of the state.

As I have argued, death, whatever its cause, marks the limits of representation. Films can neither capture death nor help us know what cannot be known. We can and do watch others die without being able to capture death's meaning or significance. Yet neither *Last Dance* nor *Dead Man Walking* acknowledges that "both death and film are negotiations with absence, and that the representation of violent death in film constitutes a special crisis of believability, a threshold of realism and its own critique."[127] In the end, whatever our particular judgments about whether their main characters are justifiably or unjustifiably condemned to death, neither film invites us to do more than comfortably embrace the conceptual categories of responsibility and representation that justify the apparatus of criminal punishment and keep the machinery of state killing in place and operating.

Notes

I am grateful to Amrita Basu, Carol Clover, Marianne Constable, Lawrence Douglas, Tom Dumm, and Joel Handler for their helpful comments on a previous draft of this essay. An earlier version was published in *Yale Journal of Law & the Humanities* (1998).

1. Friedrich Nietzsche, *The Birth of Tragedy and the Genealogy of Morals*, trans. Francis Golffing (Garden City, N.J.: Doubleday, 1956), 211–216.

2. Thomas Dumm, "Fear of Law," 10 *Studies in Law, Politics and Society* (1990), 29.

3. Nietzsche, *The Birth of Tragedy and the Genealogy of Morals*, 189.

4. Herbert Morris has famously suggested that persons have a moral "right" to be punished. This right, he suggests, is realized when "we permit the person to make choices that will determine what will happen to him and second, when our reponses to the person are responses respecting the person's choices." Morris, "Persons and Punishment," in *Human Rights*, ed. A. I. Meldren (Belmont, Calif.: Wadsworth, 1970), 127.

5. For a useful discussion of the significance of these moral tents and legal doctrines see Jennifer Culbert, "Beyond Intention: A Critique of 'Normal' Criminal Agency, Responsibility, and Punishment in American Death Penalty Jurisprudence," chapter 9 in this volume.

6. H. L. A. Hart, *Punishment and Responsibility: Essays in the Philosophy of Law* (Oxford: Clarendon Press, 1968). Hart claims that "all civilized penal systems make liability to punishment for at any rate serious crime dependent not merely on the fact that the person to be punished has done the outward act of a crime, but on his having done it in a certain state or frame of mind or will" (p. 114).

7. Sir William Blackstone, *Commentaries on the Laws on England*, vol. 2, ed. William Carey Jones (Baton Rouge, La.: Claitor's Publishing, 1976), 2175. Also Aristotle, *Nicomachean Ethics*, Book 5, chap. 8, trans. W. D. Ross (Oxford: Clarendon, 1925). In the modern law of criminal responsibility the language of vicious will or depraved state of mind has receded. More often, criminal intent is framed as a question of fact, the relevant issue being whether the defendant had knowledge of the likely consequences of the prohibited nature of his act. See George Fletcher, *Rethinking the Criminal Law* (Boston: Little, Brown, 1978), 397.

8. William Connolly, "The Will, Capital Punishment, Cultural War," chapter 8 in this volume.

9. For a discussion of the nature of this challenge see Wendy Lesser, *Pictures at an Execution: An Inquiry into the Subject of Murder* (Cambridge, Mass.: Harvard University Press, 1993).

10. Michel Foucault, *Discipline and Punish: The Birth of the Prison*, trans. Alan Sheridan (New York: Vintage Books, 1977), 9.

11. *Id.*

12. See Austin Sarat and Aaron Schuster, "To See or Not to See: Television, Capital Punishment, and Law's Violence," 7 *Yale Journal of Law & the Humanities* (1995), 397.

13. Lesser, *Pictures at an Execution*. And, as Dolan and Dumm argue, this crisis of representation is not limited to the domain of punishment. "[T]he struggle over the *representation* of politics in the public spheres of late twentieth-century America has become the single most important force shaping political life in this country." See Frederick Dolan and Thomas Dumm, "Introduction: Inventing America," in *The Rhetorical Republic: Governing Representations in American Politics*, ed. Frederick Dolan and Thomas Dumm (Amherst: University of Massachusetts Press, 1993), 1.

14. On the legal definition of those boundaries in the context of capital punishment see Sarat and Schuster, "To See or Not to See," 417–424.

15. For a general treatment of the difficulty of representing pain see Elaine Scarry, *The Body in Pain: The Making and Unmaking of the World* (New York: Oxford University Press, 1985). Also Austin Sarat, "Killing Me Softly: Execution and the Technologies for Taking Life," in *Courting Death: The Legal Constitution of Morality*, ed. Desmond Manderson (London: Pluto Press, forthcoming 1999).

16. Richard Johnson, *Death Work: A Study of the Modern Execution Process* (Pacific Grove, Calif.: Brooks/Cole Publishing, 1990), 5.

17. Foucault, *Discipline and Punish*, chap. 1. Also Jacques Derrida, "Force of Law: The 'Mystical Foundation of Authority,'" 11 *Cardozo Law Review* (1990), 925.

18. Hugo Bedau, *The Death Penalty in America* (New York: Oxford University Press, 1982), 13.

19. Lesser, *Pictures at an Execution*, 37.

20. Foucault, *Discipline and Punish*, 50.

21. One thing that typically has not been a subject of public display has been the executioner's identity. The anonymous executioner is, at once, a stand-in for the community in whose name the execution was carried out and a sign of the "shame" attached to those who turn our bloodlust into blood-thirsty deeds. See Geoffrey Abbott, *Lords of the Scaffold: A History of the Execution* (New York: St. Martin's Press, 1991); and Roger Callois, "The Sociology of the Executioner," in *The College of Sociology* (1937–39), trans. Dennis Hollier (Minneapolis: University of Minnesota Press, 1988).

22. Petrus Spierenburg, *The Spectacle of Suffering* (Cambridge: Cambridge University Press, 1984). Also Steven Wilf, "Imagining Justice: Aesthetics and Public Executions in Late Eighteenth-Century England," 5 *Yale Journal of Law & the Humanities* (1993), 51.

23. Foucault, *Discipline and Punish*, 48–49.

24. V. A. C. Gatrell, *The Hanging Tree: Execution and the English People, 1770–1868* (New York: Oxford University Press, 1994), chap. 2. See also Peter Fitzpatrick, "'Always More to Do': Capital Punishment and the (De)Composition of Law," chapter 5 in this volume.

25. Foucault, *Discipline and Punish*, 58.

26. *Id.*

27. *Id.*, 57.

28. As Gatrell argues, "These crowds behaved and spoke in terms which polite observers grew less able to understand. Many crowds acquiesced in what was done by the law and affirmed its righteousness. The hanging of murderers was usually approved. But when humbler people hanged for humble crimes, they could act like a Greek chorus, mocking justice's pretensions." See *The Hanging Tree*, 59.

29. Foucault, *Discipline and Punish*, 59–60, 63.

30. Johnson, *Death Work*.

31. Franklin Zimring recently called on scholars to broaden the focus of death penalty research and claimed that the increasing unresponsiveness of policy makers and courts to social science evidence concerning capital punishment sets researchers "free of the constraints that might apply if such work was relevant to immediate decisions on executions." Franklin Zimring, "On the Liberating Virtues of Irrelevance," 27 *Law & Society Review* (1993), 12.

32. For two fine examples of such work see Robert Burt, "Democracy, Equality, and the Death Penalty," *Nomos* 36 (1994). Also Hugo Adam Bedau, "The Eighth Amendment, Dignity, and the Death Penalty," in *The Constitution of Rights*, ed. Michael Meyer and William Parent (Ithaca: Cornell University Press, 1992).

33. See, for example, David Baldus, George Woodworth, and Charles Pulaski, *Equal Justice and the Death Penalty: A Legal and Empirical Analysis* (Boston: Northeastern University Press, 1990).

34. This approach to the study of capital punishment is more fully described in Austin Sarat, "Capital Punishment as a Fact of Legal, Political, and Cultural Life: An Introduction," in this volume. For an important precursor of my approach see Louis Masur, *Rites of Execution: Capital Punishment and the Transformation of American Culture, 1776–1785* (New York: Oxford University Press, 1989). See also John Sloop, *The Cultural Prison: Discourse, Prisoners, and Punishment* (Tuscaloosa: University of Alabama Press, 1996).

35. David Garland, "Punishment and Culture: The Symbolic Dimension of Criminal Justice," 11 *Studies in Law, Politics, and Society* (1991), 191.

36. *Id.*, 193.

37. *Id.*, 195.

38. On the semiotics of punishment see Wilf, "Imaging Justice."

39. Emile Durkheim, *The Division of Labor in Society,* trans. George Simpson (New York: Free Press, 1933).

40. George Herbert Mead, "The Psychology of Punitive Justice," 23 *American Journal of Sociology* (1918), 577.

41. Sloop, *The Cultural Prison,* 3.

42. See Norman Mailer's, *The Executioner's Song* (New York: Warner Books, 1979).

43. These films appeared at about the same time (1996) and were intended for a mass audience. They came out at a time of deepening public support for capital punishment and increasing impatience with the delays that frequently attend the movement from death sentences to executions. As any attentive American who lived through the 1970s, 80s, and 90s knows, the politics of law and order have been at center stage for a long time. From Richard Nixon's "law and order" rhetoric to Bill Clinton's pledge to represent people who "work hard and play by the rules," crime has been such an important issue that some now argue that we are being "governed through crime." See Jonathan Simon, "Governing through Crime in a Democratic Society," unpublished manuscript, 1997. In the effort to show that one is tough on crime the symbolism of capital punishment has been crucial. These films are but two examples of this symbolization.

Last Dance and *Dead Man Walking* are important interventions in the debate about capital punishment, but, as I argue in this paper, their interventions, while significant at the level of some of our most significant cultural categories, are quite circumscribed in the questions raised about capital punishment.

I make no claims here about the representativeness of these films. My purpose is to read them as cultural productions. Yet it might be worth noting that both films are examples of one type of death penalty film, which I label the sentimental tale. These films focus on a biographical or autobiographical reconstruction of the condemned, raising questions of responsibility and repentance. Other death penalty films, which I label injustice tales, take as their central thematic the question of whether the condemned is really guilty, that is, whether an innocent person will be executed. (The classic of this genre is *I Want To Live.*)

44. See, for example, Michael Tonry, *Malign Neglect: Race, Crime, and Punishment in America* (New York: Oxford University Press, 1995).

45. Connolly, "The Will, Capital Punishment, and Culture War." See also Wendy Brown, *States of Injury: Power and Freedom in Late Modernity* (Princeton: Princeton University Press, 1995); and Homi Bhabha, "Anxiety in the Midst of Difference," 3 *Critical Inquiry* (1997), 75.

46. The very title of the film *Dead Man Walking* emblematizes a crisis of representation. The title invites the viewer to imagine the impossible—a dead man walking—and it conveys the undecidability of death in the sense that death row inmates are described as dead men before they are actually put to death. I am grateful to Susan Schmeiser for pointing this out to me.

47. Perhaps Edmund Burke had it right when he suggested that in certain domains the imagination is more powerful than the senses. "The imagination," he said, "is the most extensive province of pleasure and pain as it is the region of our fears and hopes and all of our passions." See Edmund Burke, *A Philosophical Enquiry into the Origin and Our Ideas of the Sublime and the Beautiful,* ed. James Boulton (London: Routledge and Paul, 1958), 31. Envisioning the unknown "creates a terror unequalled by actually seeing the object of fear." See Wilf, "Imaging Justice," 64.

48. "Our death, which is intended for us alone, is the one experience of our life that we

can't directly experience. . . . We can have access to the event only indirectly, by extrapolating from the experience of others." Lesser, *Pictures at an Execution*, 135.

49. Writing about the end of public executions in the mid-nineteenth century, Masur notes that it "marked the triumph of a certain code of conduct and set of social attitudes among the middle and upper classes; it symbolized a broader trend toward social privatization and class segmentation; it turned the execution of criminals into an elite event centered around class and gender exclusion rather than communal instruction." See Masur, *Rites of Execution*, 6.

50. In this context to be for capital punishment is, so it is said, to be a defender of traditional morality against rampant permissivism, of the rights of the innocent over the rights of the guilty, of state power against its anarchic critics. To oppose it is to carry the burden of explaining why the state should not kill the killers, of producing a new theory of responsibility and of responsible punishment, and of humanizing inhuman deeds. Proponents of state killing, Connolly contends, put aside "the instability . . . [of] . . . categories of will and responsibility." At the same time, they highlight "the theatricality of the state's power to kill, and the promise to make state punishment 'morally proportional' to the act." See Connolly, "The Will, Capital Punishment, and Culture War."

51. Others have pointed toward such a reading of *Dead Man Walking*. "The movie *Dead Man Walking* . . . fails to deliver the same unequivocal abolitionist punch as the book. . . . [V]iewers are torn about whether or not this is even a film with an anti-capital punishment point of view." See Carole Shapiro, "Do or Die: Does *Dead Man Walking* Run?" 30 *University of San Franciso Law Review* (1996), 1144.

52. As Baudrillard suggests, in regard to capital punishment, "the thought of the right (hysterical reaction) and the thought of the left (rational humanism) are both equally removed from the symbolic configuration where crime, madness and death are modalities of exchange." Jean Baudrillard, *Symbolic Exchange and Death*, trans. Ian Grant (London: Sage, 1993), 169. And, all of this is carried on against the background of cultural divides that are becoming ever more intense as they become more complex and unpredictable.

53. Shapiro contends that *Dead Man Walking* "leaves the audience clueless about the systematic inequities and arbitrariness" of the death penalty. See Shapiro, "Do or Die," 1145.

54. See Robinson v. California, 370 U.S. 660 (1962).

55. Morris, "Persons and Punishment."

56. See Morisette v. United States, 342 U.S. 246, 250 (1952).

57. Stephen Carter, "When Victims Happen to Be Black," 97 *Yale Law Journal* (1988), 421. Robert Gordon calls this conception of responsibility "narrow-agency." It frames wrongs as "done by specific perpetrators to specific victims; the remedy is the limited and negative retributive sanction of the criminal process." See Robert Gordon, "Undoing Historical Injustice," in *Justice and Injustice in Law and Legal Theory*, ed. Austin Sarat and Thomas R. Kearns (Ann Arbor: University of Michigan Press, 1996), 36.

58. Carter, "When Victims," 421–422.

59. Id., 426.

60. Gordon, "Undoing Historical Injustice," 38.

61. Such stories are precisely the kind that defense lawyers in capital cases typically deploy in the penalty phase. See Austin Sarat, "Speaking of Death: Narratives of Violence in Capital Trials," 27 *Law & Society Review* (1993), 60. Also James Doyle, "The Lawyer's Art: 'Representation' in Capital Cases," 8 *Yale Journal of Law & the Humanities* (1996), 428–434.

62. At least in one sense, no matter whether one favors individualist or structuralist explanations, it is important to recognize that there is an asymmetry between the cultural life of crime and of punishment. While we are bombarded with representations of crime, punishment, as I suggested above, is almost invisible. See Alison Young, *Imaging Crime* (Lon-

don: Sage, 1996). The scene of criminality is a familiar one, a common though not unproblematic sight for most citizens; the scene of punishment is neither familiar nor common. The result is that the bridge between crime and punishment works primarily at the rhetorical level, or the level of imagination. Seeing the scene of crime, confronted with its graphic depiction, we are left to identify a responsible agent and imagine a just punishment.

63. Many death penalty films are structured around a relationship of the condemned and another person who befriends them, or takes up their cause. In these films we are invited to see the condemned through that person. Harding contends that "these secondary characters are pivotal" in that they are often able to see the human face behind the monstrous deeds that brings someone to death row. If these characters can see beyond the crime, then perhaps so can the viewers of the films. See Roberta Harding, "Celluloid Death: Cinematic Depictions of Capital Punishment," 30 *University of San Francisco Law Review* (1996), 1172.

64. But in each film there is a problem of how *we* identify with their caring for and about the condemned. In *Dead Man Walking* it is Sister Helen's deep religious conviction that moves her; in *Last Dance*, it is Rick's growing attraction to Cindy that moves him.

65. See Alison Young, "Murder in the Eyes of the Law," 17 *Studies in Law, Politics, and Society* (1997), 44–45.

66. On the power of such photographic evidence see Kristin Bumiller, "Real Violence/Body Fictions," unpublished paper (1991). Also Jennifer Mnookin, "The Image of Truth: Photographic Evidence and the Power of Analogy," 10 *Yale Journal of Law & the Humanities* (1998), 1.

67. Young, "Murder in the Eyes of the Law."

68. For a discussion of the uses of this imagery in capital trials see Sarat, "Speaking of Death."

69. For an empirical examination of the reactions of jurors in capital cases to photographic evidence see Austin Sarat, "Violence, Representation, and Responsibility in Capital Trials: The View from the Jury," 70 *Indiana Law Journal* (1995), 1103.

70. This moment is a reminder of the stark fact that when law runs out, sitting just beyond law is the power to pardon, a plenary power of the executive. See Kathleen Dean Moore, *Pardons: Justice, Mercy, and the Public Interest* (New York: Oxford University Press, 1989). The haunting specter of executive clemency depends on the will of a single person, who sits as an omnipotent force with the power to grant, or save, life. To enlist this power, as Davis reminds us, requires the fashioning of persuasive narratives, narratives of the kind that Rick tries to provide for the Governor. See Natalie Zemon Davis, *Fiction in the Archives: Pardon Tales and Their Tellers in Sixteenth-Century France* (Stanford: Stanford University Press, 1987). Yet, as *Last Dance* so vividly demonstrates, no narrative can guarantee clemency.

71. This is, of course, the classic anti–capital punishment argument made by Albert Camus, "Reflections on the Guillotine," in *Reflections on Capital Punishment*, Albert Camus and Arthur Koestler (Paris: Calmann-Levy, 1957).

72. Sarat, "Violence, Representation, and Responsibility."

73. Scarry contends that we only can know pain through images of weapons and wounds. See *The Body in Pain*, 16.

74. A truth is revealed to the film's viewers that was not available at her trial, since evidence of her use of crack before the crime was suppressed by an incompetent judge during the penalty phase of her trial.

75. On the transformation of Karla Faye Tucker, see Beverly Lowry, "The Good Bad Girl," *New Yorker*, February 9, 1998.

76. In so doing Cindy plays out a powerful theme in contemporary legality. The more law is challenged by theories that insist on the contingency and fluidity of identity, or on the effacement of the subject in modern conditions of danger (for one example see Thomas

Dumm, *Democracy and Punishment: Disciplinary Origins of the United States* [Madison: University of Wisconsin Press, 1987], 7–11), the more it seeks to affirm "that individuals are completely responsible for their actions. . . . [Law] needs an autonomous, rational, self-determining individual to assume the position of the cause of events that disrupt the pattern of everyday life in an ordered society. And it must affirm this figure without skepticism." Culbert, "Beyond Intention."

77. See William Connolly, "Evil and the Imagination of Wholeness," in *Liberal Modernism and Democratic Individuality: George Kateb and the Practices of Politics*, ed. Austin Sarat and Dana Villa (Princeton: Princeton University Press, 1996).

78. Peter Brooks, "Storytelling without Fear? Confession in Law and Literature," in *Law's Stories: Narrative and Rhetoric in the Law*, ed. Peter Brooks and Paul Gewirtz (New Haven: Yale University Press, 1996), 115.

79. For an elaboration of the state of the doctrine see Culbert, "Beyond Intention."

80. Shapiro, "Do or Die," 1153.

81. *Id.* See also Harding "Celluloid Death," 1177.

82. The film presents a transposition from the verbal to the visual where the verbal is at least initially given priority as an accurate rendition of events. On the significance of such transpositions see Carol Emerson, *Boris Godunov: Transpositions of a Russian Theme* (Bloomington: Indiana University Press, 1986), chap. 1.

83. Jimmy Cagney plays the lead in *Angels with Dirty Faces*, one of the earliest death penalty films.

84. Sarat, "Violence, Representation, and Responsibility."

85. On the significance of victim impact statements see Austin Sarat, "Vengeance, Victims and the Identities of Law," 6 *Social and Legal Studies: An International Journal* (1997), 163.

86. William Connolly, *The Ethos of Pluralization* (Minneapolis: University of Minnesota Press, 1995), 47.

87. *Id.*, 45.

88. This imitation of law initiates the scene of danger. Law, we are reminded, always establishes a terrain of danger from which law itself can never fully protect us. See Dumm, "Fear of Law." In this case, it is Walter and Hope's respect and fear of law that becomes the lynchpin in their victimization.

89. Morris, "Persons and Punishment."

90. Fitzpatrick, "'Always More to Do,'" 123.

91. Peter Brooks, "The Overborne Will," *Representations* (forthcoming) (typescript pp. 10 and 12).

92. Callins v. Collins, 62 U.S.L.W. 3546 (1994), Scalia, C.J., concuring.

93. Harding suggests that "[b]y alternating shots between the dying Matthew and the victims the film maker poses many questions to the audience. The physical position of Matthew's body resembles that of his victims. Does that mean that Matthew is also a victim? Is it done to tell us that this penalty is acceptable by reminding us of the victims as their killer is dying? Or, does it mean that the death penalty is futile because all that has been accomplished is the taking of three lives instead of two?" See "Celluloid Death," 1176. In addition, Shapiro argues that "the movie indicates that Poncelet confesses and is redeemed only *because* of his death sentence." See "Do or Die," 1153.

94. Connolly, *Ethos of Pluralization*, 64.

95. On the priority of the imagination see Burke, *A Philosophical Enquiry.* Also Lesser, *Pictures at an Execution.* Lesser contends that murder stories are about "what must be imagined, what can't actually be seen—what can't, in any verifiable way, be known" (142).

96. For a discussion of those prohibitions see Sarat and Schuster, "To See or Not to See."

97. A useful analysis of representational realism and its significance is found in Colin McCabe, "Theory and Film: Principles of Realism and Pleasure," in *Narrative, Apparatus, Ideology: A Film Theory Reader*, ed. Philip Rosen (New York: Columbia University Press, 1986).

98. *Id.*, 180.

99. *Id.*

100. As Young notes, "In film theory, analysis of the cinematic gaze pays attention to the suturing of the audience into and by the scenes displayed on the screen." "Murder in the Eyes of the Law," 32. For an example of what Young suggests, see Teresa de Lauretis, *Alice Doesn't: Feminism, Semiotics, Cinema* (Bloomington: University of Indiana Press, 1984).

101. Lesser, *Pictures at an Execution*, 40.

102. Ron Steffey, "Witness for the Condemned," 69 *Virginia Quarterly Review* (1993), 607. Also Susan Blaustein, "Witness to Another Execution," *Harper's* (1994), 53.

103. Steffey, "Witness for the Condemned," 614, 618.

104. As Fitzpatrick notes, "[T]he site of execution . . . is a place which is qualitatively different to what surrounds it." "'Always More to Do,'" 14. Joan Dayan says about the death chamber, "In this place of disposal, even the making of ghosts is defeated." "The Blue Room in Florence," 85 *Yale Review* (1997), 46.

105. Catherine Russell, *Narrative Mortality: Death, Closure, and New Wave Cinemas* (Minneapolis: University of Minnesota Press, 1995), 7–8.

106. Lesser, *Pictures at an Execution*, 234.

107. Fitzpatrick, "'Always More to Do,'" 119–120.

108. Lesser, *Pictures at an Execution*, quotes David Bruck, a prominent death penalty lawyer commenting on the prospect of televising executions as saying, "'The truth of the matter is that the public's imagination of what this must be like—and I say this having seen two of these executions take place—the public's imagination is much truer than what they would see on TV'" (p. 42). What he says about television would seem to apply with equal force to the representational realism effected in *Last Dance* and *Dead Man Walking*.

109. Robert Cover, "Violence and the Word," 92 *Yale Law Journal* (1986), 1623.

110. The much publicized execution of Robert Alton Harris is a telling example of the drama of the last-minute stay and of the increasing pressure to compromise law's highest values and aspirations in order to turn death sentences into state killings. See Judge Stephen Reinhardt, "The Supreme Court, The Death Penalty, and the *Harris* Case," 102 *Yale Law Journal* (1992), 205. Also Evan Camiker and Erwin Chemerinsky, "The Lawless Execution of Robert Alton Harris," 102 *Yale Law Journal* (1992), 2225. During the twelve-hour period immediately preceding Harris's execution, no fewer than four separate stays were issued by the Ninth Circuit Court of Appeals. Beneath the headline "After Night of Court Battles, a California Execution," the April 22, 1992, edition of the *New York Times* reported the tangled maze of last-minute legal maneuvers that immediately preceded the death in California's gas chamber of Robert Alton Harris. As in many previous executions, the hope of clemency or the possibility of a stay of execution was in Harris's case pursued until the last minute. Ultimately, in an exasperated, and unusually dramatic expression of Justice Rehnquist's aphoristic response to the seemingly endless appeals in capital cases—"Let's get on with it"—the Supreme Court took the virtually unprecedented, and seemingly illegal, step of ordering that "no further stays shall be entered . . . excepted upon order of this court." The Court scolded Harris's lawyers for "abusive delay which has been compounded by last minute attempts to manipulate the judicial process" (*New York Times*, April 22, 1992, 22). In so doing, it displaced Harris as the soon-to-be victim of law and portrayed law itself as the victim of Harris and his manipulative lawyers. To defend the virtue of law required an assertion of the Court's supremacy against both the vexatious sympathies of other courts and the efforts of

Harris and his lawyers to keep alive a dialogue about death. With this order, the Court stopped the talk and took upon itself the responsibility for Harris's execution.

111. For an interesting analysis of this public outrage and its translation into judicial opinions, see Anthony Amsterdam, "Selling a Quick Fill for Boot Hill: The Myth of Justice Delayed in Death Cases," chapter 7 in this volume.

112. Laura Mulvey, "Visual Pleasure and Narrative Cinema," in *Narrative, Apparatus, Ideology: A Film Theory Reader* (New York: Columbia University Press, 1986), 201.

113. Cindy Liggitt dies with a single gasp, her face reflected in the glass through which Rick and we see her death. She dies in his eyes and through him in ours. Death is given its meaning, death redeemed, through acts of viewing. However, unlike Rick, whose presence is crucial to Cindy, the witnessing audience to the film of an execution "becomes . . . a non-existent presence, an invisible crowd of spectators who yield up nothing on behalf of the performer." Lesser, *Pictures at an Execution*, 205.

114. Lesser, *Pictures at an Execution*, 60.

115. Fitzpatrick, "'Always More to Do,'" 3.

116. This theme is explored by Michael Madow, "Forbidden Spectacle: Executions, the Public and the Press in Nineteenth-Century New York," 43 *Buffalo Law Review* (1995), 461.

117. Russell, *Narrative Mortality*, 24. This disavowal occurs in *Death Man Walking*'s visual reminders that we really are not there, even as the film provides a sight of that which is forbidden to us.

118. *Id.*, 48.

119. *Id.*, 46.

120. Jean François Lyotard, *The Postmodern Condition: A Report on Knowledge*, trans. Geoff Bennington and Brian Massumi (Minneapolis: University of Minnesota Press, 1984).

121. William Connolly, *Identity/Difference: Democratic Negotiations of Political Paradox* (Ithaca: Cornell University Press, 1991), 209.

122. *Id.*, 179–180.

123. Carol Clover, "Law and the Order of Popular Culture," in *Law in the Domains of Culture*, ed. Austin Sarat and Thomas Kearns (Ann Arbor: University of Michigan Press, 1998), 3.

124. The shouting of the demonstrators is contrasted with the cool dispassion of the death squad that manages Cindy during her execution. In addition, a close-up of two nuns carrying signs that say "Thou Shalt Not Kill" suggests the ironic indeterminacy of a message that could apply with equal force either to Liggitt or to the state that is about to kill her.

125. Connolly, "The Will, Capital Punishment, and Culture War," 193.

126. Stephen Heath, "Narrative Space," in *Narrative, Apparatus, Ideology: A Film Theory Reader*, ed. Philip Rosen (New York: Columbia University Press, 1986).

127. Russell, *Narrative Mortality*, 23. The "violent deaths" to which Russell refers apply both to the death of the victims and to the executions in *Last Dance* and *Dead Man Walking*.

INDEX